Swimming Up the Tigris

UNIVERSITY PRESS OF FLORIDA

Florida A&M University, Tallahassee
Florida Atlantic University, Boca Raton
Florida Gulf Coast University, Ft. Myers
Florida International University, Miami
Florida State University, Tallahassee
New College of Florida, Sarasota
University of Central Florida, Orlando
University of Florida, Gainesville
University of North Florida, Jacksonville
University of South Florida, Tampa
University of West Florida, Pensacola

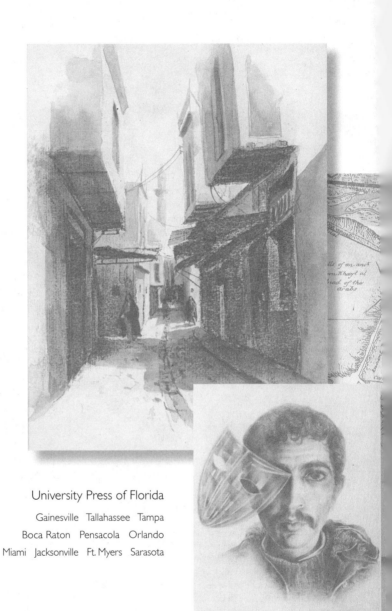

University Press of Florida

Gainesville Tallahassee Tampa
Boca Raton Pensacola Orlando
Miami Jacksonville Ft. Myers Sarasota

Swimming up the Tigris

Real Life Encounters with Iraq

Barbara Nimri Aziz

Copyright 2007 by Barbara Nimri Aziz
Printed in the United States of America on recycled, acid-free paper
All rights reserved

12 11 10 09 08 07 6 5 4 3 2 1

Library of Congress Cataloging-in-Publication Data
Aziz, Barbara Nimri.
Swimming up the Tigris : real life encounters with Iraq / Barbara Nimri Aziz.
p. cm.
Includes bibliographical references and index.
ISBN 978-0-8130-3144-6 (alk. paper)
1. Ethnology—Iraq. 2. Iraq—Social conditions. 3. Iraq—Foreign relations.
4. Iraq War, 2003—Personal narratives. 5. Aziz, Barbara Nimri—Diaries. I. Title.
GN640.A97 2007
306.09567—dc22   2007012101

Title page credits: Street scene, by Abdel Ameer Alwan; self-portrait, by Hazem al-Mawally;
19th-century British map of the River Tigris.

The University Press of Florida is the scholarly publishing agency for the State University
System of Florida, comprising Florida A&M University, Florida Atlantic University, Florida
Gulf Coast University, Florida International University, Florida State University, New
College of Florida, University of Central Florida, University of Florida, University
of North Florida, University of South Florida, and University of West Florida.

University Press of Florida
15 Northwest 15th Street
Gainesville, FL 32611-2079
www.upf.com

Harka Gurung,
who understood the dream, the obstacles, the
challenge, and the necessity of making a difference

Contents

Illustrations

Field Notes

Preface

I arrived in Iraq in early 1989. The atmosphere there was calm and welcoming. Eight years of battles between Iraq and Iran were over. It was called the "war of attrition"—mutual self-destruction, nourished by outside powers. It produced no victor, only martyrs, weeping mothers, and a warrior leadership.

Foreign correspondents had left for new killing fields. Citizens, exhausted by war cries and deaths, found the tranquility invigorating. Like Iranians, Iraqis were eager to rebuild and move ahead into the high-tech world. In Washington, London, and Tel Aviv, certain international players may not have been willing to see Iraq advance and (as we now know) they were laying plans to thwart any regional ambitions by its leader. Their preparations would emerge into the deadly policy they called "containment"—actually "dual containment," since it applied both to Iran and to Iraq. It would take the form of an embargo.

Meanwhile, Iraq's leader, his ego distended with military prowess, had his plans. He sought a new position of regional dominance. Blindly, he was leading his nation toward disaster.

I did not know this, of course, when I embarked on my first assignment in Baghdad. Being a social anthropologist, not a war correspondent or political analyst, my interest was on social life in a land whose people had largely been ignored by the departed journalists. Iraq offered unlimited opportunities for this visitor's pen. And I sought to meet as many citizens as I could and write about this very worthy Arab people as part of our world community. What journalists call "human interest" stories were waiting for dispatch; professional women worked in every field in Iraq; modern art filled the galleries. The early history of this land had boundless records to add to our world history. As a modern nation, Iraq's accomplishments in health and education needed to be known too.

I was warmly received, not by officials but by women and men eager to rejoin the world community from which the war had excluded them for eight years. In three visits before the blunder in Kuwait, I saw a great deal and I spoke to many vibrant, forward-looking people. I was smitten with admiration and pride in a sister Arab nation. I was fortunate to know archaeologist Walid al-Jadir; he arranged for me to spend some days in the home of Abu and Um Mohammed in Yussefiyya district near his university's excavation site. "Of course she can stay here alone," retorted the professor to a nervous colleague. "She's an anthropologist." He respected my professionalism and expected me to put it to good use. Al-Jadir also knew I would honor the values of my hosts.

I never forgot those early weeks; I revisited Um Mohammed to greet her son, a POW returning from Iran, and to see her grandchildren grow into young adults. However, most of my early interaction was with urban women and men, mainly professionals, and their children. The numerous times I visited during the subsequent embargo years took me into almost every corner of Iraqi society.

As I write this, I am aware that the country may not exist according to its twentieth-century borders. Certainly Iraq's pre-embargo civil society is buried under the present rubble. Although it is not gone. Also concealed are the convulsed economy and quaking social order of the thirteen years this book covers.

Yet this collection is not intended to be a history, whatever tumult and transformation Iraq has experienced in these years. Nor is this an ethnography of a vanished tribe—in this case, a nation-state. This book is as much an account of the American political and economic agenda on Iraq as it is about the Iraqi experience.

Washington's 2003 military assault and occupation is indisputably part of the United States' wider imperial design. More than dominance, it is a plan for worldwide conquest that began well before Saddam Hussein or the Taliban were viewed as enemies. We also need to understand that the American scheme in Iraq is not the work of one administration or political party. The embargo war on Iraq, although instituted by a Republican administration, that of G.H.W. Bush, was wholeheartedly embraced under the Democratic administration of Bill Clinton. So when we seek explanations for the origins of the eventual problems and assign responsibilities, we need to keep this in mind.

This testimony of the embargo war is also a review of the legality and the morality of a systematic campaign to destroy a people. It was a scheme to inflict suffering but also to drive millions into exile and to tear away the foundation of a civilization. The culture that Iraq fostered and protected, whatever the follies and evils of any leader, is critical to the dignity and perpetuity of modern Arab and Muslim civilization as a whole. In the American and Israeli quest to conquer that region, it had to dislodge Iraq from Arab and Muslim history. The particular leadership of Iraq at this juncture was and is irrelevant to the overarching American aim.

While this scheme was being implemented, the wider world was watching with growing disbelief and indignation. The malice of Washington's campaign may have escaped American citizens. It did not pass unnoted by hundreds of millions of people around the globe—people with "civilizational" memories, people who had rid themselves of colonial rule and advanced along a modern course, yet were still nourished and motivated by the experience of vital early civilizations coursing through their veins. They did not like what they saw being done to Iraq.

The venality in the embargo strategy can explain two important developments. First is the eventual fierce response by Iraqis to occupation. Remember that a child who was ten years old in 1991 when the first Gulf War ended and the embargo took hold—old enough to understand injustice and assign blame—watched his parents humiliated and his family life eroded, his basic needs denied, his people's achievements assailed, his homeland utterly isolated, and his very name loathed. He would be twenty-two at the time of the U.S. invasion. He is now twenty-six—an age to determine a new course, to build a house, to take up arms. Young Iraqis comprehend the wrongs done to them, wrongs carried out by a nation professing a free press and democratic ideals.

Second, the effects of the embargo war reached far beyond Iraq. That embargo, not the occupation of Iraq, accounts for the shift, beginning in 1991, in world opinion against the American, British, and Israeli governments who are seen as co-conspirators in the assaults on Iraq. This unfavorable opinion is not confined to Muslim peoples. It is shared by the people of Asia, Africa, and South America—that is, most of humanity. Whether this opposition is manifest or not by governments, it exists in powerful, ever widening popular expression. Much of the world's people, unlike Americans, observed the embargo first as an unfounded campaign against a regional leader. They also saw this (American) extremism in moral terms. The punishment meted out to Iraq was totally out of proportion to any crime. It also exposed the West's double standard—a critical failing (whose gravity Western governments and populations do not comprehend). The majority of the world's people could not accept that deceit. The result? America as a nation would become judged on moral grounds. This may account for the current level of worldwide hostility toward the United States.

As a portrait of the United States through the embargo war lens, these essays illustrate the complicity of American media outlets with their government's political agenda on Iraq. Rather than fulfill their role of furnishing facts and stimulating thought and debate, American media on the whole promoted the anti-Iraq policy and then advanced the campaign to attack Iraq when they endorsed the weapons hoax and other fabrications. Yes, the *New York Times*, perceived as a liberal newspaper, apologized for its lack of responsible coverage in the period leading up to the 2003 assault on Iraq. This shift came only in 2006. With that admission, the paper was pardoned and its upstanding reputation was reaffirmed (within the United States). How can such irresponsibility be so readily excused? This and other broadcast media knew very well what they were doing at the time; they knowingly chose to assertively support Washington's political and military agenda with slanted data and "planted stories." They will do so again.

And what about the U.S. public? February 15, 2003, worldwide antiwar protests erupted, bringing millions into the streets. For Iraqis, already firmly in the enemy's crosshairs, it was too little and too late. Those marchers were naïve, they say. When troops, warships, and bombers are en route to their killing mission, it is too late to parade with paper banners and ballads. Since 1991, information about the wickedness and fraud of the sanctions campaign was available. Few journalists and human rights advocates chose to visit Iraq to find out the truth in the early years of the blockade; fewer still would write forcefully about it. Ramsey Clark and his small group, International Action Center, were active from the outset, documenting U.S. crimes in the 1991 Gulf War, then the mounting devastation wrought by the embargo war. Forceful writers like Geoff Simons, Felicity Arbuthnot, and John Pilger were joined by British parliamentarian George Galloway, Margarita Papandreou of Greece, and dismayed United Nations officials who served in Iraq. Facts were easily available through their reports. Yet journalists, scholars, and NGOs chose to ignore them. In these violent days when the West's errors are so horrifyingly clear, we cannot say, "We did not know," or "This wasn't done in our name."

Having been a member of the university community in the past, I watched for signs of leadership from fellow scientists and humanists. Their silence was stunning. This was in the 1990s, not the post 9/11 era of Homeland Security wiretaps and "campus watch" vigilantes. With few exceptions, our scholars failed in their professional obligations. They shied away from debating U.S. government policies; they did not support their embargoed peers in Iraq or rally to protect priceless antiquities during the 1990s. Now (2007) is hardly the time to write petitions condemning assassinations of Iraqi professors or lost antiquities.

I hope this collection will help people realize that we Americans and Europeans are far less the free thinkers we believe ourselves to be. We are less well informed than we claim to be. We boast of freedoms to print or say anything. But this free will is largely a myth. If our "alternate press" is confined to the extreme margins, only accessible with great effort, those voices do not contribute—as they must in a democracy—to a healthy, useful national debate. We may have a liberal press, but at times of imperial hubris, we have no debate. We need to draw on the abundant sources worldwide—in print, Internet, and broadcast media, and in more languages than English. We need to mobilize our energies sooner, as soon as we begin to doubt our government's policies. We need to read the signs of our government's malfeasance earlier. Above all, Americans need to accept their fundamentally conservative, emotional, and heavily (bordering on extremist) "nationalist" character. Because of this character, two important institutions, our universities and our press, fail us at vital moments.

Around the world today, people whose lives our government may control, and whose own leaders may not meet our idea of benevolent, are far better informed than are Americans. Ignorance may be forgiven in some circumstances, but not when we are citizens of a nation that is so frighteningly powerful. Whether we like it or not, each American is an intrinsic part of this imperial superpower. Unknowingly and even involuntarily, we still benefit (at least in the short term) from this nation's imperialist actions and from its often brutal, rapacious conquests. Citizens cannot claim to have no responsibility.

Finally, you will see when you read these accounts that not one Iraqi I know and write about is a "victim." They are targets, marked by our government for elimination. As long as we perceive other people as victims, we are locked into an unhealthy, patronizing mind-set that promotes imperial agendas. I write about these individuals—Hanna and Gaya, Jabra, Sabaar and Mehdi, Ali, Amal and Adnan, Manal and Abu Farah—in order that you may recognize them as citizens of a wider world.

Acknowledgments

My thanks go to the many, many Iraqi women and men, some named in this book and others unnamed but forever remembered. They received me, trusted me, and taught me about their land and their experience in the years covered by this collection. They made it possible for me to write about Iraq as I do. Where I could contact individuals for permission to quote them by name, I do so; otherwise I employ pseudonyms. In two chapters—"Adnan in America" and "Mehdi"—that focus on individuals, I fictionalized the stories to a degree and altered the names because of the intimate nature of my reports on their personal lives. Yet all the events I recount there are true, based on my direct observation or on firsthand accounts by both men.

A book whose scope covers so many years takes me back to my earliest days in Iraq. I published some dispatches, but it was mainly through my reports to Pacifica-WBAI, the radio station in New York where I still work, that I found deep concern over U.S. policies in Iraq starting in 1990 at the time of the invasion of Kuwait. Over the years, fellow Pacifica Network producers Laura Flanders, Patricia Guadalupe, Hugh Hamilton, Valerie Van Isler, Samori Marksman, and Ginger Otis among others ensured that my reports from Baghdad were widely broadcast at a time when interest in the subject was slim and when the public did not want to look critically at U.S. policies in Iraq. My articles on Iraq were published in international newspapers and journals, including *Natural History*, the *Christian Science Monitor*, and *Middle East International*, but I am especially grateful to *Toward Freedom* editor Greg Guma and to International Action Center director Sara Flounders, who saw that my reports reached the activist community of Americans who cared about the situation at an early, critical period.

One cannot work under the difficulties of war without the support of friends who open their homes and hearts: in Iraq, Jordan, Palestine, Algeria, Lebanon, Egypt, and in the United States, I was sustained especially by the friendship of Ron David, Veronica Golos, Selma al-Radi and Qais Awqati, Mohja Kahf, Salma K. Jayyusi, Etel Adnan, Lenore Foerstel, Muna Atway, Laila Atshan, Um Yasser, Suha and Asia Taraiki, Aseel Nasir Dyck, Adnan Yusuf, Suad al-Rahi, Gaya and Mohammed and their children, Hiyam Taher, Hussein Ibish, Ahmed

Mehdi, Mohammed Deek, Rosemari Mealy and Sam Anderson, Suzy T. Kane, Amal Khuderi, Nita Renfrew, and Dara M. Taher. In the preparation of the manuscript, I had the good advice, steely support, and dedication of Elizabeth Boosahda and Rachida Mohammedi. Cartographer and web designer Aydin Baltaci kindly prepared the map; my colleague, Arabic scholar and translator Mansour Ajami, provided the transliteration system for the Arabic words and phrases in the text. Poets Lamea Abbas Amara, Lisa S. Majaj and Zaid Shlah kindly allowed me to include their poems, and artists Burhan al-Mufti and Abdel Ameer Alwan gave permissions for the inclusion of their drawings. My special thanks go to Felicity Arbuthnot. To all, and especially to my colleague, fellow journalist Nermin al-Mufti, for her years of companionship and guidance, I am deeply grateful.

Harka Gurung, to whom this book is dedicated, read and commented on specific chapters and, as he had for decades, provided needed words of encouragement along the way, although he did not live to see this publication. He is in the heavenly company of many dear Iraqi associates.

Abbreviations

CPA	Coalition Provisional Authority
DU	Depleted uranium, a highly radioactive substance employed in conventional weapons
FAO	Food and Agriculture Organization
IAEA	International Atomic Energy Agency
IMF	International Monetary Fund
MOI	Iraqi Ministry of Information
MOU	Memorandum of Understanding, a protocol agreement related to a UN resolution
OPCW	Organization for the Prohibition of Chemical Weapons
RCC	Revolutionary Command Council, Iraq's highest decision-making body
UNSCR	United Nations Security Council Resolution
UNCC	United Nations Compensation Commission
UNICEF	United Nations Children's Fund
UNMOVIC	United Nations Monitoring, Verification, and Inspection Commission
UNSCOM	United Nations Special Commission

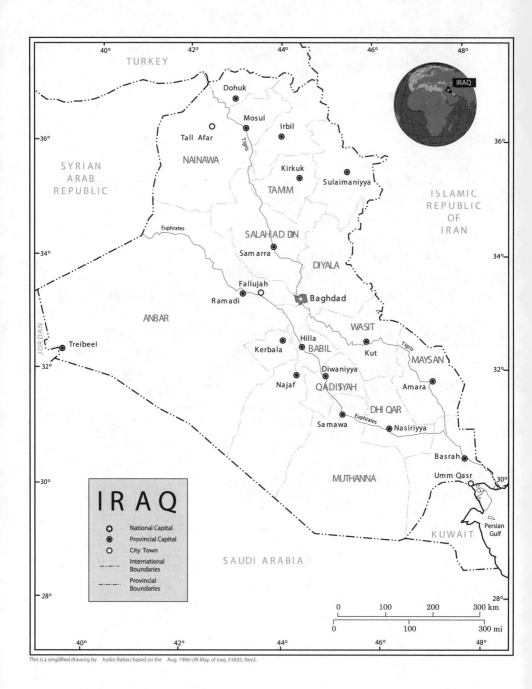

IRAQ

- ✪ National Capital
- ◉ Provincial Capital
- ○ City Town
- -·-·- International Boundaries
- ·-·-· Provincial Boundaries

This is a simplified drawing by   Aydin Baltaci based on the   Aug. 1996 UN Map of Iraq, #3835, Rev2.

Introduction

Oh, for those quiet, beguiling years of the United Nations embargo. Thirteen lonely years, yes. After 1998, we changed. We asked, "Why are we chasing those Americans?"

Late, so late, we understood Washington was not our friend. Worse. Do you know America made the whole world our adversary?

You say I am Turkman, she is Kurd, her husband Sunni. How?

We are Iraqi! You will never change this.

We made mistakes. We grew dependent on the West for our food. Here, between the great rivers where agriculture began! Imagine. So the embargo starved us. We returned to our fields. We plowed our Iraqi earth. It blessed us with wheat. We repaired our cars ourselves; we ended our wasteful habits.

We exposed the United States, Britain, and the UN with their phony democracy. Month by month their double standard became clear to all. Washington controls the UN; it is clear. "Why does no one protest?" we asked. Our children, little children, understood, too.

We know the aim of the United States and Israel is to destroy us as a protector of *Umma Arabia*, the Arab nation. We support a free Palestine, yes. We help families of martyrs, yes.

Am I a Baath Party member? I am. I am not ashamed to accept service in my government. You call it Saddam's gang. It is my government. We love Iraq. Why not? There is much to love in this land.

Our young felt the greatest pain. How they had loved the United States! Iraq—our Baath Party—sent many, many students there.

Naturally, the young thirst for knowledge. And they managed to master computer technology despite you.

Even our leaders changed. We decided we would accept payments for oil only in Euro currency. We studied international laws.

We felt we could overcome the blockade with new allies and hard efforts. That was before September 11, 2001. From that day, we saw another war coming at us. We waited for the attack. How we would fight back, we did not know.

Iraqis watched the entire world transect their history during the years I visited and revisited them under the UN-sponsored and U.S.–imposed global embargo.

The statements above are some Iraqi opinions. They reflect a changing worldview, a process that took ten years. They felt abused. They grew defiant. Once wholehearted admirers of the United States, Iraqis developed into strident adversaries.

Iraqi people and their government, whatever the mistakes of the Baath leadership and however tyrannical their president, made repeated, genuine efforts to legally meet UN and U.S. embargo demands. They did so even though knowing the blockade was unjust and fraudulently manipulated by Washington. Former UN weapons inspector Scott Ritter affirms Iraq's pre-1998 compliance and disarmament in his 2005 exposé, *Iraq Confidential.* His revelations affirm what other monitoring agencies and intelligence sources concluded: Iraq was not a military threat.[1]

Through the twelve and a half years preceding the American invasion of Iraq in March 2003, Iraqis as a people were mercilessly penalized and pushed to extremes, forced to cling to life, isolated internationally, and tyrannized at home. Up to two million perished as a result of sanctions-induced illnesses. Millions fled. The rest somehow struggled to retain their sovereignty, self-respect, and well-being.

With the 2003 military invasion led by the United States, Iraqis would have their chance to face their enemy and fight, by whatever means.

Signs of the resistance to occupation were slow to emerge. But the imperial design of the invaders, implemented by Paul Bremer III during his yearlong tenure as ruler of Iraq, doubtless helped an opposition movement take shape. American greed, perfidy, and miscalculations are amply recorded by investigators of the ongoing debacle in Iraq.

This collection of essays, written during the years of embargo and the first weeks of invasion, reveals an earlier source of Iraqi determination to resist. In exposing the malice perpetuated by Washington against Iraq, I suggest there were deep-rooted motives behind Iraqis' hostility toward the American "liberator."

Preparations

"They will welcome us in the streets of Baghdad with songs and flowers," U.S. leaders told their soldiers and their voters as they ordered American bombers and battalions to move into "the land between two rivers" in 2003. This scenario, we now know, was naïve at best. Possibly, it was an outright fraud knowingly committed by U.S. and British war planners. Continuing investigations by individuals inside the United States and by European analysts are uncovering abhorrent realities of the U.S. invasion and occupation of Iraq. Lies are sifted from truths. Military excesses are revealed. Massive profiteering is laid bare. Unmitigated racism, torture, and abuse are detailed. Death and suffering seem unstoppable.

The embargo was a preparation for America's assault—an assault that would catapult the United States into a position of world dominance. It was meant to weaken the leadership and disarm the nation. What really happened in those buried years leading up to 2003? We need to examine the blockade era from the Iraqi point of view. The treacherous embargo set the stage for entrenched opposition. In fact, Iraqi understanding of their adversary shifted dramatically during that time. The nation essentially reversed its perception of the western powers and the embargo. That shift would bear on how the invading forces were received. Not inconsequentially, the Iraqi experience would also bear on world opinion—in its favor.

Today, the embargo years are a marginalized era. But revisiting Iraqis' experiences, we can grasp how Iraqi society was already undergoing a significant transformation. The people would not welcome their self-professed "liberators." And once occupation forces were within their reach, they emerged into a formidable resistance movement.

As we review their years of hardship under that "embargo war" which U.S. critics rightly identified as the real weapon of mass destruction, we may begin to understand how, in some respects, Iraqis' military and ideological response to occupation today mirrors how the West treated them during the decade that preceded it.

For twelve and a half years, American and British governments employed the United Nations to conduct a remorseless campaign against Iraq's people, its culture, and its economy. If not technically illegal, the blockade was immoral. The UN economic embargo's aim was ostensibly to drive Iraqi troops from Kuwait. It was continued in order "to ensure Iraq was disarmed," and it was extended "to force a change of leadership." In reality, it had a wider, long-term goal. The embargo was the public face of a sinister strategy to obliterate modern Iraq. It ignited a process of social disintegration aimed at demolishing a people's will. It was a carefully crafted campaign. Perhaps no analyst has better comprehended this strategy than historian Richard Drayton. The embargo, he explains, was designed to "destroy the collective memory" of this pivotal Arab nation—what he terms the "decay and default model" of warfare.[2]

Embargo as an Immoral War

The blockade on Iraq, a multipronged aggression unprecedented in its nature, was in effect from August 6, 1990, until May 9, 2003. It became, for a nation of 20 million, a supreme trial. On the aggressor's side, it was a measure of America's coercive power. For the world, it was a moral test. Nations initially endorsed it, gradually reflected on the truth of it, and then opposed it.

The embargo did little to weaken Baath Party rule within Iraq. (It actually may have strengthened Saddam Hussein at home.) Meanwhile, the regime of sanctions left its mark on every single citizen—from the infant born into it, to its Republican Guard troops, the artist, the mechanic, the doctor, the bureaucrat, the grocer, and the herder. Hardships reached every corner of the nation. Iraqi diplomats found themselves ostracized. Iraqi expatriates, American for decades, became suspect along with other Arab Americans. World citizens attempting to offer assistance were threatened.

While their leadership remained firmly in place, Iraqis asked themselves new questions—not about their ruler but about the UN and the United States. They were shocked at injustices meted out to them by the embargo rulers. Ultimately most citizens concluded that their onetime friend, the United States, was bent on destroying their country.

The UN embargo was more than punishment for the military invasion of Kuwait. In the Iraqis' view, and gradually in the view of many people worldwide, UN treatment of Iraq was immoral, and as such it altered world perceptions of its perpetrator, the United States.

Iraq's suffering exposed injustices and trickery that few associated with modern western powers. The manner by which Washington enforced the siege on Iraq revealed its double moral standards. Perhaps even before Iraqis accepted this reality, others observing the thrashing from afar understood the treachery it embodied. Iraq's treatment under embargo eventually polarized the world and world opinion. Prejudiced news coverage by the U.S. media of Washington's stand against Iraq came under scrutiny. Globally, people recognized the bias of the western press in supporting U.S. policies. Iraq's experience lay bare the hidden agendas of a professed democracy and the moral hypocrisy of western civilization.

Day by day, individuals and nations decided not to comply with the embargo. They saw the UN's impotency. If they dared not directly confront the great powers and if they could not act collectively, they found ways to circumvent the odious embargo design. Each in turn initiated contact with Iraq. Individuals and nations decided to visit Iraq, to trade with Iraq, and to send aid to Iraq.

A number of states reopened embassies in Baghdad. They sent delegations to investigate. As important as any humanitarian assistance was the emergence of a moral solidarity with the besieged people. Solidarity of any kind with Iraq meant a choice—a choice between right and wrong. Solidarity here carried ideological implications. This moral alliance would sharpen the rift between East and West, between people of Muslim faith and the West because solidarity with Iraq signified defiance to U.S. will.

As the 1990s ended and the embargo pounded away, a new spirit was born within the region. By the end of 1998, world opinion on Iraq was polarized. On one side, mainly in Anglophone nations, Iraq's punishment had to continue. On the other, the siege had to end.

Despite tremendous hardships and obstacles, Iraqis had not lost everything. With a few friendly nations willing to barter, and a handful of individual sympathizers, Iraq opened a new course of action.

Their president did not matter as much as their nation. Every Iraqi I encountered, even in their grief and poverty, experienced growing pride as a people surviving an immoral war by embargo. That pride blossomed as they buffeted punishments meted out by so-called western democracies. With renewed energy and new sources of building materials, machinery, food, computers, and clothing, Iraqis pressed ahead with repairs and new construction and stepped up technology. "We have accomplished far more under these sanctions than most third world nations can manage without a siege," said Mustafa al-Mukhtar. That was likely true.

Once Iraq decided to proceed without waiting for the UN approval, things improved remarkably. I recall the visible transformation of Baghdad in just a few months between the fall of 1998 and the spring of 1999. Small businesses had opened, including computer schools. Color reappeared on shop fronts and walls. Houses were trimmed in blue, yellow, and green. Bright plastic fixtures welcomed shoppers and workers. Advertisements shone out from billboards. The sounds of bulldozers clearing debris and the sight of cranes in the city sky were new. Doctors saw more of their patients recover. Families once more strolled the gay streets of their towns at night.

In midsummer 2001, I sighed with gratification on receiving a short letter from Iraq. Postmarked "Baghdad, July 16," its few quiet words drowned out the millions of bleak words filed from Baghdad over the decade: "Iraq is now recovered from the insult America did to us," wrote Dr. Karim, a physician. His letter offered testimony that a hurdle had indeed been breached. It was more than a message of hope. It announced a moral victory over the United States. We barely had time to savor the triumph.

Fifty-six days later, on September 11, six thousand miles away, four planes were hijacked in U.S. skies and Iraq's fate was reversed. U.S. and British intelligence sources reportedly linked the 9/11 perpetrators and Iraq. Iraq could attack the West with its nuclear weapons in under an hour, they said. Soon, enough people believed the claims to support a U.S.–led military assault on Iraq. The bombing and occupation of Afghanistan had not satisfied the American public, still hungry for vengeance after 9/11. It was intent on greater retribution, however weak the evidence.

Four years into occupation, it is hard to grasp the chaos. Iraqis live in utter turmoil on a scale few can imagine. On one side, the Iraqi insurgency seems excessive, totally lacking in civility. On the other, the invasion and the occupation expose deceit, fraud, and cruelties by the occupiers that shock and shame people around the globe. After the attacks of September 11, 2001, most Iraqis knew their land was fixed in the crosshairs of American guns. From that day until the invasion of their homeland nineteen months later, they were subjected to sustained psychological warfare that no one outside even noticed. They watched preparations for another assault on their nation while far away the game of democracy and consensus was played out for willing, war-nourished spectators. As one Iraqi youth noted, "It is like watching a film in which I am the main character. The film is complete; the scriptwriter and directors know the outcome. I can only watch it unfold frame by frame."

The invasion that brought American troops into the center of Baghdad and expelled the Baath leadership lasted barely a month. In those few days, the invaders destroyed what the people had slowly, painfully, and proudly rebuilt during twelve years of remarkable determination and toil.

Iraqis initially offered little opposition to occupation forces. How could they fight? Iraq's air force had been out of operation since 1990. Its missiles were disarmed. Its troops were hungry and ill equipped. Soon after Baghdad was under U.S. command, Washington declared the mission of regime change "accomplished." Then it turned to economic and civil conquest. That fraud took less than two years to unravel.

Critics of the failed U.S. liberation of Iraq say Washington had no governing plan for the country following the military conquest. U.S. military management may have been defective or carelessly conceived. But there was a clear plan to "colonize" Iraq. Following the resignation of the first U.S. administrator, Lieutenant General Jay Garner, Paul Bremer put in place a complex and pointedly American capitalist economic agenda. Bremer was described as an American "terrorist expert," but his appointment may have derived from his close association with former U.S. secretary of state Henry Kissinger, whose vile aims on Iraq were no secret. With regard to the eight-year Iran-Iraq war, he is said to have commented, "Too bad they both can't lose."[3]

Transforming Iraq by American Authority

From May 2, 2003, until June 28, 2004, Iraq was ruled by the Coalition Provisional Authority. CPA chief Bremer was endowed with the powers of a viceroy. He set in place a series of administrative laws to transfer Iraqi resources into American hands. Special "orders" regarding Iraqi assets are detailed along with other features of the economic occupation of Iraq by Pratap Chatterjee and investigative journalist Naomi Klein. Those laws were designed to assign Iraq's economy to Washington's long-term advantage and ensure that Iraqi sovereignty would be compromised well into the future. Bremer himself is hardly mentioned today. But Klein's research reveals how during barely 13 months Bremer "pushed through more wrenching changes in one sweltering summer than the International Monetary Fund could enact over three decades in Latin America." First Bremer fired 500,000 state workers, mostly soldiers, as well as doctors and teachers. He flung open borders for unrestricted imports: no tariffs, no duties, no inspections, no taxes. He privatized two hundred major Iraqi state-owned companies, the largest state liquidation since the collapse of the Soviet Union. He set up a court and appointed administrators and judges to try Iraqi leaders. He funded the court with a budget of $128 million appropriated by the U.S. Congress.[4]

Under Bremer, billions of dollars in what was described as Saddam Hussein's (recovered) cash store disappeared. Under U.S. military control, hundreds of millions of dollars held in the Iraqi Central Bank vanished. Bremer appropriated for American needs in Iraq billions of dollars of Iraqi assets abroad, frozen since 1990 when the embargo first took effect. Bremer laid the ground for the billion-dollar-a-week budget to manage and rebuild "liberated" Iraq. Under this American administrator, early no-bid contracts were awarded to companies like Bechtel and Halliburton, which were known for their close ties to high U.S. officials. Bremer instituted a law that the CPA would award contracts only to coalition partners. He enacted a radical set of laws unprecedented in their generosity to multinational corporations. Bremer's "Order 39" allowed foreign companies to own 100 percent of Iraqi assets (outside the oil sector); they could transfer 100 percent of their profit out of Iraq. "A capitalist's dream," wrote the *Economist* of Bremer's Iraq, Klein notes. "Using legal loopholes, foreign investors who came to Iraq during a seven-month Bremer-protected period could sign forty-year contracts to buy up Iraqi assets."[5]

Klein describes how during his short CPA governance Paul Bremer spent or locked in for future projects more than $19 billion of the $20 billion Development Fund for Iraq (DFI, all of whose money came out of Iraq oil revenues, established by the UN) and how the UN handed over $5.6 billion to the CPA for Iraq by January 2004, with UN Security Council Resolution 1483 authorizing the CPA to administer this fund.

Foreigners were hired over Iraqis at ten times (or more) the rate a job could have cost. At the same time, the CPA left Iraq's sanitation, electricity, and water systems in disrepair. Iraq's "liberated" citizens looked on helplessly. As if this were not enough, they had to endure the plundering of their culture.

Cultural Assaults

Looting began as soon as Baghdad was "secured" by U.S. troops. The storming of the universities, libraries, and museums was first reported as an uncontrolled outburst of public anger toward the deposed Baath leaders. "The Iraqis were exploding with hatred," we were told. Outsiders believed it, but Iraqis knew that this myth was another element of the occupation strategy. Some Iraqis were able to identify the looters as foreigners. (They later learned these were thugs brought in from jails in Kuwait and elsewhere, then secreted away.) They followed the route of trucks carrying crates of loot to Jordan. They noted the tons of crated museum booty under American military "protection" at the Baghdad airport awaiting transfer abroad. It did not take long to discover that U.S. forces unlocked the museums and libraries to facilitate the work of the thugs.

Today forty thousand precious Iraqi artifacts have been catalogued by experts as missing, presumably destroyed or in the hands of dealers and curators across the world.[6] Iraq's modern museums housing the work of celebrated contemporary painters and sculptors also were wrecked and their treasures were carted away. Ashes of burned books blew into the dust of the city.

Iraqis quickly understood this burst of violence was not an impulse but part of the wider American design. It planned to first de-Arabize the nation and second to rid Iraq of its human and material treasures, that is to say, its history—a major source of the Iraqi (Arab) intellectual and cultural drive for excellence. In this way, the Americans calculated, the country would never again be a source of inspiration to its own citizens or to others. Iraq had for millennia been a repository of Arab heritage. Stamping out evidence of this might be a way for the West to cut off Arab people from their history and to remove Iraq from its exalted place in Arab consciousness. Few non-Arab observers have understood this as well as Cambridge historian Richard Drayton. In his 2005 essay "Shock, Awe, and Hobbes," Drayton defines a "'decay and default model,' whereby a nation's will to resist collapsed through the imposition of social breakdown." He argues that contrary to reports that post-invasion destruction was caused by failed U.S. planning, "evidence is that this was at least in part a mask for the destruction of the collective memory and modern state of a key Arab nation and the manufacture of disorder to create a hunger for the occupier's supervision."[7] If we accept this scenario for the 2003 chaos, the same logic is even more appropriate to explain the twelve and a half years of embargo.

Moreover, the apparently wild, dramatic plundering of Iraq's museums eclipsed the systematic looting of more strategic centers. U.S. troops swiftly removed official Iraqi government documents from targeted offices: the oil, defense, interior, foreign affairs, and health and education ministries.

Files of diseases and death rates laboriously assembled during the embargo are gone. So are education ministry files from which students draw transcripts and other certification they need to apply for advanced training or study abroad. Iraq's seized home ministry files, on the other hand, provide their new owners with a mine of information about visitors to Iraq, information yielded by surveillance, and the names of anyone arrested by Iraqi security. Trade ministry and foreign affairs files would also furnish details on Baghdad's contracts and discussions with foreign powers and individuals. This is an intelligence windfall for the new authorities.

Weapons of Mass Destruction

The history of the search for WMD is widely known. Press revelations are ongoing about Washington's claims of Iraq's capacity to attack Britain and United States. It appears certain that American and British leaders (as well as Israel) knowingly exaggerated the military threat of Iraq. Colin Powell's presentation of evidence of Iraq's threat before the UN General Assembly in 2002 convinced few, and it shamed the office of the secretary of state.

Washington's notorious "Plame affair" grew out of the White House's attempt to discredit a former U.S. ambassador who accused George Bush of mishandling intelligence to justify the Iraq war. Within months of the Iraq invasion, a team led by U.S. weapons expert David Kay, after an exhaustive inspection of Iraq in 2003, declared to the UN and Congress that Iraq possessed no weapons of mass destruction. The disarming of Iraq by UN inspectors before 2003 documented by former marine and weapons inspector Scott Ritter augments evidence from other sources, namely, the International Atomic Energy Agency and the head of the UN Chemical Agency, Jose Bustani, that by 1997 Iraq posed no danger.[8]

Some critics propose that if President George W. Bush (along with Britain's Tony Blair) really concocted WMD intelligence to win support for his invasion, it is a very serious crime. Although the constitutional legality of the Iraq war is discussed with increasing seriousness in the American press and among a few members of Congress, it is unlikely those responsible for the ruse will ever be prosecuted.

Revelations in the western press meanwhile do little to mollify Iraqis. Their country continues to be stripped of resources—oil, agricultural, and intellectual—in accordance with U.S. design for the benefit of U.S. companies, its people polarized into sectarian factions on a scale never known in the past.

Oil Production

If oil exploration, refinement, and transport in Iraq are not yet completely privatized, they are under way. Iraq's rich southern oilfields are "protected" by American troops so that American companies can have unfettered access to the oil. That is the plan, a plan that is relentlessly being sabotaged by insurgent attacks on oil facilities. Refineries as well as pipelines and extraction facilities are so badly damaged that Iraq cannot furnish its own citizens with petrol and cooking gas.

Iraq's northern oil fields are in dispute with Kurdish leaders laying claim to the key northern city of Kirkuk as Kurdish property. Kurdish companies have long controlled passage of oil from Kirkuk fields north to Turkey. Fees from this trade give Kurds considerable economic leverage.

It is uncertain today where revenues from Iraq's oil exports are deposited. There is general agreement that oil drilling and refinement have been so badly disrupted that production for local needs and for export is far below the 2003 invasion level. In a January 5, 2006, statement summarizing conditions in Iraq, Ramsey Clark accused the Bush administration of stealing Iraqi oil through oil production sharing agreements with their puppet Iraqi government, agreements that give the lion's share to U.S. companies. Clark argues these oil deals were "the main interest in [U.S.] policy of overthrowing the Iraqi government in 2003."[9]

Food Production

In addition to the destruction of farms and the disruption of farming on a daily basis by U.S. troops, a transformation is under way in Iraq's agricultural industry. Critics suggest that mainly American companies licensed under the Bremer laws have instituted practices unfavorable to Iraq.

First, Iraq's priceless national "seed banks" of more than 1,000 varieties of seeds related to its plant breeding program were either destroyed or removed from the country. World grain experts describe this store as "a genetic time capsule containing Iraq's agricultural heritage." Meanwhile, according to a critical review of U.S. food aid policy in Iraq, Jeremy Smith, writing in the *Ecologist*, accuses the U.S. administration of "setting out to totally re-engineer the country's traditional farming systems into a U.S.–style corporate agribusiness." According to Smith, American companies have assumed the task of retraining Iraqi farmers, using U.S. imported seeds.

Smith charges American agribusinesses with deceit in their Iraq cultivation programs. He says American universities and businesses are misleading Iraqi farmers when they introduce high-yield seed varieties of crops said to double production. According to Smith, farmers are promised soaring production levels and may "be only too willing to abandon their old ways and use of diverse seed varieties in favor of the new technologies." Out will go traditional methods, critics warn. And in will come imported American seeds that require new chemicals—pesticides, herbicides, fungicides, all ready "for sale to Iraqis by U.S. companies." The general aim of U.S. agricultural aid in Iraq, say Smith and others, is to teach Iraqi farmers to grow crops for export. "Traditional varieties developed over millennia are forsaken in favor of a few new hybrids, all owned by giant multi-nationals. Under the guise of aid, the United States has incorporated [Iraqi farmers] into the global economy." They charge that American miracle varieties displace the diversity of traditionally grown crops through this process (labeled "biopiracy" by international environmental activist Vandana Shiva), and through the erosion of diversity, the new seeds become a mechanism for introducing and fostering pests. They predict that the Iraqi farmer will find himself legally bound to the new technology by regulations imposed through Paul Bremer's "Order 81," which forbids Iraqi farmers to save their seeds.[10]

In conclusion, Smith says, "What America has done is not restructure Iraq's agriculture, but dismantle it." It is a practice occurring worldwide, but there is greater concern in Iraq, since thousands of varieties developed there over many thousands of years of agricultural experiment are ultimately the best suited for local conditions and offered a priceless treasure for world agriculture.

Intellectual Resources

The intellectual rape of Iraq is not limited to its physical treasures—art, artifacts, architecture, and books. Iraqi doctors, scientists, engineers, and researchers have been leaving. Thousands fled during the embargo, and the drain has accelerated in recent years. Iraq's neighbors, from Jordan to the Gulf States, and European nations welcome these refugees' advanced skills.

A more sinister development began after the U.S. invasion. Intellectuals are being kidnapped and assassinated. Medical doctors and scientists representing a broad range of expertise from agriculture to oncology and hydrology seem to be most often targeted. According to a 2005 report from the Iraqi Research Center in Baghdad, at least 58 professors, 150 physicians, and dozens of scientists at institutes and ministries have been murdered since April 2003.[11] Hundreds more were reported kidnapped and have not been heard from again.

Who is responsible? "Unknown assailants," say officials. U.S. and Iraqi security services show little interest in these crimes. Persons I interviewed in Iraq are certain these murders are not the work of common criminals but are planned assassinations. They suspect they are ordered and paid for by a foreign agency committed to "cleansing" Iraq of its intellectual heritage. Targeting of Iraqi intellectuals continued in 2006, with the imprisonment of professors for various crimes including "ideological support of the resistance."

These murders and the imprisonment of scientists and other intellectuals by U.S. authorities hasten the rush of remaining intellectuals abroad and exacerbate the deterioration of the nation's education system. Throughout the 1990s, Iraq was able to attract some students from neighboring countries based on its long-standing reputation for excellence. Educational training here was valued even during the embargo. That is no longer the case.

A general atmosphere of lawlessness is widespread in Iraq today. Guns are easy to obtain, and most households are armed. Some Iraqis working with the occupiers have become extremely wealthy. Their prosperity only aggravates widespread poverty and despair.

Across Iraq, burglaries and holdups are common and unchecked. Kidnapping for ransom—women and men—is a regular occurrence. Individuals we visit in this book have been forced to sell their property and borrow money to pay ransoms and secure the release of their loved ones. Others find their kidnapped family member dead, no matter what they do. Everyday crimes of this kind are not sectarian, say Iraqis. They often take place in full view of patrolling foreign soldiers, a message to people that the coalition occupation forces are not concerned with general security of the population. They may even be involved in the crimes.

Prison Abuses

Iraqis say that even under their despised former president they never experienced the house searches and detentions on the scale they are subjected to under U.S. occupation. Searches by American troops that seem designed to humiliate Iraqis are a deep source of public animosity.

Across the country, hardly a family has been spared intrusive house searches by gangs of U.S. troops. These raids often end with family members hooded and hauled away. It is estimated that to date (early 2006), up to 200,000 Iraqis —mainly men but also women—have been detained in American prisons inside Iraq. The number held at any one time is impossible to know. One NGO reports that the United States holds Iraqi detainees in as many as thirty-four prisons that its forces operate in Iraq.[12] In 2004, the gruesome nature of those detentions and criminal behavior of U.S. personnel came to world attention in what has become known as the Abu Ghraib scandal.[13] Abu Ghraib prison is one of dozens of U.S.–run detention centers inside Iraq where atrocities occurred. The abuses did not end even after details of torture sent shock waves around the world and U.S. authorities ordered investigations.

For a short time, the American public became absorbed by revelations concerning U.S. torture of Muslims. With the publication of more outrageous revelations, especially through photographs, public criticism of the U.S. administration increased.

For Iraqis, the issue is not *how* or *if* the United States can legally engage in torture, whether torture methods are effective, or who is responsible. Mistreatment at the hands of Americans, the daily humiliations and abuse they experience, cannot be mitigated by investigations, admissions, or compensation, they say. Mistreatment has nothing to do with Iraqis' Muslim values. Ill-disciplined occupation soldiers were not the problem either. To Iraqis the source of this maltreatment is a foreign culture. For them, the prison revelations were further evidence that the United States is indeed a racist and immoral society.

A major feature of the widespread abuse of Iraqis, inside and outside prison, is persistent and apparently systematic use of a range of tactics aimed at public humiliation. Iraqis believe this is part of an American policy of disempowerment. It is a daily occurrence—in the streets and in homes as well as behind prison walls.

One of the earliest published photos of Iraqis stripped and paraded naked appeared well before the Abu Ghraib scandal. It was taken in May 2003, during the first month of the occupation. The photo shows four young men, completely naked, standing in a residential city street. They are overseen by heavily armed U.S. soldiers. The photo caption says the men were picked up as looters, caught raiding the university. Punishment? They were stripped and sent on their way.

Throughout the occupation, Iraqis regularly have been subject to humiliation and insults by young American soldiers. Troops raze homes, search and destroy household property, hood captives, frisk girls and women, and much more. While each occurrence may seem short-lived, they have a serious cumulative impact.

The effect of what is seen as American racist treatment bears heavily on the Iraqi conscience. It fuels deep bitterness toward the United States in general.

The lack of sanitation services and serious shortages of water and electricity are part of the same policy of humiliation, one designed to make them feel worthless, powerless, and uncivilized.

Iraqis were able to repair their essential services after the 1991 bombings of their cities, and they managed to keep utilities functioning even during the blockade. They knew it could be done. So when the occupation authorities refuse to provide these services, Iraqis understand this as a political decision by the United States. Their comments on the absence of basic services are underpinned by a deepening sense of injustice. These hardships wear them down and make them feel impotent. On the other hand, the wrong impels them to fight on.

Trials of Iraqi Leaders

The high profile court proceedings of Saddam Hussein and others listed in the U.S. "55 most wanted" announced in April 2003 are bankrolled by a special fund set up by the United States. Televised proceedings against a handful of captives began in 2005, with the ex-president as their star defendant. Saddam Hussein's court appearances provided graphic copy for journalists. At the same time, his defiant words offered dispirited Arabs across the world reassurance that someone, even such a criminal, spoke for their victimization and their indignities.

Saddam Hussein's trial may have been a U.S. strategy to mollify Iraqis, to demonstrate how America has brought law and democratic process to their country, although commentators dispute its legality under international law. People associated with the trial have been assassinated and witnesses are hidden from view. The indictments were limited as well. For example, Hussein was not tried for genocide because, some say, he might have entered evidence implicating American executives and politicians. That would have proved embarrassing to his captors.

The trial of their ex-president did not seem to have interested the Iraqi public.[14] Doubtless, many would have been happy to see their former dictator summarily shot. Others staged public demonstrations in support of Hussein. Most, I suspect, would rather see security services and courts attend to immediate problems like street crime. Neither U.S. nor Iraqi authorities mention setting up a truth and reconciliation commission.

More important than the "show trial" of the ex-president is the nontrial of many thousands of Iraqis captured by U.S. troops, wounded, detained, and badly treated in U.S. prisons in the country. One of those "most wanted" captives is Dr. Huda Saleh Mehdi Ammash. Like hundreds and perhaps thousands of others, she was detained by the U.S. military. She was given no opportunity to answer charges in a court of law.

At the time of Ammash's capture, she was a newly installed member of the Republican Governing Council. U.S. authorities perniciously labeled her "Mrs. Anthrax"—walking evidence of the biological WMD threat Iraq posed to the American people. She was a vicious criminal, we were told—a scientist engaged in the production of those salacious weapons of mass destruction.

Ironically, Dr. Ammash is a graduate of universities in Texas and Missouri. After completing her PhD in biological sciences in the United States, she returned home. She was a proud Iraqi committed to using science to understand diseases. Despite personal and professional hardships, she showed no open animosity toward the United States during most of the sanctions period. Throughout the embargo, Ammash continued her work at Baghdad University as a teacher and dean of students.[15]

By 1993 she began intensive cell biology research to examine the effects of the 1991 Gulf War and the embargo on the health of selected Iraqi populations. Meeting Ammash on several occasions over a four-year period, I appreciated the significance of her work in a time of difficulties. Few scientists in Iraq were able to conduct research of this kind. Her efforts needed to be known more widely, and I was able to arrange the publication of one of her articles, "Toxic Pollution, the Gulf War, and Sanctions," in which she summarized her research findings.[16]

A responsible scientist, Ammash's attention was on measuring possible links between toxicity created by U.S. military attacks on her country in 1991 and evidence of increased incidence of diseases in the population. Ammash was not interested in political rebuttals to the U.S. embargo policy. She sought to use her research to open a dialogue with others studying the effects of radiation and other war-related pollution. To that end, she was eager to discuss her troubling findings with her peers. But whenever she sent her articles to scientific journals, there was no response.

Her article noted above did not appear in a professional journal, because Ammash found herself blacklisted by her peers. Former American colleagues whom she approached did not reply to her letters. (This general cultural and intellectual embargo was first recorded in 1996 as a result of my investigations.)[17]

Ammash was shocked and disheartened by the disinterest of scientists around the world. She persisted with her research, but the rejections affected her views. In 1999, she began to criticize America's Iraq policy, but even then only mildly and not in writing. Like millions of others, she changed her view about the American people; perhaps they were responsible for their government's policy and the harm it imposed on Iraqis. Many Iraqis had already reached this conclusion.

Ammash had been deeply troubled before this by UN weapons inspectors' treatment of her and other professors when scrutinizing their files and laboratories. (After detailing one example of these inspectors' violent behavior, Ammash asked me not to repeat it. This was in 1998, and I suppose she still hoped that uncritical cooperation with the UN weapons team, whatever the circumstances, might lead to the successful lifting of the embargo.)

By 2001, Ammash had quietly forsaken the United Nations and the United States. She added her voice to those openly criticizing U.S. policy. Perhaps this was why, in 2002, she joined the Supreme Republican Council, a body headed by the Iraqi president. Doctored photos of Ammash were as venal and inaccurate as published statements claiming that she was a powerful member of Iraq's ruling elite. She found herself on the "55 Most Wanted" list drawn up by the U.S. State Department.

Ammash surrendered herself to occupation authorities in May 2003 and was locked away. She was never charged and never brought before a court. From the day she was taken into custody until late 2005, she was held in solitary confinement in the Baghdad airport prison built and operated by the U.S. military. During most of her captivity, Ammash was forbidden contact with her family.

Meanwhile, her husband and other family members actively publicized her mistreatment and petitioned for her release. It seemed hopeless at times. U.S. authorities reportedly froze the family's personal assets. From the few letters the ICRC passed on to them, Ammash's family learned of her deteriorating health. She was denied medicine for her cancer.

In October 2005, U.S. authorities informed her family, "We have nothing on Ammash; she is free to go as far as the United States is concerned. But the Iraqi government says she cannot leave prison."

Suddenly and without explanation, two months later, on December 19, 2005, Ammash was released along with several other high-profile detainees. No charges were ever filed against them. Shortly before Ammash's release, Lenore Foerstel, who was working on the Iraqi woman's appeal, managed to reach a U.S. military official inside Iraq and plead on Ammash's behalf. "I'll look into it," replied the American.

Fearing for her safety, her family pressed Ammash to depart for Jordan immediately. But she had to leave her husband behind. Within forty-eight hours of her release, Ammash's husband, Ahmed Makki, who had fought tirelessly for his wife's freedom, was arrested. According to our sources as of March 2007, Dr. Makki remains in custody inside Iraq. No charges have been made, and his family has been told nothing by U.S. or Iraqi officials.

The treatment of Dr. Ammash is a well-documented example of the merciless character of American occupation. Her case also illustrates an occupation policy that is capricious at best. Her treatment doubtless has a terrifying effect on other Iraqi scientists.

The New Iraqi Government, the Constitution, and the Elections

Iraq's exercises toward self-government are in such a fluid, ambiguous state that what you believe depends on which account you read. The U.S. government insists that Iraq is self-governing, pointing to the December 15, 2005, election as a major step not only for Iraqi sovereignty but also for democracy. American television networks trumpeted this opinion at first.

Others share the view of veteran journalist Patrick Cockburn, who claims the election proved Iraq is disintegrating.[18] He predicts it will soon be three regions: Shia, Sunni, and Kurdish. "The election marks the final shipwreck of American and British hopes of establishing a pro-western secular democracy in a united Iraq. Islamic fundamentalist movements are ever more powerful in both the Sunni and Shia communities," Cockburn writes. The triumph of the election is not for Washington but for its enemies—for example, Iran—according to Cockburn.

Others interpret statements by the respected Iraqi religious leader Ali Sistani as indicative of growing independence. Sistani reportedly insisted on an election over the objections of Washington; he saw his Shia population gain the majority of seats.

Iraqi commentators seem reluctant to accept westerners' simplistic sectarian explanations. Ghali Hassen and others argue that the entire election process was a sham. They write, "There is no democracy; the entire election was rigged."[19] Iraqis may be free to form new parties and enter their names on the ballot. But there is general agreement that a heavy American hand is involved at every stage of the election process and in every party. Washington favorites such as Ayad Allawi and Ahmed Chalabi (whose campaigns were slick and expensive) may not have secured significant votes, if the Iraqi ballot functioned at all; yet they remain lodged firmly within the circle of power.

From inside the country, many Iraqis express deep cynicism about the election process. Some of those who voted say they had little faith in the exercise. They claim ballot boxes were stuffed to reflect a desired result in a neighborhood, other boxes were lost, and in some districts, people were prevented from voting.

A major issue for many citizens is the manner in which the occupying force has skewered identity. People are involuntarily labeled Sunni, Shia, or Kurd, and they feel obliged to vote in line with what the bosses say.

Many Iraqis refuse to be so identified, and they argue that these categories are imposed, that they did not define their lives in the past and should not do so now. They fear these artificially created differences will eventually be used to rationalize the division of their country. Iraq, they admit, could fragment into three states. But they argue that such dismemberment can only be manufactured and imposed by an outside hand. It would not happen in a truly sovereign Iraq, they believe.

Noam Chomsky suggests the United States backed the 2005 election not out of a commitment to democracy but as a referendum on occupation. He accused Washington of trying to dilute the election process in order to control the leadership. In a January 6, 2006, interview in *Khaleej Times*, he claimed that Washington really did not want a sovereign Iraq and cared little about democracy there.[20] Chomsky argued that whatever party secured the majority of votes, all signs showed that everyone voted overwhelmingly for a near-term U.S. withdrawal. For Chomsky and other critics, the election was not about building an Iraqi administration; it was a vote in favor of U.S. troops leaving their country.

Iraq's constitution, which was put to a vote early in 2005 in order to lay the foundation for the new government, was drawn up with American supervision. It failed to clarify what role Islamic law would play in Iraq, and it did not guarantee universal rights for citizens on the basis of gender or religious affiliation. The new constitution was vague about how a federation of states might function within a central government. With or without an acceptable constitution, few see Iraq as it is presently constituted becoming a truly sovereign nation any time soon.

Shia, Sunni, and Kurd

Nowadays Iraq seems to be a divided population of Shia, Sunni, and Kurds occupying different regions, different parts of a city, as well as different governorates. It is an entirely new status for a people who during their modern history were Iraqi first. But recent political and military events have accentuated differences that are becoming new indisputable "facts on the ground." Moreover, the three groups are used as a framework to explain all Iraqi life.

There are doubts within Iraq concerning the 60 percent figure for their Shia majority. "There was no census to identify us according to Muslim sectarian identity," says one expatriate Iraqi. Most educated Iraqi who lived in the large cities and once constituted 25 percent of the population maintain that until the U.S. occupation in 2003, little priority was given to religious affiliation. "It was unimportant. I never asked a friend if he were Sunni. Shia and Sunni often married." They were a generation who grew up in a predominantly Arab nationalist atmosphere. They took pride in holding their identity as Iraqi above all others.

Two communities did not follow this pattern: the Christian and the Kurd. Only those identities were listed in Iraqi census in the twentieth century.

Today, the Kurdish Iraqi people may number four million, less than a fifth of the population. Kurds are farmers, teachers, engineers, and journalists, and many are successful in commerce. Their homes are in the northern governorates of Irbil, Sulaimaniyya, and Dohuk, but they have always moved throughout Iraq. A few held high positions in the Baath government. Even though the Baath government supported Iraqi Kurdish language and culture and brought Kurds into the central government, it did not tolerate Kurd (or any other minority) separatist aspirations.

Kurdish desire for a homeland was repeatedly thwarted by outside powers. But it never completely disappeared. Following the division of their ancestral land by the British when the Ottoman Empire was dissolved, the Kurds were dispersed. Flowing across several national borders, the Kurds (whose overall population may be fifteen million) were subject to political manipulation by several nation-states, and in turn they tried to secure the support of a major power, siding at one time with this, at another with that neighbor. During the Iran-Iraq war between 1980 and 1988, the Kurds who straddled the borders of the two warring countries were weakened. Their treatment during that time laid the basis for deep hostility toward Baghdad. As victims of Baghdad's purges, the Kurds won American and British sympathy, and their chance for autonomy came in 1991 at the time of the Gulf War. Throughout the embargo period, the Kurdish region was essentially a U.S. protectorate.

The British and Americans established a "no-fly" zone in the north of Iraq, enabling the Kurdish people to strengthen their leadership, build up their military and economic capacity, and flaunt Baghdad. It was also a secure base for CIA and other espionage agencies to plan their anti-Baath campaign. Israel, home to thousands of Jewish Kurds, also played an important role in this process. Today, Kurds are able to control trade flowing between Turkey and central Iraq and exert levies on oil passing through the north to Turkey.

Kurdish power increased with their assistance to the United States during its 2003 invasion of Iraq and subsequent occupation. Kurdish leader Jalal Talabani is now the Iraqi president. Kurdish fighters have been welcomed by U.S. commanders, playing an important role in the newly constituted Iraqi military. It is widely reported that Kurdish members of the Iraq military are active in U.S. military campaigns against alleged hostile Sunni populations, although most Kurds are themselves Sunni Muslims. Not unexpectedly, the alliance between the Kurdish people and American occupiers is a source of deep resentment in the country.

As Kurdish influence increases, another Iraqi minority, the Turkman, are further marginalized. They are losing their majority status in the city of Kirkuk, a location strategic to the Kurdish people for its proximity to Iraq's northern oil fields. In response to the inroads of the Kurds, a new Turkman nationalist movement is emerging. And although their numbers are small, they could play a role in growing sectarian politics, according to author Scott Taylor.[21]

Iraqi Christians represent the most ancient Christian community in the world, and they are deeply tied to their homeland. Most want to remain in Iraq, but as the community weakens, as power within Iraq is won and maintained by parties that draw on religious identity, Iraq's Christians (mainly of the Chaldean sect), like the Turkman, are further marginalized. In 1995, Chaldean Church authorities in Iraq claimed 500,000 had emigrated since 1991. The decline in their numbers since the first Gulf War continues. With the increasing polarization of the country along Muslim sectarian lines, Iraqi's Christians may find themselves with no political identity whatsoever.

How Iraq Became a Symbol of a New Imperialism and Raised New Issues of Morality in the International Community

Accepting the 2005 Nobel Prize for Literature, Harold Pinter articulates what many in the world believe. He says the world has been deceived by American and British leaders. He calls for a return to the search for truth, a search that must never cease. "It cannot be adjourned, it cannot be postponed." Politicians, he says, are not interested in truth but in power. "To maintain that power it is essential that people remain in ignorance, that they live in ignorance of the truth, even the truth of their own lives. What surrounds us therefore is a vast tapestry of lies, upon which we feed."[22]

Pinter lists the lies Washington and London employed to gain support for their 2003 assault on Iraq. He reviews the wars of the 1980s in Latin America and elsewhere—Haiti, Panama, El Salvador, Chile, Turkey, Indonesia—where the U.S. government was complicit in the murder of hundreds of thousands of people. The U.S. history of brutality must be remembered, exposed, and faced, Pinter argues. He contends that those deaths are attributable to U.S. foreign policy. "But you wouldn't know it," he says. "It never happened. Nothing ever happened. Even while it was happening, it wasn't happening. It didn't matter. It was of no interest. The crimes of the United States have been systematic, constant, vicious, remorseless, but very few people have actually talked about them. You have to hand it to America. It has exercised a quite clinical manipulation of power worldwide while masquerading as a force for universal good. It's a brilliant, even witty, highly successful act of hypnosis."

He rages, "What has happened to our moral sensibility? . . . Look at Guantanamo Bay. Hundreds of people detained without charge for over three years, with no legal representation or due process, technically detained forever. This totally illegitimate structure is maintained in defiance of the Geneva Convention. It is not only tolerated but hardly thought about by what's called the 'international community.' This criminal outrage is being committed by a country, which declares itself to be 'the leader of the free world.' Do we think about the inhabitants of Guantanamo Bay? What does the media say about them? They pop up occasionally—a small item on page six."

Calling the invasion of Iraq "a bandit act, an act of blatant state terrorism," he charges, "We have brought torture, cluster bombs, depleted uranium, innumerable acts of random murder, misery, degradation and death to the Iraqi people and call it 'bringing freedom and democracy to the Middle East.'"

Pinter's appeal stands out because he elevates these atrocities beyond a particular lie or one man's arrogance. He links them to the higher, more troubling question of morality, morality not of one man but of whole nations who pretend "it is not happening."

Eleven years ago, five years into their embargo, Iraqis asked, "Where is their conscience?" They were midway through the UN siege, and they were slowly waking to the true nature of this punishment. Across the Third World, others began to ask the same question. Iraq, the nation with a tyrant leader, ironically would become a moral standard for western democracies.

Today, abundant evidence is available exposing false linkages made by U.S. and British administrations to justify "regime change" and their invasion of Iraq. The question of Iraq's danger to the world is no longer debated. It has been well established that Iraq was not a military threat to the United States or Europe. It had no ties with al-Qaeda and no connection to the attacks of September 11, 2001, on the United States.

The American invasion and occupation of Iraq continue to be hotly debated, especially in the United Kingdom and United States, as deaths of members of occupation troops in Iraq mount. By 2005, the morality of the assault on Iraq had become an important public issue for many Americans as well as overseas observers.

Inside Iraq, the debate about the justification of their treatment took place long before—during the years of the embargo. Iraqis argue that the disingenuous American actions of recent years are simply a manifestation and an extension of its policy against Iraq begun fifteen years earlier. They claim that the United States prepared the foundation of its policy of world dominance through the UN embargo on Iraq. It is not an unreasonable claim, given what we learn from investigators of U.S. action in the UN by Phyllis Bennis and others.[23] With Richard Drayton's analysis in mind and the arguments of authors Ramsey Clark and Geoff Simons, there is abundant evidence that the United States manufactured the confrontation with Iraq to consolidate U.S. world hegemony and that it was a carefully planned long-term project.

Applying the reasoning of Drayton, we can more easily consider the treachery of the embargo, a perfidy that Iraqis came to recognize. Thus the seeds of Iraqis' opposition to the U.S. occupation, expressed in violent, widespread resistance, has its roots in that embargo period. Corruption and lawlessness in Iraq can be traced to that time, too. It is essential, therefore, that we examine those years and include Iraqi experience there in any discussion of subsequent developments. By revisiting Iraqi homes, offices, schools, and hospitals, we will understand how Iraqis view themselves and the West. In their sometimes gentle, sometimes confused, sometimes angry and bitter voices, we can detect the foundation of the resistance and lawlessness that has taken over Iraq. We may also find their capacity for restoration.

The period of sanctions also reveals fine qualities of this people. If the occupation of Iraq ends and a degree of real sovereignty is established, these people will draw on resources that are absent or obscured in the current conflict. Compassion, intellect, and energy were evident in Iraq during the embargo. Witnessing that, while following their political transformation through the embargo years, is essential.

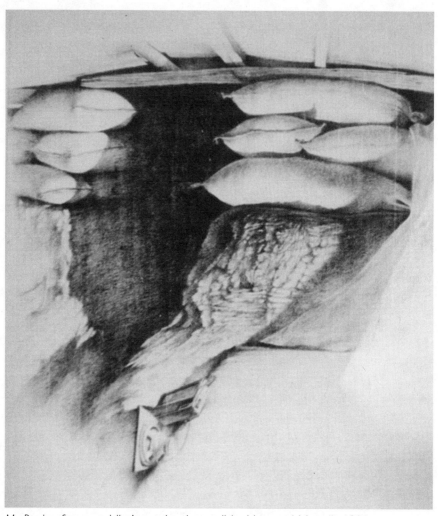

My Bunker, from a soldier's notebook, pencil, by Hazem al-Mawally, 1991.

Part 1

1

War Coming

APRIL 2002. What remains is only to pray. For twelve years, we struggled to overcome the embargo. Many of us perished. How we suffered from the siege. Yet look how we rebuilt. We thank Allah; with perseverance and love of our land, we could overcome those attempts to destroy us. It will never be the same. Perhaps we learned some lessons from this. Now all is in the hands of God. That is all we have. (e-mail from Iraq)

SEPTEMBER 11, 2002. President George W. Bush, U.S. president, will address the UN General Assembly in New York tomorrow. He is expected to announce his government's war plans. (U.S. news report)

SEPTEMBER 8, 2002. "We are praying, that is all. We have only Allah on our side." (caller from Baghdad)

SEPTEMBER 9, 2002. For the second time in a week, scores of U.S. bombers targeted Iraqi defense sites. It is not known how many were killed. "Any casualties are not our concern," said a Pentagon spokesman. Reports from the region say U.S. forces are placed in several locations around Iraq, in Jordan, and in several states in the Gulf, ready. (news report)

SEPTEMBER 3, 2002. "Inshallah, inshallah, my brother will marry next week. Inshallah. We pray for grace." (caller from Baghdad)

AUGUST 19, 2002. The UN's chief weapons inspector yesterday slammed George Bush and Tony Blair for talking up the prospect of war with Iraq. Hans Blix made clear he was not willing to accept U.S. and British claims over Saddam Hussein's terror arsenal until he had seen it for himself. Blix also attacked Mr. Bush's threat of action, admitting it was wrecking the prospect of a breakthrough on weapons inspections. (*Mirror*, London)

AUGUST 19, 2002. "My friend will help us. Do you know who my friend is? Allah. Yes, our only friend is Allah. You cannot imagine the Iraqi people. We are between Saddam and Bush. We cannot speak on the phone now. It is more difficult than ever." (Baghdad resident, by phone on business in Korea)

AUGUST 18, 2002. Officers Say U.S. Aided Iraq in War Despite Use of Gas—A covert American program during the Reagan administration provided Iraq with critical battle planning assistance at a time when American intelligence agencies knew that Iraqi commanders would employ chemical weapons in waging the decisive battles of the Iran-Iraq war, according to senior military officers with direct knowledge of the program. (*New York Times*)

AUGUST 16, 2002. "Yes, we are fine. We have a grandchild. My son is working very hard. He has grown up since he became a father. You will not know him. He and his wife are very fine." (caller from Baghdad)

AUGUST 16, 2002. Russia and Iraq plan to sign a new five-year economic cooperation agreement worth $40 billion, reinforcing Moscow's close ties to Baghdad even as the United States weighs a military attack to drive Iraqi president Saddam Hussein from power, Iraqi and Russian officials said today. (*Washington Post*)

AUGUST 15, 2002. Senator Chuck Hagel, Republican of Nebraska, who was among the earliest voices to question President George W. Bush's war plans against Iraq, said that the Central Intelligence Agency had "absolutely no evidence" that Iraq possesses or will soon possess nuclear weapons. Hagel said he was concerned that President Bush's policy . . . could create the political cover for Ariel Sharon to expel Palestinians. (press report)

AUGUST 14, 2002. Ali, in California with his Iraqi-American father for only seven months, wanted to return to Iraq. "Baba, a war is coming. Mama needs me," he wept.

AUGUST 15, 2002. Anti-Baghdad Talks Shunned by Top Kurd—The most powerful Kurdish chieftain in northern Iraq, Massoud Barzani, refused the Bush administration's invitation to attend the meeting of Iraqi opposition figures at the White House last week, Kurdish and administration officials said today. Mr. Barzani's decision to stay in Iraq indicates that a crisis may be looming with Turkey. (*New York Times*)

Randa and Nazim are building a house in Abu Dhabi. One son is there with his two babies. They are uncertain about their son Jasim back in Iraq. He can't leave. He told them: "The Iraqi military is calling all men for reserve training. The music director must report, retired diplomats, too, along with physicians, artists, and professors."

AUGUST 13, 2002. Syrian president Bashar al-Assad met last week with his Iraqi counterpart, Saddam Hussein, on the border between the two countries, an independent Jordanian newspaper reported Tuesday. Assad took with him to the meeting his brother, Maher, as well as the head of the Syrian intelligence services. In July, Assad sent a message to Saddam on the thirty-fourth anniversary of his Baath Party coming to power. (*Agence France Presse*)

Burhan's sister left for Damascus for her wedding to a Syrian boy. (Their father met the boy last year when he was in Syria on business.) Burhan is happy for her. Their parents went; so did his three aunts. Burhan could not leave Iraq. He is under twenty-five and must report to the army to train for the coming battle with the Americans.

AUGUST 13, 2003. The leader of a Tehran-based Iraqi Shiite Opposition group said . . . he favours a "political solution" to the situation in Iraq and called on the United States to avoid "any military action" against his country. "A political solution is necessary for a regime change in Iraq. We are against any attack or occupation" of Iraq, said Ayatollah Mohammad Boqer Hakim. (*Agence France Presse*)

AUGUST 2002. We will teach the American administration and the Zionist entity lessons in Jihad [holy war] and steadfastness. (*Al-Qadissiya,* the Iraqi government's official newspaper, front-page editorial)

AUGUST 17, 2002. Sama Al Baz, political advisor to the Egyptian president, said Egypt will not allow passage through the Suez Canal of U.S. ships headed to strike Iraq. He added, "Egypt rejects any military operation against Iraq, its territorial unity, independence." Al Baz said the question of UN weapons inspectors is an issue that concerns the UN and the Security Council and not Washington. (Qatar News Agency)

AUGUST 16, 2002. *Not in Our Name*—We are told a war on Iraq is needed to pre-empt a threat to the region and to free the Iraqi people from Saddam

Hussain's tyranny. As professionals, writers, teachers, and other responsible and concerned citizens, many of whom have personally experienced the persecution of the dictatorship in Iraq, we say no to war; not in our name, not in the name of the suffering Iraqi people. (Open statement by Iraqis in Exile Against War)

AUGUST 10, 2002. Saddam has ordered the formation of a 300,000 volunteer force charged with aiding the Palestinians and freeing Jerusalem from Israeli control. (Iraq News Agency)

AUGUST 6, 2002. Anglican Head Leads Christians Against Iraq War—The next leader of the Anglican Church and thousands of other Christians joined a swelling anti-war lobby in Britain Tuesday with a petition to Prime Minister Tony Blair opposing military action . . . calling a potential U.S.–led attack "immoral and illegal." (Reuters)

AUGUST 7, 2002. The American Constitution at the very beginning of the Republic sought above all to guard the country against reckless, ill-considered recourse to war. And yet, here we are, poised on the slippery precipice of a preemptive war, without even the benefit of meaningful public debate. The constitutional crisis is so deep that it is not even noticed. The unilateralism of the Bush White House is an affront to the rest of the world, which is unanimously opposed to such an action. The Senate Foreign Relations Committee held two days of hearings, notable for the absence of critical voices. Such hearings are worse than nothing, creating a forum for advocates of war, fostering the illusion that no sensible dissent exists. (Richard Falk, *The Rush to War*)

AUGUST 7, 2002. Q&A War and Iraq—Spencer Abraham, the U.S. energy secretary, yesterday insisted that stockpiling oil for emergencies was simply a matter of "overall energy security." Behind his words is a resolve to avoid increasing oil prices, which could be precipitated by military action against Iraq. (*Times,* London)

AUGUST 2002. Haidar returned to Baghdad from Germany. He'd gone to Hamburg with a visa for which he's paid 1,000 Jordanian dinars ($1,400), saved over two years working as a tailor in Jordan. Authorities at Hamburg airport said Haidar's visa was a phony; they turned him away. "Maybe Iraq is not so bad," he sighed after his return to Jordan. The next day he set out across the desert for his homeland. (report from his employer in Amman)

AUGUST 6, 2002. The U.S. is now a threat to the rest of the world. The sensible response is non-cooperation. There is something almost comical about the prospect of George Bush waging war on another nation because that nation has defied international law. Since Bush came to office, the United States government has torn up more international treaties and disregarded more UN conventions than the rest of the world has in twenty years. It has scuppered the biological weapons convention while experimenting, illegally, with biological weapons of its own. It has refused to grant chemical weapons inspectors full access to its laboratories, and has destroyed attempts to launch chemical inspections in Iraq. It has ripped up the anti-ballistic missile treaty, and appears to be ready to violate the nuclear test ban treaty. It has permitted CIA hit squads to recommence covert operations of the kind that included, in the past, the assassination of foreign heads of state. It has sabotaged the small arms treaty, undermined the international criminal court, refused to sign the climate change protocol and, last month, sought to immobilise the UN convention against torture so that it could keep foreign observers out of its prison camp in Guantanamo Bay. Even its preparedness to go to war with Iraq without a mandate from the UN security council is a defiance of international law far graver than Saddam Hussein's non-compliance with UN weapons inspectors. But the U.S. government's declaration of impending war has, in truth, nothing to do with weapons inspections. On Saturday John Bolton, the U.S. official charged, hilariously, with "arms control," told the *Today* program that "our policy . . . insists on regime change in Baghdad and that policy will not be altered, whether inspectors go in or not." (George Monbiot, *Guardian*)

AUGUST 1, 2002. Russia and China Call for UN Lead on Iraqi Policy: Growing international fears of war voiced at conferences—China and Russia called Thursday for the United Nations Security Council to take the lead in settling the dispute over alleged Iraqi weapons proliferation, as a war of words in the United States over military action increased. (*International Herald Tribune*)

The Iraq Ministry of Health began repairing the roof of the Ibn Rushd Psychiatric Hospital, the first time in ten years that any funding was available. The director has plans to make a garden in the central courtyard. "It will help to calm the patients, a pleasant setting for them to pass their time," he says. (e-mail from Baghdad, summer 2002)

JULY 30, 2002. Voices in the Wilderness and other anti-sanctions groups call on the Senate Foreign Relations Committee hearings on Iraq to include perspectives of experts urging an alternative to war. We note: Mr. Rolf Ekeus (executive chairman, UNSCOM, UN Weapons Inspection teams, 1991–97) stated on Swedish radio (interview, 7/29) that the United States routinely attempted to influence UNSCOM and succeeded in using it as a tool for their own particular interests. He expressed concern over past U.S. manipulation of inspection teams. (Voices in the Wilderness press release)

JULY 29, 2002. If, as promised, the United States does attack Iraq to overthrow its government, it will be the most notorious, arrogant and contemptuous violation of the Charter of the United Nations, the Nuremberg Charter and international law yet experienced. It would also violate the Constitution and laws of the United States. (statement by former U.S. attorney general Ramsey Clark to the UN Security Council)

JULY 27, 2002. Tony Blair has privately told George Bush that Britain will support an American attack on Iraq if Saddam Hussein refuses to accept resumed UN weapons inspections. The agreement comes as diplomatic, military, and intelligence sources revealed details of a new plan for the invasion of Iraq. A force of around 50,000 troops could be deployed within a matter of days. (*Guardian*)

JULY 19, 2002. The British press and policemen looking on chose to ignore an assault on guests attending the Iraqi ambassador's residence. As well-wishers including other ambassadors arriving for the private reception marking Iraq's national day at the diplomatic residence, they were accosted and subjected to abuse by known members of the Iraqi opposition who lined the approach to the residence. The police did not intervene, even after two guests whom the gang attacked required hospitalization. (Iraqi eyewitness calling from London)

JULY 22, 2002. Stop the War before It Starts—The attack-Iraq lobby argues that the military overthrow of Saddam Hussein is a necessary part of the war on terrorism, but there is no solid evidence that he supported the Al Qaeda attacks of September 11. Bush has emphasized the danger of Iraq's weapons of mass destruction as a justification for deposing Saddam. (David Cortright, Fourth Freedom Forum president)

JULY 25, 2002. Two years ago, my brother in England brought $40,000 to

Iraq and we went to our home town in the north and built a school. Everyone contributed. There was such a celebration. We danced and sang for three days. We felt proud we had finally overcome the adversity—the evil blockade. Now, we don't know what is going to happen to us next. (Baghdad resident)

JULY 25, 2002. Israeli strategic analysts believe that the defeat of Iraq would remove the nerve of the Palestinian leadership. "I think one of the reasons for Mr. Arafat's conduct since the outbreak of the Intifada is his belief that he is supported by the radical elements in the Arab world," says Shlomo Brom of the Jaffee Center for Strategic Studies. "If these radical elements get a blow—and this is the meaning of success in Iraq—then Arafat will know he will have no support of any meaningful element in the Arab world and he will change his conduct." (*Palestine Report*)

JULY 23, 2002. Hanna became an observant Muslim not long after her father died of a heart attack. She heard rumors: party agents kill civil servants like her father who are familiar with the inside operation of the party. "But my Baba loved the party, and the president." She does not believe those whispers. Still, she needs to be closer to God. She is expecting her second baby. She is sorry the baby will never know his grandfather. (Ramadi)

JULY 21, 2002. I do not think a war is going to happen. America has no re-placement for Saddam. The Kurds in the so-called opposition group hate each other; all want is to rule and get the money the CIA has set a side for them! Kurds hate [Ahmed] Chalabi [Iraqi National Congress leader]. People met in London just to collect a piece of the $97 million Congress allocated to overthrow the Iraqi govern-ment. (private communication, Iraqi Kurd writer)

JULY 14, 2002. When Abdella returned home in the prisoner exchange between Iraq and Iran in 1994, all his sisters and his mother celebrated. Soon after, his brother Faisal, also a prisoner in Iran, was freed. Weak from years in captivity, Faisal died barely a year later.

Two years after the embargo began, their tribe was prospering because the gov-ernment paid high prices for wheat. (Kerbala provincial farm)

JULY 19, 2002. The [British] Ministry of Defence is planning a mass mobili-sation of key reservists beginning in September stepping up preparations for an attack on Iraq. (*Daily Telegraph*)

JULY 2002. When Samer reached eighteen years of age last month, he went into the army. He's a farmer's son. He planned to start tomato production using new irrigation techniques introduced after the sanctions. Now he doesn't know when he will return to his land. (Rashdiyya village)

JULY 11, 2002. The removal of President Saddam Hussein would open Iraq's rich new oilfields to western bidders and bring the prospect of lessening dependence on Saudi oil. (*Times*, London)

2002. Manal left Iraq soon after the 1991 bombing; she recently moved back to Basra from Jordan to teach young Iraqis. Now she is planning to leave. For good. Her brother in France says he will help her. She is not going to tell her students about her plans. (Basra)

JULY 17, 2002. Turkey has agreed to back the United States if it takes military action to topple Saddam Hussein but has asked that Washington write off $5 billion in debt and guarantee that Kurds would not be given an independent state, according to news reports Wednesday. (Associated Press)

JULY 2002. Yussef became wealthy selling agricultural supplies in the blockade years when food production was high priority. Two years ago, in 1998, he built a big new house in Baghdad. Now he says he's transferring his business and family to Jordan. (Baghdad)

JULY 15, 2002. Jordan's Prince Hassan attended a strategy meeting of anti-Iraq groups, a move that may signal Jordan's willingness to join the forces ready to topple Saddam Hussein, while allowing his nephew, King Abdullah, to continue to claim it [Jordan] is against such a move. (press report)

JULY 2002. Laila has a children's wear shop, and Hala is a hairdresser in Baghdad. The two women, sisters, are married to American Arab men. They plan to leave Iraq to join their husbands. Their mother and brother want to stay on, to look after the family house. (Baghdad)

JULY 16, 2002. Assault on Iraq "a Mistake"—A former U.S. Marines intelligence officer arrives in Britain. Gulf War veteran Scott Ritter will speak to a House of Commons audience. Ritter, former weapons inspector in Iraq, believes U.S. and British troops will try to topple Saddam Hussein as soon as mid-October. He says that Iraq has no weapons of mass destruction capability. (*Mirror*)

JULY 2002. Mawafaq took a leave of absence from his job to go to Baghdad to fetch his mother. She was left alone when his father died two years ago. Mawafaq's brother is in Germany. They have a sister in Mosul in north Iraq. She refuses to leave her home, but she asked her brothers to get their mother to safety. (Missouri)

JUNE 25, 2002. The United States has reportedly moved 7,000 forces into Kurdish areas of North Iraq, in place for what may be a multi-pronged assault on Iraq. At the same time, Jordan is said to be turning over two air bases to the United States to use for air attacks from that side. (Associated Press)

OCTOBER 2002. Nazira's son is in Egypt working for a computer company. He has given up trying for an overseas PhD program in nuclear engineering, his specialty. He is Nazira's only son. She visited him there, but now she doesn't know whether to return to Egypt or stay in Iraq. (Baghdad)

JULY 17, 2002. Ankara. If Iraq becomes a democratic state, "it won't be only the people of Iraq who benefit from this, but it would be the whole world, this region. . . . Turkey stands to benefit enormously if Iraq becomes a normal country," said Wolfowitz, the Pentagon's no. 2 official, who met with top Turkish leaders. (Associated Press)

2001. After his two sisters and mother left Baghdad, Shaker stayed on to look after the family house with its collection of art and antiquities. His wife works in a school; their baby is three years old now. He promised his father, before he died five years ago, that he would never sell the family's treasures. But neither can Shaker remove them from Iraq. His mother in Sweden says get out. What shall he do with his father's collection? (Iraq)

JULY 18, 2002. Secretary of State Colin Powell was asked to comment on the response of U.S. allies being publicly averse to any kind of action against Iraq by the United States. Was it likely the United States would have to proceed alone? Powell replied, "We're in consultation with our friends about the danger that the Iraqi regime presents to them and to the world. We believe it is in the best interest of the world and the region and the Iraqi people for the regime to be changed. Obviously we're looking at options." (National Public Radio, Washington)

Ashia and Maan, her husband, sent their two eldest sons to study in England in 1999. Their plan is to send the rest of the family there, one by one. That's their hope. Maan is a senior psychiatrist at a government hospital in Baghdad; he also runs a small private clinic. He is overwhelmed with patients. "I have only rudimentary drugs. I have no way to help my people." (private communication, Baghdad)

JULY 11, 2002. Gerald Butt, Gulf editor of the *Middle East Economic Survey,* said, "The removal of Saddam is, in effect, the removal of the last threat to the free flow of oil from the Gulf as a whole." Iraq has oil reserves of 112 billion barrels (eventual reserves could be as high as 220 billion barrels), seven times those of the combined UK and Norwegian sectors of the North Sea. (*Times,* London)

2002. Ramadan's children went to Australia with their mother. He stayed in Hilla, Iraq. With his taxi service, he earns enough to live, he says. His children want him to join them. The boys phone every week pleading with their father to leave Iraq. "I tell them, yes, I'm getting ready. I never got on with my wife when we were together, so it will be the same there. I don't expect to live long anyway. I am seventy-one. If there is a war, I will take up arms to defend my land." (Hilla)

JULY 2002. Voices in the Wilderness (Chicago-based anti-war group founded by Kathy Kelly) is calling for volunteers to join their efforts to stand in solidarity with Iraq. They will join other groups of pacifists from around the world and will stay in Iraq, alongside the Iraqi people, even as the assault proceeds. (Voices in the Wilderness press release)

2002. Along with his medical colleagues, Naji had succeeded in rebuilding their general hospital in Kerbala. The sanctions almost incapacitated the work of the hospital, but gradually they brought it back and, he said, they saved a few lives. They even built a new pediatrics wing in 2001. This year Naji, a surgeon, has begun to look for a job in Germany, where he had originally studied. (Kerbala)

JULY 15, 2002. Saudi Arabia had made it clear for the past year and continues to maintain it opposes a military strike on Iraq and cannot allow U.S. planes to fly from its bases as it did in 1991. For the past five years Saudi diplomatic ties with Iraq have strengthened, and the Saudi leadership believes its restoration of ties is the best way to secure security in the region. (press report)

JULY 19, 2002. A high level Iraqi embassy official in New York who defected with his family, has applied for asylum in the US. (Reuters)

JULY 19, 2002. U.S. experts have begun a two-week training course for Uzbek military, coping with incidents involving weapons of mass destruction, officials said. The training, which began Monday, is part of the U.S. Defense Department and FBI's counter-proliferation program. (Associated Press)

Gazwan returned to his home in Baghdad after a year working in the Emirates. He said he preferred his country. He and Sousa, his wife, were unhappy so far from their families. Sousa is pregnant, and Gazwan wants his first child to be born in his homeland. After that, he doesn't know. (Iraq, private communication)

Campaigners across Europe are marching to protest the war on terrorism. Hundreds of Muslims from all over Britain have gathered in central London to demonstrate against America's recent foreign policy. Simultaneous demonstrations are occurring in Berlin, Brussels, Vienna, and Jakarta. Campaigners are planning to march to the embassy of Uzbekistan, a country they highlight as "a prime example of the war America is waging against the Muslims." (www.ananova.com)

JUNE 2002. Hala went to Dubai with her husband two years ago. They now have a baby. She asked her parents to join them. But she is uncertain about her sister, Nasra. Nasra is a government engineer in Baghdad and does not want to leave her job. "We have to help her, too," writes Hala.

JULY 18, 2002. From July 11 to July 13, a CIA-supported gathering in London of hundreds of Iraqi military and political foes of Saddam Hussein announced a virtual government in exile. At the meeting was Jordan's Crown Prince Hassan. Media reported that Jordan's pro-U.S. monarchy has "agreed secretly to allow U.S. special forces to operate from two of its air bases" when the invasion takes place. (Brian Becker, International Action Center, New York, in *Herald of Scotland*)

JULY 2002. Bushra's parents are both over ninety. Her brother and his family are trying to leave. Her sister has been out of the country for eight years. Sisters and brothers together decided that Bushra should remain in Iraq with their parents, whatever happens. She is selling as much family property as she can in order to help her brother resettle somewhere. (South Iraq)

JULY 18, 2002. Articles have appeared in the major press of U.S. allies with screaming headlines like that in the July 16 National Post of Canada: "Iraq is bound to lose, quickly, completely." On the same day British prime minister Tony Blair went out of his way to tell the members of Parliament that his government will not be compelled to discuss with them any British participation in the coming war. (Brian Becker, IAC)

2001. Tamer says he is going to university now for one reason. "It is my only chance for a visa to somewhere. Iraq, at least for the present, offers us an excellent education. This is something that I know outside governments will buy with a visa." (Iraq)

2002. California Department of Highways has added 500 Iraqi trained engineers to its staff since 1993. Almost every one is a refugee from Iraq after the embargo was imposed. (communication from expatriate Iraqi engineer, California)

JULY 18, 2002. Impact of Leaked War Plan—The administration's psychological war, or "Psyops," as it is known in military parlance, began with special intensity when a top-secret five-inch-thick dossier detailing plans for an invasion of Iraq with 250,000 troops was "leaked" to the *New York Times,* which published it on July 5. Since then, the print media and television have been dominated by a discussion of the tactics of the coming war. (Brian Becker, IAC)

JULY 11, 2002. West Sees Glittering Prizes Ahead in Giant Oilfields—No other country offers such untapped oilfields whose exploitation could lessen tensions over the Western presence in Saudi Arabia. (Michael Theodoulou and Roland Watson, Nicosia)

After Kuwait's liberation by U.S.–led forces in 1991, America monopolised the postwar deals, but the need to win international support for an invasion is unlikely to see a repeat. . . . Russia, in particular, and France and China, all permanent members of the United Nations Security Council, have high hopes of prizing promises of contracts in a liberated Iraq from a United States that may need their political support. (*Times,* London)

On a Rainy Day in San Diego

I long for you
the light rain
and autumn shedding
all my leaves
my footsteps winged
the wind my path
your face my sacred destination.
I pass solemnly along the shore
as if you are this frightful Pacific.
I wander in my reverie
There
lost in song
some wondrous cottage
snug in a shady thicket.
I wish I could live there
but time and exile
separate us.

I wonder
has spring been forgotten in San Diego?
has it stayed behind
with no reason to follow?
Alone in the green hills—
like a child—
spoiled by relatives and visitors.

The beauty of San Diego
reminds me of Lebanon
if only the bleeding would stop.
It reminds me of festive Kurdistan
celebrating with flutes and tambourines.
And the wrested homeland
—how much we have lost—
how much noble Jerusalem means to us.

The beauty of San Diego tortures me.
These silver clouds slaughter me.
How can I live in a country
where swords are sharpened daily for our people?

By Lamea Abbas Amara, 1991. Translated from the Arabic
by Mike Maggio.

2

Just Imagine: Baghdad, March 8, 2003, International Women's Day

Mohassen and her children are back in Baghdad. The Iraqi family returned from the Jordanian border after being refused entry there. They had left their home yesterday after she decided to escape the impending war.

Just imagine. Imagine years of determination to stay in your country, despite every hardship, ill health, humiliation, funerals, and loneliness. Imagine your loving husband working far away in the Arab Emirates. He phones regularly asking Mohassen to join him, to send the girls to him, to visit him if only for a few weeks.

Imagine declaring: "As an Iraqi, I will not be forced from my homeland. This is my country. I love my nation. I will not allow the Americans to take it from us, from my father, from my president, from any Iraqi."

Imagine being economically well off, yet suffering countless deprivations each day from the hard, hard blockade.

Imagine years of helplessly watching friends die before you, give up before you, depart before you, stricken by cancers, heart failures, miscarriages, diabetes, ulcers.

Imagine, with a military invasion just days away, calling your dearest friends with whom you stood for twelve years, to say, after all their pleas and good wishes, "Good-bye. *Allah karim.*"

Imagine leaving your brothers, leaving your neighbors to pray themselves through yet another war.

Imagine packing up the house, bundling paintings and wardrobe, assembling documents and a few valuables and delivering them along with the children's pet bird to your sister's house.

Imagine telling the children you did not know when they might return and whether they could take their exams in Jordan.

Imagine hasty arrangements with your employer to hold your job and instructions to the neighbor's gardener to guard the house.

Imagine ordering the taxi to the border, leaving your own car at your brother's. Imagine arguing with your weeping children about what they can and cannot take with them to Jordan, about one more good-bye phone call to a school friend. "Please, Mamma, please."

Imagine the car, piled with bags and boxes, arriving at the Iraqi border after the six-hour drive across the desert. Then the exit procedures—opening every item in your bags for inspection, filling out papers, answering questions, turning from the eyes of the officials who cannot leave. (They nevertheless graciously wish you well.)

Imagine finally pulling the children, cranky and groggy with sleep, into your taxi. You drive out of the Iraqi customs shed and turn your back on the great arch above the gateway at Treibeel, with its portrait of your ruinous president, his wooden hand held aloft. Your car moves toward the next portal and you exhale deeply. You feel no emotion as the portrait of the little Amrikyan king (Abdellah) comes into view and you arrive at the border of Jordan.

Then imagine a Jordanian customs officer handing back your papers and saying, "*Ma fi majal.* No chance. You can't enter."

Imagine another three hours, arguing, phoning your husband in the Emirates, weeping, calling friends inside Jordan to find someone, anyone, to give you clearance to cross. No chance. And there is nowhere to sleep. You feel grateful that the taxi driver agrees to return with you.

Imagine another six-hour drive through the night, all the way back to Baghdad.

Mohassen's sister rushes to her house to welcome her. They weep joyously. The next day Mohaseen finds she is flooded by a sense of relief. She had been telling her husband for years that she would stay, whatever. Tomorrow she will phone him to ask him to join them in Iraq—to spend the war together.

Just imagine our lives.

It is such a beautiful spring day. How could a war possibly be sweeping toward us?

Art galleries on Abu Nawwas Street still remain open every evening. Posters in the lobbies announce the Iraq Theater Company will stage *Gilgamesh* in the capital next week, and Laila has urged Mohaseen to bring the children to see the play. Before ringing off, Laila reminds her friend about bottled water; supplies are running low, and the price has doubled since she left for the border on Thursday. Look for a generator as well, Laila advises, although she warns that it is unlikely she will find one. The women consider combining households to wait together for the attack. Yes, that is a good idea.

Mohassen left for the border on March 7 and found herself back in Baghdad the next day.

Twelve days before the March 19 invasion, I travel to Mosul. I want to visit the hospital there but also to escape the tensions building in Baghdad, mainly among newly arrived foreigners.

Some foreign supporters of Iraq, called "human shields," vow to stand in solidarity with the country during the attack; stalwart members of international delegations arrive to urge the government to capitulate or negotiate; other newcomers are a mix of journalists arriving to cover the biggest story of their careers and expatriate Iraqis desperately trying to help their families. It is harder each day to know who is what they claim to be and what news is trustworthy. The one thing all of us know for certain is that a massive attack is imminent.

At some level there must be panic in every corner of Iraq, including Mosul. But I do not feel as nervous here as I do in the capital, bombarded by rumors, milling among nervous journalists, consulting officials who are themselves preparing to bolt at any moment.

Upon arriving in Mosul, I phone WBAI, the radio station in New York to which I am dispatching reports. A colleague calls me back eager for a story: "Tomorrow is International Women's Day." She dearly wants a radio report on how women in Iraq are coping. "Do they know women around the world are demonstrating against the war in solidarity with Iraqi women?"

The question annoys me. One does not need to ask Iraqi women or girls—or any Iraqis—how they feel. Because not long before, on February 15, on satellite television from inside Iraq, all of us viewed the drama that some Europeans considered their finest moment: mass demonstrations in hundreds of cities worldwide in a historic expression of solidarity with Iraq's people. It would remain a proud moment for many inhabitants of developed nations. People of conscience, members of peace-loving democracies said, "No war!" For us, locked inside Iraq, the worldwide protests are simply another foreign news story. Those displays do not impress the people of Iraq; they arrived twelve years late, too late. And when they calculate the numbers, Iraqis see how the fifteen million demonstrators amount to barely 0.2 percent of those western populations. Any proclamations on March 8 are bound to pass without interest inside Iraq.

March 8 is a Friday. *Youm al-Jumaa*, day of gathering, is for Muslim prayer and rest. I can feel the palpable bond of solidarity deep within the people around me. It is as solid as it is sad. Today is a time for husbands and wives, children and mothers, sisters and brothers. It is a day of commonality. An apocalypse is about to open on them. I expect not one Iraqi does not silently admit by this time that an attack is inevitable. Everyone remembers the 1991 bombings. This will surely be worse.

Can anyone comprehend the magnitude of the coming assault and what might follow? I hear no analyses, and I am in no mood to ask questions about the war stampeding into us. I ask no one if they are Sunni or otherwise.

It is a glorious spring day, a day for a picnic at the man-made lake above the great river Tigris that pushes through Mosul city. A day for the family to drive onto the hills around Nimrud, a day for children to run on the still unexcavated mounds of the city that our ancestors had built 5,000 years ago, a city that so symbolizes Iraq's presence in civilization. How can a war be closing around us? How can thousands of tanks be lined up along three borders ready to roll over us? How can thousands of planes loaded with missiles and bombs be waiting for orders to attack?

Night rains nourish the gardens on the banks of the blue Tigris and soak the wide, open hills of sprouting green wheat. Miles and miles of rolling green fields. Familiar. Serene. Spectacular.

Everything appears so tender, so vulnerable. Here and there, we glimpse apricot blossoms, delicate and white, peering from walled yards in the old neighborhoods of the city. Will they survive better than we might?

By noon the city is half-empty. Cars and vans filled with families and friends and set out toward the green hills on all sides beyond the city. Whether we are Christian, Muslim, Turkman, Kurd, Arab, or Sunni, our mothers spread plastic sheets over soft, sprouting wheat and then anchor them with bowls of cucumber and fruit. On nearby hillocks, fathers and sons pray. Car doors and trunks are flung open to catch the clean, spring air. Brothers and sisters stretch out, looking into the blue sky. Young families do not wander far from their mothers.

The city seems almost empty. The streets are quiet. Where the roadway follows the bank, above the river, a promenade waits for strollers who will arrive in the early evening. Soda vendors pass the day here, shifting their weight from one foot to the other a few yards from their battered, rusty coolers with their meager clutch of 7UP and Pepsi drinks. Clusters of two, three, or four chairs are set out on the pavement for their customers, mainly families without cars. After families depart, the vendors will stay on, hoping for a sale to the young couples who come here after dark to gaze into the river.

"*Allah ala ayyamak, ya Dejli*" (Allah, those glorious days were yours, O Tigris) is a phrase common in Mosul where this waterway is an intimate partner in people's history and modern-day fate.

The ruins at Nimrud site some fifteen miles beyond Mosul always attract visitors on Friday, although Ahmed, the guard and guide, is on duty every day.

He leads young sightseers to a small platform and invites them to peer into the ancient brick well. It is smooth and perfectly circular. He urges each child to touch the walls along the corridor and to glide their fingers over the 5,600-year-old carvings that tell histories, praise kings, and analyze their ancestors' discoveries.

Yah, Iraq. How we love Iraq.

Those incisions of cuneiform words on granitelike panels are so fine, and their edges are so keen, they appear to have been drilled only yesterday by a computerized machine. They are surely too precise to have been scored by hand. Ahmed apologizes for the scaffolding around the main gate of the Nimrud ruins. "Restoration was restarted only two years ago. For ten years, because of the embargo, things were neglected. When the repairs are complete, the museum will be as glorious as it was in the past," he says, his voice trailing off. Then he concludes, "*Allah karim*" (God is merciful). We repeat, "*Allah karim*." In reality, no one knows what the future holds.

"What is more vulnerable?" I ask myself this as I watch these families at play and while we drive through the countryside, between the fields, and back to Mosul's streets.

I notice a pickup truck heaped with cardboard boxes. Some have split open, their contents tumbling out, and the three soldiers sprawled over the load try to hold it together. The spilled cargo, I see now, are black soldiers' boots—supplies for the army that will defend the land.

Among the shops is a furniture store on the main road into the city. White plastic picnic chairs are stacked on the pavement, ready for sale. Closer to our residence, a nine-year-old girl with heavy eyeglasses is walking home. She is wearing a bright yellow jogging suit.

Which will break first when the strike comes? The glass windows of the university campus? Or the new graduate, Maher Feisel, who defended his master's thesis in French literature yesterday, the same boy who at the age of eleven (that would have been during the 1991 Gulf War) dreamed in French stories?

Which will be crushed first? Palestine or Iraq?

Who will surrender first? The man polishing his new orange Nissan taxi or those soldiers digging shelters in fields of young wheat?

Who will wear those black boots? Who will buy the white plastic chairs? And how long can Ahmed guard Nimrud?

Following thousands of other families into the city, we return to Bushra's house. I suspect most families will automatically switch on their TV sets or radios to hear the evening news. The UN Security Council has been in session today, debating "the question of Iraq." Some of us gather to watch. We hear the distinguished men in charge of weapons inspections for Iraq request more time. No vote is taken. They agree to schedule another meeting.

Because discussing international deliberations over Iraq has become a daily habit here, a few women and men talk about the latest phase of what they call "the UN stage show." Regardless of our cynicism, nothing quells the terror we feel in our hearts under our spring Iraqi sky.

Before he leaves his sister's house, when there is a moment of silence in the room, Mustafa casually offers: "I have completed my military service. I have fought in two wars, first against Iran and then against the Americans. I am not a young man, and I am sick. But I will be ready to defend my nation, and so shall my father. My son, too," he adds, smiling as he puts his hand on the back of his boy's head and leads him into the reddening evening.

Author's note: An earlier version of this chapter appeared under the title "March 8, 2003, International Women's Day in Iraq," published in *Shattering Stereotypes: Muslim Women Speak Out,* ed. Fawzia Afzal-Khan (Northampton, Mass.: Interlink, 2005). Used with permission.

Night Sky

She pleads, "Just imagine our lives."
Tilting my head to the night sky
I watch the stars shine calmly
over our small world.
From wherever we are,
Baghdad is not so far.

by Lisa Suhair Majaj, from *Geographies of Light*, forthcoming

3

Adnan in America (Forget about Iraq), 2001

Well before the March 2003 invasion of Iraq, Iraqis who had settled in the United States and had chosen to forget Iraq were not sheltered from the chaos, the follies, and visits by U.S. intelligence agents, the hatred, the embargo, threats, or appeals for help. Adnan, from a town not far from Mosul, left Iraq more than twenty years before the invasion and never returned. Yet here he was, in California, floundering like a desperate refugee.

Adnan and his American wife of eleven years were driving to the Los Angeles airport to welcome his son. Unlike her husband, Liza was cheerful about their visitor. This reunion had been her idea. After she learned that her husband had a grown son in his family's home in northern Iraq, she was determined to bring the boy to live with them. Adnan was never as eager as Liza about this, but he finally agreed. They faced many obstacles. Even now, he felt apprehensive. The boy was a complete stranger to Adnan, having been born five months after Adnan left Iraq to study in the United States. The young father-to-be had intended to close that chapter of his life for good when he set out for California. But Iraq kept intruding into his new life, with its wars and finally, after the blockade.

Adnan gripped the wheel tightly as he drove on. Hovering in front of him was the bright face of Ali, the face he knew only from a photo on their kitchen counter. He had looked at the photo every day for three years, since Liza convinced him they should bring the boy to live with them. Ali's broad forehead was the same as his father's. Like Adnan, he was also tall.

"He's a man now." Adnan had to remind himself of this. Ali was aboard the 3:00 p.m. flight direct from Ankara on June 12, 2001. Today would be the boy's first encounter with his father.

Ali's mother began preparing her son to leave Iraq after his fifteenth birthday. At eighteen, he would be drafted into the military. She saw no signs of the embargo's end. His father had been sending her money for Ali since the embargo began. That was not enough. She knew it would be possible for Ali to reach Turkey where one of his father's brothers lived and would help him.

Tens of thousands of Iraqis had escaped via Turkey through the Kurdish hills since the 1991 war. Many left reluctantly, forced by the blockade to seek another home. But Ali had never been separated from his mother and grandmother. He might never again see her or his grandmother. He did not want to leave. When he turned eighteen, the family prevailed. Besides, under Iraqi law, he was now the responsibility of his father. Before they could get him a passport, another year had passed. With it in hand, Ali needed just three days to reach Ankara. Living with his uncle in Turkey, he waited almost another year. Finally Uncle Jamal announced that the boy's American papers were ready. It was time for Ali to go to his father.

A Product of the Good Years

"Do you think he speaks English?" asked Liza. She was growing more apprehensive as the miles between their home and the airport lessened. Ali would actually be with them, in their home, tonight. It suddenly occurred to her that she might be unable to communicate with him.

"Of course," said Adnan. "We all learned English in Iraq. Ali is—" He stopped, realizing that he, too, was uncertain, uncertain about what Iraqi kids studied nowadays, uncertain about Ali's abilities. They spoke in Turkman whenever he and the boy talked by phone. Iraq had changed so much during the embargo years. Education was not what it had been. Adnan heard that schools had deteriorated. Health services had become decrepit, even for those who had money. Whenever Adnan found someone going to Iraq or to Turkey, he sent cash: $400, $1,000, sometimes more.

Still, the family appealed to Adnan to take his son. There was no future for young Iraqis at home; there could be another war. The American couple finally decided to concentrate on getting Ali out of Turkey. For three years this had been their priority.

Liza gently gripped Adnan's arm as they drove on. Her buoyancy and faith had led them to this point. "We'll find a school for him if he needs to study English. At twenty, he'll learn quickly."

Twenty years. That was how long it had been since Adnan left Iraq. Yet, throughout these twenty years, Iraq's fate still disrupted Adnan's life and engulfed him emotionally. Perhaps it was because Adnan never really made a clean break with his homeland or with his family. The first time he went abroad was in 1972. He was twenty-four, and he had accepted a government teaching assignment to Saudi Arabia.

The 1970s, depending on your politics, was a good time for most bright and ambitious young Iraqis, especially those from rural backgrounds and humble provenance.

Education, already of a high standard, was expanded to embrace every child. Graduate schools, technical colleges, and research institutes were created. Education was free, and possibilities for most young Iraqis, girls and boys, who completed university were limitless. They would become an ambitious, daring, urbane middle class of modern Iraq.

After finishing school, graduates leaped ahead along paths opened by the aggressive Baath leadership. The Baathists intended for their socialist system to become a model for other Arab nations. They claimed there would be no distinctions among Iraqis in the modern state. Although the Party ensured that power remained in the hands of a few and favored Sunnis, their policy promoted minorities, especially bright children, in line with a policy to demonstrate equal opportunity. As long as they were not communists and they didn't question party policy, Turkman boys like Adnan found plentiful opportunities.

Adnan left Mosul to study French at a college in Baghdad, then shifted to art history and from that to fine art. He never imagined this would become his passport to the United States twelve years later. Growing up in the 1960s and 1970s, he and others in his generation did not seek to escape their homeland. Committed to a program of rapid modernization, Iraq expanded facilities to train their own professionals and put them to work. Graduates found exciting and well-paid careers at home in agricultural and solar energy labs, civil engineering projects, publishing, fish and forestry institutes, schools, hospitals, universities, museums, and the oil and chemical industries.

Assignments in neighboring Arab states were also open to young professionals. French colonizers hadn't allowed Algerians to use their own Arabic language, and after the French left, hundreds of Iraqi graduates headed to North Africa and elsewhere to teach Arabic. After Adnan arrived in Saudi Arabia to teach Arabic, he convinced the education ministry in Jeddah that Saudi youths should learn to paint and sculpt, and so he taught art. This, he claims, helped him endure an otherwise dreadful two years at what he called an outpost in the desert.

When Adnan returned to Iraq, he moved to the capital. He was twenty-six, and he easily merged into a vibrant community of artists within Baghdad's new middle class. Almost all these artists found work as teachers, and many sold their work to private collectors. Purchases of paintings, ceramics, and sculpture by ministries and other government institutions supplemented the income of most artists. This was in accord with government policy. Across the country, the work of Iraq's contemporary artists hung in government offices, meeting halls, schools, and clubs.[1] The Baathists had committed themselves to the arts, especially plastic and visual arts, perhaps thinking that visual art was less politically troublesome for them. As the same time, policy makers understood how visual art could serve as a powerful medium to represent the accomplishments of contemporary Iraq and build bonds with other nations. Contemporary artists were also seen as carrying on the legacy of Iraq's unmatched 10,000-year history in the arts. The prehistoric figurines, the jewelry designs, innovations in metal fabrication and ceramic technology, the mosaics, engravings, architecture, pottery, and the first books—all from Iraqi's glorious past—were preserved for global humanity by its artists. (Writing, a significant part of Iraq's special contribution to human civilization, did not fare as well in modern times. Creative writers were seen as notoriously critical people who should keep their political opinions to themselves, except to praise their leader.)

Iraqi artists, even during the monarchy (1921–58), benefited from generous government support; this was expanded under subsequent governments and continued up to the time of the blockade. Iraq's national galleries sponsored international exhibitions along with regular showings of contemporary Iraqi work. They also hosted frequent seminars on modern literature and arts, making certain that invitations went out to foreign teachers, critics, and artists. Before 1990 in Baghdad, in any month of the year, one could stroll through an exhibition and view the work of Vietnamese, Cuban, Indian, Pakistani, Chinese, Tunisian, Brazilian, or Czech artists. The visual arts were so well established that it withstood the pounding blockade. Iraq's artists actually flourished in the sanctions era, finding new private markets in the absence of government support.

Free Ride on the Baath Bus

In its zeal to glorify itself and enhance its own international goals, the government provided funding for bright young people to advance their skills. This often involved studying overseas. Painters and musicians went off to England, Italy, France, Czechoslovakia, Russia, Austria, and the United States. America appealed to Adnan. And indeed, he was accepted at the California School of Design in San Francisco. He would finally see the treasures collected in Western museums, learn new technology, and meet his Western peers. The scholarship was for five years, which meant Adnan might defer his military service and delay his marriage as well.

Postponing military service was easier than avoiding married life, however. Before his departure, Adnan's family arranged his marriage. His protests were useless. And even though he told his wife he did not want to stay with her, she soon became pregnant with his child.

The baby was not yet born when Adnan accepted the government award. Since the scholarship included family support, Adnan felt no guilt about leaving his wife behind. (This simply delayed the man's coming to terms with his past and his Iraqi identity.)

The art student from Mosul arrived in California in 1981. Who imagined Iraq would be embroiled in a war with Iran within a year? The country had entered a time of deepening nationalism and rapid economic growth. As one Iraqi graduate reflected thirty years later: "Our vision of ourselves was not simply excelling among the Arab states. We saw ourselves as once again world leaders in science, archeology, literature, playing a central role in new advances in civilization—as we had three thousand years earlier. When we went away to study, we were not seeking to be as good as the British, German, or American scholars and practitioners. We would be better because we would augment our own tradition with whatever we learned outside. Our government had the resources to supply us with everything we needed to continue our research, our art, our publication."

Few Iraqis passed up opportunities for advanced training. Most women and men who left Iraq during that period genuinely planned to return to help advance their nation. They knew many opportunities awaited them. They preferred to forget that behind the government's largesse was a party leadership with little tolerance for opposition, a policy that circumscribed the limits of intellectual pursuits, a military eager to evince its worthiness. Unless they met an exiled Iraqi communist abroad, these students could forget about what their government had done to them as well. Iraq's new leaders may have been generous, expansive, and visionary in some ways. But they were quintessentially military men committed to one-party rule and obedience.

Adnan had ignored the anticommunist sweeps during the 1960s in his country. He knew men and women who escaped to Cairo, Damascus, and Europe. Their fates seemed far from his interests. He had never associated with the communists. He had one ambition: to roam unfettered and indulge his passion for painting. With the party ready to care for a wife and baby, Adnan could concentrate on his own needs. In California, he did just that.

Not Difficult to Forget Home

Once a month, Adnan drove to the Iraqi consulate in Los Angeles to collect his allowance. He met the officials whose job was overseeing Iraqi students abroad. Among these men, Adnan was able to converse with a depth and glee not possible among his American friends. He talked with the consul in their real Iraqi language; they rediscovered places and people they knew at home. Using the consulate phone, Adnan called home to his mother and his wife. Because he had a baby son, the office pampered Adnan more than other students. He did not know and did not care if the consulate sent an intelligence agent to follow his movements around the city and at college.

For the first two years, Adnan shared an apartment near Oakland with Nidal, a Palestinian architecture student.

Adnan made friends quickly. He became known as the guy who was always available when someone needed help. With his generous stipend from Baghdad, he had no financial worries, not even when war between his country and Iran erupted in 1982. When he read stories about the war in local papers, it seemed his country could not lose; Iraq was always on the verge of overpowering the enemy, according to U.S. news reports. After all, America was supporting Baghdad. If he thought about the conflict, Adnan agreed with American intelligence that the Iranian religious revolution was dangerous and that the new Islamic regime had to be crushed. In any case, the war seemed remote, confined to a few frontier areas in the east and south and certain to end soon.

Two more years passed; the battle between Iran and Iraq lumbered on. Many sons were dying, and the nation needed more fighters. It was time for this Iraqi to go home. A letter arrived from the Ministry: "You have been on government stipends for more than four years. Your training is over. You are needed to help defend the motherland."

Adnan missed his next visit to the consulate. They phoned him: "Your check is here. We are waiting for you. *Ya ibni* (son); *Habibi* (dearest), you know about our new rules for military service."

He missed another appointment to pick up his stipend. In fact, he never went to the consulate again. Not on Iraq's national day or on President's Day. He didn't show up for the celebration parties in 1988 at the end of the war with Iran either.

"Forget Iraq," Adnan told himself repeatedly. He wasn't really an Iraqi anyway. He was Turkman, and he resented how Iraq touted its love for sister Arab states and its glory in defense of Arabism. After four years in California, the Turkman from Mosul felt how little he had in common with Egyptians or Palestinians.

Following his rebuff of the consulate, Adnan thought they might send someone to kidnap him. They did not, but his father telephoned and sent telegrams. "You have deserted your country. You will be jailed. Come home while there is still time for us to help you." His wife wrote a postscript: "Your son will soon go to school. Come home." Adnan was repulsed; he could not understand why. A new thought came to him: "To hell with Iraq."

Embracing America

Liza and Adnan drove steadily toward the airport. There had been a long pause in their conversation. They passed a glossy Tommy Hilfiger billboard on the highway, and Liza was able to vent her anxious feelings. "Ali must be as tall as you are. Shall we plan a shopping trip to outfit him tomorrow?"

Adnan tensed at the reminder of his son's maturity. "We're taking him to meet your parents tomorrow. Your mother is sure to buy him a whole wardrobe."

"They'll love him," Liza concluded. Adnan felt reassured.

In 1986, after that angry letter from his father and the reproachful words of his wife, Adnan really appreciated how special America was. It was free. Families did not arrange marriages. No American woman accepted a man she had not chosen. Americans were free to love. He knew this after he met Liza; she helped him feel, for the first time, what American love is. Americans were also free to resign from a job and to move to another city—to travel anywhere—and to start a new career. Americans were ignorant of tribal names. Who asked what family you belonged to or how beautiful your wife was?

Adnan also found himself questioning his government. Iraq was not a democracy. His people were not free to travel. Men were forced into military service. His new homeland was not in a foolish war with its neighbor. (He conveniently ignored U.S. adventures in South America and its blunders in Vietnam.) Iraq's parliament was a sham. Only the Iraqi military could remove Saddam Hussein, and they could only do that by murdering him.

Any news from Iraq reaching America was about war, only war. Iraqi men were dying. Iranian boys were killing them. What could Adnan do? To answer his doubts, the Iraqi embassy in Washington sent an officer to meet Adnan. They drank together and talked about America more than about Iraq, but the man insisted Adnan should return home. "Every Iraqi must serve the motherland," he gently reminded the painter. "The war will soon be over anyway. You can rejoin the college here. After all, America is our friend in this war. It will always welcome us."

The now cosmopolitan boy from the Kurdish hills often felt lonely. He longed to see his grandmother and mother and to sit with his village friends. But it seemed Iraq had become a place full of chaos and soldiers and funerals.

The prospect of returning to a wife he felt nothing for—she was just a village girl—helped further distance Adnan from his country. He did not allow himself to imagine being the father of a four-year-old boy.

Adnan went underground. He quit his studies at the institute and moved in with Liza in her apartment near the city center. He found work easily, first as a waiter, then as a private art teacher. With both of them working, they managed easily. Adnan's life with Liza during the next three years sped along: work, parties, days at the beach, exhibits and lectures, a fishing trip, Christmas and birthdays with her family, hanging exhibitions, a few sales, a group show, a spree in New York City. He and Liza settled into living as a couple. She was energetic and ambitious. She had money in trust from her parents, so their continued comfort was ensured. And she loved Adnan.

If anyone remembered where Adnan's homeland was, they never mentioned it. He himself heard nothing from Iraq for three years.

One summer day, Iraq's war with Iran ended as abruptly and as irrationally as it had begun. Adnan should have welcomed the news. Instead, he felt unsettled. He did not know why.

Liza viewed the cease-fire between Iraq and Iran as a chance to stabilize their lives. She was ready to marry Adnan. "You must write your family. Find out whether your wife expects you to return," she urged.

A reply from one of Adnan's brothers arrived within a month: "Your wife is more capable than you know. She doesn't need you now. I advise you to forget about Iraq. You would be jailed if you set foot in your motherland again." The letter said nothing about their son.

If the immigrant had his way, he would resolve to purge Iraq from his life forever. His first wife was far away. Who would report his Iraqi marriage? He would never return there. It was simpler for him to forget.

Liza insisted otherwise. If they were to marry, Adnan would have to be legally divorced. Liza's parents had met the artist and liked his quiet voice and his attention to their daughter. They hired a lawyer, and within two years his divorce was being processed. Adnan did not have to return to Iraq. There was no alimony payment. Best of all, no one mentioned his child. By 1990, weeks before the invasion of Kuwait, he received the papers, and within a month he and Liza were married. Another year and Adnan would have his citizenship. Now he could finally forget Iraq.

They moved to downtown Los Angeles and bought an apartment with enough space for his studio. They had many friends. Adnan was invited to show at a respected gallery. His work began to sell. He found commissions.

Then came August 1990 and Iraq's blunder in Kuwait. Adnan called Mosul and was able to reach his mother. She reassured him all of them were well. She urged him not to come home.

The American press became openly, fiercely anti-Iraqi. Saddam Hussein became a monster, and any Iraqi was suspect, even those long settled in the United States. Liza's parents cautioned their son-in-law that, as an Iraqi, he was certain to be watched by American intelligence. An FBI agent stopped by their apartment. The exchange was polite. Liza wisely insisted on staying with her husband; she gripped his hand tightly throughout the interview. No, Adnan assured the man, he had no ties with Iraq. He was just a painter. He had no political interests.

Adnan did not call Iraq for many years. He and Liza stayed away from meetings organized by antiwar activists. The immigrant had never associated with Iraqis in Los Angeles, although he knew many lived there. Somehow American friends learned about Adnan's origin; however American he felt, he found himself now tainted with "Butcher Saddam's" brush. The gallery postponed his exhibition. Two commissions were canceled. The couple received fewer dinner invitations. Adnan could not forget that he was Iraqi after all.

A message from Baghdad reached him months after the winter 1991 bombings ended. His younger brother Salam had died; another brother had fled to Turkey. His 93-year-old grandmother was still alive, and his parents were managing. They were all in the north, in their village. Phone contact with them was impossible.

Adnan scoured newspapers for reports from Iraq. What few articles he could locate spoke of hunger and disease caused by the embargo. There was simply no food. Medicine was unavailable. The sanctions on Iraq, barely in place for a year, were wreaking havoc across the country. Phone and mail services were cut. He heard rumors that no one could enter Iraq and no one could leave.

Into the second year of the embargo, a friend in Baghdad finally reached Adnan. "I have a message from your family. Your son is twelve. His mother wants you to take him. They are starving. You must help them."

During the next four years, Adnan and Liza's contacts with Iraq were fitful. Occasionally they phoned Turkey and his brother passed on fragments of news. Messages from the family outside Mosul repeated: "We are well. Don't worry. Send money for your son."

Adnan sought out people traveling to Iraq: a journalist, an Iraqi family, and an anti-sanctions group in San Francisco. He took cash to them with a phone number in Baghdad and a name in Mosul. He sent $400 the first time, then $600, and then $1,000. Young Ali would need $500 to purchase a passport.

Whatever they sent was consumed just in feeding the family. Any message arriving from Iraq, even after he had just dispatched a bundle of cash, said: "We are well, but send money for your son."

Adnan tried to help. He could not bear to think of his mother in such need. Eventually a journalist working in Iraq was able to get a copy of Ali's birth certificate, and she passed it on to Adnan. Liza began filing forms for Ali's immigration. She tried to convince her husband to go to Iraq where the process would be faster. "Liza, you do not know Iraq," he told her. He was certain he would be jailed for evading military service.

Finally the boy's uncle in Ankara managed to get Ali out of Iraq. He kept him with him in Turkey until his American papers were ready.

Earlier this month the boy turned twenty. And today he was aboard a plane descending toward Los Angeles airport, within moments of seeing his father. As Adnan left the parking lot and walked nervously, hand in hand with Liza, toward the arrivals lobby, he thought, "Finally I can forget about Iraq."

Postscript. During the first year of Ali's stay with his father, he was celebrated and pampered by Adnan and Liza, her family, and the neighbors. After the United States invaded Iraq in March 2003, Ali wanted to go home. He missed his mother. He had not yet found a job, and he had no American friends. U.S. intelligence agents visited both Ali and his father. They came to the house twice. Ali was troubled as he watched his father being questioned. Adnan appeared helpless and showed no feeling for his motherland.

Adnan suspected one of the agents who visited them met Ali again and recruited him for a U.S. mission because, not long after, without telling his father, Ali signed up to join the army. "I can translate. My country needs me. I can help take care of Mamma." Liza and Adnan argued with the boy for days. It was no use.

Ali left for a training camp in Georgia to prepare for posting to Iraq. He never reached Iraq. He turned up at his father's home a few months later, sullen and nervous. The boy's interest in Iraq had vanished. All Adnan could learn from Ali was that he and some other Arab boys, all American recruits for the Iraq mission, had fought with other soldiers, some of whom had returned from action in Iraq. Ali and the others were in jail for days before they were released from military service. "They said dirty things about Iraqis" was the only explanation the boy gave.

4

Mehdi

Mehdi was almost the same age as Adnan (see chapter 3), and he had a daughter as well as two boys. These Iraqi youths, like Ali, eventually would confront the 2003 invasion into their country. Before that they too braved the long block- ade. Within America, their once callow lives would be swept up by a rising political torrent.

In 1970, these two fathers entered Iraq's national agenda as young men on the cusp of careers in a stable and promising nation. Mehdi progressed along a different route than the painter, although their careers were launched by the same education system, designed to identify and advance Iraq's brightest young people in the service of an ambitious modern country.

Mehdi's culture and temperament led him into the Iraqi Foreign Service, and barely three weeks before the invasion of Kuwait by Iraqi forces in August 1990, this affable Iraqi diplomat arrived in the United States. He had previously only visited New York for short periods on urgent government business. This assignment was for a full term.

Advancing through the Iraqi Foreign Service, forty-four-year-old Mehdi found himself as a first secretary, assigned to his country's mission to the United Nations in the glamorous metropolis. This was a dream posting for him, after eighteen years with the ministry.

At the UN headquarters he expected to find dear friends from across the world. He would live in a high-rise Manhattan apartment and, most impor- tant, he would have his chance to travel across this fabled land.

The first secretary brought all the family: Suha, his beautiful, urbane wife, and their three children. Before this posting, they'd been in Dacca, Lagos, and Jakarta. Parents and children alike were keen to experience this country first- hand, to get to know this generous, colorful people—the Amrikyan.

Mehdi had served in Iraq's Foreign Ministry during the nation's most pros- perous years. By 1990, Iraq was on the verge of being recategorized by the UN from "developing" country to "developed," an infrequent occurrence in the world.[1] Mehdi was twenty-two when the Baath Party consolidated its rule in 1968. Nationalist, socialist ideals adopted by the new republic appealed to him. He and his peers respected European cultures but rejected European colonialist ambitions, which they recognized as an enduring threat. "The time of foreign control, political or economic, is over," said Mehdi's mentors. "You are a servant of the Arab nation. We judge you by your work and by your loyalty. The time for privileged families is over. We all eat from the same plate, and every Arab is equal to his brother."[2]

Across Iraq, class differences weakened after the 1958 revolution and were further diluted when the Baathists came to power.[3] Names of once notable families—many of them tribes—were sometimes invoked. People may recognize the sons and daughters of former mayors, ministers, and governors, but none enjoyed privileges based on that provenance. Although, following the British practice—priority in high government postings awarded to Iraqis of Sunni faith—ability and performance were essential to advancement. In personal relations, especially among newcomers to an office or city, your place of origin was what others first wanted to know. In his personal life, tribal identity was paramount for Mehdi.

Until the arrival of the blockade in 1990, high-ranking military and intelligence officers, ministers, and other key government figures lived simply and mixed freely with the general public. Their homes were not ostentatious, and their cars were indistinguishable. Saddam Hussein's inner circle was always the exception.[4]

For the most part, belief in Arab nationalism and meritorious service were the primary guides to success in Iraq. Whatever their level of training, most educated Iraqis became civil servants because all services and resources and most industries were nationalized under Baath rule. Jobs in medicine and foreign affairs carried the most prestige. The latter included nonparty members. Salaries were adequate, but employment benefits were especially generous. Neither nationalism nor rewards account for Iraqis' standard of excellence and professional commitment, however. Those qualities certainly preceded Arab nationalism and the Baath Party. Notwithstanding their historical achievements, even during the early twentieth century, Iraqis earned respect for their competence, their generosity and accessibility, and their ease in merging into any cultural environment.

Mehdi was a typical bureaucrat of the Iraqi Foreign Service. He was from a well-known tribe in a village near Fallujah, West Iraq. He was a team player, quick-witted, and possessed an astonishing memory. During his compulsory eighteen months of military training, he was selected for the Foreign Service where, because of his sharp intelligence and cautious nature, he was promoted above men and women who were more urbane.

Foreign service afforded Mehdi a degree of social status, yet he never changed his simple lifestyle. He was proud of that. When he visited his tribal village, he sat as an equal with the farmers, teachers, and health workers. Most of them were his cousins anyway. On his overseas commissions Mehdi's standard of living was not much different than at home. At their bungalow in Dacca, when Mehdi was with the Iraqi embassy in Bangladesh, he and Suha hosted cookouts in the lush monsoon gardens where Mehdi could be seen helping the servants. Dacca is where Mehdi grew to like curried fish. His government provided abundant aid to Bangladesh, mainly in education and electrification. All three of his children learned to speak Bengali there.

Now the family had arrived in what he regarded as classless America, a nation where your village or grandfather's status was unimportant, where rewards were based on merit. They were in a land whose citizens, Mehdi's generation felt, most resembled Iraqis.

A New Agenda

The Iraqi diplomat and his wife were settling into their apartment on the fifty-fifth floor, and the children were excitedly preparing for their first day in an American school, when Iraq made that fatal miscalculation—its invasion of Kuwait—and found itself at war. Leading the assault against Iraq was the United States, the nation Iraq most admired among the western states. Overnight, America had become its enemy. Virtually the entire world was lining up behind Washington against the Baath nation. Thirty-three countries were preparing for war on Iraq's twenty million inhabitants.[5]

Private Iraqi citizens as well as officials were dumbfounded to find themselves ostracized wherever they appeared. In a stroke, Iraqis had become the focus of international censure and, incomprehensibly, raw hatred.

One after another, Mehdi's family would return to Baghdad. Hanna, their daughter, was engaged, and since her fiancé would be called into military service, their marriage was moved ahead. Mehdi's wife, Suha, was a forthright woman. She declared that she had never really wanted to live in America. She fought with the neighbors. "Why should I have to defend my president? Why did the world suddenly and irrationally care so much about those indulgent, cultureless Kuwaitis? Their emir is only a creation of the British empire in any case," she retorted. "Like the king they imposed on us." Unhappy and angry, she decided to go home with Hanna. The boys stayed on with their father.

He had little time for his sons. The embassy in Washington was forced to close, and then it was ransacked by American agents.[6] This compelled Mehdi's office to assume responsibility for Iraq's affairs in the United States as well as carry on its work in the world forum.

Iraqis visiting the United States in those months found themselves stranded.

Prohibited from boarding planes even to travel home, and threatened on the street, sneered at by American colleagues, they called the mission for help. Mehdi was meanwhile assisting his ambassador in negotiating the release and the transport of American workers and their families held in Iraq (between the start of the crisis August 6, 1990, and Christmas).[7] Private companies with operations in Iraq were threatening Iraq with legal action over damages to their property and danger to their staff. And hundreds of journalists were clamoring for visas to Iraq.

Mehdi's office had to tackle all these crises at the same time that it carried out the increasingly demanding political negotiations between Washington, Baghdad, and the UN Security Council.

Obstacles confronted the staff at every turn. Doors that had always been open to Iraqis were closed. "Friends" became unavailable. Informed by Baghdad that Iraqi forces intended to withdraw from Kuwait, the mission staff found itself with awesome responsibilities. With their Washington embassy destroyed and sealed, it was up to Mehdi's office to convey Baghdad's policy to the American government and negotiate with other missions at United Nations.

Iraq's ambassador's attempts to inform the White House about their intended deployment from Kuwait seemed thwarted. No one was available to negotiate with.

Washington would not respond to Iraq's overtures. Any televised statement by the Iraqi president showed him defiant and uncompromising, although this was not the policy indicated in memos from Baghdad's foreign office. This left the Iraqi diplomats confused. Journalists were phoning for comment about rumors of Iraqi soldiers looting, raping, and killing in Kuwait and of Baghdad's intention to blow up Kuwait's oil installations. The Foreign Office issued statements, but international press reports seemed to invalidate them.

Mehdi watched helplessly, incredulous when the entire UN General Assembly with the exception of five abstaining nations voted to condemn Iraq.[8] The Security Council, with a vote of 13–0, had already imposed mandatory sanctions on Iraq (Resolution 661). When the U.S. Congress voted for war, news coverage shifted to the urgent dispatch of hundreds of thousands of allied troops and war machinery to Saudi Arabia, where the assault on Iraqi troops would be launched. Diplomats from friendly UN missions told their Iraqi counterparts that war plans were for real. "The U.S. and British are going to whip you."

Meanwhile Iraqi students, government-sponsored scholars at American colleges, phoned Mehdi's office, frightened and in need of advice. Fellow students were shunning them and calling them ugly names. U.S. intelligence agents had come to interrogate them; neighbors were threatening them. Several were evicted from their apartments. The besieged diplomat's sons now pleaded with their father to let them go home.

Following the speedy imposition of UN Resolution 661 embargoing Iraq on August 6, Iraqi assets in U.S. banks were frozen. Fifteen apartments leased by the mission for its staff, each rented at three to four thousand dollars per month, had to be maintained. New York landlords were threatening the mission with lawsuits. The Iraqi education consul found himself without funds to pay students their monthly stipends.

Mehdi and other embassy staff worked around the clock, often sleeping at the mission office. They were certain the crisis could be diffused, despite transparent and formidable military preparations by the Americans and British. Iraq could not last a day against the assembled forces. Iraq did not want a war. Dispatches from Baghdad repeated their intention to withdraw from Kuwait.[9] Their government was ready to capitulate. But nobody was listening to Iraq's representatives.

No Letters from Home

On January 17, 1991, at 7:10 p.m. New York time, the American-led assault began.

In their office, Iraqi embassy staff huddled together, smoking, tapping their feet nervously against the parquet floor, while they stared, stunned and helpless, as their nation was being bombarded on television. Over 700,000 troops were lined up against Iraq, 110,000 air sorties were launched, and over 4,000 missiles were fired. There was no fight. This was no real war! Communications with the foreign office in Baghdad were intermittent and useless at this point.

The most painful sight for Mehdi was the collapse of bridges over his land's great rivers. He watched televised replays of the bombing of Jisr Muallaq, a suspension bridge in Baghdad. Tears flowed as he gazed at the torn bridge near Fallujah, the town where he grew up. Nasiriyya Bridge was in tatters, too. Suha, unable to reach her husband by phone, sent a short message through the ministry on the first night of the assault: "We are alive. Keep the boys with you as long as you can."

As the bombing wore on, the staff at the UN mission sat bewildered, unable to grasp the extent of the calamity. The first secretary didn't have much work those forty-two days.

Finally the bombardment stopped, and a cease-fire was signed. But the end of the attacks brought no relief to Mehdi and his people. Months earlier, oil shipments had been halted. So had all imports. His country was heavily reliant on food and agricultural and industrial imports and totally dependent on foreign medicine. Nothing could enter Iraq by road, air, or sea. Mehdi's family needed cash. Legal claims arrived at the office from American creditors. Even prepaid medical and food supplies en route by sea when the embargo was imposed were not permitted to dock at Iraqi ports or cross a land border. Inside the country, food stores had been bombed, heightening the food crisis.[10] Without refrigeration, every family's food stock was rendered inedible. Reports of hunger spreading across Iraq reached New York. The Iraqi dinar was a fraction of last year's value. Mehdi's allowances were cut, and his salary was reduced. His colleagues at the foreign office in Baghdad sent notes asking him for medicine for their families. This continued during the six years Mehdi was in New York.

Caution Was Not Enough

Mehdi's boys survived the animosity of classmates and the cutbacks to their household budget. Khalid, seventeen, and Mahmoud, twelve, were sophisticated lads, modest and thoroughly trained in diplomatic protocol. They concentrated on their schoolwork and stayed close to home. "People will try to provoke you. Be prepared. Be polite. Walk away. Keep your passport with you, and don't volunteer anything about yourself," Mehdi cautioned them. During the three years following the war that the boys stayed on in the United States, they handled themselves well.

Mehdi was proud of his sons. Even when Khalid was apprehended and jailed for a night, his father was sympathetic. The problem had erupted on a quiet summer night while Khalid was having a soda at a nearby store with boys from his building. When a petty thief made a grab for some items at the doorway and fled, the cashier sounded the alarm. Feeling they had nothing to fear, the Iraqi and his companions waited. But while the police were questioning them, Khalid casually volunteered that he was the son of an Iraqi diplomat. Seeing the startled expressions of the policemen, he realized his mistake. Too late. "Oh, Saddam, eh?" one of the officers replied, moving toward the boy. "We know your type." Khalid reflexively raised his arm in defense, and both officers lunged at him. In a stroke, they had the Iraqi teenager in their patrol car and they were gone.

Khalid later told his father how he had been stripped naked at the local precinct. The police also took his passport. "Let's see if Saddam can help you now," said one officer to the young captive. "I've got a brother over there. If anything happens to him, you'll all be dead, you Arabs."

"Think your type can take American citizens hostage, do you?" added his partner, who passed the Iraqi boy to a third man who led him away. "Saddam f--cks a goat!" Khalid heard one policeman yell.

The boy stayed locked in a room at the police station until a UN liaison official found him the next day and took him home. Mehdi had never seen his son so grim-faced. His clothes were soiled. One of his socks was missing. "I hate this country," he said in a whisper when he sat with his father and told him how the police had spoken.

Mehdi tried not to show his rage. "You did nothing wrong. You did not hide that you are a son of Iraq. I am proud of you. *Ya ibni*, oh, my son, you watched those American cops and robbers movies," he said, trying cheer up the boy. "Well, now you've seen the real thing. How many diplomatic kids have this inside view of America?"

But the boy's hurt was too deep. Yes, he had been enchanted by the city, and his friends at home had envied his "golden opportunity" in the Big Apple. "Baba, please, I want to go home," he told his father the next morning. Everything had changed. Khalid left after a few weeks, before spring semester ended. By summer's end, Mahmoud would join his brother and the rest of the family in Baghdad. Meanwhile, for four more years, Mehdi lived a bachelor's life.

In August 1995, Mehdi was nearing his fifth full year in New York. Iraqis were finally accepting the need for long-term strategies. Diplomatic ties with nations across the world had to be reestablished. "We can do it." Mehdi was certain. "Our friendships are enduring. We will not repeat our mistakes. We are a patient people. We are adaptable."

Iraqis began to realize that the embargo might not be lifted. Not in a year or two or three. Maybe never. Poverty and other hardships were going to be with them for a long time. Work at the mission in New York became routine for the first secretary. And he was no longer the only bachelor. One after the other, families of his associates returned to Baghdad, needing the support of their extended families there and unable to bear the hostility they experienced in New York, even within the UN. The Iraqi resolved that he could have no American friends and that he would never see the Rio Grande, Tennessee, or Texas.

A Secret Excursion to Coney Island

With the arrival of the hot summer days of 1995, Mehdi resolved that he must go to the beach, something he had long wanted to do. The forecast of another sweltering day in New York afforded the diplomat the chance to visit Coney Island and swim in the surf. Before Mahmoud left for home, he promised that the two of them would spend a day at the seaside. "This is the only American beach you will see," he said to the boy. "The original Brooklyn Dodgers came from there. *The Godfather* was filmed there. Anyway," he added cheerfully, "I'm not going to let politics stop me from taking a swim in the great Atlantic Ocean!" Mahmoud didn't really care about Brooklyn. He rarely went out anymore. Yet he understood how few pleasures his Baba enjoyed; besides, Baba would soon be all alone in New York.

By 8:30 on Sunday morning, father and son were on the train heading toward Coney Island. From the moment he entered the subway car, Mehdi felt pleased with himself. He felt he was being swept into a tribal celebration as the crowded train sped through the tunnels of the city and toward the sea. More families boarded at each stop, and by the time the train was crossing Brooklyn, the aisles were dense with passengers. Puerto Rican, Mexican, Indian, Chinese, East European, Caribbean, and African people pressed close around the two Iraqis. The diplomat welcomed this intimacy.

In his everyday life, the Iraqi father shared little with these fellow travelers. Unlike them, he was not an immigrant but a member of the privileged diplomatic corps. He had a company car and a driver at his disposal during the week. He had tax-free privileges and diplomatic immunity. Expensive suits (all bought before the war) hung in his uptown apartment closet. He possessed a first-level UN pass and received paid home leave.

Yet here he sat in knee-length shorts and his baseball cap, rolling through Brooklyn on the D Train heading for a poor man's holiday at a noisy public beach. He felt barely distinguishable from the immigrant Honduran father, clutching a cooler full of sodas and steadying a little boy between his legs as the subway car rushed toward the ocean.

Mahmoud was absorbed with his sports magazine. Mehdi was smiling into the crowd, happier than he'd been in a long, long time. "*Allah karim*," he whispered. "By the generosity of Allah. I'm here today, thanks to the embargo."

Young Mahmoud would rather be visiting the spacious suburban homes of wealthy Iraqi exiles they knew on the North Shore of Long Island. But going there needed special permission from the U.S. State Department. Since 1990, Iraqi diplomats to the UN were forbidden to venture beyond the five boroughs of New York City without approval—a travel restriction imposed by Washington. Thus today's subway trip to Coney Island in Brooklyn.

"I prefer this," the Iraqi father thought, pressing his lips together determinedly. "Why should we—Iraq, a sovereign nation—submit an application to the American government to permit us to have a simple picnic? Never!" He surveyed the families around him. "Even these immigrants whose child wears a shirt handed down from her older sister has more freedom than our Iraqi diplomat!" he mused.

The subway train rolled along above ground, then slowed as it pulled into Coney Island station. The entire train quickly emptied amid a new burst of glee and hurried instructions as each parent gathered children and hauled stuff onto the platform, down the stairs, into the street, and toward the salty, windy open space. Iraqi son and father followed the crowd. "Hmmm," mused Mehdi. "No quarantined bench marked 'Iraqi,' and no gateman asking to inspect our passports."

For the past six years, all but the Yemeni and Cuban diplomats at the UN had avoided Iraqis. Even Bangladeshi officers he had known in Dacca stopped speaking to Mehdi. A few times, when things slackened at the office, the lonely diplomat went to a bar near his apartment in search of new faces. He met nice people there, just amusing themselves for the evening.

Invariably he was asked where he came from. He could have told them anything: Indonesia, Bangladesh, Guatemala, Tunisia. "Iraq," he always replied, lifting his head, staring straight into the eyes of the American. The Iraqi couldn't betray his homeland, even during a casual encounter. The strangers backed away. So he gave up those forays.

He liked the singers Reba McEntire and Bonnie Raitt, although he heard them only now and then on television. At home, Mehdi played some cassettes of Iraqi music that men at the mission circulated among themselves. He liked melancholy Iraqi songs. "I feel my sadness is not mine alone. I am less lonely. I feel better."

Swimming with the Tide

The Foreign Service officer from Baghdad stood among the picnickers on Coney Island. It gave him the sensation of intimacy, something he had rarely known during these five years. "We are all equal," he thought. He watched an infant crawling over its mother's legs. The child was about the age of Hanna's baby girl, his first grandchild, whose little face he had not yet touched.

Father and son walked across the beach and halted close to the thundering surf. Mahmoud spread a blue bed sheet on the already warm sand and bought drinks from a passing vendor while his father pulled off his shirt, inhaled the Atlantic air, hoisted the waistband of his swimsuit, and set out for the open water.

It wasn't his beloved Euphrates or the canals near the farm at home. But the farmer's son from Fallujah didn't think of his childhood in Iraq now. He just languished in the cold, salty water, feeling swathed and protected by the cries of happy children and the gentle push of the sea against his body. He felt a thousand miles from the UN.

"Things change. In our part of the world, life is always changing," Mehdi often said to friends. He thought therefore that life for his Iraqi people was bound to improve soon. Surely the sanctions could not go on much longer.

Orange Square, by Burhan al-Mufti, 1998.

5

"I Love My Country"

Forgetting war and the hardships and sadness it creates is sometimes possible. Adnan (see chapter 2) escaped to a distant land; he believed he had managed to disappear inside a gentle American family. Mehdi (see chapter 3) became a more devoted civil servant; he sought solace in music; he walked for hours in the anonymous streets of Manhattan; he took secret excursions to beaches crowded with humble families.

In Baghdad, men and women found relief in simple exchanges—lewd jokes about a scandalized U.S. president, new metaphors for their tyrant Iraqi chief. They noted the time when night jasmine bloomed. They counted spy satellites. They circulated family news from overseas—from someone who "did not forget their Iraq."

The vicious embargo pounded insistently at their doors, however poor, however privileged the house. Iraqis' sovereignty was being ripped away from them and shredded before their eyes. Yet somewhere inside its history and language, coursing through its rivers and sweeping across its deserts, Iraq offered up sustenance. More than once, inside the Iraqi land, my friends and I also found ourselves able to taste some sweetness in this depleted earth. We broke through the unbearable loneliness from civilization.

The Best Companions

We were three Arab women on an uncommon sanctions-busting outing. It was 2000, a full ten years since the UN had voted to lay siege to Iraq and almost two years since Iraq had switched to a policy of defiance to the U.S.–led blockade. This was surely one of the few times when citizens and their leader were in accord. Everyone joined the plan with gusto, pride, and hope. Iraqis appeared less tormented, even though they still moved through each day facing deprivation, illness, and worry. I spent a good part of my assignments documenting hardships. Suffering was so immediate, and I was committed to getting reports back to the still nascent anti-sanctions movement in the United States. It seemed frivolous or disrespectful to put that aside and say, "Let's have a holiday." Yet I did just that.

I was blessed with dear friends. One loaned me his car and driver; others took me to their favorite places to enjoy the pleasures of the land. We would motor into the open countryside beyond Baghdad and visit a rural market and an archaeological site. To hell with the embargo.

It was a Friday, the weekly holiday. We crossed the sleeping city and reached its outskirts by 8 a.m. We were headed south. My companions, Amal and Nermin, are trusted friends but especially dear to each other. Twenty years separate them in age, but they have the same deep love for Iraq, a land they are forever discovering. Each woman devotes herself to rebuilding the nation. And each has a son she has raised alone.

Nermin is a brilliant journalist, always finding new stories, eager to interview any newcomer who crosses her path, ready to pursue any subject. She is one of those whose work and life are totally intertwined. She lives in daily competition with her teenage son over the use of their home computer.

Amal's son, Munir, now thirty, left home to take up a job in the Emirates after a brief marriage. When the embargo struck, he had completed his MA in physics and expected to win a place at a U.S. or British university. But his applications were repeatedly turned down without explanation. Finally, he received a letter from a Canadian university specifically saying it was prohibited from accepting Iraqi students in "sensitive" fields such as physics. It was a bitter blow for Munir and for his mother.

Amal works from dawn until late at night in her gallery. She is proprietor of a private boutique and an aficionado of contemporary arts and crafts. I doubt if there is anyone else in Iraq able to manage what Amal has accomplished in her art center.

I am a visiting journalist long past my twenty-fifth trip into Iraq. Veteran enough to find ample companionship among Iraqi friends, I risk evenings and days doing what I wish, with whomever I wish. Amal had often talked about a drive into the countryside. Nermin was always ready for a break. I needed it, too. I knew I might earn a scolding from the Ministry of Information, whose "facilitators" are supposed to accompany me whenever I travel outside the capital. Those men were always charming and unobtrusive (see chapter 16). They were also helpful. But today's excursion could not include them. My friends and I would have more fun on our own. And we had Yussef, our driver, if a man was needed.

My first encounter with Amal was on my second visit to Iraq, in 1989, before the Kuwait fiasco and the 1991 Gulf War. Our introduction had been bristly, and it did not portend our eventual camaraderie. I was revisiting Baghdad to research a story about professional Iraqi women, and I was directed to Amal's boutique, an art gallery of contemporary treasures in cloth, ceramics, canvas, and wood. I burst into the shop with my camera, expecting to take some photos and depart. Amal rushed at me, barring my exit. "How dare you? Who are you? You cannot come and go just like that. Tell us about yourself. Sit down. Take tea with us." I was properly chagrined and duly allowed myself to get to know Amal and her friends.

Because of the 1991 war, the magazine story was axed. But I had been smitten with this land.[1] I resolved to return and find out about the bizarre turn of events. The terrifying retaliation was excessive, and I suspected at that time that Iraq's foolish venture into Kuwait was a trap, perhaps set by Washington. Certainly the scale of the Gulf War to liberate Kuwait and the punishment inflicted on Iraq through UN resolutions could not be satisfactorily justified by either American oil interests or human rights concerns. (The possibility of Iraq's entrapment warrants more attention after the 2004 revelations by "economic hit man" John Perkins.)[2] In 1991, simply examining the unreasonable terms of the blockade, I was convinced that the embargo was unjust and part of a malicious long-term agenda. Given Iraq's heavy dependence on imports, a blockade was perilous. My suspicions were reinforced by Iraqi economist Mustafa al-Mukhtar, who referred me to a September 1988 Pell Bill (S 2763) passed by the U.S. Senate to boycott Iraq economically. Mukhtar suggested the Pell Bill, redrafted in 1990 as HR 4585, was the model for the April 3, 1991, UN Resolution 687 imposing economic sanctions on Iraq.[3]

Well into my mission, perhaps in 1994, Amal introduced me to Nermin. I was attracted to the Iraqi reporter by her good humor. But before long I realized how skilled a journalist she was and how profound her knowledge of Iraq was. She is the only Iraqi I know who has been to every corner of her country as a journalist. She traveled on assignment to the battlefront during the Iran–Iraq war. She studied Iraqi history, and she keeps herself fully informed about current developments, economic and social, as well as archaeological news. She is also well versed in Islam, which she practices with deep faith. Her fund of knowledge and mastery of detail puzzles me because I found her files and her home always in total disarray. Moreover, Nermin talks incessantly. In the fleeting intervals in her chatter and jokes, she somehow picks up the latest details on any issue. I find her to be one of the best informed people in the country.

Before 1990, Nermin or Amal would have driven her own car into the countryside. Now the embargo had reduced both vehicles to wrecks. So we borrowed a friend's 1988 Toyota Crown and hired his driver for the day. Given the state of war created by the siege and the heightened security, we knew we would face many checkpoints. Perhaps because of the newfound hope infusing Iraqis after 1998, we felt confident we would handle any questions from police along the way.

A Sanctions-Busting Day in the Countryside

Winter is not the best time for a fling in the Iraqi countryside. Since my assignment was nearing its end, my friends wanted to make this excursion before I departed. Besides, we never knew when the three of us would next meet.

Our plan was to visit an ancient site. You can do this almost anywhere in Iraq. Nermin had selected the mysterious Um al-Ukhaidar ruins beyond Kerbala, which were not far from a village market Amal wanted to visit. Along the way, we would enjoy a picnic near some water.

It had been raining lightly since the early morning. "Just imagine," noted Nermin, smiling. "The first shower of the winter! *Allah karim.*" This rain was long overdue, and the hungry desert consumed each drop as it fell. The rain was auspicious. This is a world where nine months can pass without a single wisp of a cloud in the sky. Not during the burning summer but rather in these chilly winter months do we see rain here. The winter rains of Iraq are decidedly for the land. Even city dwellers are mindful of the long months when the land waits for this nourishment. Every Iraqi has some relative living on a farm. An aunt or grandmother, a brother or uncle will be herding sheep, pruning trees, harvesting olives, collecting grass, or repairing machinery. Indeed, whether they inhabit apartments in Damascus or Beirut or they live in the suburbs of Cairo, Algiers, or Baghdad, I find that few Arabs are without any tie to a village and a farm. So many of our most savored foods—butter and cheeses, olives and fruits—are prepared only in those farmhouses. To enjoy them, we have to go back, even for a day. Amal's family plot is in north Baghdad, adjacent to her house on the riverbank; Nermin's is in Kirkuk.

On the main road south of Baghdad, we passed the towns of Mahmoudiyya and Yussefiyya. We passed farmers assembling in the main intersection of Mahmoudiyya with their goats, sheep, and chickens. In another hour, this would become a crowded country market. Amal spotted some handcrafted items hanging outside a shop and shouted to Yussef to stop. But Nermin said no. "Just imagine. It is hardly 9 a.m., and she wants to shop." She instructed Yussef to press on. We passed a road sign reading Kerbala, 50 km.

Kerbala has its own traditions and a reputation for its fine ceramic work and weaving. Kerbala sweets are also special. Amal again asked Yussef to halt the car as soon as we reached the central market. "I must find some *darja* cloth; it's manufactured only in Kerbala. From *darja*, we make the most delicate kind of *abaya* cloak," she added, turning to me. Yussef also wanted to stop in order to pray at the Al-Husseini mosque, near whose gate we had just arrived. Did this mean he was the Shia Iraqi among us? Not at all.

Nermin decided that on our way home we would halt here for as long as Yussef and Amal wished. Yussef could pray, and Amal could search for *darja*. They both assented to Nermin's logic and her commanding but reasonable manner. Yussef's lips moved in prayer as he drove slowly past the front of the great mosque. Its glistening golden copula and four radiant towers and the tile work across the walls are without comparison. No one could not want to pray here!

We left the fabled city, which along with Najaf was inundated by Iranian pilgrims, even during their years of hostility with Iraq.[4] We continued west onto an arid, uninhabited expanse over a single-lane tarred road that Amal—who had become our navigator—assured us led to Ein al-Tamr village. The oasis there was one of our destinations. Only a line of electric poles running on one side of the road indicated to me that we had not altogether left modern civilization.

Nermin must have sensed my disquiet. She said, "By 1980, all of Iraq was electrified. Our government gave this priority. We knew electricity was the foundation of any modern society. So did the Americans who bombed all our power stations." She punctuated the comment with her habitual reproachful glance. "We know what's behind the U.S. game." How this woman was able to identify my curiosities and then address them, adding an important political spin for this journalist, I could not comprehend. What a treasure!

Directly ahead of us lay the Saudi border. We were already deep into America's southern "no-fly" zone. This is the area comprising a third of Iraq identified by warring western armies as "the Shia South." From the outset of the blockade, American and British fighters regularly bombed these regions, which they forbade Iraq to fly in (and defend with radar stations); thus the euphemism "no-fly" zone. Today we ignored the danger, although those regular military intrusions were a deep and disturbing insult for Iraq. The UN ignored the contraventions, and the rest of the world somehow accepted the attacks as legitimate.

Nermin spotted a solitary car driving toward us. "*Habibiti*, my dear. Would you like to go to Saudi Arabia?" She knew I might go there on Hajj someday, but not otherwise. She had already made Hajj more than once in pre-embargo times when Iraqi Airways operated like any normal airline.

The foreign car whizzed past us. "That's a Saudi car. If we continue on another 125 miles, we will reach the border. Just imagine."

I thought, "Isn't Saudi Arabia allied with the United States in the embargo war? Who could be driving from there to Baghdad?"

"Businessmen," volunteered Nermin, again reading my thoughts. "Americans are in Baghdad for business. Why not Saudis or Kuwaitis?" Nermin's journalistic instincts never waned. My entire day was interposed with my friend's political and economic elaborations. I loved it.

On both sides of the road, the land seemed to be a flat, stony desert. It was not. Nermin pointed out rows of large plastic hutches to our right. "Tomato farms. Yes, thanks to the embargo, we have been forced to produce more of our own food. Do you know the agriculture ministry offers free land to farmers who build vegetable gardens using the new drip irrigation? Thanks to our embargo-smugglers, we can obtain the tubing we need from Syria and Lebanon," Nermin said cynically.

I had already learned how, almost four years into the embargo on black market trade, the Iraqi government had been able to expand cultivation. Without a doubt, the policy had averted the terrible famine set in motion by the UN blockade.[5]

"Look there! More hothouses," Nermin said. "You know, Iraqis cannot eat anything without tomatoes. With new technology, we now produce more tomatoes, even out here! We never used this land before the war. No one grew vegetables here because there were no canals. We have learned a lot because of that bloody war and the embargo. Just imagine."

Agriculture, although constrained by lack of many essential components and still short of what was needed, had taken on renewed importance in Iraq after years of government neglect. With the embargo abruptly severing imported food supplies in 1990, within two years the whole population was facing starvation. This fertile valley between two great rivers, the cradle of civilization, had abandoned its natural resources and become dependent on chemical and other supplements. Fertilizers, spraying machines, water pumps, and other essential technology became unavailable under the blockade. Two years into the embargo, the government finally moved to counter the disaster. It decreed that all arable lands should be planted with wheat. Farmers were paid handsomely. Call it a bribe. Or coercion. It was a crisis. Iraqis had to be fed. "From all this suffering, we realized that food is more important than oil," Nermin grumbled good-naturedly. "How could we forget the origins of Mesopotamia?"

We often talked about Iraq's import dependence. Nermin and others spoke about it as if making a sad confession. "Some Baath policies were good. But the party made serious mistakes, for example, allowing fields to lay fallow. During our war with Iran, young men left the countryside to fight. We did not have enough farmers. The Americans arranged for letters of credit for us so we could import whatever Australian and American grain we needed. Imagine! That's why Iraq could not feed itself when the blockade hit."

Amal did not join in these talks. She had brought a map of Iraq, which she spread over our laps in the back seat. Amal was always so well prepared. "Look. Here is al-Ukhaidar! Ein al-Tamr must not be far."

"It's just north of here," offered Yussef. "They call it Shuthathah."

Amal moved her finger up the map and over the lake near Shuthathah, following the blue line that passed through al-Fallujah and al-Ramadi and continued northwest.

"Al-Furat." Euphrates. Amal spoke as if this were a distant memory.

I thought, "Her house in the capital lies on the Tigris, and I know she cherishes that spot. She repaired the house after the bombing and lives in comfort there." I could not understand her melancholy, never having sung the songs of these rivers, heard poems of celebration, watched their waters rise and fall year after year, waited for the birds to return to the reeds on its banks, splashed as a child in the canals flowing through the countryside, or grasped how its waters are channeled across a whole land to support this civilization. After all, this is where irrigation was introduced to human civilization and enabled humankind to flourish.[6]

Amal traced the course of al-Furat on the paper, lingering for several minutes. Nermin, who appreciated Amal's mood, was silent—uncharacteristically so. I thought, "There are some things one simply cannot understand about Iraq unless you know these rivers."

The Sanctions Debate inside Iraq

"We need another hour before we arrive at Ein al-Tamr," announced our navigator. Putting her map aside, Amal reached into the picnic basket she had prepared for us. This stash was to be our lunch, and it was barely 10 a.m. Never mind, time for a snack. Pulling out cucumbers, she proceeded to peel one in her lap and we resumed chatting.

The evening before, my two companions had attended a meeting of a women's association. Iraqis could not meet without discussing the siege, and this was no different. "We must debate the issue of sanctions among ourselves and decide on a united action," insisted Nermin, repeating last night's arguments for my benefit. "We are not totally helpless. We have alternatives.

"Media is a major issue. Can we ignore it? Should we make a real effort to help the international journalists produce stories about our hardships and the injustices and how the blockade is really only punishing the simple people? Or should we become isolationist and fortify our own institutions? If so, then we must become self-sufficient."

Amal had argued for the latter approach: "We were too dependent on foreign imports and too accepting of western ideas. We have no choice. We must be self-reliant. I said this frankly last night. Let's face this. Our leaders must accept it as well."

Oddly enough, although rather late, Iraq ceased chasing international media, abandoned its attempts to please western powers and the UN, and by working with new friends found ways to thwart the embargo. (Commerce was illegal, according to the UN.) Trade was still crucial to Iraq's survival, so although the country became somewhat more self-sufficient than it was in 1990, Iraq remained heavily dependent on imports.

Other women at that meeting believed it was still possible to impact the western media and thereby get the truth to the American people. This bloc held that if the American public knew the truth, they would surely change Washington's policy. This camp was growing, but they were still a minority. Even after almost a decade of failure to have the sanctions lifted, many Iraqis continued to argue that the international media was needed to put Iraq's case to the U.S. public. One cited the UN health report recently carried by Reuters, the British international news agency. Another saw the resignations of Denis Halliday, Hans von Sponeck, and Jutta Burghardt, all ranking UN officials in Baghdad, as a sign of progress.[7] Yet most of the women taking part in the debate had reached the conclusion that the press, especially the American media, had not been helpful in exposing the truth about Washington's heartless blockade against Iraq.

Nermin laughed contentedly, recalling the way the meeting ended in cheers for Hanna, who had stood, her arms raised high. "'No one, not even the UN secretary general, questions the illegality of these "no-fly" zones. I say dump the UN.' That's Hanna. I agree with her. Our leaders have to abandon the policy of appeasement. Their idea of friendship is outmoded. In politics, there is no friendship. As the devil Kissinger says, no?"

A decade into the embargo, Iraqis were finally losing their naiveté about foreign media. Whether the authorities had accepted the realities about politics and friendship, I could not say. But people were discovering how CNN's Middle East broadcasts differed from what was shown to Americans on CNN at home. Interviews by the Baghdad-based CNN team were either heavily edited and reduced for the U.S. edition or excluded altogether. Iraqis learned that a Baghdad correspondent's report about the terror of the blockade usually went unaired when it reached her headquarters. It was increasingly evident to everyone at the Press Center moreover that correspondents who seemed too sympathetic to Iraq were rotated out by their bosses. Everyone acknowledged that the best reports, done by poorly funded freelancers, often working for "alternative" media, were hard to locate in the U.S. media circus. Reports by Korean or Spanish TV teams were never seen by Americans.

"Last night's meeting ended without a resolution, despite Hanna's appeal," Nermin admitted.

Amal countered, "Most of us are now convinced Iraq doesn't need the international press. If we believe we must become self-sufficient in food, let us declare our independence of the press as well."

The same debate was going on in homes, offices, and schools around Iraq and, I suspect, inside the Baath Party's highest councils as well. Support for a total disengagement from the West was growing. Many who had initially felt they could turn world opinion around were now abandoning that idea. No one had been left unaffected by the embargo. I knew not a single Iraqi who had not felt humiliated and helpless at some point in these hard, hard years. Young Iraqis were especially bitter. Many were becoming more religious. They began to reject the cultural values of their parents and the ideals of western democracy they once embraced so enthusiastically. Support for a more isolationist approach was growing. Amal found herself allied with this group, yet still she had mixed feelings about the West. "No one can accuse me of being anti-Western. I studied at an American high school. I like France. I like to visit France. I like Europe. But that is different from depending on them to help us. I will not beg," she said firmly. "We must simply learn to make things ourselves."

As journalists, Nermin and I had a different argument. We still believed our news could affect public opinion. As long as we continued our work, we were committed to trying to affect policy debates. Corporate media was inarguably anti-Iraq; we knew this. But we had not lost our faith that individual Americans, if they could somehow be reached, would become allies of the Iraqi people and would oppose Washington's war policies.

The discussion came to an inconclusive end. Yussef slipped in, "I thought you wanted to forget the embargo and Amrikya."

Amal passed each of us cool slices of cucumbers. I let the fragrant moisture slide down my throat. Whatever their botanical classification, we Arabs (perhaps Italians, Greeks, Iranians, and Turks as well) treat cucumbers as a fruit.

We sometimes eat it unpeeled, either in bites or sliced. We eat it freshly clipped from the stem, snap off the dry, bitter end, and munch it like a crispy apple. In our Arab sitting rooms, we pile cucumbers on a big round plate already heaped with oranges, grapes, bananas, and grapefruits and offer them to guests. Cucumbers are cool and moist, as portable as an apple, as aromatic and succulent as a melon. Melon and cucumber are the sacred water vessels sprouting from our Arab desert—a gift to any pilgrim.

As Amal skinned each cucumber and passed it on to us, she collected the shavings in her lap. Then, gathering a few strips of those wet skins, she began to wipe her forehead and cheeks with them. "We cool ourselves in the summer like this," she explained, as she pressed the peels up and down her arm. She bathed her face in the same way and invited me to follow her example. I took some cucumber peels from her and wiped my face. It was not a hot day, but the sensation on my skin was lovely.

Growing Up in the Iraq Landscape

"You know, I feel more affection for al-Furat than for the Tigris. Look how very green it is!" Amal was peering out the car window at the watercourse running parallel to the road. Every time we came within sight of a waterway, she became possessed by the river. "Notice how trees are growing all the way down to the waterline. I like to sit on a riverbank under a tree. I can't do that on the Tigris near my home; there the river is always muddy and reedy. Our Iraqi birds along al-Furat are different, too."

Nermin expressed less sentiment for these rivers, perhaps because she grew up in the hilly north, in Kirkuk, with only mountain streams. Nermin lives in Baghdad, but she often travels to Kirkuk to see her mother, her brothers, and her son. Kirkuk is normally a three-hour bus ride from Baghdad, usually more during the embargo because of breakdowns on the road. She never visits her hometown without going to see her two friends who work as archaeologists there. They are busy on the Arab'kha excavations in the city center.

Nermin knows almost as much as these experts do about this ancient site. Arab'kha is its Sumerian name, and it is still in use today. For centuries Arab'kha lay buried under modern-day Kirkuk. Nermin herself fought to convince the authorities that, after six years of interruption because of the cursed blockade, excavations should restart. "Restoration is slower, but at least it was under way again, *al-Hamdulillah*."

Nermin was born in Kirkuk, and she is an ethnic Turkman. She speaks Turkman as well as Arabic and English. And she understands Kurdish because many Kurds live around Kirkuk. Turkman though she may be, Nermin says, "I am an Iraqi first." She is a resolute Arab nationalist.

Nermin speaks Hungarian, too. She studied in Hungary after completing her first degree in journalism in Baghdad. Since she was in high school, Nermin wanted to be a journalist. Once she entered college, she switched from medicine (where Iraqi educators direct their best students) to journalism. That's a rare shift in Iraq. She later won a scholarship to study in England, but before that she spent two years in Budapest, where she completed a diploma in journalism.

Today Nermin is arguably the most widely traveled correspondent in the country. She covered the Iran–Iraq war, accompanying Iraqi troops from the southern border to the hills of the northern governorates. She knows the Kurdish region well, and she returned there during the embargo where she knew U.S. and Israeli agents were planting roots to strengthen that alliance against Baghdad. She confronted two men she knew were Israelis, exposing them by the slight defects in their Turkman accents. She could do nothing to remove them, but she insisted they know that she (and her government, even under the embargo) were not fooled.

During the Iran–Iraq war, this woman reported from the frontline on the battles between her countrymen and Iranian boys the same age. She hadn't planned to be a war correspondent; she wanted to write about archaeological discoveries, ancient history, and the social issues that modern Iraq was facing. But during the twenty years she's been a journalist, Iraq has been at war. So reporting on wars and the embargo has become her expertise.

In the Middle East and in India, one still encounters people they label "Renaissance men"—experts of contemporary and ancient alike, able to recite early love poetry and recount stories from ancient folklore, then critique the arts and offer commentary on current political affairs. These *ustad* will entertain admirers with a limitless collection of original verses, too. Nermin doesn't write poetry, and no one addresses her as *ustadah*, but she is truly a Renaissance woman.

It was Nermin who directed me to Qsair, the ancient Christian site near Kerbala, recovered by archaeologists from the Iraqi Department of Antiquities after 1991. Iraqi historians suspect that Qsair, which they say may have been a church or a monastery, is the oldest Christian structure in the Middle East. "This would make it the oldest in the entire world!" I remarked when Nermin told me about it.

"Of course." She smiled (that's what makes us so special). "Just imagine."

Urged by this remarkable woman who rarely was mistaken about her history, I decided to visit Qsair one day in 1997. Few people who I questioned, including other Iraqi journalists, could recall it. Its discovery by archaeologists had been reported in the Iraqi press some years earlier, but because of the embargo, it was ignored. On my first excursion to Qsair, I set out only with Hassien from the Ministry of Information Press Center. It was near Kerbala, so he expected local people would direct us to the site without difficulty. "Just imagine," said Nermin, amused when I returned to Baghdad without having found the place. "Imagine hunting for a Christian monastery in the holiest Shia city, a town of mullahs and Iranian pilgrims. Did you think this was Rome? Some anthropologist you are!" She told many people about that folly, but I was proud that I had tried, and I would seek out Qsair again.

If not for the embargo, Qsair would surely be restored and listed in tourist guidebooks by now and have a place in Christian history. It would also be a government-protected antiquity. Instead, there was no restoration of the site, no security, no guidebook, not even a road marker. And at the time of my visit, few Christian scholars had even read about Qsair. It simply lay there, exposed to thieves who, under the flag of the merciless UN embargo, enjoyed a license to loot.

Under the siege, few visitors go on day outings, and still fewer write articles about the glories of Iraq's past.[8] By 1997, the Iraqi president's office was financing renewed excavations at a few sites across the country, but not on the pre-embargo scale, when the government had so generously funded archaeological research and protected valued sites. Iraq under siege could not counter the looting that had begun when the guards and staff of those cites lost their jobs, found work elsewhere, or were bribed by the thieves.

Qsair did not completely escape notice by certain interested outside parties, however. When I told Doni George, director of documentation at the Iraq National Museum, of my visit to Qsair, he shared this story with me. In 1996, he said, a university in Paris successfully lured away the young Iraqi archaeologist, a student of George's, who had worked on the site under his supervision. They offered the Iraqi a scholarship to complete his doctorate in France, and he jumped at the opportunity, as most young scholars would. Under the embargo, the offer was especially seductive, and the young man was somehow persuaded to bring to Paris the original photographs and other important documents he had collected from the Qsair site. The Department of Antiquities felt it could not bar this student's chances for advancement, so it allowed him to travel abroad. Only after he had departed, explained George, did they discover that he had taken with him all of the documentation on Qsair that was stored at the museum. George and other staff did not know if the student would ever return to Iraq. It was one more embargo battle lost.

In 1999, I made a second and this time successful attempt to visit Qsair. This time Hassien and I contacted the archaeological office in Kerbala beforehand, and a staff member led us directly to the site. We reached Qsair only after a drive of several miles over a desert track and then a half-hour hike. Stone blocks that had toppled from the walls lay in piles here and there. I ran my finger over a stone in the remaining wall, and the surface fell away like sand. Shards of pottery lay about. The archaeologist guiding us had worked on the excavation, and he knew the design of the original structure. He pointed to various features of the stone building as well as a stone water channel and a nearby cemetery. It had withstood two thousand years of wind and rain and wars. But would it survive this embargo?

Al-Ukhaidar and Ein al-Tamr

On this outing with Nermin and Amal, our destination was not Qsair but al-Ukhaidar and Ein al-Tamr. Both are located in the general vicinity of Qsair southwest of Kerbala. Al-Ukhaidar is a deserted castle, one of many great Iraqi structures that had survived the centuries. Ein al-Tamr is an oasis town renowned for its sweet dates and its pure spring water—hence the name *spring of the date palm.*

We reached al-Ukhaidar first. It was colossal. Yet as massive as it was, even Nermin, who had visited it before, had failed to spot it from a distance. Suddenly there it stood, majestic and silent, rising from the flat, dry plain to greet us. "Just imagine," said Nermin. "We still don't know exactly what it served as. Perhaps a castle or a fort built for an exiled prince. Perhaps a kind of monastery. Maybe a trading center, since this place was once a main route between Basra at the head of the Persian Gulf and the commercial center of Aleppo in Syria."

There was no sign of a water supply and no village. Neither was there vegetation, apart from a low, solitary tree standing by a mud brick shelter at the edge of the road.

"Let's call the guide," suggested Nermin. Surely she was joking! We had seen no sign of life whatsoever. Yet suddenly a man appeared, smiling at us from the doorway of the shelter. A tourist office?

The guide invited us to examine English and French language brochures describing al-Ukhaidar. I bought a folder of postcards and noted in the corner of each card the words "Printed in Japan, 1985."

The man's name was Ahmed. He really was the local attendant, and Nermin invited him to accompany us. By the time we reached the end of the ramp and stood at the great arched entrance of the fort, Nermin had learned that Ahmed earned 6,000 dinars a month, had studied up to class 10, had served in the army (in Kuwait), was the father of four children, and lived with his family in a nearby town, riding to and from work on a bicycle. He had worked at al-Ukhaidar for twelve years, learning its history from scholars who occasionally visited.

Ahmed affirmed that al-Ukhaidar's character and its location in this lonely, arid place still baffled archaeologists. They could not explain who had occupied it or why it was so heavily fortified. The whole structure is well preserved, and its exterior wall is intact. Sixty-five feet high, the wall completely encircles what must have been a settlement. This outer fortification is the main feature of al-Ukhaidar, towering above the tallest inner buildings. That encompassing wall encloses 29,000 square meters of space, says the brochure. Even though it is massive, its total effect is one of astonishing grace.

Historians have found no other trade centers with this kind of protective wall and battlement. Oddly, no inscription has been found that would indicate who built it or when, and there are no written texts about its construction or provenance. At first, researchers suggested the building at al-Ukhaidar was from the Abbassid period (eighth to thirteenth centuries A.D.), while others said it could be earlier, perhaps pre-Islamic. Eventually, after more research and studies of its decorative elements and construction methods, it was concluded that it was indeed Islamic, dating to the earliest century of Hijra, soon after the founding of Islam in 622 A.D. This still did not explain its location at this particular place or the heavy fortification.

We climbed the steep stairway to a turret and walked along the narrow, perfectly straight corridor that joins the outer and inner walls and completely encircles the complex. The refined, simple geometry of the walls and corridors awed me more than did its great size.

"Look here. A pigeon warren!" Nermin called me to examine what she found under a stairway in the inner living quarters. "Just imagine. The Iraqis kept pigeons to send messages across the country." Nermin knew I would be more impressed by this kind of sociological detail than by the size or age of a castle. Al-Ukhaidar intrigued me even more when we walked across the tile floors of rooms that Ahmed pointed out had been bathrooms. He directed our attention to the drains along the bottoms of the walls. "According to the architectural features of each," he explained, "we know one bathroom was for summer and one was for winter use."

Imaginary sounds of those cooing ancient pigeons were now augmented by splashing bathwater, cries of children, stomping of horses, calls of mothers, and the thump and bang of workers' tools. When al-Ukhaidar was occupied by thousands of families and their animals, there must have been gardens and orchards spreading in all directions. Traders passed through here en route to and from the port of al-Basrah in the Gulf, three hundred miles south, and the commercial centers of Syria, six hundred miles to the north.

Amal's Gifts

Amal had initiated today's outing. Whenever I was in Iraq, I could count on Amal to suggest an excursion—to a film showing, to a riverside café, or into the wilderness. Amal was an anthropologist, the practical type. Her collection was on display in her extraordinary shop in Baghdad, al-Beit al-Iraqi (Iraqi House), and it was filled with contemporary work, both crafts and fine art that Amal has assembled from across her country.

Al-Beit al-Iraqi itself was a traditional Ottoman house with rooms opening into a central garden courtyard. It was located on the eastern approach to Jumhuriyya Bridge, which spans the Tigris near the south end of al-Rasheed Street. The house belonged to her father, but the family had not lived in it for many years. "It was the residence of the archaeologist Seton Lloyd for a time, and I can tell you stories about Gertrude Bell, the explorer and writer, who also stayed here," says Amal proudly.

Showrooms of garments and furnishings, ceramics and wall hangings, carpets and paintings were arranged with the simplicity and elegance that Amal's eye bestows on all her work. The west end of the garden is enclosed by a yellow brick wall with latticed window openings. Beyond it flows the Tigris.

Amal converted each wing of the house into a gallery, and each is filled with art. "Every item here is Iraqi," she asserts. Once, examining the fine fabric of an *abaya* cloak, when I remarked that it looked southern Arabian, I was swiftly rebuked. "That cloth is Iraqi," she snapped. Amal takes great pride in the authenticity of her collection, and she has chosen each article with care. This is an Iraqi showplace. "Nothing here is imported; every piece is Iraqi," she insists, and she can tell you the provenance of each piece in the house. "This *abaya* is from Mosul. Look at the weave, the fluting. Feel the wool. That one is particular to north Iraq, worn only by Turkman women."

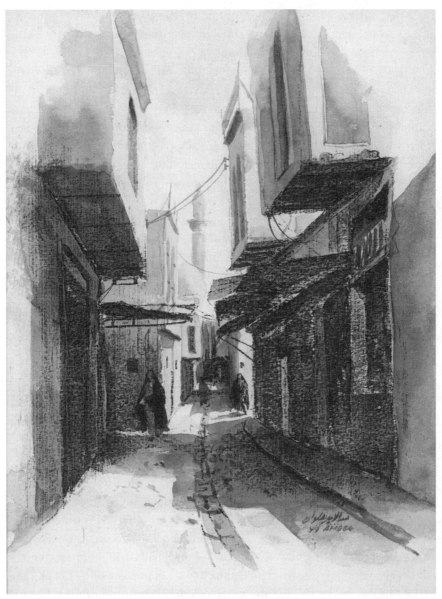

Kerbala city street, charcoal, by Abdel Ameer Alwan, 1999.

Al-Beit al-Iraqi was also a gallery of fine art, displaying work by ceramicists, glass workers, and wood carvers. Three framed miniatures by the renowned water-colorist Abdel Ameer Alwan hung in one vestibule.

When I first visited al-Beit al-Iraqi in 1989, calligraphy classes were under way. In those days, Amal scheduled weekly evening lectures and concerts to showcase one or another Iraqi art form. Her gallery was one of several centers of intellectual activity in the capital at that time. One by one the others closed. Apart from the French Cultural Institute (reopened in 1999), only al-Beit al-Iraqi survived as a cultural center into the year 2000 (even though it was badly damaged during the 1991 war because of its proximity to the bridge, which was repeatedly bombed).

It took Amal barely a year after the war to repair the windows, walls, and portico of her center and reopen for business. For a long time, there were few clients, and she found it harder to find professors available to give a lecture. Yet she persisted. By 2002, a few more embassies had reopened, and many journalists were arriving to cover the crisis over the weapons inspections. The garden of her shop became a locale for political discussions between Amal, Nermin, and other Iraqi patriots meeting foreign journalists and other delegations. As late as February 2003, a group of Japanese anti-sanctions activists arranged an exhibition of drawings by Japanese children and young Iraqis. A final gasp, it was sad and bracing at the same time. The house was packed with Iraqis during those weeks, perhaps because we needed every living twig to cling to.

Shopping with Amal

Less than an hour after departing from the arid plain around al-Ukhaidar, Yussef drove into Ein al-Tamr. As we passed through large stands of trees, we could smell the spring water that meanders a few hundred feet through a palm grove before pouring into a crystal clear pool. A genuine oasis! This water was renowned for its healing powers. Indeed, the town had been built to accommodate Iraqis seeking respite from their ailments. It became known as Ein al-Tamr because of this hot spring and the prized dates that grow around it.

Before the embargo—always before the embargo!—Baghdad and Kerbala families motored here to picnic near the pool. Amal remembered a cluster of cottages that vacationers could rent near a charming public park, and she led us there for our picnic. We found the cottages boarded up and the lawn a mass of weeds and overgrown grass. "Bloody embargo," uttered Nermin.

Amal was forlorn yet determined we would not be denied our picnic. She instructed Yussef to take us to the town center. There we found benches and tables near the creek and shaded by large, leafy trees.

"Bread, we must have bread," announced Amal, and she headed toward the market stalls, leaving us to unpack our spiced cream cheese, butter, sausage, and fruit. In a moment, Amal reappeared. She was empty-handed. "No bread. Everyone here has finished their lunch. And the bakery is shut. We simply must have bread. We are Iraqi. We cannot have a meal without bread," she insisted, and she approached a young man resting nearby. They spoke for a moment, and she returned looking very satisfied. "He will bring bread from his house," she announced, joining us at our table. We had hardly poured our tea when the youth arrived with four enormous flat loaves hanging over his arm. He laid them before us. Declining a mug of tea that Nermin offered him, he left us with a blessing that we enjoy our meal. "It is only bread. This is the custom," Nermin assured me, noting that I seemed a little uncomfortable about the gift. "Everyone will have plenty of bread at home, and it will be fresh. Every house has a surplus. We are travelers. They want us to have whatever we need. If not for this embargo, we would have been taken into the man's home and feasted with a specially prepared meal."

Yussef, Nermin, Amal, and I finished two of the loaves with our cheese and spiced meat. Amal rolled up the remaining loaves and put them in her hamper. "This kind of bread is not available in Baghdad. This is made from whole wheat and cooked in a *tannour* oven. Besides, the farmers wouldn't accept it back."

Amal told us to pack up. She would be back, she said, and she headed toward the clusters of women sitting not far from the road with basket-ware spread over the ground around them. She had come here precisely to buy the woven mats they made from stripped palm fronds. She quickly picked out half a dozen mats and four baskets. "They are rather rough," she explained to me, "but they have their character. These designs in the weave are distinctive to this town."

Before departing, we purchased three ten-kilo sacks of the best variety of Ein al-Tamr dates from a stall that Amal chose. These would be distributed among friends in Baghdad.

The small town disappeared behind us, and the terrain again looked like uninhabited desert. Before we reached Kerbala, we passed two herds of camels—first a cluster of twenty or so animals, then a herd of several hundred. Both Nermin and Amal were enchanted. "Look, there's a white camel," Amal sighed. Several colts trotted beside their mothers. "I thought only foreigners were entranced by camels," I remarked, watching how the women gazed lovingly at the passing herd.

The sight of the lumbering creatures awoke Amal's anthropological spirit. "They have their peculiar mating practices, you know. As the male and female couple, the others in the herd form a circle around them and turn their backs to the mating pair in the center."

At this point Amal confided that she might like to visit Saudi Arabia. "There is a famous camel fair in Arabia. When herders gather there, they sample the camel milk, and from the flavor of the milk they can identify the area that camel was raised in. They can distinguish the taste of the milk just as wine tasters in France can determine the locale of a particular wine."

"Just imagine," sighed Nermin.

It was still raining, although only lightly. We hoped the rain would increase. The land needed water.

Some hawks flew overhead through the darkening sky. And as we neared Kerbala, palms once again appeared on the horizon, long straight rows, bending slightly away from the wind.

"I love my country," whispered Amal.

First Letter Since

dearest alwarda,
so i am still alive full of tears and pain
without any feeling
just asking: was saddam so precious
that iraq was the price?
baghdad is not baghdad i knew
so i came back to mother's.
In coming days we will keep in touch, inshallah.
Love, Nermin

April 29, 2003

Part 2

6

There Goes the Medical System

The prohibitions against the sale or supply to Iraq of commodities or products, and prohibitions against financial transactions with Iraq, contained in resolution 661 [6 August 1990] *shall not apply to foodstuffs and medicines.*

UN Security Council Resolution 687, section F, paragraph 20.

Within two years of the approval of SCR 687 by the United Nations—the world body mandated to protect the vulnerable and to promote peace—Iraqis faced a medical catastrophe and famine. How could this be?

In the episodes and lives recorded in foregoing chapters, we may possibly begin to imagine some of the hardships, chaos, and transformations Iraq was subject to under embargo. (If we cannot imagine, at least we possess more facts, including testimonials by real people.) Around the world, few noted the embargo exemptions listed in paragraph 20—foodstuffs and medicines. But we can be certain every Iraqi knew. Every schoolchild, every woman and man, every Baath and nonparty citizen, every soldier and artist read and clutched the words in paragraph 20. Each day their deprivations mounted, they recalled them. They grew more angry.[1]

Much of the world recognized the double standard in U.S. policy in regards to Palestinian rights. Now that intelligence extended to Iraq, and for many, this affirmed how inveterate western racism and anti-Muslim prejudice really was. Iraq was being singled out for punishment beyond any reasonable standard. Worldwide, as this became increasingly undeniable, anti-American sentiment multiplied.

The exemptions in paragraph 20 existed only in law—on paper. Using political threats against other nations and emphasizing supplementary clauses aimed at neutralizing this provision, the American administration ensured that these exemptions could not be effected. It should have been clear from the start that if this continued Iraq was doomed, but it took its leaders eight years to grasp the reality. The goalposts kept moving.[2] It was useless to wait any longer for international law to support them. Iraq had to fight back.

By 1998, a new, defiant spirit (a healthy one, in my opinion) had taken hold within the country. By then, 1.5 million Iraqis had perished, perhaps more.[3] Debates over strategies accelerated. They took place in every Iraqi household and in the councils of power, that is, the Revolutionary Command Council and the Iraqi cabinet presided over by the president.

Iraq's food production had improved despite enormous obstacles created by the embargo. Some essentials, such as clothing, paper and plastic goods, electrical and phone cables, spare parts for machines, seeds, vaccines, and animal feed, were entering the country through trade prohibited by the United States. More than basic consumer and industrial supplies were needed. Only in late 1998 did Iraqi citizens and government officials really focus on devising pragmatic policies to save themselves. Change required imagination; it meant abandoning some Baath socialist economic ideals; in some cases, it needed great daring, or promise of profit, or both. Baghdad had to look to new partners abroad. Thus Iraq began to chip away at the deadly embargo.

UN Security Council Resolution 986, which arranged (subject to complex outside management) for the food and medical purchases in exchange for controlled oil sales, turned into a scam and a multibillion dollar theft. It proved to Iraqis that the West was intent on their destruction while engaging in wholesale procurement of their nation's revenues. Iraqis gradually realized that the siege might never be lifted. Then came heightened confrontations with the UN weapons inspectors, some of whom Iraq suspected were U.S. spies. The acrimonious exit of UNSCOM from Iraq at the end of 1998 was followed by a gratuitous and murderous U.S. bomb attack on the country. That finally resolved Iraq to reconsider their attempts to comply with ever increasing UN demands. It declared that UNSCOM could not return until certain conditions were guaranteed.

By now Baghdad had opened avenues for private trade with neighboring countries, however illegal it might appear to the United Nations.[4] The country continued to sponsor international festivals and competitions. It brought visitors, including musicians and writers, to stimulate cultural life. Bribes and extra benefits were accepted as the norm, whether to enhance agricultural production, secure generators and cables to run the electrical system, restart the poultry industry, obtain computers for doctors, engineers, and the universities, or meet presidential indulgences or security needs.[5] Ultimately, the skies over Baghdad (see chapter 13) would also reopen to commercial flights. At first, these excursions were labeled "humanitarian" to circumvent American warnings that any commercial interaction with Iraq was illegal under the terms of the UN embargo.

None of these ventures could rebuild the collapsed health sector. Without new sources of revenue, humanitarian services remained in a desperate situation. Without adequate salaries, civil servants (teachers, city clerks, street cleaners, security guards, professors) were leaving their jobs. Not everyone could emigrate; many former government employees took up peddling and other means of self-employment. Oddly, petty capitalism offered enough income for many families to feed themselves.

To stem the exodus of its educated class, the government levied exit taxes on trained professionals seeking to travel. The departure tax for doctors was excessive, and some who chose not to leave opened private clinics. These flourished, but they could never replace the general hospitals.[6] Still, perhaps their success led ministry officials to rethink their socialist commitment to universal free medical treatment. The country was losing its physicians (as well as professors), adding to the urgency of finding new solutions. One answer was partial privatization of the health system to help increase physicians' income. Accordingly, citizens would have to bear part of their hospital costs, even though they were poorer and sicker than ever. Private hospitals and clinics had existed in Iraq before the revolution, but now they became a beacon for change because of desperate circumstances.

The crowning glory of Iraq's socialist structure, its free, high-quality health system, was to undergo privatization. This was an indication of the degree to which Iraq was prepared to change in order to push back the scourge of the embargo.

A Collapsing Infrastructure

It was like a mudslide, beginning with a barely perceptible creep as soon as the embargo took effect in 1990 and developing into a massive, unstoppable tide within three years. Nothing could slow its advance. It would bury in its path the foundations of an earlier way of life: international accolades for Iraq's health standard, the pride of its practitioners, and the socialist philosophy that built it.

It didn't matter that hospitals hardly functioned anymore. Never mind if the health care system had shrunk to a fraction of its former capacity. Forget about the thousands of doctors who just gave up and left the country. Iraq's tattered medical system had to be redesigned.

Across the country, hospitals became a barometer for the vicissitudes and ills in the whole of Iraq following the Gulf War and the imposition of the embargo.

First there was no medicine. Medical journals were halted; so were communications with physicians and medical researchers abroad. Then hospitals deteriorated to the point where they were barely hygienic. All this was happening while the rate of diseases and malnutrition was soaring. At one point, with little to offer the sick, some hospitals shut most of their wards. Iraq's excellent network of rural health centers had ceased to exist within a year of the start of the embargo.

Five years later, Iraq's health services continued to deteriorate. At the medical level, many once common surgical procedures were no longer practiced because of broken facilities and departed specialists. Hospital diagnostic equipment and beds were broken, light and air-conditioning fixtures needed repair, and sanitation was wanting. Hospital libraries were in tatters. The simplest medicines were unavailable, and advanced drugs were out of the question.

With the implementation of SCR 986 signed in 1996, some new medical equipment could be ordered from outside. It was paid for out of the special oil revenue fund set up by the UN to control Iraq's oil production.[7] Those supplies slowly began arriving in the country in mid-1997. By this time, hospitals were almost beyond repair, and their medical staffs were much reduced. Had such a crisis occurred anywhere else in the world, nongovernment organizations would have rushed forward to donate entire hospitals and fly in doctors to assist, and foreign governments would have eagerly allocated relief funds for emergency medical centers. But this was Iraq, where "Saddam massacred his own people." American authorities warned any sympathizers to stay away. Apart from those designated by the UN, no NGOs arrived to help, and no additional budgets were allocated for their work, even though the massiveness of the needs was well documented from early in the crisis by observers like Ramsey Clark.[8] The UNICEF office in Iraq was authorized to engage only in preventative health programs; its director continually complained of insufficient funds to meet their needs. Human rights professionals concentrated on Saddam's crimes and had little time for American transgressions here.

A Decaying Socialist Medical Model

During the 1980s, many socialist nations around the world shifted to capital-generated economies. With the U.S.–driven globalization (free market) agenda, privatization was forced on or adopted by governments who previously funded their health and education sectors from public funds. Iraq, forced by the U.S. policy of "containment," was out in the cold. Credit cards were useless here, Iraqis could not obtain letters of credit, and no legal commercial exchange (through banks) in Iraq was possible. Thus normal market forces, the International Monetary Fund, and World Bank regulations could not advance privatization here.

If the world cared little for Arab nationalist ideology, at least it had to recognize that Iraq had built an exemplary health care system with a highly capable and dedicated corps of health professionals. Before the embargo, Iraq had provided free education for its people; this included medical training. Iraq even offered free medical training to non-Iraqis, especially Palestinians. Instruction in medical schools had been in English, the only Arab state where this was so. Many graduates from Iraq's medical colleges had gone abroad, mostly to the United States and Britain, for advanced training, all at public expense. At home, doctors had been guaranteed good salaries, free housing, well-equipped hospitals, ongoing opportunities for training (through seminars at home and overseas), sophisticated (imported) drugs, and first-rate diagnostic equipment. Public hospitals had been considered superbly equipped. A patient recommended for treatment in a foreign hospital had received government support for travel, surgery, and postoperative care. At home, all citizens had received free medical treatment. What few small private hospitals existed had been inferior and could never attract the best surgeons and specialists.

So generous was the government in health matters that Iraqis may have become overly dependent on pharmaceuticals and high-tech treatments. Few doctors showed any interest in alternative remedies: Chinese innovations or ancient treatments, special nutritional or herbal therapies, or the experiments of the Cuban people who had been facing sanctions for much longer.[9] Like Americans, Iraqis sometimes opted for surgery when it was unnecessary; they regularly sought drugs for ailments that required only simple herbal or nutritional treatment. So wholeheartedly did Iraq's health professionals embrace trends and fashions from Europe and the United States that by 1990 they had convinced most Iraqi women, both urban and rural, to abandon breastfeeding in favor of bottled milk for their babies.

A Downward Swing of the Pendulum

The embargo's effect on Iraq's health system was immediate and devastating in every sphere. Medical journals ceased to arrive from the day SCR 661 was passed (August 6, 1990). Iraq's stock of medicines, almost all imported, was swiftly depleted. People dependent on life-saving drugs died in the early months of the blockade. Broken machinery, all foreign made, could not be repaired. Physicians who obtained work overseas did not return.

The population suffered the following effects:

- a spiraling mortality rate for diseases and ailments once easily treatable
- the return of diseases once eradicated
- a rise in the increase of cancer at the same time that all cancer drugs and radiation needs were cut off
- poor diagnostic procedures
- underweight births
- the spread of infections in a weakened, malnourished population

The catastrophe was well documented.[10] Annual comparative statistics were assembled by authorities in all governorates of Iraq, although journalists and NGOs generally cited foreign investigations, as if they were more reliable. Not only did Iraq's death toll rise sharply. Many people endured prolonged suffering and fatal complications because of malnourishment, bad hygiene, and lack of drugs. Surgery had to be performed without the aid of anesthesia. It was a nightmare for the medical profession. Doctors simply did not have the tools they needed. They were further distressed because they could not consult with colleagues abroad.[11]

By the mid-1990s, a few government hospitals were able to repair their most critically damaged facilities using donations solicited from individuals in the emerging upper class, farmers who benefited from wheat production and merchants who profited in cross-border trade. Kerbala and Najaf hospitals financed renovations with solicitations from visiting pilgrims to holy places in those cities. (They were exceptions.)

Adoption of partially private services in public hospitals began in 2001. This was seen not as a retreat from socialist principles but as a strategy to cope with the growing shortage of doctors and professors of medicine. Administrators may also have been seeking ways to hold on to its rapidly dwindling professional class in general. It was an essential element in Iraq's secular urban society. A strong educated class was needed to balance encroachments by newcomers in the city from farms and villages, to innovate in science and technology, and to project Iraq's modernism. The latter's rural values had begun to eclipse the cosmopolitanism of the educated urban class. The country had lost so many of its professionals—architects, doctors, professors, designers, writers, and other creative people, even singers and musicians—that if this trend continued, leaders feared the collapse of any "progressive," secular community in the cities. Indeed, under occupation the trend accelerated. The latest ranking professional to abandon Iraq because of biased and ill-trained administrators was Iraq's top cultural official, archaeologist Doni George. In his August 26, 2006, statement to the press in England, reported in the *Guardian,* Dr. George warned that the State Board of Antiquities was now controlled by al-Sadr, the Shia party founded by Muqtada al-Sadr, which with thirty seats in parliament controlled a number of ministries at the time. "I can no longer work with these people. They have no knowledge of archaeology, no knowledge of antiquities, nothing." Resignations like George's are as lethal for Iraq as the hundreds of assassinations of professors, researchers, and medical specialists since the 2003 invasion.

A Pilot Project

In 2001, the Ministry of Health announced a new two-tier plan of health care. Those who could pay more got more; those who could not pay even the minimum fees (sometimes only a few pennies per visit) got less. Although Iraq's new health management plan is now redundant, it is worth reviewing. It demonstrates how a country tried to cope with a collapsing socialist system.

Iraq's deputy health minister, Khalid Jamil Mahmoud, outlined the plan to me at the time it was initiated. (It was impossible for me to assess his personal opinion about it.) "This reform will generate funds to maintain our hospitals," he explained dispassionately. "The idea is to get our people to fully participate in operating our hospitals. The purpose is not to tax the poor." He spelled it out. "Tier A fees for wealthier patients are still very low—from 10,000 to 60,000 Iraqi dinars [$5–$30 at the 2001 exchange rate] for treatment that includes surgery, food, and a room. In Tier B, where a person is totally without resources, we ask the hospital to absorb the cost of care. [The fixed daily rate for a private room is the equivalent of $10, $1 for a bed in a public ward.] Thus far, we provide medicines free of charge at all our hospitals. Since 1997, we have purchased them through the 'food-for-oil' plan. Let us be clear. These new fees bear no relation to the real cost of health care. Ninety-five percent—the hospital building, its furnishings, and medical equipment—is still borne by the government. Psychiatric hospitals and centers for communicable diseases are exempt from the levy."

A Fundamental Change, Nevertheless

Government and private hospitals alike were obliged to adopt rates fixed by the Health Ministry, and until the 2003 U.S. invasion, doctors reported that it was well managed.

Surgery was the most costly item, although fees were modest by any standard. A heart operation, for example, might be 500,000 Iraqi dinars, equivalent to $250 at that time. Kidney surgery might cost the same as a heart operation; a hysterectomy was listed at 150,000, a thyroid operation 75,000, and a cesarean 50,000. Minor operations were fixed at a fraction of these costs. The deputy minister explained that none of the income from an operation went to his ministry. "Revenues are retained by the hospital, with a specified 20 percent assigned to the surgeon, 5 percent to the anesthetist, 5 percent to the radiologist, and so on. This arrangement separates our ministry from the administration, so payments do not seem to be a tax on the public." Officials called the fees incentives because they were designed to increase doctors' incomes and encourage them to remain at work. According to the scheme, after specialists are paid, a hospital can distribute the remaining funds according to its needs. After the plan was introduced, it was not unusual to meet someone seeking a specific amount of cash for a particular operation that someone in the family needed. Those who could not raise even these amounts died.

Dr. Umaya, the doctor who drew my attention to this initiative, was a radiologist. (She herself succumbed to cancer in 2003.) Even though the plan would benefit her as a doctor, she knew it meant increased hardships for most patients. "The admission fee is a mere hundred dinars (the equivalent of five cents), but some families will be unable to pay. Iraqis are already turning to local healers or to home remedies out of desperation. We know of many cases where a family does not bother to seek out medical care with us because they are so poor." She noted that doctors could waive the new charges, including the admission fee. But she doubted that many would.

Not a Single New Medical Center in Twelve Years

Given the terrible state in which Iraq found its hospitals by 2001, the new scheme seemed reasonable. At least health centers could purchase paint and materials to repair beds, windows, fans, electrical wiring, pipes, kitchens, and laundry services and start restocking their libraries and pharmacies. However, with their health facilities so dysfunctional and decrepit by 2001, billions of dinars (hundreds of millions of dollars) were needed to bring the standard even up to its 1990 level. Much more of everything was needed to address the terrible health conditions wrought by the embargo.

The ministry had completed only 15 percent of urgent hospital repairs according to their 2001 budget. "Not a single new hospital has been constructed in twelve years," said the health official when he reviewed general conditions for me. "By any standard, our facilities are inadequate." All 1,200 health centers that once provided care for towns and villages across the country were nonfunctional, even in 2001. "Our ministry has been able to repair barely 5 percent of them," the official admitted. He did not know whether they would ever be restored. "Without these local clinics, all responsibility for health care has fallen on the hospitals, increasing their already heavy load."[12]

Miraculously, despite limitations and obstacles, by the summer of 2001 it seemed the deathly slide had been checked. Through the food-for-oil scheme, critical diagnostic equipment and computers were bought and delivered to hospitals, and patients' records could be properly assembled and analyzed. Through their new computers and Internet hookups, doctors were also able to access medical journals.

For the first time in ten years—since the embargo began—I stood with hospital administrators watching new medical wings under construction. The grind of those bulldozers and the whirr of cement mixers were sweet sounds.

Inside, the staff proudly pointed out private rooms for the wealthier class of patients. Bathrooms and wards for general patients were newly fitted and painted. At another large regional hospital, workmen were laying a foundation for a small cardiac wing. Beside it rose another building. That would house the hospital's new pediatric ward. Costing $20,000 to $50,000 (40–100 million dinars), it was financed not by the Health Ministry but by funds raised privately by enterprising doctors and other medical staff. CT and MRI scanners, sonar machines, and basic heart monitors were installed at a few hospitals. Ambulances began arriving in 1998. Imported through the Memorandum of Understanding of SCR 986, they were contracted by the ministry and distributed to centers around the country. So valuable were they and subject to resale abroad by profiteers, they had to be securely locked away when not in use. Because of U.S. government designation of computers as "dual use" items that might serve military purposes, the UN disallowed the import of computers for hospital use. This prompted the Iraqi authorities to encourage "private" import of computers, and suppliers were found, mainly from the Arab Emirates (see chapter 9). By 2001, a few doctors in Iraq owned personal computers and could purchase pirated medical CDs (at $3 each). Finally they could begin to keep abreast of medical developments abroad.

A Different Kind of Revolution

On the surface, the introduction of the two-tier system of health care in Iraq may not appear to be a radical change. It is difficult to know how many medical professionals decided to stay in the country because of increased income. By the time of the 2003 invasion, citizens had not yet been required to pay for medicines, but many special drugs were still unavailable. And the causes of so many diseases and illnesses—pollution, bad sanitation, radiation, malnutrition, lack of pesticides—continued unchecked.

Availability of physicians would also be affected by the decline of Iraq's educational system as it, too, was forced to reform. In 2001, a medical student's education was still wholly financed by the government. In 2000, Iraq passed a law permitting graduates to buy out of their education debt obligations. Up until then, it had been obligatory for all Iraqi professionals to take up government service following graduation; anyone who tried to avoid this faced punishment. This was a major reason why many Iraqis, if they left the country on government scholarships, never returned. They feared imprisonment if they did so. Although Iraq announced an amnesty for these expatriates after 1995, only a few dared to test the new law. After 2001, when it was possible for any graduate in Iraq to pay off the debt with cash, many engineers and doctors took advantage of the opportunity. Unburdened, some left the country; others opened private businesses. This was a further step in the privatization of Iraq's education system.

The next generation of Iraqis is unlikely to see anything comparable in terms of facilities or opportunities available to them before 1990. At a time when poverty has become the norm and many find it difficult to feed and clothe their children (free school lunches ended with the imposition of the embargo in 1990), Iraq's young, except for those few families who have grown rich from embargo-related enterprise, face more hardships.

Iraq had seemed beyond the reach of privatization policies sweeping the world behind the American-driven globalization agenda. Ironically, although Iraq was banned from world commerce, privatization burrowed through the wretched embargo and into one of its most sacred public sector strongholds.

One had to admit that the incentive system implemented by the Health Ministry was bearing fruit. And government's encouragement of free trade (or smuggling, since it was untaxed by Baghdad and unlawful, according to the UN embargo) helped save the country from a worse disaster at that time.

Man Growing Flowers, by Burhan al-Mufti, 1998.

It's Difficult for Me

It's difficult for me to be in a classroom where
Everybody is on George Bush's side
And I'm on Saddam Hussein's side, because
It's hard to explain to them;
George Bush started the war in the Gulf.
And I don't think it was a good idea
To kill 500 people.

Hamdi, age 9, 1991, New York

7

One Iraqi Child and Her Father, 1996

Surely the saddest words any doctor has to utter are "Nothing can be done." Hundreds of thousands of times, Iraqi physicians sighed and said, "We can do nothing." They have known what had to be done. They could have saved many of their patients—before 1990.

Before the blockade, spinal surgery was conducted in two of Iraq's hospitals. After 1990, the only solution for a patient was to seek help outside. In the past, this would have been easily arranged and financed by Iraq's Health Ministry. Today, a doctor only can say, "Try." Probably fewer than one in a million needy children have received help abroad. How the Almighty chose that soul, we cannot even ask.

Taking Chances with Strangers

I first met Abu Farah in Jordan. He was a complete stranger, and he was glaring at me across the width of a conference table that separated us. It was an uncommon gesture in our culture. "Why is he staring at me like that?" I thought. Surely I was the one who ought to be scrutinizing him. Never mind. My longtime friend Ahmed had brought us together. I trusted him. The issue at hand was urgent.

I had a mission, and we had pressing business to complete. I was about to hand some precious mementos, letters, photos, and other things to Abu Farah. People abroad had entrusted these to me since there was virtually no other way than by hand to get these to their loved ones inside Iraq. A boy needed a document from his father overseas to obtain a passport. The family of a deceased woman was sending a token of hers to Kerbala Al-Husseini Mosque; grandparents in Mosul longed for photos of grandchildren in California. Cardiac units needed any amount of life-saving drugs. Medical journals had been gathered for a hospital library. I had promised to deliver these papers and medicines.

I had expected to go to Baghdad from Jordan, but I had to return to New York before my visa arrived. "I will find someone for you," offered Mohammed. He was a Jordanian with business interests in Iraq. He understood the importance of these gifts. "Come to my office tomorrow. We will look after it."

That was where I found myself seated across from the man introduced to me as Abu Farah. The Iraqi said barely a word throughout the exchange. How I wished his hazel eyes and thin lips would reveal a hint of warmth. He just stared. His face was slender and sallow, and his slight moustache was almost white, although he looked hardly more than forty-five. Apparently he did not feel it necessary to assure me that he would do what I asked.

"Abu Farah is departing for Baghdad in the morning. You can trust him to deliver the gifts," Mohammed said quietly. The stranger carefully itemized the information I gave him on a piece of paper: names and phone numbers of each anxious Iraqi family and their sender's information. He worked silently, taking each envelope, attaching to it an individual note with the details written in Arabic. He made a master list, signed it, and passed it to Mohammed, who made a photocopy for me. We parted.

"This Is Manal"

Eight months passed before I could return to Iraq. On my way through Jordan, I again met Mohammed, who gave me his friend's phone number. "I'll phone him to expect you."

Abu Farah came to the Palestine Hotel within an hour of my arrival in the capital. This time he was smiling broadly. He did not mention the items I had left with him, and neither did I. Months earlier, each sender had informed me that their relatives had phoned to thank them for the gifts.

Abu Farah was keen that I meet his family, and I accepted his dinner invitation for the following day. When I arrived at his house, I found two children along with Umm Farah waiting at the door with gleeful smiles, hugs, and kisses. (Kisses are a customary greeting to a visitor, even a stranger, arriving in an Arab home.) The children led me inside. Once we were seated in the parlor, another girl quietly entered. She silently sidled over to her father and collapsed against his chest. She knew she was his favorite.

The girl's thin face was almost hidden by luxurious, shiny black hair. She looked in my direction for a fraction of a second. Then she buried herself deeper between her father's knees, her eyes down, her pointed chin thrust against his chest. Abu Farah picked up his daughter and settled her on his lap. His eyes were sparkling. He teased her, whispering into her ear, and turned back to me, his face radiant. The rest of the family was silent, standing somewhere out of my line of vision. They seemed not to exist in this scenario.

"This is Manal. She is the dearest to me," Abu Farah said. By now, I had realized the girl had some kind of disease that seemed to affect her spine and limbs. "She is twelve. My second child and the smartest! She is excellent in Arabic, and she is beginning to study English. Isn't this so, Manal? Tell our guest," he added, pressing his face into her hair. The child still did not speak, but he continued playfully whispering to her.

In careful, precise English now, he proceeded to explain Manal's disease to me. "Arthrogryposis," said the father slowly. "Doctors call it scoliosis. Manal has severe scoliosis." Taking his daughter's arms, the former accountant and now adventurous merchant gently extended the child's hands toward me; next he held one of her feet, lifting it to show me how distorted it was. "Come," he said, instructing the child, who walked with some difficulty, to lead us upstairs to her bedroom. He told her not to be shy and to remove her shirt and turn around so he could show me her spine. "The discs. They are fused together." Manal's father seemed to know the disease intimately, and as he spoke, he traced his finger from the base of her skull down her spine. "It will require many operations. They must cut the discs free. In the past, in Iraq, our doctors could treat such things with surgery. Not now."

Abu Farah continued talking as he helped his daughter dress. "Do you think there is a hospital in America that can help my beautiful child? We know that she may die within a few years. But we want to try to keep her with us. I will pay. I will do anything." Throughout this exchange, Manal's mother was not far away. But Abu Farah clearly assumed full responsibility for the girl. His arms embraced her like a soft bed of flowers the entire time we sat together.

We returned to the parlor. Abu Farah now fixed his eyes on me with the same intensity as on our first meeting. This time, however, he was smiling warmly. "Can you find help for Manal in your country?"

A Job Offer I Did Not Want

A quiet trembling seized me. If my disquiet was evident to him, I did not care. This is not my job, I thought. What medical contacts did I have in the States? None. Why didn't he approach the United Nations or one of the visiting medical delegations?

I did not want this responsibility. I had had no success with what few attempts I had made to help people obtain visas or admission to colleges. This was more difficult, more complicated. It was not merely a medical matter. An American family must take care of the child after her operations. A visa had to be secured. Travel expenses had to be found.

Few Americans were extending sympathy of the extent this child needed. In my mind, I retraced the names of humanitarian organizations I knew. Fellowship of Reconciliation arranged for Bosnian children to travel to the United States for treatment. But that was Bosnia. There was a Palestinian children's health service. Palestinians found some support (as victims) in the United States, despite their political losses. A Muslim-run humanitarian effort for Iraq was based in Wisconsin. But did it take on medical cases?

Iraqis were low priority for humanitarian groups in the United States, perhaps because of political obstacles they had already encountered. Compared with other disaster victims, help for Iraqis under embargo was feeble. One medical group in Stony Brook, N.Y., ferried a few children out of Iraq. Their arrival in Baghdad was highly publicized; they were heaped with praise and somehow managed to secure permission to fly out in UN aircraft. Inside the United States, that group worked in near-secrecy, however, and I suspected their motives. As for my meager efforts thus far, they had been confined to getting help to Iraqi medical teams. I always maintained it was better to equip Iraqis who could attend to thousands than to bring one victim out of Iraq. Physicians in Iraq felt disempowered by those international gestures and rightly said, "Give us what we need, and *we* can save our children."

The U.S. State Department was stingy with visas for Iraqis. Washington wanted only one-way travelers from Iraq.[1] Even if we found travel funds, a hospital, and a host family, getting a visa would be an enormous obstacle.

I had no idea where to begin. This was not the first time I had complained, "This is not my job." I recalled the day I trudged through markets with doctors purchasing bed sheets and light fixtures for their hospital. My colleague, Dr. Karim, a cardiologist, gently retorted, "It is not my job either." This mission was more complex. I felt helpless and daunted by the obstacles that flashed through my mind. Yet I found myself replying, "I will try."

"We will need photos and a doctor's certification," I advised, trying to pinpoint something concrete with which to begin this undertaking.

"No problem," replied the father. "I have photos. I have her X-rays. I have a doctor's report—with a statement of why this cannot be done in Iraq. I have her school records, too. She is at the top of her class. Tell me when you need the papers, and I will have everything ready for you."

Two days later, he gave me all of his daughter's files on a CD as well as in hard copy. I was impressed. Few computers existed in Iraq at that time. I was heartened. Seeing how organized and single-minded the father was, I began to think that we—that is to say, he—might actually achieve this impossible goal.

Abu Farah also disproved the notion that only an Arab son deserved this much attention.

"Get Manal Ready to Travel"

Shortly after returning to New York, I copied the documents from Iraq and sent them to two organizations. Perhaps, I reckoned, if these agencies are familiar with my radio dispatches on Iraq, they will be responsive. Any reply would take months in any case. So I put the matter out of my mind and hoped Abu Farah would not phone to harass me about the applications.

He did not have to. I initiated a call to him barely a month later.

I felt I had won a lottery when I received an e-mail from the director of one of the two agencies to whom I had sent Manal's records. "Tell the family to get the child ready to travel." *Al-Hamdulillah*! Praise Allah for his grace.

Could it be so uncomplicated? I picked up the phone and dialed the organization's office. A decision of this magnitude needed affirmation. "Yes, we have found a sponsor. Please contact the child's parents. They do not need to come with her. We will find an Arab family here to host Manal. We are working with another organization (the agency to whom I had sent the duplicates). We will arrange the hospital."

There was still no Internet connection in Iraq—the embargo again—and it took me several attempts to reach Baghdad by phone. Abu Farah was pleased by the news, but he did not seem at all surprised. "No problem. She is ready," he said quietly. I thought I heard him laugh. Or was he weeping?

There were delays as the hospital negotiated how many operations it would commit to. At one point I feared the main sponsor might cancel. The first hospital backed out, and another had to be found. Their services had to be gratis. Manal required several operations, and it was not easy to obtain a commitment. So I had the awful job of calling Abu Farah to warn him that we might not succeed. He seemed unruffled. "You will succeed. But please explain to them. I need to be with her."

It would be the first time in the girl's life that she would be separated from her father. She might not manage without him.

"No parents," came the reply. The sponsor was firm, and Abu Farah did not press me further. As with all his earlier preparations, he facilitated important official matters. Before long he had arranged Manal's passport and an exit permit. They learned the name of the Iraqi-American family in California who would host Manal. This family had four children, and their house was just an hour from the hospital where the child would be treated.

Only Abu Farah accompanied Manal by car from Baghdad to Amman. The twelve-hour drive was the sole means of entering and exiting the country at that time. Abu Farah accepted it as a blessing; his daughter needed to rest. Her flight to Los Angeles was leaving the next day. In the morning, hardly five hours after Manal and her father reached the Jordanian capital, Mohammed drove them to the airport.

Manal seemed determined to proceed unaided through the departure lounge, and she moved slowly toward the gate, away from her father. Abu Farah followed each labored step she took, ready to spring after her. In her arms, she clutched a small bag of gifts. At the door of the ramp, she stopped, twisted her head around, and let it drop onto her shoulder. Slowly, she lifted her face upward in a farewell nod to her father. She was wearing bright yellow slacks and a T-shirt with a tiger embroidered on it.

Mohammed held his friend's shoulders for a long time afterward. "I have never seen a man like this," he later told me. "The little girl did not cry. It was her Baba who was sobbing like a child."[2]

Flower Chasing Butterfly, by Burhan al-Mufti, 1998.

8

Books Break Sanctions

"We could not read," said the tormented, disoriented Iraqi woman. "The electricity. The thunder of bombs across the city."

This incapacity is not an incidental item in war's depravity. Not a victim, not collateral damage. This was another target of the siege against Iraq, against the civilization it inherited and the Arab values it embodied and also protected.

In April 1991, I returned to Iraq barely three weeks after the Gulf War bombings ended. During those terrifying few months, I'd been unable to reach anyone in Iraq. Now, although somewhat apprehensive, I sought out women and men I knew from earlier visits. Gaya Rahal Ghani was such an Iraqi. She was a Baghdadi intellectual, an archaeologist, and an adoring reader.

At our reunion in the devastated city, Gaya, in her characteristic manner, was not voluble. Some spoke about the terror of the air strikes and listed people we knew who were dead, who had gone mad, who had fled, or who were immobilized by outrage and disbelief. Gaya Ghani's pithy remark about books resonated through a long tunnel of sorrow. Everyone had spent weeks without electricity; each was submerged in anxiety, waiting for the next roar of bombers, the coming rally of explosions, the need to rush here and there for supplies. Reading would have calmed this book lover, maybe distracted her, and helped her connect with her past—in order to bear the future.

It is well known that writing was first developed in Iraq and that libraries existed in this ancient land as early as five thousand years ago. In addition to literary achievements in the Abbassid period (750–1258), ancestors of modern Iraq played important roles in all fields of intellectual pursuit, including medicine, mathematics, and astronomy. In their modern lives, Iraqis are passionately enthusiastic readers. The availability of books from around the world is vital to their existence. "Written in Cairo, printed in Beirut, read in Baghdad" is a well known and frequently quoted maxim denoting the centrality of books in Iraqi life. So it was quite reasonable, despite paper shortages, deteriorating hotel facilities, blocked imports, and reduced conference funding, that Iraq should host Mahrajan al-Marbid, the gathering of writers. Every year throughout the embargo, they convened this literary festival.

Al-Marbid had become more than a symposium to promote Arab national values and bonds. This gathering was a rebellion against the blockade because the embargo proved to be as much a cultural siege as an economic one. Iraq's enemies knew that books are as important as food and electricity here.

Rejoicing in Baghdad

Normally empty and often gloomy, the lobby of Melia Mansour Hotel filled with laughter and gossip for a week every winter. The al-Marbid poetry festival was under way. When poets, critics and publishers from neighboring Arab countries converged here, they transformed the hotel. The city then became a cozy, animated intellectual carnival.

Most of the visitors who gathered at Mansour this week in 2001 knew Iraq well. The festival was like an alumni reunion for them. Some had been students here. Many attended seminars and celebrations in Baghdad before the blockade. Al-Marbid was an occasion for renewing essential bonds; colleagues, lovers, ex-husbands, and teachers were here. These women and men came to recite poetry and listen to other bards. They also brought an unequivocal political message. "It is to break the sanctions. This gathering is one of the ways we fight sanctions: to say, 'We are still here, still living.'" Buthaina al-Nasiri is a writer and a publisher based in Cairo. Every winter, you could find her at al-Marbid.

Some sympathizers traveling to Iraq carry teddy bears to draw attention to the absurdity of the U.S. sanctions policy that lists the toy among banned exports to Iraq. Most foreign visitors and journalists tour hospitals. Only a few inspect a school. Some offer token packages of random medicines collected from friends. Precious few donate pencils to a school. Hardly any western sympathizers, few as they are, bring Iraqis something to read.[1] This mission carried armfuls of books to al-Marbid, including visitors' own published work.

Buthaina is originally from Iraq. She arrived two weeks before the festival, in part to visit her family but also for another gathering. "We celebrated the 500th anniversary of the founding of Beit al-Hikmah, House of Wisdom, last week. In November, Baghdad will host a celebration to mark the 5,000th year of the origin of writing! Here! In Baghdad! Can you imagine?" Buthaina asked. The question was rhetorical. She lifted her eyebrows, amused, looking directly at me. She knew I could not imagine. People raised in the West can't even comprehend 1,000 years of progress. How could we imagine this pride and the enduring effect of literature in their everyday lives?

"Celebrating 5,000 years of history and doing so under an ugly American blockade is another means of challenging the West.

"Praise of literature is a policy we in Iraq embrace. It is a good policy, a policy to say we care not only about food and medicine but also about civilization. The West will say we are wasting our money, reading instead of giving people food, and so on. But these celebrations are very important. They support us spiritually; they help us to stand and fight the sanctions."

Demitasses of drained coffee pile up and ashtrays overflow. Laughter rises from every cluster of men and women in every corner of the hotel. When one writer departs to meet a friend, another slips into her vacated seat. Calls fly across the room as one hails another into their circle or fixes a rendezvous. The staff of the Ministry of Information seem never more relaxed and delighted by their efforts as during this week when they are hosting Arab writers.

This is the final day of Iraq's seventeenth annual al-Marbid festival. Colleagues have spent days and nights reminiscing, and new friendships are fused. Performances by individuals over the previous five days aroused acclaim and debate about past recitations and new works. New poems celebrate Iraq's defiance of U.S., British, and Zionist assaults. Verses glorifying Palestinian resistance are as numerous as songs for Iraq. Writers do not forget the link even if politicians and journalists ignore it.[2]

Solidarity in the Family

Al-Marbid is a party for writers, editors, and publishers. This year's guests arrived from Algeria, Sudan, Egypt, Yemen, Lebanon, Syria, and other Arab states. Before 1990, al-Marbid was even more international. Then delegates from Vietnam to Mauritania, Morocco to Kuwait mingled with Yugoslav and Australian poets. The UN embargo had changed a lot of things. It could not bury al-Marbid.

Invitations went out from the Ministry of Information as broadly as in the past, although fewer responses were received. No Asian or European poets came to Baghdad after 1990. Despite some intellectuals expressing sympathy with Iraqis, few risked actually coming to the country, even for a literary gathering. Sadly, the Arab literary giants Mahmoud Darwish and Adonis declined al-Marbid as well. But in recent years, with increasing hardships and Washington's inexorable pressure on Iraq, other Arab intellectuals insisted on demonstrating unity with Iraq. As one by one, Arab nations distanced themselves from the United States, they initiated rapprochement with their sister state. More writers joined the thin columns of visitors to al-Marbid.[3]

I make my way through the huddles of Iraqis and their guests in search of Buthaina. She waves me to her coffee table, an arabesque-sculpted stand cluttered with papers, books, and cups. With her sits Ahmed, her Egyptian husband, an artist and illustrator, and Dunya Saadi, an Iraqi woman who is an English-language scholar. I hurriedly fix an appointment with Dunya to hear more about her translations of American novels. Then Buthaina and I leave Ahmed and the young translator to find a quiet corner for our interview.

"I come here every year. I come to see my people, my friends, and my home. *Ishtar*, which I founded eight years ago, is devoted mainly to literary work from Iraq. I come to see what my compatriots are doing. I select manuscripts, take them to Cairo to publish, then distribute as widely as I can. It is a way to break the embargo." Noting my look of puzzlement, al-Nasiri continues. "Yes, to break the sanctions. Because of the UN embargo, Iraqi writers cannot publish their work as they did before. Today, most middle-class families here cannot even afford to purchase a new book—if they can find one. Before 1990, Iraq published two thousand titles annually, thanks to government financing. Now, almost nothing is printed here—perhaps fifty titles a year—and that covers all subjects.

"They cannot get paper," she interjects, without stopping to explain that problem.[4]

"By publishing Iraqi literature in Cairo, *Ishtar* at least provides a chance for others around the Arab world to keep in touch with our writers. I give my Iraqi colleagues the opportunity to publish their work outside the sanctions wall and to affirm their rights as writers."

Buthaina al-Nasiri, wiry, ebullient, and attractive, started out as a short story writer. She left Iraq during the Gulf War. For the last eight years, she has lived in Cairo with Ahmed. Together they manage their publishing house, *Ishtar*.[5]

More to Write About

Iraqi visual artists have actually flourished during these hard years. In contrast, one hears little about the besieged nation's writers. We would be mistaken if we thought creative writing had been abandoned, however. "They are astonishing me, every time I come here" exclaims Buthaina. "I know you expect the opposite. You expect people living under these conditions would just break down, unable to write, to do anything creative. On the contrary, they are amazingly productive. I don't know how to describe it, but," she pauses, then, certain of what she wants to say, continues. "I envy them. It is not easy to understand the values we fight for." Buthaina was clearly excited and proud of her compatriots. "In Cairo, where I have everything I need, I haven't produced any new novel these past years. On the other hand, my people in Iraq are writing like crazy people and publishing. They publish in small editions to distribute among their friends. They are doing everything to say that they are standing and fighting. They are fighting for life.

"Of course they write about conditions around them," Buthaina says. "But there is more, something no one would have expected. Sarcasm appears in their new writings. You couldn't find this in the past. It is emerging . . . as if they need to devise ways to endure hardship. We find fantasy in their new work as well. A means of escaping their sufferings? Perhaps.

"There are abundant jokes, too. This fresh Iraqi humor is strange for us living in Cairo because you know Egyptians are famous for being jesters. Their jokes are popular everywhere. In the Arab world we turn to Egyptian stories to lighten our lives. In recent years, people have become so serious in Egypt. I don't know why. But they ask me, when I return from Baghdad, 'What is the latest joke from Iraq?' Iraqis poke fun at anyone and everything: local politics, the American president, Arab kings. But their jokes are mainly about themselves."

Through her publications, Buthaina al-Nasiri strives to keep Egyptians and other Arabs better informed by selecting honest articles about Iraq and printing them in a newsletter that she produces from her Cairo office. "I distribute it mainly among Egypt's literary public. Most of the articles I reprint are about the siege. I find them on the Internet and translate them. Many are written by Europeans and Americans who visit Iraq."

Until Next Year

From the first to the final days of al-Marbid, writers exchange stories about themselves and gossip about lost colleagues—those who had left Iraq, who had abandoned writing, who had died—and new manuscripts and new voices. Since many of them are editors as well as creative writers, they are eager to plan new projects. They sign up authors to send them new articles, and they map out plans for new collections.

"Oddly enough, just being in Iraq inspires us visitors," reflects Buthaina. "Iraqis are described as readers, the great readers of the Arab world. When I visit my family here, I ask my grandchildren what they want. They don't want chocolates or toys, only magazines and books. Before the embargo, the Ministries of Information and Education had abundant funds for publishing. Books were cheap, too. Not only Iraqi works, but also Arab creative work. Arab writers from all over came here with their manuscripts and they published their work within a week. When the sanctions end, we will be as before."

I had, of course, read about Iraq's historical role in human literary history, from the example of *Gilgamesh* (a Sumerian legend in epic poem form, the oldest known work of literature) to the abundant cuneiform libraries of the great cities of Sumer and Ninevah.[6] In 1989, I had the honor to tour the Sippar site at Abu Hatta. My host was Walid al-Jadir, professor at Baghdad University and director of excavations there. Fingering the clay shelves of the library index he had unearthed and identified impressed me deeply. But a two-volume set of books printed in 1968 that I came upon during that same visit, when I was browsing in a Mansour district bookstore, influenced my work in Iraq more profoundly than anything else. Learning about that publication and its editor, Ahmed Sousa, sealed my admiration for contemporary literary pursuits. (Ten years later, I found myself in his private library with his remarkable daughter and biographer, Aliya Sousa.)

Su-Ren Bookstore was opened in 1989 in Baghdad by Nasra al-Saadoun and a colleague. The Iran-Iraq war had ended barely four months earlier. Although books from overseas were unavailable because of the war, Su-Ren displayed an unusual and broad collection of Iraqi publications. *Idrisi's History of Geography* was a profusely illustrated two-volume set. It cost 60 dinars ($180 at the 1989 exchange rate). I bought it. I could see at once what an extraordinary compilation this was. Written by Dr. Ahmed Sousa, it was published by the Iraqi Engineering Association, a government-funded organization.

Sousa died in 1983, but I was able to locate Aliya Sousa in 1998 through my colleagues Amal and Nermin. I quickly recognized that this woman was more than the daughter of an important writer, historian, and civil engineer. She was a scholar. And she chose to defy sanctions by producing books!

Her father's library, now carefully secured in her home, housed Sousa's published articles and books, his private letters, sketches, and photos, and his unpublished works. Dr. Aliya had become custodian of all this. She knew what a treasure this was. Most important, she was engaged in compiling Ahmed Sousa's unfinished work, including his autobiography, arranging for new editions of out-of-print books, and translating others from Arabic to English. She had also begun writing his biography. This was her mission, one she worked at daily, into the eighth year of the blockade. The embargo had forced schools to cut back, wiped out government-funded publications, and left universities handicapped. All this was in her charge when Aliya Sousa was killed in her office at the UN headquarters in Baghdad on August 19, 2003.

Between 1998 and 2001, I interviewed Dr. Aliya four times. During my two visits to her family home, we sat in her father's library. I was able to examine some of his work, including manuscripts and private letters, and to see how beautifully and carefully everything was maintained. "He was a very organized man, very organized," she confided. So was she.

I felt honored to be in the Sousa home. My hostess was generous with her time. She shared anecdotes about her father, his early life, and his education, and she told me some of her plans to make his work more widely available. She possessed extraordinary focus and determination in that aim.

Dr. Aliya did not explicitly tell me this project was a means of resisting the embargo. We both knew it was. I was aware that she was proceeding with a sense of mission and urgency, without compromising her high standard of scholarship. As a scholar, she knew some things could not be rushed. She took up employment as an economist at the UN's Iraq office to help finance her private research and publication. (With the arrival of the blockade, government support was no longer available. She was seeking outside publishers.) As long as she was able to work on her library, Iraq had a promising future.

The following is transcribed directly from taped interviews, drawn from our three conversations.

"My father was a son of Babylon. He was born in Hilla. From an early age, visiting construction sites, he was fascinated by the engineering of canals, and this led him to his interest in excavations of our early Iraqi history."

Sousa authored fifty books; the last was in press when he died in 1983. All his books are in Arabic; most were published by the Iraqi Ministry of Information. In addition to his research materials, Sousa kept copies of thousands of pages of correspondence including his private letters, early newspaper columns, and scientific commentaries. Many of his scientific papers, individually published, were ready to be assembled as new collections. No one was better suited to see that this was done than his daughter. She was highly educated in Arabic, French, and English. She studied in Paris, London, and the United States. Although not an engineer, she spent so much time discussing his work with her father when they were together that she became intimately familiar with the subjects he wrote about.

Sousa's research in various fields of civil engineering resulted in books directly concerned with Iraqi civilization. He was a prodigious scholar. He combined an early interest in the two fields of irrigation and archaeology into a vast area of scholarship, applied engineering, and publication.

An Arab nationalist from his youth, Sousa began writing in support of Arab values in the early 1920s when he was a student in Beirut. His earliest articles were published in his hometown newspaper in Hilla and in Lebanese journals. By the time he set out for graduate studies in the United States, Sousa's Arab nationalist and anti-Zionist positions were well known. He would later write a classic study on the history of Arabs and Jews, part of which was translated and published in English. It is a highly regarded reference book without parallel, although not easy to locate.

Sousa first studied civil engineering. His focus was on hydrology stemming from his early interest in irrigation, hence his huge three-volume publication, *The Planning of the City of Baghdad*. That work in turn led to his research on the 1,200-year history of irrigation. (This was in addition to his *History of Irrigation in Iraq*.)

Sousa left Hilla in 1920 for the famous American University of Beirut. From there, he went to the University of Colorado for a second degree in civil engineering (1928). After Colorado, he joined Johns Hopkins University for his PhD. "His doctorate was in political history, and the subject of his thesis was 'Capitulations in the Ottoman Empire.' His research of how western governments undermined and then reconquered the lands of the Ottoman Empire was motivated by my father's growing suspicions of western imperialist aims in the Arab lands. He feared what the United States, the United Kingdom, and the emerging Zionist state would do to undermine and destroy the Arab nations. My father was a deeply Arab nationalist man as well as an Iraqi nationalist."[7]

Sousa's interest extended to comparative religion. "He spent a great deal of time in the States and back home reading philosophy and religion. This grew out of an attraction to Islam, his boyhood friendships with Muslim lads, his Jewish family history, and perhaps his marriage to his first wife, Mary, in 1932. She was from Iowa, a Christian woman. Growing up among Muslims, my father abandoned Judaism early in his life and became Muslim. In 1936, after studying at al-Azhar University in Cairo, he officially embraced Islam.

"That was motivated as much by his love for Iraq and its Muslim heritage as by his opposition to Zionism. He never considered himself anti-Jewish, and he exhorted Arab Jews to oppose Zionist ideas." This personal history helps explain Sousa's nationalist writings, his dedication to Iraq, and his studies and publications in comparative religion. These were among his lesser-known works, which together with her father's letters Aliya Sousa was assembling for publication when we spoke in 1998 and on other occasions in Baghdad.

Aliya Sousa felt that her father's most outstanding contribution was his historical work in hydrology and archaeology. "All the modern projects in Iraq are located in the same places where ancient irrigation structures were. There are certain places in Iraq that are especially suitable for irrigation. This had not changed. My father made very detailed studies of ancient irrigation systems, and this led him repeatedly back to our ancient history." By 1931, Sousa was an employee of the Irrigation Department in Iraq's Ministry of Communications. "His work on ancient irrigation projects led him into the study of early civilizations, and through that he discovered that our ancient Babylonians were the world's first cartographers, with line drawings alongside the cuneiform script. They drew the first maps we have. My father published an atlas on Iraq's ancient maps."

Some of Sousa's work was coauthored. "There was one book, a huge volume, *The History of the Planning of Baghdad*, that he wrote with the historians Mustafa Jawad and Naji Marouf and the architect Mohammed Makkiya. My father's articles in that volume are on irrigation in Baghdad. That was his specialty. He and his dear friend Mustafa Jawad wrote another book, *The History of Irrigation in Baghdad.*[8] That book remains a major source on the history of Baghdad. On this same subject, his favorite, he has twelve important research papers; I am now preparing to publish them."

Another study Dr. Aliya was working on was her father's two-volume *History of Mesopotamian Civilization*. "In this, he combines his research on ancient irrigation, archaeological discoveries, and other textual historical sources. It was his last contribution, a huge two-volume work, which he never saw. He died while it was being prepared for the press. It is translated by a colleague." (We do not know if this translation was from Arabic into English.)

"I checked the terminology and prepared the footnotes for this book. It was a big job. It took me years. The Iraqi Ministry of Information also published this. It was a very costly production, but it was sold at a nominal price—trivial, really. Many thousands of copies were printed.

"Among my father's other work published by the same ministry is *The Development of Arab Civilization from Ancient Times*. In this, he addresses Mesopotamian civilization and the controversy between Semites and Sumerians.

"Then, of course, there is his classic study for which he is also famous, *Arabs and Jews in History* (Al-Arab wa 'l-Yahood fi 't-Tarikh). A summary from this was translated into four or five languages and published in Switzerland, but only a summary. The importance of my father's contribution here is his reading of the Old Testament through archaeological discoveries. Hitherto, scholars read the ancient history of Palestine through the Old Testament, which was less reliable. Archaeological discoveries are accepted as indisputable, not the legends of the Old Testament, which had been the accepted guide to the interpretation of the ancient history of Palestine. *Arabs and Jews in History* has been reprinted five times since 1972 by the Ministry of Information and Culture. I have been asked to approve a new reprint.

"Ahmed Sousa taught for only one year in the 1970s. He found teaching exhausting; he wanted to conserve his energy for his research. In 1957, when he retired from his job at the Department of Irrigation, he received a modest pension and lived on that. He continued to publish commentaries; he sometimes criticized the work of government hydrology engineers. He came under fire for his views from former colleagues in the Department of Irrigation. They tried to have his commentaries banned. They were unsuccessful, I am glad to say, and he continued to express his professional assessments in the press.

"My father was active in the Iraqi Academy of Science, where he devoted much of his time after he retired. He was engaged along with others in the Academy's Arabic terminology project. It was a long-term project on which all the members of the Iraqi Academy worked. They were engaged in Arabizing scientific and other terms applied in different areas of scholarship. Volumes, volumes, were published from this effort. When not at work there or in his own library, my father could be found at the Iraq National Museum. He went there every day to consult books. The museum houses a very important library, and he spent long, long hours there."

Ahmed Sousa left three unpublished manuscripts at the time of his death: "Al-Idrisi and Arabic Geography," "The Arab Peninsula: Cradle of Semitic Civilization," and an autobiography called "My Life during Half a Century." These were finished manuscripts, according to his daughter, and she was planning to publish them.

"Occasionally, but not often, my father attended symposia outside Iraq. Sometimes he took my mother, Najat, and me. I was their only child, born after ten years. So when I came, for him, it was a gift of Allah. He considered me a friend, and he communicated intellectually with me."[9]

If we remember the deprivations precipitated by the long, malicious embargo, then every effort to write, to debate ideas, and to somehow get one's writings printed becomes a truly remarkable feat. It should convince any people lacking even a small fraction of the literary history of Iraq of what pride in one's civilization can do.

Author's note: Book titles are taken from my interviews with Buthaina al-Nasiri and Aliya Sousa and are not precise translations of the Arabic titles. In the interest of scholarship, we list below the approximate English titles of books written or edited in Arabic by Ahmed Sousa.

Sousa, Ahmed, ed., *Idrisi's History of Geography.* 2 vols. Baghdad: Iraqi Engineering Association, 1968.

———. *History of Irrigation in Iraq.* Baghdad: Ministry of Information, n.d.

———. *History of Mesopotamian Civilization.* Baghdad: Ministry of Information, n.d.

———. *The Development of Arab Civilization from Ancient Times.* Baghdad: Ministry of Information, n.d.

———. *Arabs and Jews in History.* Baghdad: Ministry of Information, 1972.

Sousa, Ahmed, and Mustafa Jawad. *The History of Irrigation in Baghdad.* Baghdad: Ministry of Information, n.d.

Sousa, Ahmed, Mustafa Jawad, Mohammed Makkai, and Najim Arrouf. *The History of the Planning of Baghdad.* Baghdad: Ministry of Information, n.d.

9

Just Business

Noble ideals like supporting literature and restructuring institutions as with Iraq's two-tier health plan helped to offset the destructive effects of the embargo. Promise of easy profits had a role to play, too.

Any commerce with Iraq was illegal according to the UN resolutions, and the United States, self-appointed enforcer of the blockade, did its best to intimidate and punish would-be trade partners with Iraq. Across Iraq's land borders this approach was unworkable. From the Iraqi side, vigorous exchange was initiated through a new laissez-faire policy: smuggle what you can. Willing Iraqi entrepreneurs found suppliers.

Baghdad levied no tax against the underhanded imports. It also did not impose price controls, a remarkable break from past policies. We can expect the leadership used this venue to secure goods for itself. Not on the scale that the foreign press would have us believe, namely, that anything entering Iraq was for the arming, pleasures, and profits of Saddam Hussein. Not at all. In fact, the import of essential staples probably saved the country from famine in the early years of the embargo.

Initially, roads were the only means of transport, and some supplies had to be conveyed under harsh and dangerous conditions. Trade was restricted to dinars at first; Iraqi merchants had no access to foreign currency and little to barter in exchange. Yet, for anyone determined to venture across Iraq's unfriendly borders, profits could be considerable. Cash rewards for farmers had proved effective. Now merchants were mobilized.

If Saddam Hussein benefited, so did his neighbors.[1] No countries were more affected by Iraq's change of fortunes than Turkey and Jordan. Jordan appeared to be Iraq's dearest political ally. During the Iran-Iraq war (1980–88), Iraq shifted to a consumer economy—its farmers and laborers were on the battlefield—with the majority of imports coming primarily through Jordan. My first visit to Iraq was in 1989 via Iraqi Airways. I was the only journalist aboard, the rest having left after the Iran-Iraq cease-fire a few months earlier. The flight was nevertheless full. My fellow passengers, about sixty-five men, were Jordanian businessmen seeking contracts. Jordan's spectacular growth and fortunes derived from profits in Iraq.

Companies who had profited during Iraq's war with Iran still looked to Iraq to sustain their good fortune. I was startled when I arrived in Amman from Iraq, the bleakness of life there still fresh in my mind, to hear the woes of Jordanian merchants, from drug manufacturers to seed suppliers. As they sat in soft leather chairs in their trim offices and sipped aromatic coffee, their sole concern seemed set on how the embargo affected their profits.

> We need Iraq; she is the richest country in this area. We've just concluded three contracts totaling $20 million, mainly for vegetable oil. We supply Iraq under a special protocol agreement with Jordan. It's approved by the UN. We do not produce vegetable oil ourselves. We buy most of what we need from the United States, soy and corn oil, and we process it here. Half of what we export to Iraq, 45,000 tons, originates in the United States. We are paid from the Central Bank of Jordan's reserves of dollars from Iraq's oil supplies to Jordan. (Director of a private company, Amman, 1997)

Iraq had no Wall Street, no stock market, no consumer index. The only statistics posted during the decade (apart from the price of crude oil after Iraqi oil began to flow following the signing of SCR 986) were registers of the rise in diseases and underweight births.[2]

In Jordan, scores of businessmen regularly traveled to Baghdad in search of trade contracts. They did not lack compassion for their suffering neighbors. But their view of Iraq was little changed from ten years earlier—a limitless consumer market. Under embargo, and during open hostilities, Iraq was a major source of profit for Jordanian suppliers. They were eager to tap it. Petty consumer goods were filtering across Iraq's mountainous borders with Turkey and Iran. The bottom end of that cross-border trade is portrayed with intimacy and acumen by Iranian film director Bahman Ghobadi. His film *A Time for Drunken Horses* focuses on children employed as packers and carriers lugging consumer goods by horse across Iran's mountainous frontier with Iraq. Those supplies were simple household goods and cheap clothing. They reflected Iraqis' most urgent needs. Inside Iraq, in market stalls and shop windows, I noted these same items on sale. "From Iran," the vendors told me. Among their basic requirements in those desperate early years of siege, one found children's toys—plastic balls, stuffed animals, and colorful miniature playthings. Fundamentals of survival.

Jordan's trade with Iraq, by contrast, was largely on an industrial scale. Here it was legal.

We're a new company. We produce magnesium and batteries. Since 1989, we've been producing about $10 million worth a year, 60 percent of which is destined for Iraq. We made a bid last week to supply batteries to Iraq—an order for 2,000. We expect that to increase. Since 1990, export of cables to Iraq is prohibited. The new UN resolution 986 has approved $1 million in the first phase for cables for the Kurdish area. It's not much, but we submitted a tender.

Before 1990, Iraq imported $20 billion worth of goods every six months. Every six months! The UN is allowing $1.2 billion in the first six-month phase. It won't make a difference to the quality of life of Iraqis. None. But we can live nicely on this. (Abdul Rezk, company director in Amman, Jordan, 1997)

Pressure on Baghdad increased to let citizens share new profits. In 1975, the Baath government, in line with its austere socialist philosophy, restricted private development. In 1987, it extended possibilities in the private sector to Iraqi citizens, allowing co-ownership by private groups, but with the majority of shares held by state-owned companies. In 1995, a new doctrine issued by the Iraqi president gave Iraqis, including government bodies, authority to operate on the basis of self-financing. It lifted restrictions on imports and opened the economy to increased private investment by Iraqi nationals.[3]

I wouldn't risk it. Even if Iraq permits outside investment, it's still unstable. There was a cable company in the south, al-Nasiriyya Company, that imported copper from Saudi Arabia. The Saudis bought the raw material from Chile, Zaire, and Oman. That al-Nasiriyya plant's capacity was 15,000 tons. It was bombed in the 1991 war. Destroyed. They can't produce anything there now; anyway, they have no raw materials. They need more from outside than ever. We are trying to get contracts to supply them with finished cables. (Syrian investor, 1997)

The forty-two days of attacks on Iraq from January to the end of February 1991 knocked out the electrical system across Iraq. That in turn led to the spoilage of thousands of tons of frozen meat, emergency government supplies stored in refrigerated warehouses. Poultry farms were decimated when electrical supplies were cut. For months, no meat was available in Iraq. The crisis was exacerbated by other factors. For example, sheep herders decided to export their stock rather than slaughtering animals for local consumption. This "adjustment" continued through the decade.

Farmers transport 10–15 sheep packed into a small pickup truck to the frontier, either the border with Saudi Arabia or Jordan. They unload the animals and herd them across on foot. No one can regulate it. It's a long border, and the herders know all the routes. On the Jordanian side business partners pick up the sheep and truck them to their own camps. Of course, it's illegal. They mingle the Iraqi animals with their own, and no one can tell the difference. You can buy a whole sheep, Iraqi, good quality for 10 Jordanian dinars ($15 in 1996)—more than Iraqi families could afford—compared to the Jordanian price of 40 JD ($60) an animal. (Palestinian truck driver on the Amman-Baghdad route, 1996)

To conserve its limited supply of sugar, Iraq halted commercial production of candies after 1991. This had an unfortunate social impact: children were refused the simplest treat to ameliorate hardships they endured.

Not only was sugar rationed. Packaged candy was dependent on the availability of cello wrapping paper, a product of the chemical industry. Since chemical imports were under embargo, neither candy nor other paper-wrapped items were available. In 1997, after packaging equipment was allowed into Iraq by the UN, production resumed.

We are now producing propylene products to send to Iraq. We are setting up a new plant. In the past Iraq consumed 10,000 tons of packaging material produced from imported raw materials. Their factories are destroyed. The plant currently under construction is not for the local market. Jordan is too small. Saudi Arabia, Syria, and Egypt have their own plants, so that is not a market for us. Our only market is Iraq. (Jordanian company director, 1996)

In 1991, desperate for food, Iraq ordered farmers to plant wheat on all arable fields. It paid them a premium for their produce. Anything farmers managed to grow was sold only to the government. More land was turned over to grain production. Even nonfarmers with some capital to invest (professors and dentists, accountants and attorneys, normal city dwellers) leased land and began to plant wheat as well. Along with ordinary farmers, these grain producers became wealthy by growing wheat for the government. After only five years, thousands of farmers reportedly possessed more money than they could spend. Iraq had a new wealthy class.

There is no more government trade in Iraq now; it's all in the hands of private operators, new people. These new rich, wealthy from growing wheat and smuggling, were created by the Iraqi regime. They are allowed to expand without government oversight. In many ways, they are free. But that doesn't mean the government isn't involved. Ultimately the regime can take it all back. Saddam and his sons can say, "Yes, I sold it to you, but I want it back. Now." What can an individual do? Everything is ultimately the government's. It's all one system. The companies are phony as far as being private goes. They pay no tax, legally. But they have no security. The president takes a cut in any case. He can take over any time. Everyone understands this. (Jordanian professor of business administration, Amman, 1996)

Most of Iraq's food reserves were destroyed in the 1991 bombing. Whatever remained was depleted within a few months. Food had to be found, anywhere. Iraq gave its herders, farmers, and merchants a license to find food and sell at whatever the market would bear. Enterprising dealers set off into hostile territory, reopening abandoned desert roads, slipping through unmarked mountain passes. They pioneered avenues of commerce that continued up to the time of the 2003 invasion.

Iraq's old industrial families are finished. We don't know the names of the new millionaires yet. They are families from tribes and villages whose men crossed into Iran, Syria, Turkey, and Saudi Arabia to buy food and bring it into Iraq. It all began with food. There was no food in Iraq in 1992.

Food—that was all they bought at first. After they made huge profits, they began to look for new investments. They were the only ones who could afford fleets of cars and other government supplies when the government decided to sell off many of its assets. (Iraqi expatriate relocated in Amman, Jordan, 1995)

In September 1996, Washington expressed its disapproval with France over a major oil deal that the French oil giant Total had made with Iran.

Why are the Americans furious? News reports refer to this deal as between Total and Iran. Actually, it was with Iraq! It was signed between private dealers in Iraq—men with government connections—and Total Oil Company. It's outside the terms of the United Nations plan for Iraq." (Iraqi expatriate in Lebanon, 1996)

On threat of heavy fines, the U.S. Commerce Department expressly forbade any American citizen or company to engage in commerce with Iraq. No transactions were possible with Iraqi banks, no transfer via credit card, no letter of credit.

A Jordanian firm announced a 110-ton food and medicine donation to Iraq in 1998. Between 1996 and 1999, Jordanian pharmaceutical companies became the leading drug suppliers to Iraq. New plants opened. Sizable profits were made. This boon continued until Iraq was able to buy medicines through its UN-regulated oil revenues. Thereafter its contracts went to its pre-1990 suppliers in Europe, to the dismay of Jordanian firms. They argued that they had saved Iraq during its bleakest years.

News item: "American troops boarded an oil tanker in the Persian Gulf bound for the United Arab Emirates, claiming it carried illegal Iraqi oil. The Iraqis are selling oil on the sly, U.S. officials claim. The crew was detained, along with the ship and its contents, which were handed over to Kuwaiti authorities."

Off Sadoun Street in central Baghdad is a showroom piled with heaters, electrical compressors, generators, refrigerators, air conditioners, copper pipes, and other small industrial fixtures. If you want computers within a few weeks, the proprietor Falah can probably get you a shipment.

> Our goods come by sea on small ships. Yes, they are sometimes seized by U.S. and Kuwaiti patrols and turned back to Dubai and Abu Dhabi. The shipper has to pay—we don't know whom—to get them back. He absorbs the loss. We try to buy the same shipment when it is sent out again. It's more costly the second time.
>
> It's a game. Sometimes our shipment gets through and the next guy's doesn't. Next time it's the reverse—part of the cost of doing business in war.
>
> I was a broker in Dubai and Abu Dhabi in the 1980s. My family was a major importer. We had government contracts to install and decorate offices and other buildings. In 1990, we were asked to leave. We lost our investments but not our bank assets. They were returned.
>
> I came back to Baghdad in 1994. In 1996, I returned to try to collect on payments the Dubai government owed. I was unsuccessful. I came back to Iraq and gradually, with my contacts in Dubai and other Gulf countries, began importing goods we needed here. I get orders for luxury goods, from $1,000 to $10,000. Some, like computers, are used but still good. Tax here in Iraq is low; the government wants to stimulate this kind of import. Our profit margin is barely 1–3 percent because we have to keep our prices low. (A. Falah, Baghdad-based dealer, 1998)

Many items are still banned under a proposed new "smart sanctions" (eventually set out in SCR 1409, May 2002) ostensibly designed to lighten the hardships of the blockade.[4] They are what Washington designates as possible "dual-use items"—materials that could be adapted for military purposes. They included Sony PlayStations, angised (a heart medication), isordil and other chemotherapy drugs, laser instruments, chlorine and graphite, many types of computers, and scientific journals.

> I'm not a producer. I'm a business agent for foreign companies specializing in high-tech equipment—phone and solar systems. I sell to the military. I used to work with the American company Johnson Controls, which built Saudi Arabia's early warning system. I lost that contract at the time of the Gulf War.
>
> A Spanish company is interested in working with us to supply Iraq with phones—an exchange system with 40,000 lines. They said they would take payment in oil (outside UN control and therefore risking confiscation). They will work through the Arab Emirates. They want the business.
>
> We're not worried. Iraq can manage to pay us. (Jordanian business agent, 1998)

In 2001, Iraq's Ministry of Trade organized a book fair for foreign suppliers. It drew forty vendors selling mainly university medical, historical, and scientific texts. Starting in 1995, this ministry sponsored a general trade fair in Baghdad. It grew larger every year until, by 2001, even Kuwaiti companies joined. The 2000 fair attracted 1,500 exhibitors from forty-five countries, with many of the participants arriving by plane for the first time.

Like the large trade exhibitions, the book fair was held in Baghdad. By UN embargo rules, such trade was still forbidden. But more and more nations flaunted the ban. Even Egyptian suppliers were daring to do business in Iraq by then.

The 2001 book fair was the first such exhibition Iraqis had seen in twelve years. Teachers and students, retired military, artists, and doctors flocked to the tables. All the medical books and most of the scientific textbooks were in English, many published by American firms. Prices were high, but somehow Iraqis produced the cash.[5] By the end of the week, almost all the stock was sold, and the departing vendors, their pockets bulging with Iraqi dinars, assured us they would be back next year.

> Iraq is rich. Iraqis are big spenders, always have been. They have only a third the population of Egypt, yet they consume almost as much as Egypt's 60 million people. Iraq is the biggest market in this area. We will ship in much more stock for the next book fair. (Egyptian bookseller, Baghdad book fair, 2001)

In late 2000, Iraq-Jordan commerce took a temporary downturn. Jordanians had benefited from a trade protocol arranged by their American friends, and under this Memorandum of Understanding, many Amman-based companies profited. Then Iraq announced that Jordanian merchants could no longer act as middlemen between Iraqi buyers and foreign contractors. Licenses would henceforth be assigned only to Iraqis.

> Iraq is finished. They are importing low-quality goods from Egypt, China, and other Asian countries. The Iraqis have lost their values and have been corrupted by kickbacks. Any party member who can buy an import license jumps into the business; no experience, no training, just connections. It is impossible to work with them. There is no business ethic and no law in the country now. (Jordanian industrial supplier, Amman, 2001)

Two years later, following the invasion of Iraq, Amman was to enjoy a boom of unprecedented proportions.[6] During the preceding decade, Jordanians noted disproportionate construction across Amman: grand hotels, expanding medical centers, little-used new highways linking Israel, Jordan, and Iraq. "Who are these being built for?" Jordanians wondered. "What do these investors know about Jordan's future that we do not?" The explanation came with the U.S. invasion of Iraq. It seems that years earlier, Jordan was identified and developed in anticipation of the invasion and occupation of its neighbor. All signs point to a long-term economic strategy for Jordan as the main supplier for "occupied" Iraq, further proof that the U.S. invasion had little to do with al-Qaeda or Iraq's possible possession of threatening weapons. After 2003, hotels that had sat empty for a decade were overflowing; journalists, soldiers, NGO agents, security companies, government officials, and merchants were pouring in from all directions—Israel, Turkey, Russia, Saudi Arabia, Poland, Philippines, and Japan, but especially from the United States. Jordan would be fine.

Abu Ghraib, a Story

An Iraqi fellow named Fawzi wanted to declare how brave he was in fighting the American invaders. He did not really join the resistance, however. Instead, he hid in his own house for three months. When he emerged to greet his friends in the village, all were happy to see him. They all knew that, although he was a feisty fellow, Fawzi had no courage at all, certainly not what he claimed. They asked him: "Fawzi, what's the story? Where have you been all these months?"

He replied, "Don't you know? I was arrested by the Amrikyan. They put me in Abu Ghraib prison. You know the place. I survived three months of torture."

Everyone doubted Fawzi's claim. "How can we believe you? Give us proof of what happened to you."

"I don't need proof. I swear before God, I was in that hellhole."

Fawzi was known to be a slacker. So the villagers insisted he give them evidence. Under pressure now, Fawzi had to think quickly. "I have internationally recognized proof," he retorted.

"What is it?" demanded the crowd.

"All of you have seen the famous Abu Ghraib photo of the pile of naked prisoners. How come you didn't see me? Did you notice the fourth ass on the right? That's mine!

10

Who Gets What

Embargoed Iraq was a great source of profit. But benefits to local traders could not match what United Nations agencies reaped during those years. For a non-profit agency, its gains were considerable. They were also legal. Aside from any questionable dealings privately engaged in by UN employees, the agency funneled billions of dollars to its staff, contractors, subagencies, and dubious or nefarious claimants, all through its offices, in accordance with sanctions laws, all overseen and carefully monitored by the self-appointed overseer, Washington. No UN action on Iraq went forward without America's involvement and approval. So later U.S. claims of the agency's corruption in its Iraq program are either spurious or were purposely overlooked in order to be used against the UN should it step out of line.[1]

Journalists and other public regulators showed little interest in UN accounting over Iraq during the blockade years. In contrast, Iraqis kept themselves informed as to who got what. But they were helpless. UN administrators likely considered themselves immune to judgment by their weak and starving wards who utilized their waning energy to seek out a few doses of medicine, a visa to another land, or, best of all, employment as a local UN gardener or driver. In any case, any UN indulgence or graft would be eclipsed by the excesses of Saddam Hussein. His was the moral standard, so any overseer could always point to Saddam's indulgences as the bottomless hole swallowing up Iraqi revenues. He was the sole culprit, stealing millions from his hapless, terrorized subjects. The press loved copy on the president.[2]

After we appreciate how Iraq's embargoed income was allocated, exposés about Halliburton and Bechtel and other U.S. companies profiteering in Iraq after the 2003 invasion make more sense. Likewise, we can appreciate Iraqis' bitterness and their resistance. The new profiteers followed the precedent of an international institution with the highest credentials.

The Story of a Tractor

Under the close watch of a highly paid UN monitor and overseen by committees at UN headquarters, a new John Deere tractor is purchased for $47,000. It is then sold for $5,000, then resold to a car dealer. It is displayed on his lot, listed at $7,000. It disappears, then resurfaces in a neighboring country, operated by a wealthy vegetable farmer who has no bill of sale but who paid below market value for it. It looks like everyone wins, except the original buyer. Who is that fool?

Iraq's pecking order is well known: first, Saddam Hussein and his family, then high-ranking Baath party officers and ranking military, followed by importers and other traders who somehow managed to secure prized licenses.[3] If we exclude for the moment foreign NGO employees and UN weapons inspectors—who, although generously compensated, are not part of the Iraqi social system—next in rank come proprietors of enterprises where Iraq's elite eat and shop. Ranking technocrats in important ministries are next, followed by a coterie of celebrities, including physicians who keep the presidential circle happy and healthy. A nascent rich class includes the embargo-spawned gentry: families with capital and ambitions who responded to the food emergency by leasing huge parcels of land and hired others to work it. They saw the benefits of farming after the government launched the protocol to stimulate grain production. Some traditional farmers, rural families who benefited from excessively high wheat prices when the country was on the verge of famine, join that rank. Gazwan Mukhtar, an engineer and close observer of Iraq's capricious economy, explained the process. "They moved into our cities where they built grand houses. Soon they found new investments: transport, electronic goods, construction. They didn't need foreign exchange. With Iraqi dinars from wheat sales, new fortunes arose." Mukhtar included embargo-bred petty vendors in an up-and-coming class. "These are men who, assisted by their children, push carts through the streets from morning to night. They hawk cigarettes, candies, hot tea, sometimes vegetables. They appear to live in penury, but they are comfortable, better off than civil servants."

Police and rank-and-file intelligence agents and some ministry personnel come near the bottom. The majority of Iraqis, including salaried ministry employees, share the crumbs that manage to reach them from UN imported stock.

"Who gets what" is no secret in embargoed Iraq. Handouts from the top are sometimes publicly announced, such as the leaders' gifts of millions of dollars for impulsive and often flashy "presidential projects." The embargo made him a "public benefactor." Saddam Hussein built schools for the retarded, financed sports festivals for the youth, and funded archaeological research. Those funds came from his private account. In 2001, Iraqis were informed that their president had donated millions of dollars for a new cancer hospital. Eighteen months later, the medical team assigned to administer the project still had not set up a board, and no contractors had been called. But the beneficence of Saddam Hussein had been recorded.

That same magnanimity financed construction of a mosque in Baghdad. It was to be the world's largest. This and similar projects were accepted presidential indulgences, like his gifts to individuals who somehow win his favor. One heard stories of his handouts of oil contracts (a letter authorizing sale of 100,000 or more barrels of oil) to random beneficiaries. "Here is the license. Find your own buyer, pay me 15 percent, and the rest is yours." Buyers, it seems, were not hard to locate. They paid those ad hoc agents for a multimillion dollar oil shipment as if it were just a boatload of fish.[4]

How much did those private sales generate for the president? Who were the buyers? How was the money transferred? It is difficult to say. The accumulated revenue could have amounted to several billion dollars.

Shocking? Scandalous? But why is this arrangement more outrageous than the many billions of dollars of Iraq's money, also oil revenue, forcibly deposited in a French bank in New York, with more than 30 percent skimmed off the top beforehand by the United Nations? Only a minor portion of the remaining revenue was allotted for actual purchase of emergency food and medicine. Moreover, those supplies were often contracted at above-market value, sometimes of low quality, with no legal protection to the buyer (Iraq), for a near starving population—the Iraqis who actually own the oil!

Where the Money Comes From

Iraqi money held in the New York branch of Paribas Bank, a private French firm, accumulated from what was internationally regarded as Iraq's legitimate oil revenue. It was income from oil that Iraq was compelled to sell according to terms laid down by Washington and approved and managed by the United Nations under the official cover of SCR 986. By the end of phase 12 (six years of the food-for-oil program), UN-supervised oil sales had generated some $20 billion in revenue. (In his 2004 exposé of U.S. profiteering, Pratap Chatterjee cites $46 billion in accumulated Iraqi oil revenues between 1996 and November 2003, when SCR 986 finally ended.)

According to the Memorandum of Understanding defined by SCR 986 and signed May 1996 by Iraq and the United Nations, income generated by this "legitimate" sale could not be paid directly to Iraq. It had to be deposited in the Paribas Bank escrow account to await UN approval of contracts for necessary goods—contracts that must pass scrutiny by the notorious UN 661 Committee. The UN exerted its sovereignty in the agreement by speedily paying its administrative staff salaries and expenses from that fund. Then it engaged in lengthy committee reviews to consider Iraqi's needs before tendering contracts, some of which had been sitting for years awaiting decision. There was a general understanding that the 661 Committee passed on or rejected submissions on the dictates of its American members, who in turn were directed by Washington.

Numerous contracts were rejected or held up by this committee, often at the expense of suffering Iraqis. Out of the $20 billion in revenue from oil sales between 1997 and 2002, the committee put on hold requests worth more than $7.1 billion.[5] Unallocated funds remained in the French bank. Contracts "on hold" included materials essential for Iraq to repair its electrical system and its crumbling communications network, to restore its water purification system and mend oil production plants, to purchase supplies for schools and hospitals, and to furnish medical essentials. Food is also purchased from this fund. While 661 approval was pending, the money lay unused, and it was unclear to whom the accruing interest belonged—the United Nations, the bank, or another entity. Anyone but Iraq. In 2001, the deputy director of the Central Bank of Iraq, Abdul Munim, could not confirm to me whether the accumulating interest on this account accrued to Iraq or not. It seems dispensation of that interest was overlooked in the contract signed between the UN and Iraq in 1996! (Investigations in 2006 were still trying to trace the whereabouts of what remained in that account as well as frozen Iraqi assets since 1990.)

This Is for Me, and That Is for You

Before looking at just how the UN supervised purchases destined for Iraq and who gets what, let's review how Iraq's oil-embargoed revenue was assigned. In the first six phases (between 1997 and 1999) of the UN plan, accumulated revenues in the special UN account was $19.8 billion. Of this gigantic sum, the 661 Committee released $5.9 billion to contractors for approved supplies in all sectors. This amounted to an average of $327.70 per person during those three years: just over $100 a year, a monthly allocation of just $8.23 per Iraqi. Moreover, $8.23 was not a family's food allowance. Rather, this amount included allocations for medical supplies as well as approved imported materials for all sectors of the society.[6]

Meanwhile, the UN set aside $6.8 billion of the $19.8 billion for itself—the administration of its Iraq programs—and for payments to Kuwaitis and other foreign nationals making compensation claims for alleged hardships suffered as a result of the 1991 invasion and war. The United Nations Compensation Commission controlled the largest share of Iraq's oil revenues.

Starting with the imposition of the blockade on August 6, 1990, Iraq became a major income for the world body. First confiscated funds, then Iraq oil revenues, supported the UN's New York–based staff (with more than two hundred employees, including the 661 Committee) and their expenses, UNSCOM weapons inspectors and their expenses (including the UNMOVIC team headed by Hans Blix, who from 1999 to late 2002 had yet to set foot inside Iraq), and all Iraq-based staff and their expenses. How much these UN bodies had gobbled up by 2003 is nearly impossible to tabulate, since the agency is understandably circumspect about its windfall from Iraq. We know, however, that annual salaries could amount to about $120,000 per person. (One report cites monthly salaries for some UN personnel at $15,000 to $20,000 per month!) Add to this tax-free salary, entitlements to pension, health, dental, and travel expenses, home leave, accommodations, and an array of backup services. Staff posted in Iraq required briefings, training programs, translators, high-powered vehicles, helicopters, mess halls, offices, and advanced security and communications equipment as well as drivers and mechanics, gardeners and cleaners, guides and office staff. This was part of the UN operating expense and therefore part of Iraq's dues. In addition to their salaries, foreign staff received a daily living allowance of $100[7] (in 2000, per diem was reduced from $300 to $100). A conservative estimate of Iraq's cost of maintaining 3,000 UN employees over three years at an average $100,000/year/person would amount to almost a billion dollars in annual salaries alone. Actual costs could have been double if one included obligatory employee benefits and support services, travel, insurance, etc.[8]

Meanwhile, Iraqi fathers and mothers lined up for their monthly ration: 9 kg. wheat, 2 kg. sugar, 3 kg. rice, salt, tea, and an allocation of cooking oil. Families with children under the age of five had to apply for additional milk rations. Proof of residence was required of every household member.[9]

Every Iraqi understood how their individual ration, which was supposed to guarantee them a daily UN recommended caloric intake of 2,470, compares with provisions for the foreigners brought to supervise the allocation of these meager allowances. Each Iraqi knew that most of their oil income was consumed by the UN and by the thousands of people making often fraudulent compensation claims through UN agencies.

Every Iraqi knew that their oil revenues supported the indulgences, whims, and extravagant expenses of Richard Butler, director of the hated United Nations Special Commission (weapons inspection committee) and his large team. With difficulty, Iraqis forced to work with UNSCOM continued to cooperate. Their official complaints were never made public. Privately, however, after the

December 1998 exit of the inspection team, rumors circulated inside Iraq about UNSCOM members' abusive and destructive behavior.

Between 1995 and December 1998, in the course of seven rounds of weapons inspections, 3,200 UN inspectors arrived in Iraq. The Iraqi Ministry of Foreign Affairs reported that 11,000 inspectors were received in Iraq between 1991 and 1997. Between December 1998 and November 2002, after UNSCOM had withdrawn voluntarily but was not permitted to return, salaries continued for the weapons team, now newly assembled and called UNMOVIC. Financing of both agencies came from the food-for-oil account.

This rape of Iraq was conducted in full view of Iraqis. Weapons inspectors were one team. In addition, the UN sent in hundreds of highly paid "food monitors." They were there ostensibly to ensure that Iraqis' allocations are not stolen or, worse, diverted to their own leadership or to their defense forces where their sons were serving. All these UN employees were salaried and housed, given health care, entertainment, phone calls home, etc., siphoned from the same bottomless Iraqi pot of oil.

Iraqis suspect that the thousands of military sorties by U.S. and British planes over their territory (the notorious "no-fly" zones), and the bombings they execute on these missions, are also billed to the UN's Iraqi account. But they could not confirm this. The U.S. administration claimed these patrols were necessary to protect Iraqis—the Kurd and Shia inhabitants of northern and southern Iraq—because these people were under threat by Saddam.[10]

The UN-controlled Iraq oil account was tapped for compensatory damages against Iraq. These were administered by the UN Compensation Commission based in Geneva. The commission reviewed and passed on requests from companies and from tens of thousands of foreign workers (Egyptian, Vietnamese, Filipino, Israeli, etc.) who sought compensation from Iraq. Their often fraudulent claims were for hardships suffered: for example, unemployment as a result of Iraq's invasion of Kuwait or its missile attack on Israel. The commission was reportedly still operating into 2006, still drawing on Iraqi funds to pay claimants.

Iraqis were justifiably outraged by this piracy. The dealings of their president may not have troubled them as much as the UN's legitimized embezzlement scheme: 661 was better known as "oil-for-food" as if it were a humanitarian program.

The picture of abuse got worse. Approved contractors—companies who supplied basic staples such as rice, wheat, sugar, and oil, as well as those who exported medicines and equipment into Iraq—were not expected to negotiate lower prices. They were businessmen, and they were taking nothing from starving and sick Iraqis. The UN paid their invoices and did not worry about overpricing.

Under the terms of the Memorandum of Understanding (MOU), Iraq had no legal right to compensation for any goods damaged in shipment, nor for expired medicines, nor any other problem related to a faulty product in these contracts.

Some merchants admitted to me that their prices might have been above actual market value. "Iraq is rich!" is the uncensored refrain heard from foreign suppliers of cooking oil, sugar, rice, and other staples. Iraq, they say, is not looking for bargains. They insist that Iraq accepted paying high prices in order to gain some political leverage with a supplier's government. If Iraq favored contracts from dealers in Jordan, China, France, or Vietnam, it was understood those countries might in turn take a more favorable political line toward Iraq. This may have been true. The policy was not unlike Washington's "favored nation" trade policies. Iraq's choices were limited, and a favorable outcome for it was far from assured.

Given the legalized profiteering we describe, a 250 dinar handout to a soldier posted on a lonely road, or the 3,000 dinars a policeman might accumulate on his shift, or a 5,000 dinar inducement for a ministry employee to sign a document were of little moral significance to anybody in Iraq. Iraqis grew to believe any crumb plucked from the monster known as the UN food-for-oil program was justified.

Backstage at the Circus: 1, 2, 3

Before 1990, Iraqis were widely known for their exemplary work habits. Their civil service was almost unmatched for its efficiency and ethical standard. Theirs was a culture where bribery, fraud, and embezzlement were unheard of. Corruption was almost absent across Iraq. Twelve years into sanctions, Iraq had evolved into a corruption circus.

When it was first proposed, Iraq was reluctant to accept the UN food-for-oil scheme. At the time, one Iraqi minister observed, "It was designed to turn Iraq into one huge refugee camp." One wonders if he envisaged the real monster it would breed. Iraq had indeed become a kind of refugee colony. But the funds set aside for administration were so plentiful and so unprotected that in the first years of its life, this creature had effectively taken over Iraqi society. It had unraveled the bureaucracy, destroying all sense of professionalism and self-respect, corrupting young and old, leaving waste and crime in its wake and providing fortunes for foreigners, stashes of cash for its president while hardly affecting the level of nutrition or health care for the average Iraqi. An Iraqi man, woman, and child's share remained at $8.23 a month!

Naked injustice and fraud arrived in 1997 with the purchase of the very first $3.5 billion of Iraqi oil offered on the world market after the Gulf War. Expedited without delay, according to Iraq's trade minister, the "first shipment of legally purchased Iraqi oil was delivered to an American company in Texas."

Step 1: Since Washington expressly forbade American companies to engage in commerce with Iraq, any U.S. oil purchase from Iraq was facilitated through a third party. Payment was deposited directly to the UN-assigned French bank for transfer. It was paid to a supplier whose contract had first to be examined and approved by the 661 Committee.

Step 2: Oil was delivered to the United States while twenty million Iraqis on the brink of a famine had to wait many months more for the arrival of their first food shipment in six years! As Iraqi economist Nasra al-Saadoon raged, "Iraqi oil had arrived on the world market and affected world prices months before a single tablet of medicine was even seen in Iraq." It was an ominous beginning.

Once a purchase is authorized by the United Nations and shipment is under way to Iraq, goods pass through a process that seems designed to be exploited. The authority licensed to make purchases against oil sales was the Iraqi government. For example, the Ministry of Agriculture negotiated with a contractor, say, a Vietnamese rice exporter. When approved by the 661 Committee, the supplier received payment from the UN's designated French bank account. Then it shipped the rice to the Iraqi Ministry of Agriculture warehouse.

Step 3: The Iraqi government could not be trusted, said the UN. It insisted that shipment and distribution of food and other supplies to Iraqis be overseen by UN staff—hundreds of officials paid from the UN Iraq account. These $100,000.00+ salaried foreigners were posted at Iraq's borders and among twenty-two holding/distribution centers around the country. They oversaw and inspected the shipments. With their perks and salaries, those men and women were doubtless beyond suspicion in what happened to the rice they inspected. They were there to protect starving Iraqis from Saddam.

Iraq may have been paid $2,000 a ton (about $1 a pound) for Vietnamese rice. It was far too costly for the average Iraqi. The government therefore subsidized food imports in order to keep it affordable to the citizen, selling what it had imported to wholesale distributors (who were not permitted to import directly) for $.20 a pound.

Step 4: That distributor extracted his margin and sold at $.25 a pound. He did not necessarily sell it directly to the householder, however, but to another wholesaler who marked it up to $.30. And so on until it reached the consumer at perhaps $.40 a pound. At each stage, the distributor took a cut. Before the embargo, these agents may have been salaried ministry officials or workers whose factory closed due to sanctions. One can understand why a person would resign a civil service post to become a food supplier under the siege.

Hoarding and reselling of food by middlemen became widespread. It was common for hunger to drive a parent to buy from racketeers. The Iraqi administration seemed unable or unwilling to check the exploitation, although the Iraqi government meted out excessively harsh punishment to a few profiteers after sporadic clampdowns.

The UN became so despised inside Iraq that, by 1999, it feared attacks from the public on their more than two hundred foreign staff members. All UN offices and garages were fortified with ten-foot-high fences and extra security guards, and foreign employees carried two-way radios outside the office. Expatriate staff were not allowed to travel without a guard, and all were transferred into secure lodgings away from the general population, again for safety reasons. Even public restaurants were off limits to them.

In 1998, by the end of the second phase of the plan, as food and medicine became more available and the calamity evolved into a subdued catastrophe, Iraq began to import nonfood needs, including heavy machinery. Now came opportunities for even bigger fortunes.

From Circus to Spectacle

Iraq needed every kind of machinery, from ambulances to water pumps, tractors, generators and cables, and hospital diagnostic and surgical machinery. Some of these items cost tens of thousands of dollars each. A state-of-the-art cardiac machine may have a price tag of a quarter of a million dollars. Given the levels of deterioration and the breakdowns in Iraq after years of sanctions, contracts had to be made for fifty, one hundred, or more machines. New tractors were needed. Wheat production had become a high priority, and tractors bought during the 1980s had long ceased to function. By the fourth phase of the food-for-oil program, Iraq finally secured permission from the UN to import tractors. These were supplied by a U.S. firm via Russia (since Americans were forbidden to engage in commerce with the embargoed nation). For the American supplier, a 2 percent commission to the "paper contractor," the Russian agent, was a minor item in his budget. His income for two hundred tractors at $47,000 each totaled $9.4 million.

Iraq's Ministry of Agriculture bought these tractors. But how would these precious machines be distributed? Many thousands of farmers needed a new tractor. But few could afford the market cost. So like the rice, the government again subsidized the purchase, this time dropping the price from $47,000 to $5,000. It was still beyond the reach of most Iraqi farmers.

The government had to distribute the tractors. Often, those able to afford a tractor didn't really need one; he bought it anyway at the government subsidized price of $5,000. The $5,000 buyer might be offered $6,000 for the machine. Like the grain merchant, he could resell at a small markup. And so it went.

One ministry official happened to spot a new tractor for sale at a used car dealership in Baghdad. He noted it was the same model his office had bought and distributed four months earlier. Suspecting the vehicle was illegally acquired, he reported it to the local police. By the time authorities investigated, the tractor had disappeared from the compound.

One can suppose that a similar fate befell costly generators, medical equipment, and other machinery. Fortunes made in this arena matched or exceeded the illegal (as defined by the UN) imports of computers, washing machines, stereos, and other consumer goods transported to Iraq by boat from Dubai, the Arab Emirates, Qatar, and other Gulf nation suppliers.

With each level of corruption established, another seemed to sprout from it. Another source of profit derived from deals made between suppliers and ministry officials who negotiated contracts, in other words, kickbacks. The first case I learned of was a shipment to Basrah port of two hundred minivans. They were to be used as city buses. The market value of each was $15,000. Supplied by an Asian firm on contract with the Ministry of Transport, the shipment was legal, that is to say, approved by the 661 Committee and inspected by UN monitors on entry at Basrah port. The ministry sent two hundred drivers to Basrah to bring the new machines to Baghdad. The vehicles were offloaded and put on the road for the 180-mile journey. According to my investigations, only thirty-seven of the two hundred reached Baghdad without breaking down en route.

The order of Asian minivans was the first publicized case of a supplier charging market prices but sending defective goods. There was no investigation, and there were no replacements. Uday, the president's much-hated son, announced that the dumping of inferior goods on Iraq's market would be severely punished. Despite this, these practices continued.

Every sort of inferior product, from surgical scalpels to cooking oil, medicines and X-ray machines to buses, became commonplace in Iraq. Neither the UN through whom the orders pass, nor Washington, nor Iraqi officials were willing or able to halt the practices. Local newspaper reports of infractions led nowhere. Before long, Iraqi government employees wholeheartedly joined with the UN in the thievery. Meanwhile, foreign critics of the Baath regime kept their focus on the excesses of a few presidential palaces.[11]

News item: An Iraqi is charged with killing two UN staff and wounding seven others in the capital earlier this year. . . . Fu'ad Hussein Haider, 38, is accused of killing two United Nations Food and Agricultural Organization employees. On June 18, 2000, Haider burst into the UN office, opening fire. . . . At the time Haider said he was planning only to take the UN officials hostage to protest UN sanctions imposed on Iraq. His demands, he said, were aimed at alleviating hardships caused by the embargo. (Reuters, December 19, 2000)

It was only the August 2003 suicide attack on the UN compound in Baghdad that seemed to raise international awareness that the UN could be a source of abuse by outside powers and the focal point of Iraqi resentment. The world was shaken by what it saw as an outrageous assault against a venerable institution—unless one understood how "who got what" in Iraq. Haidar's action and the bombing of the UN Baghdad office were not acts of madmen.

Denis Halliday, who resigned in protest to the UN's sanctions policy on Iraq in 1998, dared to admit the attack could have been a result of accumulated outrage over UN complicity with Washington and London: "When you think it through, why not? We, the UN, have been tainted and corrupted by our presence in Iraq and the work that we have done in Iraq at the beck and call of the Americans and the British. For twelve years, the UN tortured Iraq. There is hardly an Iraqi family, for example, that has not lost parents or children or extended family unnecessarily due to the consequences of UN sanctions. So the UN is a hated entity. The Security Council has been corrupted. It has become an instrument of American foreign policy. It is very simple, really. So why are we surprised?"[12]

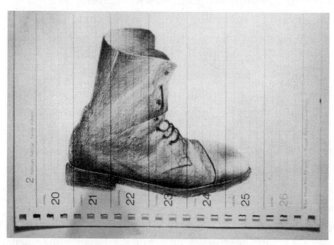

Soldier's Boot, pencil, by Hazem al-Mawally, 1991.

▌▌

Trade or Aid?

When I announced to a humanitarian worker upon my arrival in Baghdad in November 2000 that I had flown in from Athens on an Olympic Airways jet with a European delegation, I expected he would be thrilled. Ours was the latest of several airlines that had challenged the American blockade. "It's all for business," he grumbled. He was not pleased.

"What do you mean?" I retorted. Flying here was exceedingly risky. Many attempts had failed. "These flights help break the air embargo. We overcame huge obstacles in order to confront the U.S. ban. The sanctions are crumbling!"[1]

This man, despite his mission as a humanitarian aid provider, did not share our sense of victory. "They are here for their own benefit," he muttered. He also resented the idea that foreigners were arriving in Baghdad by air. Unjustified luxury! He had spent several years in Iraq as director of a religious charity. It was not easy. Like everyone else, he had to endure the grueling overland journey to and from Jordan. Communications were inadequate. So much was needed, and his resources were limited. He was probably lonely, not only for his family but because there was no community of NGO workers in Iraq. In his view, our delegation had traveled in comfort, and worse, some visitors might be here in search of profit.

The 102 passengers on Olympic Airways Flight 3598 opposed what they concluded was a misguided U.S. policy and a violation of international norms. They were artists, journalists, parliamentarians, doctors, and other activists. Among us were a handful of business people. But the flight was far from a profit-making venture. Most delegates were on their first visit to Iraq, people who for ten years had watched the progress of the blockade with grief and anger. Recognizing the injustice of the blockade and the malicious U.S. role in the embargo, they had decided to travel to Iraq to demonstrate solidarity with its people. They sought ways to help stimulate the Iraqi economy and share its rich culture. Some may have sought contracts to develop projects here, something the Iraqis were eager to facilitate.

A few weeks before our flight, a successful international trade fair in Iraq had attracted hundreds of exhibitors, all engaging in what the UN judged to be illegal commerce. That trade fair and the arrival of other delegations by plane exposed a weakening of the United States' embargo policy. Things appeared to be changing, for the better, for Iraq.

Why? Because every visit and every exchange was in defiance of the unreasonable blockade on Iraq. Political activists had a single agenda: to oppose what they believed was an unjust and cruel U.S. policy. Businesspeople came with a dual purpose. They sought contracts, although without guarantees. But all embarked on this trip knowing that their arrival in Iraq was in itself a political statement of some significance. People who had feared visiting Iraq in the past were now joining with ideologically motivated activists because any commerce with Iraq was a circumvention of the embargo. If investors were prepared to defy the American blockade, it marked a new stage in the campaign against sanctions.

Why didn't veteran humanitarian workers like this man see these trade delegates in a more favorable light? Trade might be better than aid. This is what Iraqis had been requesting since 1991. "Lift the embargo so we can trade, and we will look after our own people," said Iraqi administrators.[2] I never heard them or regular citizens plead for aid.

In some cases, humanitarian relief is essential. But aid cannot sustain a population of twenty million. Moreover, for ten years, appeals by humanitarian groups with firsthand experience in Iraq had had no impact. There was no way they could address Iraq's needs. The silence these NGOs encountered was not what the aid business calls "donor fatigue." It was political. Interested NGOs had even been harassed or threatened by U.S. authorities. "Stay out of Iraq," they were told, "or we will shut down your projects elsewhere."[3] On its side, Baghdad did not see foreign aid as a solution. Iraq was not a refugee camp of a hundred thousand people. No NGO program could address an entire nation on the verge of collapse.

So why was any NGO in Iraq? "To give testimony to the hardships. To inform the world about the massive suffering and the rampant diseases created by the embargo." This was the argument given to Iraqi authorities, based on the presumption that Americans and Europeans, paragons of democracy and champions of universal human rights, would come to the aid of Iraqi people. A better-informed citizenry would demand policy changes, the argument went.

So the activists wrote. They lectured. They made films. They brought small delegations of their countrymen to Iraq and showed them the hospitals, the polluted streets, the beggars, and the Amariya air raid shelter where hundreds perished when allied planes bombed it.[4] They quoted UNICEF, FAO, and WHO statistics about underweight births, congenital deformities, infant mortality, and rising cancer rates.

Perhaps a few more sympathetic (or curious) delegates decided to visit Iraq as a result. Perhaps a few more articles about suffering children were published.

Iraq's humanitarian crisis was unparalleled. Iraq was not a poor country. If it were, how could it pay for all those UN research teams and food monitors? How could it finance thousands of weapons inspectors conducting tens of thousands of searches inside Iraq, including in its schools and libraries? How could it pay hundreds of sanctions committee employees in New York overseeing the food-for-oil program? How could Iraq compensate the tens of thousands of foreigners (individuals and companies) for their purported losses in the Gulf War? Those UN committees and the food and weapons inspection programs in Iraq were not "feel good" projects. They were highly lucrative exercises.

Were those well-paid staff acting as humanitarians as they compiled research reports and argued over what was to be banned from Iraq, which company was to be contracted, and who was to be compensated?

UN operations related to Iraq is a multibillion dollar business. It was an operation of unprecedented proportions funded by Iraqi oil revenues, siphoned off the Iraqi people, and channeled through a monstrous bureaucracy that offered rich rewards to all the foreigners associated with it. One critic even suggested that Iraqi program profits were used to sustain the UN headquarters in New York.

Doubtless some UN staff members work tirelessly and with the genuine aim of relieving suffering. But humanitarian aid is an industry today. And for many of its officers, it is very profitable employment (see chapter 9).

Humanitarian gestures we saw in Iraq during those years were largely feel good efforts. It makes us feel good if we speak for the underprivileged. It makes us feel good when we give a woman a can of milk and a child a teddy bear. It makes us feel good when we take on the role of caregiver to the world's poor.[5]

Aid is also a process that (inadvertently or by design) removes responsibility for a nation's welfare from its own leaders and assigns it to outsiders, mostly western administrators. This development was probably behind the initial UN food-for-oil scheme. That is: "You cannot trust Saddam to feed you, but you can trust us." The embargo hardships may have been part of a strategy, working hand in hand with support for an internal coup, to weaken the population's reliance on Baghdad.

Any aid agency that understood Iraq had to admit that by 2000, unofficial commerce was a major factor in preventing the nation's total disintegration. Yes, a few merchants, mainly Iraqis and Jordanians, made huge profits, and the Baathi surely received a handsome cut. But the administration must be credited with economic reforms that stimulated growth. It opened its huge stockpile of wood and metal piping, steel and concrete; it opened the door for cheap imports of paint, glass, wiring, tiles, and iron frames. The new rich farmers indulged themselves with luxuries and then began to invest their wheat profits in the construction of new buildings and businesses (restaurants, currency exchange, transport services); they also donated funds for hospital reconstruction.

That same season when flights began to arrive, it seemed a shipload of fresh paint also reached Iraq. Up until then, the urban landscapes were more drab every year. That autumn, the city was brighter than I had ever seen it. It drew merchants from Turkey, Syria, Lebanon, and Jordan. They brought with them ice cream machines, household goods, clothing, fine shoes, car and truck parts, and electronic goods. Iraqis seemed to be heading out of that awful UN embargo pit.

12

A Little Loot

Business was not all "gaamar and honey."[1] It was political, and it was effective. Private trade bolstered the economy when it was introduced in Iraq midway through the embargo. (Any U.S. administration committed to worldwide privatization would normally herald this shift.) At the same time, free enterprise undermined Iraq's moral social fabric. It could do nothing to bring back industry, and it produced few jobs. It probably made Saddam Hussein and his circle richer and more insatiable. Ironically, he was more powerful, too.

Iraq's expanding trade may have been a punch in the hated face of Washington. At home it generated inequalities and bitterness. Iraqis found it hard to sustain their deep pride in their nation. Baathi socialist ideals were in freefall. Family values were hard to maintain, and tribal solidarity could be bought. Free trade may have saved Iraq's sovereignty for the present. It may have foiled the Americans for the present. But it brought with it a terrible disease that infected almost everyone: corruption.

Want to Buy a Buick?

Early in 1991, I was offered a great deal in Beirut: a new American car for only $4,500. I was approached with this proposition during the weeks when American bombers were pounding fertilizer factories and milk plants, electrical installations, ministry buildings, food stores, and water plants across Iraq.

Bargains like this glistening new Buick were "Kuwait models." Like thousands more cars, this "hot" Buick was booty taken during Iraq's short-lived and reckless occupation of its neighbor. A 1991 Sabina for under $5,000 may not be a bargain today. But this was 1991, and the top of the Chrysler line was listed at almost five times as much in the States. In Lebanon, the price would certainly be higher *if* one could find a legitimate dealer. (Auto showrooms in the war-torn country didn't exist.)

Between August and December 1990, while Iraqi forces occupied the country, perhaps thousands of new or nearly new vehicles were driven across the Kuwait-Iraq frontier heading further north. Their destination? Beirut, where they could easily be sold. Lebanon's civil war was nearing its end, but the country was still ungovernable. Anything could be found in Lebanon—no papers were needed, no government inspections, no taxes. Registration numbers on cars were erased; for a small fee, new plates were arranged. People came from across the Mediterranean to Beirut for loot. Here was an ideal place to market the "Kuwait models."

"Every Kuwaiti family has three or four cars," recalled one looter. "When they fled, they had time to load just one. We found the keys in the others they left behind. They were free!"

Convoys of glistening new cars—Chevrolets, Buicks, Mustangs, Nissans, and Toyotas—rolled out of villa driveways and dealer showrooms, from government warehouses, from wherever they were parked when their owners abandoned them. "I returned to Kuwait six times in five weeks, each time bringing back another beautiful Buick. Every trip, I made $750 to $1,000," boasted one Palestinian driver. He seemed pleased to recount the piracy. "We organized ourselves into convoys of six. Each of us took one car. In Beirut, we dropped off our loot, then drove back together in an old car to collect the next consignment."

Some of the booty was delivered to Baghdad to be distributed as favors by the president and his generals. Iraqis favored the American models.

Kuwait offered up plenty of booty in the five and a half months it was in foreign hands. Some Iraqis were astonished when they learned how their troops had indulged in piracy. The loot their sons stole did not trouble them as much as the breakdown of military discipline. That was new to them.

Iraqi veterans of the Kuwait occupation later reported: "There was so much—so many cars, all just sitting there. Each house had several cars, freezers, all kinds of appliances, electronics, and other beautiful things. We found computers and hi-fis in every room. Auto showrooms sparkled with new models and shelves of supermarkets brimmed with rows of delicacies we had never seen before," they confessed. "We had thought that our life in Iraq was comfortable," one Iraqi told me. "Seeing the Kuwaiti luxuries, we later asked ourselves: 'If we were not always at war, we could enjoy these comforts too.'"

The Baath government set the standard for lawlessness. It speedily ordered the removal to Baghdad of Kuwait's museum treasures, libraries, university equipment, art collections, and probably official documents. Why then should soldiers not fill their vehicles with smoked meats, chocolate, French cheeses and wines, silver trays, carpets, and cameras? Hundreds of trucks were dispatched, bound for Baghdad.

Kuwait remained bitterly aggrieved by the 1990 invasion and extracted heavy retribution. There may be some truth to the reports that thirteen years later, Kuwait was involved in the 2003 looting of Baghdad following the American invasion. Knowledgeable Iraqis who observed the pillage of Iraq's museums and libraries claim that the culprits were foreigners, mainly Arabs, flown into Iraq from Kuwait for that treachery. Those men, they say, were criminals collected from their Kuwaiti jails to carry out that plunder in exchange for their release.

I arrived in Iraq in April 1991, within three weeks of the cease-fire.[2] A story had circulated about Iraqis tearing Kuwaiti infants from incubators in a maternity hospital. A British investigative medical team, Physicians for Human Rights, had announced in March 1991 that this story was a fabrication. Testimony from doctors at that hospital proved that the American charges were phony. Then a journalist discovered that the rumors had originated with the daughter of a Kuwaiti official who worked with a Washington-based public relations firm to create such scenarios. Together the White House and Kuwaiti authorities had come up with the ruse, and before it could be disproved, the lie had served its purpose. Public opinion swiftly turned against Iraq when the story was relayed worldwide. Even Amnesty International had hastily added its endorsement. Congress and shocked Americans offered Washington unqualified support for a military campaign "to liberate Kuwait." Thirty-two nations joined the attack. The assault was merciless. Not even reports about bunkered Iraqi soldiers buried alive by sand-plowing machines sweeping across their meager fortifications moved anyone to call for investigations of war crimes. Their "highway of death" in retreat was heartlessly termed as "a turkey shoot" by allied forces. Who cared whether the fleeing trucks carried loot or Iraqi sons and brothers? Any Iraqi loot would become trivial compared to what the Kuwaitis would eventually exact.

Avenging Social Wrongs

War exacerbates racial tensions and divides people who have been peacefully living side by side. This happened in Kuwait. Some foreign-born workers became pirates overnight. None that we heard of were the South Asian domestic servants who labor in the suburbs of Kuwait and who might have had deeper grievances. These pirates were reportedly office workers, teachers, and middle managers. They owned cars, lived in comfortable although modest apartments, and saved their money. They were not poor. But they were angry.

Some of these workers had lived in Kuwait for as long as twenty-five years. Their children were born in Kuwait. They were refugees from other wars, and Kuwait was their only home. Yet they were denied Kuwaiti citizenship. Their sons could not attend college in Kuwait. Even a Palestinian or Lebanese who worked for a Kuwaiti company all his life was not permitted to retire there. When his employment ended, he had four months to leave. It was hardly fair, especially when those Arabs felt their culture was far superior to that of their masters. Many had higher degrees than their Kuwaiti bosses. It was they who ran Kuwait's schools, factories, offices, and hospitals. They claimed they did the real work that made Kuwait rich.

Arab expatriates in Kuwait viewed a Kuwaiti as hardly more than a nomad. His culture could not compare with achievements of the Umayyad and Abbassid civilizations; it had none of the refinements of Jerusalem, Damascus, Cairo, and Beirut. "They are rich, yes. We all know they were mere fishermen and desert dwellers barely a generation ago. The Emir al-Sabah, their ruler, is a creation of British colonizers. They and the rest of the Arab 'kings' are pawns. The British, and now the Americans, used them to control our riches after they discovered oil in those lands."

Although under 50,000 Palestinian refugees called Iraq home, Iraq's arrival in Kuwait gained it new heroic stature among Palestinians, officially as well as in the street. Palestinian leader Yasser Arafat endorsed Iraq's entry into Kuwait, a move that would cost him dearly. When Kuwaitis reoccupied their homeland, they expelled Palestinians and froze their assets.[3] After he saw the fierce world opposition to the August 12, 1990 invasion, Saddam Hussein attempted to link his pullout from Kuwait to Israel's withdrawal from occupied Arab lands, a proposal that surely fueled a more determined assault against him. During the embargo years, the Iraqi leader's continued assistance to Palestinians under Israeli occupation added to Iraq's eventual demonization in the U.S. in particular as a supporter of terrorism.

Retributions

After Iraq's defeat in Kuwait, the tables turned. It was Iraq's turn to be cleaned out. This time the raids were conducted through bombings, intimidation, coercion, poverty, and more Security Council resolutions to establish the food-for-oil program and manage a compensation fund (SCR 687, paragraph 19) for Iraq's foreign "victims."

The first pillaging of Iraq was self-inflicted in a promising but doomed rebellion. It began during the U.S. ground war of February 1991, on the heels of forty-two days of air bombardments. Encouraged by American promises of military support, Iraqi rebels attacked government symbols of power, Baath party centers, museums, and archaeological sites. (They did not attack schools, libraries, or regular administrative offices, as happened in 2003.) The insurgents, referred to as Shia, are said to have emptied a dozen regional museums of their prized antiquities. This booty would soon find its way, often through American soldiers, to foreign markets. The pillaging of antiquities continued throughout the embargo.

Other predators pounced on Iraq in the confusion and despair following its defeat in Kuwait. Iraqis sank into poverty and turned in all directions in their desperation. Many sought asylum outside. Prisoners of war held in Saudi Arabian camps were offered visas to settle in the United States and Europe. Impoverished women went to Jordan in search of work, only to find themselves snared into the underworld. Parents withdrew their children from school and put them to work in the streets. Perhaps as many as four million skilled, educated Iraqis, including the majority of Iraq's Christian community, left in search of a new life in Australia, Europe, South America, and neighboring Arab lands. The Emirates, Bahrain, and Saudi Arabia welcomed Iraqis, especially their engineers, professors, and doctors.

Next, the pseudo-legal plundering of Iraq got under way—the plundering of the entire country under UN sponsorship through a humanitarian scheme designed, they said, to address the suffering, ensure security for the region, and address Iraq's crimes in Kuwait. In reality, the plan was deeply nefarious. It sported labels like "war compensation," "food monitoring," "weapons inspections," and "sanctions reviews." It surpassed anything that Iraq's troops managed during their short, stupid fling in Kuwait. The loser in a war normally pays the heaviest price, but the retribution devised and applied against Iraq would be on a scale not seen before.

Kuwait demanded the return of stolen goods, compensation for damages, and an outstanding role on the UN's Geneva-based Compensation Commission. That is a body established to funnel money to foreign claimants for personal injuries, corporate losses, personal property losses, and loss of work.

By 1995 alone, the Compensation Commission received 217,513 applications. It quickly developed a reputation for endorsing questionable claims. Applications for compensation had to be verified by former employers, in this case Kuwaitis. And it is widely rumored that many of them authorized payouts that they knew were exaggerated or completely fraudulent. So numerous were the claims that this committee was still at work in Geneva in late 2002, its funds drawn directly from that bottomless UN Iraq account.[4] Needless to say, the Iraqi government had no power whatsoever over the commission's judgments.

According to Alain Gresh, who has conducted investigations into the alarming inner workings of this commission, the UNCC is essentially controlled by its American representatives.[5]

Although excesses and corruption by American companies under the U.S. occupation seem to be well documented by reporters and in 2007 would eventually lead to investigations by the U.S. Congress, few journalists bothered to investigate the UN payout schemes during the sanctions era and these abuses remain in obscurity. It was only Iraqi oil money. Every Iraqi knew the shocking details, however, since UN accounting was transparent.

While the Iraqi government was powerless to check the abuse, not unreasonably it sought ways to circumvent restrictions. Private deals could be made with shadowy businessmen, even Americans. On their side, American businessmen now joined the parade of profiteers, promising political rewards to Iraqi officials. And whereas Iranian and Syrian suppliers dealt in consumer goods, the Americans were after industrial-scale contracts.

I Mean Business

In early May, 1998, I was sitting in the lounge of Baghdad's upscale al-Rasheed Hotel eavesdropping on an American and an Iraqi discussing business at a nearby table. The American said, "I can buy anything for you—generators, heavy construction machinery, transport trucks. If I have to agree to take oil or gas by a pirate ship to Dubai, I'm going to do it. I want to make money. I'm not here in Iraq for the excitement. I'm like you. I want something from my work, and I'm willing to take a risk. I need an order now. This embargo is going to end, and when it does, we'll be ready."

Al-Rasheed was where journalists from the major papers and television networks lodged, where ranking foreign delegates were hosted, and where the wealthier businessmen conducted transactions with Iraqi officials. Voices were always kept low here.

One met few of the low-budget freelancers and anti-sanctions workers at al-Rasheed. They found the hotel too removed from the neighborhoods and shops populated by Iraqis they needed to be near. And the idle men positioned around the lounge who they believed to be secret police made them uncomfortable.

These dawdlers did not appear interested in the business being discussed nearby where I sat. But I could not resist an opportunity to do some surveillance of my own. I leaned over my notebook, listening.

The American repeated, "I need an order for some big stuff: transformers, other big electrical equipment."

Such a conversation would not normally arouse my interest. Most business with Iraq had to be done in person because Iraq's communications system, destroyed in the war, was unreliable. American businessmen were rarely seen here before 2003. Throughout the siege, the U.S. government prohibited commerce with Iraq. Legally Americans could not travel to Iraq. They could not attend the trade fairs or make any agreements. Any business they conducted they had to route through a third party, usually a Jordanian, a Korean, or a Russian agent. By 1998, however, missing out on trade opportunities in Iraq, a few enterprising U.S. merchants arrived to take a share of the booty.

I adjusted myself in the soft leather chair with my back to the men. The American did most of the talking. "I've spoken with the people from Bill Beverly Company. They'll take a letter of credit from Iraq. Can I get that with easy terms?" The American was not circumspect. Letters of credit were outside the terms of the UN embargo agreement. This was not a legitimate business deal.

"I've got to have an order now," continued the visitor. His manner was stereotypical—firm, slightly threatening, and imbued with authority. The Iraqi he was addressing, perhaps a Ministry of Trade official, seemed timorous. He was clearly there to listen and would likely have to consult his superiors.

The American was offering equipment that the government badly needed—generators and transformers. Most of Iraq's requests for heavy equipment to rebuild its infrastructure had been held up by the 661 Committee. The Iraqis had no clout with 661 members, so they had to seek other possibilities. Now the subject seemed to have changed.

"He's not going to come unless I get the deal." The American continued with a mild but unmistakably threatening tone. "Either you give me an order, or I won't put in a word for you. I've got to get something out of this. I'm here because I'm looking for something," he persisted. A contractor stood to make tens of thousands of dollars in commissions from industrial orders.[6]

The American then moved on to another subject, a multimillion dollar plan to be launched when the sanctions ended. The Iraqi partner grew more interested. Even a corrupted official could melt at the mention of Iraq without the siege.

The American spoke with confidence. "We are in discussions about a deal with General Motors. Beverly [an influential U.S. intermediary] has agreed to take me to General Motors when I get back. I'm going to meet a very senior person at GM, and I'll present everything to her. I assure you we can get Chrysler to set up a jeep production plant in Iraq. Mitsubishi can't do anything for you. With GM behind you, we can supply millions of cars here."

A General Motors or a Mitsubishi factory was possible only in a post-sanctions Iraq. Was this the main appeal of this meeting for the Iraqi? Offering the American an order for generators to "pay for this trip" seemed rather petty. Now the visitor was promising to put in a word with an agent who would then possibly approach the U.S. car manufacturer.

How far ahead was this? If a major U.S. corporation was making plans for a post-sanctions era, could a policy change be under way? On the surface, this seemed unlikely.

The global anti-sanctions movement seemed to have peaked by 2000, after air flights became regular. Iraq was an old story; a coup seemed impossible; life seemed to be less tenuous; many journalists had left Baghdad. Washington's position on Iraq remained bellicose and uncompromising—nothing new. There was talk about a new United Nations sanctions law (eventually implemented by the UN as Resolution 1284). "Smart sanctions," the press called it. Although it might relax the embargo, a long list of what they called "dual-use" (military/civilian) items remained banned. Copper wire, medical radiation equipment, scientific journals, and chlorine are a few of the thousands of essentials exempted in SCR 1284. Iraq could not move forward with rebuilding or legitimate commerce. The UN also made it clear that sanctions would remain as long as the UN weapons inspectors were not readmitted.

Surely investors at General Motors would not open a discussion about putting a factory in Iraq without strong indications of sanctions coming to an end. Did this businessman have an inside track?

"The best thing is for me to speak directly to Naji." Naji was said to be as powerful as any cabinet minister, with close ties to the Iraqi president. The American was not naïve. "If you get me the order for the transformers, I can begin to work on the Jimmy Carter thing for you."

Another post-sanctions lure? This visitor knew Iraqis placed much confidence in the former American president. A sympathetic word would surely help their effort to lift the blockade, they believed. "My first priority is to get a meeting here with Carter. He's going to Cuba soon. Cuba's also under embargo. Carter is due to meet Castro and make a statement against sanctions there. If he can make a statement on human suffering in Iraq . . ." His voice trailed off.

After the Iraqi left, the American sat quietly, looking out at a garden of cactus trees enclosed in a glass courtyard. The hotel's Muzak played a Frank Sinatra melody. The secret service regulars sat passively, perhaps wondering where to seek medicine for a cancer-riddled wife or child. No one at al-Rasheed was peddling radiation machines.

Palm grove, watercolor, by Abdel Ameer Alwan, 2001.

13

Skies over Baghdad, 2000

No challenge to the U.S. containment policy on Iraq was more effective, or more harmful, depending on your point of view. Flying an airplane to Baghdad had to be tried. Control of the skies was a benchmark of the blockade. It had to be breached.

If Saddam and his Baathi could not be ousted in a coup, something Washington openly advocated, at least the U.S. military kept control of Iraqi skies. Since 1991, only the Americans could determine what entered Iraqi airspace. As long as Iraqis were kept out of their sky, they would feel humiliated and helpless. Daily the enemy sent in fighter craft to bomb northern and southern Iraq. U.S. aircraft destroyed ripening wheat with incendiary bombs and policed the ban on commercial flights. Even official UN flights into Iraq needed Washington's nod. Nothing insulted Baghdad's sovereignty like the air missions by U.S. and British warplanes. Their gratuitous bombing missions in the "no-fly" zones killed and maimed hundreds, and no country protested. At times life seemed indeed like the Stone Age for Iraqis.

Thus when anyone defied U.S. supremacy of Iraqi airspace, it was a major advance. Millions cheered when passenger planes began to arrive in Baghdad.

"Iraq 002, We Have Visual Contact"

At 10:05 a.m., November 11, 2000, Margarita Papandreou, former first lady of Greece, turned to her companions in the cabin of Olympic Flight 3598 from Athens: "Ladies and gentlemen, we had just entered Iraqi airspace." Her voice was soft, but it was underlain with tension. The danger was not over. Much could happen before we reached Baghdad Airport. Nevertheless, cheers erupted. Many of us embraced one another gleefully. Someone shouted, "We've fucked America!"

Most of OA 3598's passengers had never seen Iraq. All gazed down at the expanse of the northern Iraqi plains. No river or village was yet in sight; we could see nothing to distinguish the 10,000-year-old civilization. Yet we could not take our eyes off our quarry—this vast, blighted land of 20 million deserving souls, forgotten, trudging over dirt roads, sending out handwritten messages on scraps of paper while the rest of the world raced along high-tech pathways.

At 11:40, the aircraft began its descent. The crackling radio communication between the OA pilot and controllers on the ground was like a sweet poem. As their exchange flowed out of the open cockpit, I placed my tape recorder in its direction: "Flight OA 3598 to ground control." Our pilot's voice was calm, professional, sanctions-free. So was the Iraqi's.

"Iraq 002. The runway should be in your sight. Can you make a visual?" came the reply from the control tower at Baghdad's international airport.

"Iraq 002. Roger. Visual contact 118.7."

"Happy landing," Baghdad signaled back.

The purser took the cabin phone: "Ladies and gentlemen, please fasten your seatbelts. The time is 11:55, Baghdad time. The temperature outside is 27 degrees. We will be landing in Saddam International Airport in five minutes. Thank you for flying with Olympic Airways."

Margarita Papandreou was a resolute activist. She had joined Ahmed Ben Bella, Ramsey Clark, George Galloway, Kathy Kelly, Nawal el-Saadawi, and other international figures in challenging the legality of the UN embargo. Like them, Papandreou directed her energies to political actions more than to humanitarian relief. A defiant flight into Iraq appealed to her. Not many could pull off such a scheme, and at several points it seemed her plan might not succeed. Olympic Airways is the flagship of Greece, not a private craft. Thus its arrival in Iraqi skies carried considerable weight.

Washington did its best to thwart any such flights. Within months following the Olympic Airways landing, Syrian, Russian, and Jordanian national airlines would introduce regularly scheduled flights into Baghdad. No American group was able to successfully arrange a flight from U.S. soil. But European activists had some success.

Our delegation of 102, mainly Europeans, had assembled in Athens to fly to Baghdad on this mission in solidarity. Olympic Airways agreed to take the group. Papandreou, whose son was minister of foreign affairs at the time, spent six months planning the flight. The embargo-busters included powerful Greek legislators, media and business people, as well as members of the European Parliament, an official from Médecins Sans Frontières, activists from three other European nations, four Canadians, and five Americans. Iraq's ambassador in Athens arranged landing rights at Baghdad, and Olympic Airways secured permission from Damascus to enter Iraqi airspace via Syria. Visas were issued by the Iraqi ambassador in Athens. On November 9, all of us had arrived in the

Greek capital. We were scheduled to fly out the next evening. Then a problem arose.

Just hours before our departure, the UN office contacted Mrs. Papandreou on her cell phone. "The UN can allow the flight to proceed only if you submit to us the name and occupation of every passenger," they stipulated. She didn't like this. She delayed our departure to discuss the crisis with delegates and with the airlines. Could OA attempt the flight without UN permission? Of what importance were our names? She asked each of us for permission to pass on our names. We agreed. But she would demand assurances from the UN that this information would be given to no one else. The UN gave her its sovereign word. By nightfall the list was compiled and submitted. Two hours later, Papandreou's cell phone rang again. It was not the UN. The caller identified himself as a U.S. State Department officer. "I am calling from our embassy in Syria. American authorities here and in Athens are concerned about the inclusion in the flight of "certain undesirables," he said stonily. "They must be removed from the flight before you can proceed." Papandreou was furious, first because the UN had passed her list to the Americans, and second, because of this demand. We had already delayed our departure by twelve hours. Papandreou stood her ground.

"We are going ahead with everyone in our delegation," she told the American, and she abruptly closed her phone. Next morning, we lifted off from Athens. If we were nervous about an American attack on us, it did not show.

A Pinprick of Light

Two years earlier, on a clear, moonless evening, I had happened to look up at the black sky above Baghdad and noticed an odd light. I was walking with friends toward their car. When we were together or with other survivors of the embargo, we ate and joked and talked late into the night. Tonight we were invited to a home in northern Baghdad for dinner. Leaving my work behind in my hotel, I could sometimes forget that I was in a nation engulfed by this awful war and the blockade.

I stared into the sky to the south, deliberating on that tiny light: "Too far to be a tower; too close for a star." I listened for the sound of an airplane engine. Nothing. I peered at the spot for another few seconds. It was not moving. "Look there, Yasmine. What is that light?"

Yasmine and her husband, Mohamed, seemed unconcerned and continued walking toward their car. Seeing I was transfixed by my discovery, Yasmine came and took me by the arm. She did not peer into the sky. She knew what that light was. "Sa-tel-lite," she announced curtly.

"AM-RI-KY-AN sa-tel-lite," she said, this time with greater emphasis, her voice rising, mocking. "We have many in Iraq," she said, grinning.

"They cannot be television satellites," I said. "Not here."

"You don't know?" Yasmine asked reprovingly, raising her eyebrows. "Look. They are all over Iraq." She flung her arm skyward toward a similar light on another horizon. "See how interested your governments are in us? We Iraqis, we are so important. When we take our bath or scratch our crotch, when we buy our measly vegetables or visit our sick mother, when we go to dinner with a journalist, you watch everything we do. We soooooo interesting!"

The couple laughed as they hustled me into their car, and we drove off. My naiveté was as absurd as all those satellites whirling around. I peered over my shoulder through the car window, seeking out those tiny American specs of light hovering in the Iraqi sky. My hosts shook their heads, amused. "How could you, a reporter, be ignorant of these things? Have you never seen a U.S. military satellite?" I had not, not knowingly.

For Iraqis, these probes are so common that they hardly mention them. Nevertheless, the presence of these peeping toms penetrates deep into their psyche. They represent the loss of their sovereignty. It is not amusing.

Satellite probes may be more sinister than occupation by troops on one's soil. Yasmine could not bring herself to admit it openly, but I suspect she and others feel unprotected, vulnerable.

The Iraqi government can do nothing. And the public is aware of how utterly helpless its leaders are against these all-seeing machines. They cannot ask the light in the sky what it wants or how long it is going to stay. They cannot hit it, turn it off, or chase it away. They cannot report it to their meteorological office or call in the Iraqi air force. Neither can they forget it.

All the time, day and night, Iraq is being watched by these whirling detectives. When they first saw these probes, people were intrigued—not by satellite technology but because yet another eavesdropper had arrived in their midst. The mukhabaraat, Iraq's intelligence service, was already well established. After Washington announced its support of a coup to topple Saddam, tens of thousands more agents were put to work watching the citizens. Now comes this high-tech spy, suspended there in the sky, eavesdropping on *those* fellows.

At some level Iraqis find this humorous. A big spider has arrived to watch the little spiders scurrying about. The predator watches twenty million pitiful antlike creatures—men and women crawling to and fro to collect crumbs to eat. "The Americans know more about us than our own government does. They know EVERYthing." Yasmine's stress on *every* did not pass unnoticed. "Every" is Saddam Hussein.

These prying eyes in the sky can detect tennis ball–sized items and read license plates. After more than a decade, these hovering cameras will have mapped every inch of their country over and over. "They know everything about us. So why are they still there? And why haven't they located Saddam?" asks the citizen who is crushed by the sanctions. "It must be to tell us or him: 'You have no power. You are a rodent in a cage. When we are ready, we will snuff you out. Meanwhile, sell your oil, throw us your best engineers, scientists, and doctors, smuggle out your antiquities, finance our operations at the UN, and terrify the Gulf states into signing defense pacts with us.'"

Empty Skies Depend on Your Point of View

Apart from those menacing spy lights, the skies over Baghdad were pretty empty because of the American and UN ban on commercial flights. Not in the two "no-fly" zones that cover most of Iraqi territory, however. There, planes regularly patrol the sky. Those craft are foreign fighter jets. U.S. and British attack planes move uninhibited through Iraqi skies. No Iraqi aircraft is in sight. On the ground, villagers, doctors, and police rush to the bombsites to tend to the wounded.

The invading planes regularly occupy Iraqi air space. Between 1991 and 1995, 11,400 sorties flew those courses. Between December 1998 and May 2001, their missiles killed 1,400 Iraqi civilians and wounded 1,850. Any villages, schools, or shepherd encampments that happened to be in their paths were destroyed.

These flights and their bombings are completely illegal. This was affirmed by former UN general secretary Butros Butros-Ghali in an interview with journalist John Pilger.[1] "No mention is made of the no-fly zones in any UN resolution, and the missions are conducted without a UN mandate," says Butros-Ghali emphatically. "The flights have no reasonable military purpose; they have never been sanctioned by any international authority."

The two rogue superpowers purport that their flights are protecting the Iraqi people from attacks by Saddam Hussein. They ensure that Iraqi planes do not enter these zones. So why do they fire bombs into Iraqi towns? "Any attacks by U.S. aircraft are in self-defense," riposte Pentagon officials. "We only attack when 'threatened' by Iraqi ground fire or 'targeted' by Iraqi radar defenses." During the twelve years that these attacks had become commonplace, neither the UN nor any world court has condemned them.

Iraqis living outside the zones, between the 33rd and 36th parallels, may not face these daily threats, but this does not mean they enjoy any sense of security.

Any high-flying aircraft must be a foreign plane, probably an American spy plane. Iraq can do absolutely nothing to thwart its mission.

Iraq has no fighter planes, no bombers, and no antiaircraft power or missiles to reach the invaders. Before the January 17, 1991, assault on Iraqi troops that drove them from Kuwait, realizing it could not possibly counter the attackers, Iraq moved its fighter jets and commercial aircraft into neighboring countries: Yemen, Iran, and Jordan. Those three hundred planes continued to sit on those distant tarmacs at least until the 2003 U.S. invasion. To keep its highly valued pilots and aircraft mechanics in shape, Iraq allowed them to work with airline companies in friendly North Africa and Asian countries.

Only the UN is exempt from this fly ban, and even then, U.S. approval is necessary. Just as the UN possesses a reliable, advanced communications system (Iraqi-funded, SCR 687) for its UN staff convenience, the UN also flies its peace-blue helicopters in and out as needed, also at the expense of Iraqis. Occasionally a foreign medical team on a mission to save an Iraqi child or a sick journalist is permitted to board a UN aircraft. These planes do not use the national air terminal but slip into a private airstrip fenced in by electronic wires and out-of-bounds to Iraqi nationals.

Care is taken to ensure that no Iraqi, however vital their need, enjoys such privileges. Under this sanctions regime, dozens of critically ill Iraqis, traveling to Jordan by car in search of urgent medical assistance, perished en route.

"We Shall Fly"

International flights to and from Iraq ended in 1991. The UN sanctions resolution prohibited all commercial exchange with Iraq. The very first challenge to the ban came only in 1997. Iraqis called it a humanitarian mission: the plane carried 104 Iraqi pilgrims destined for the Muslim Hajj, a sacred obligation for Muslims. Saudi Arabia had agreed to accept Iraqi pilgrims destined for Mecca by plane. Washington, as anticipated, said "No." The UN, following its master, denied the application. The Hajj flight could not proceed.

Saudi Arabia remained silent when the Iraqi minister of endowments and religious affairs, Ahmed Saleh, asserted, "Shoot us down if you want. Let Allah decide what is our fate. We shall fly." And they did, arriving in Jeddah on April 9, 1997.[2]

The Hajj flights became a precedent for more challenges to the mean-spirited ban. The Mecca flight inspired courage in others to defy U.S.-dictated terms of the embargo. If pilgrims are exempted on a humanitarian basis, they argued, what about shipments of medicines and other essentials?

AmeriCares, an American relief organization whose aims in Iraq were questionable, became the first NGO to receive clearance from the U.S. Department of Commerce. With a well-known actor among its passengers, the flight drew some U.S. media attention when it arrived in Baghdad in April 1998.[3] Although some critics suspect a hidden political motive behind that AmeriCares flight, others with determinedly embargo-busting agendas began to organize similar humanitarian missions. An Egyptian delegation of eminent writers, film stars, and other celebrities boarded an Egypt Air flight to Baghdad. They, too, were taking aid to Iraqis. A group of mainly Jordanian sympathizers flew from Amman, using a Royal Jordanian aircraft. One after another, throughout 1999 and 2000, planeloads of visitors landed in Baghdad until the pretense of carrying food and medicine was dropped. A Russian aircraft landed in Baghdad with the minister of foreign affairs on board, and a high-level Syrian delegation followed suit. The leader of the United Arab Emirates donated a new passenger aircraft to Saddam Hussein, who passed it on to Iraqi Airways.

The Americans could do nothing to stop these missions short of blasting them in midflight. It seemed that the Baghdad airport would soon be in full operation. Washington had to concoct new obstacles.

By late 2000, in an attempt to reassert its authority, the U.S. Commerce Department announced that any further flights to Iraq would be subject to tighter regulations. A flight insurer had to obtain clearance from the United Nations (meaning in effect the United States). This rule succeeded in thwarting some flights but not all. Jordanian Airways, Syrian Air, a Russian company, and a few Eastern European carriers decided to take the risk.[4] Several eventually instituted scheduled flights into the besieged capital.

Some Europeans intending to defy the Americans capitulated under threat from Washington. One was a Belgian carrier chartered to fly a European delegation to Iraq. It was organized by George Galloway, a British Labor Party member of Parliament at the time. U.S. authorities acquired foreknowledge of it and simply informed the Belgian carrier, "If you go ahead with this, none of your aircraft will be permitted on American soil." The flight was canceled.

On another occasion, Jean-Marie Benjamin, a French-Italian active in anti-sanctions efforts, had assembled an impressive list of dignitaries in France to fly an anti-embargo mission from Orly Airport to Baghdad. Delegates were about to depart when they were informed that the flight could not proceed. French authorities had bowed to U.S. pressure. That same day, a ranking French official was scheduled to meet with Secretary of State Madeleine Albright, and the government decided it could not risk a rebuff from the Americans. Missions could also be thwarted by a country denying over-fly rights, and the Americans turned to threats against countries granting permission for any over-flight to aircraft destined for Baghdad. European governments were particularly skittish.

Only the most determined, resourceful activists were able to find partners willing to personally insure their plane in order to circumvent the U.S.–UN barricades. Jean-Marie Benjamin and George Galloway were resolute in their challenges to Washington and London over the flight bans.

Galloway, a leading British proponent of lifting sanctions, defied his own party and the British secretary of state, Peter Hain, with a daring escape plan. And it worked. According to journalist Felicity Arbuthnot, a member of Galloway's Great Britain–Iraq Society,

> Galloway invoked the formula he had used two years earlier when he organized the "Big Ben to Baghdad" bus journey. This time, on the pretext of a "pilgrimage to the continent," Galloway flew from Manston airport in Kent, South England, to Sofia in Bulgaria. His aircraft was a private jet borrowed from his friend, the Bulgarian president (who scorned the UN ban). They stopped in Sofia only to refuel and in the dead of night flew on to Baghdad! To drive his point home, on landing at Saddam International Airport, Galloway phoned the private home number of the British minister, rousing him with a cheerful "Good morning from Baghdad, Peter!"

Hain's reply is unprintable, said Arbuthnot.

Jean-Marie Benjamin, a Catholic priest and activist mulling over his options in Rome, was not to be outdone. An accomplished musician and orchestra conductor in France before becoming a priest, Benjamin used his public standing as a musician and his contacts in Rome to garner support against the blockade on Iraq. He recruited a wealthy Italian adventurer to join him on the trip to Iraq; the man would loan Benjamin his plane and personally put up the insurance. Together they located a pilot willing to take the craft and its two passengers through hazardous skies. From Rome they flew to Amman, Jordan. Filing their flight route at the Amman airport for Damascus, they secured permission to take off. The small aircraft headed north according to plan. But just before it entered Syrian airspace, it slipped east and into Iraqi skies. The Italian team ignored pleas and threats from Jordanian air authorities to turn back.

Benjamin's plan had been prearranged with Baghdad. To ensure their scheme was not foiled, an Iraqi assistant drove to Jordan a week earlier to hand over the coordinates of Baghdad airport.

"It was a little scary," admitted Benjamin when it was all over. "We were not in contact with Baghdad air control for more than two hours as we headed south-east, flying very low sometimes, but we followed the Euphrates until we made contact with air control at Saddam Airport. It was like a carnival at the airport when we landed there. 'We beat the Americans. We fooled the Americans,' people cheered. Morale was the highest I had seen in all those years," recalled the priest. "It was worth the problems that lay ahead."

Benjamin and his patron stayed on in Baghdad, leaving the pilot to make his way home alone. He had confirmation from Jordan to fly into Alia Airport direct from Baghdad. But upon landing in Amman, he was arrested. Jordanian authorities confiscated the plane and jailed the pilot. Benjamin only learned this when he reached Jordan a week later by road. "It took a lot of strings from our Italian embassy in Jordan to get the pilot and aircraft released. The pilot was a good guy, not at all upset."[5]

Some Children

Some children in Iraq—
kids,
died.
I am sad about that, because
I'm their language.

Rami, age 10, March 1991, New York

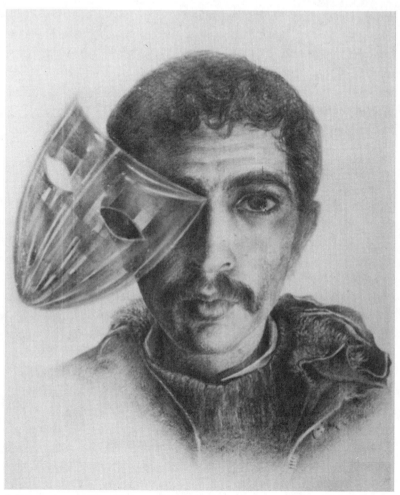

Self-portrait, pencil, by Hazem al-Mawally, 1991.

14

One Farmer's Message

Five national airlines were making weekly scheduled flights into Baghdad by the end of 2001. American legislators were wringing their hands in frustration and actually using the phrase "crumbling sanctions" to describe their Iraq policy. U.S. attempts to instigate a coup to oust the Baathi had failed.

Were it not for the September 11 attacks on the United States, Washington would have been at odds over how to reverse their weakening position vis-à-vis Iraq. Less than a year earlier, Iraq had made a major move in its offensive against the siege and the American administration, indeed, against American economic dominance. Baghdad declared its oil could now be bought only in euros. It must have sent shivers through Wall Street as well as the White House. Publicly, the United States dismissed the announcement, and the declaration received meager press attention and then only after Iran also said it would adapt the petroeuro standard in 2002.[1] At the United Nations, where Iraq applied for the new arrangement, the United States tried, without success, to thwart the move. The UN agreed to Iraq's request on November 9, 2000. The Iraqi initiative astutely played off competition between the U.S. and European economies. It pleased European buyers who took advantage of the chance to strengthen their new currency. Optimism within Iraq had reached a peak by early 2001.[2]

Life was still very hard for most Iraqis; the spread of disease could not be halted. Yet living standards were improving. Radical economic reforms and ingenuity were having some positive effect. Iraqis had good reason to feel jubilant. It was a long, hard battle.

Years of debate preceded the reforms in every house and garden and teashop, as well as within powerful Baath circles. Ironically enough, it took the gratuitous attacks on Baghdad (Operation Desert Fox) ordered by President Bill Clinton in late 1998 to bring it to maturity. For four days, firing 415 missiles and 600 laser-guided bombs, U.S. planes pounded Iraq following the exit of inspectors from the UN Special Commission on Iraq (UNSCOM).[3] It was a watershed event for Iraq. This was proof of their charge that the UN was embedded with U.S. spies and that UNSCOM was controlled by Washington.

Outside Iraq, the December 1998 assault caused few diplomatic waves, although some critics suggested Clinton's order to bomb was a tactic to divert attention from his impending impeachment. Inside, it marked the nadir of Iraqis' patience. They no longer distinguished between Washington policy and the American people. They no longer needed journalists to "tell the truth." They no longer trusted the UN to abandon what for them was an evil complicity with the United States.

Over the years I have often marveled at the unqualified cooperation that Iraqis extended to foreigners. This degree of hospitality was unreasonable. The Iraqi public appeared to welcome journalists and other foreigners arriving amid their devastation. How was this possible? Iraqis were neither solicitous nor seeking favors. Theirs was genuine Arab hospitality. Still trembling from the U.S. battering, Iraqi friends invited me to stay with them when I arrived in Iraq following their army's shameful defeat in 1991. We had known each other in 1989. Painfully, they recalled forty-two nights of relentless bombings. One father, when he received me in his home, felt he had to explain his son's rebuff: "He won't speak. He was in the war, the only survivor of a platoon of twenty-eight men."

Others, still traumatized, guided me through destroyed factories, crumbling schools, and dreary offices in disarray and without phones. Later they led me into hospital wards to witness the dying. When I needed clerical help, they provided what they could, faded copies cranked out of duplicating machines salvaged from long discarded stock. Year after year, they labored with a dysfunctional phone system trying to set up interviews or transport for me. Phone communication in the capital was poor, and connections to other cities were impossible—a direct result of the bombings and the UN embargo. Without uttering a word of complaint in our presence, year after year, they did what they could to help visitors.

I doubt if this courtesy was something engineered or ordered by the Baath authorities. Officials were doubtless told to be accommodating; they should avoid political arguments with us; they should not tell us their personal problems. But the kindness and tolerance I experienced was not limited to civil servants. I encountered it wherever I stopped: shops, schools, hotels, and restaurants, in the street, in taxis, and in private homes.

I was so struck by the absence of hostility, I asked Iraqis to explain. "You are our guests," came the reply. "We know this aggression was not your action. Your government did this. You and your government are not the same." This was civility. Call it old-fashioned grace. (On another level I felt it was also naiveté.)

Moreover, many of these women and men felt certain that the world would eventually respond to the injustices hurled at them, that they would not be punished for Saddam's excesses. Some Iraqi officials actually felt likewise.

The embargo was applied to Iraq's mail, banking, and phone services.[4] In addition to these physical obstacles, Iraqis' personal and professional contacts were cut: diplomats, former professors, business colleagues, and relatives were mute. They expected this could not last long.

For some, the presence of a journalist was somehow reassuring. Through us, Iraqis could feel connected, even if we were there to serve other masters and we stayed only a few days or weeks. The country had been traumatized by the massive blockade. People found themselves isolated. The very idea was unbearable.

"Iraq is not forgotten" was a common welcome to any visitor. It was as genuine as anything I had experienced in my many years of traveling around the world. These people's view of us as forerunners of some impending rapprochement was naïve, nevertheless. I was there to support them, but I somehow felt their leaders misjudged the lengths to which western powers would go to further punish and destroy Iraq. They were misguided in believing journalists could reverse U.S. policy on Iraq. They continued to distinguish between the U.S. administration's policy and the power of its citizens, perhaps because their own government was so alien from its people. Iraqis also expected journalists to be completely sympathetic to their woes.

The siege would end soon after the Gulf War, Iraqis believed. They had signed a cease-fire with U.S. generals! Saddam Hussein had been a stalwart friend in the past. "We sold our oil to U.S. firms, and we certainly see our trade with American companies resuming soon," Nizar Hamdoon, Iraq's ambassador to the UN for seven years, assured me in 1996. He saw no reason, he said, why his government and Washington should not resume their friendship. "As soon as oil sales are restored, things will move ahead," he asserted quietly.

This gentility ended abruptly. Tariq Aziz announced this after the December 1998 bombing. He identified the United States, the United Kingdom, and Israel as the real axis of evil. "Together," he said, "these countries have brought this havoc upon us; they intend that the embargo will never end."

Fathel, a poultry farmer, expressed the general Iraqi position in his own words. "Your Clinton is an animal. Look at his foolishness. All of you, why do we let you come into our great land? What do you want here?"

I met Fathel on February 1, 1999. This was six weeks after the December 14–18, 1998, bombing ordered by President Clinton. The spy-loaded United

Nations team of weapons inspectors, headed by Richard Butler, had departed in a huff, charging Iraq with not cooperating. As we later learned, their hasty departure was a tactic that UNSCOM coordinated with Washington. Within hours after the group's voluntary exit from Iraq, Clinton ordered a military assault on the country. Whether the bombing accomplished anything militarily is unlikely. It did not intimidate Iraq. The country was already subjected to almost daily attacks in the north and south (those benign "no-fly" zones, a British-American invention with no legality whatsoever). In the forty-one months between December 1998 and May 2002, according to data compiled by Iraq, those forays killed 1,142 Iraqis and wounded another 1,863.

The December 1998 assault held immense significance in Iraq. That week was the beginning of Ramadan. At one level the assault was an insult to Islam. Second seemed to be a cruel attempt by Clinton to eclipse his sex scandal at Iraq's expense. Moreover, the targets of those American missiles, Iraq claimed, were installations identified and flagged by UNSCOM, which Iraq had suspected was working closely with American and Israeli intelligence agencies. That attack convinced Iraqis it was useless to think that cooperation with weapons inspections might lead to the lifting of sanctions. The United States would block any progress in that direction. Farmer Fathel and millions of other Iraqis reached the same conclusion. They said "enough": they had waited long enough; they had cooperated enough; they had had enough of the United States, Israel, and the United Kingdom triumvirate that they held responsible for their woes. Now they extended blame to the British and American public—men and women who, up to now, they assured themselves, bore no responsibility for their governments' aggression against Iraq. They would no longer cooperate.

Fathel recognized me as soon as I stepped from the car. On my visit to his farm six months earlier, I remembered, he had been rather sullen. He was nevertheless patient and instructed his manager to answer my questions about how they had restarted production after eight lost years. Their stock was wiped out by electricity cuts in the 1991 bombing. Feed, previously imported from Canada, was embargoed. Rusted and broken machinery was scattered across his property, and several abandoned poultry sheds stood silent in the overgrown yard. Fathel and his father had managed to rebuild the business, but it was only a shadow of what it had been. The price for imported chicks, vaccines, and feed, now brought from neighboring countries, was high. Machinery was almost impossible to come by.

This villager had survived because he converted his land to wheat production when the government was paying premiums for grain. Life was still not easy for the family; this villager had no brothers to help, and his father was ill.

I was accompanied by a Ministry of Agriculture officer—a woman—a technical expert from the regional office, and Ali from the Ministry of Information Press Center in Baghdad. The three of them stood by, speechless, while the poultry farmer berated me. I glanced at them. All three looked on in astonishment. Or embarrassment. Or satisfaction. Ali, as my custodian, tried to intervene: "She is simply a journalist. What Clinton does is not her responsibility." Fathel ignored him. Moving forward, he placed himself between the nearby poultry sheds and us, barring my advance. "You come here again and again to see how poor we are. You take photos of us in these dirty clothes. What will you learn from my chickens? Don't you have chickens in your country? Why have you come back? To see how efficiently you destroy our people, our children? This is your country's work. Go away."

The man was really angry. This may have been a longed-for opportunity to speak directly to his adversary. I did not need Ali to translate, and I think he was content to remain silent. [It would not be easy for my hosts to utter Fathel's irate words in English.]

What could Ali do? He was a hapless MOI employee. I had worked with him before. Like his colleagues, he was trained to tolerate foreigners and act as a liaison (or a buffer) between us and the experts we interviewed. In my experience, these low-level and amiable civil servants never criticized visitors, however rude or stubborn we might be. And they never openly criticized the United States or the United Kingdom. So it was up to the farmer. "Do you think an Iraqi chicken is different than an American one? The same way you think our heart is different and an Iraqi child without food is different than your American baby?"

Apart from some blasts at the United States and the United Kingdom from Saddam Hussein (well publicized, since the western press never lost an opportunity to show the man's snarling face), Iraqi officials usually met us with courteous and conciliatory gestures. One ambassador judiciously avoided criticizing Washington when I asked him about the UN food-for-oil program being negotiated at the time (eventually known as SCR 986). It was evident to many of us that the scheme was an American maneuver designed not for Iraqi people but for U.S. political advantage. Yet that emissary dispassionately commented: "We hope the Americans will understand Iraq's needs. We do not see this policy as an attempt by the United States to further burden us." Months earlier, his boss, Foreign Affairs Minister Mohammed Al-Sahaf, had been less ambassadorial. In New York for the vote on the proposed plan, he received me at Iraq's UN Mission office. "We will refuse," he asserted. "SCR 986 is nothing but an American scheme to make Iraq one enormous refugee camp. It is another plot to assume indirect control over our oil revenue and to weaken us." (In May 1996, Iraq agreed to the plan, and the UN appointed committees and budgets to implement it.)

Even after Clinton's order to attack Iraq in 1998 and the outrage it generated within the country, Iraq continued to issue visas to journalists, although on a more restricted basis. As always, officials courteously received those of us who traveled there. This farmer had the temerity to risk expressing his views. I knew he spoke for the millions who were seething with outrage.

"You are all dogs. What kind of civilization do you have over there? You Americans. And the British and Zionists, your partners. Yes, you have better bombs than all the world. What kind of civilization have you? Do you know how old Iraq is? Here, on this soil where you stand, we have ancient cities. Who translated the Greek texts into Arabic and preserved them for the world? Who wrote novels and poetry when you were still living in the trees?"

Should I have felt gratified that men like Fathel were not running the government? They would surely have banned all reporters.

Up to now, Iraqi moderates who urged continued dialogue with the Americans had prevailed. An Iraqi diplomat confided to me how he and others working closely with their president "were vigorously engaged in damage control" over foolhardy statements made by him during the early years of the conflict. "Every government needs seasoned diplomats to neutralize a leader's tactlessness." He admitted that defiant posturing by the Iraqi leader frequently threatened to shut down all dialogue and negotiation with other states. In his rambling, often clumsy interviews with western press, Saddam Hussein sometimes made things worse for Iraq.[5]

The debate over how to respond to the sanctions continued for years. After the December 1998 episode, the other side won the day. Iraq's tolerance had reached its limit.

For eight years, Fathel and millions of others had said, "Welcome to our country," even in the midst of appalling hardships. They provided grim statistics about their stillborn babies, deformed fetuses, and shoeless schoolchildren. They admitted how impoverished families sent girls away. "Here, see how we live. See our scrawny limbs. See our empty pharmacies, our vacant libraries, our boarded-up tourist offices, our idle bank clerks. See the young leaving their motherland." These were not accusations but appeals.

This from a culture that disapproves of displays of grief and poverty to outsiders. That Iraqi attitude was evident even in the United States. When a chairwoman at a fund-raiser told those assembled how Iraqi women were forced into prostitution by poverty, a group of American Iraqis stormed out of the hall.

In Iraq, I witnessed daily displays of this self-esteem. A vendor pushing his fish cart turned his back to a camera lens. A beggar on the pavement shook his empty fist menacingly. Iraq's women's federation refused to discuss cutbacks on women's rights with a visiting delegation. Doctors tried to bar foreigners from entering hospital wards and were tempted to throw those teddy bears back at visitors to maternity hospitals. "A toy! What is this meant to do for us?" they exclaimed in sheer disbelief when the tour had passed.

Iraqis did not voluntarily display their impoverishment. They resisted journalists' pressure to do so. Eventually, however, some agreed to comply with policy decisions urging them to put aside their pride and to share their hardships. By seeing the grief the blockade causes us others will be convinced of the injustice of the embargo, went the argument. World opinion would be swayed in our favor, they assured themselves.

That approach proved fruitless. It did not help. And many Iraqis independently refused to concede.

The resentment of employees was palpable as I walked through a dilapidated plastics factory. Electricity rationing made production almost impossible, even if raw materials were available. More than one factory manager did not welcome me. When my MOI guide pressed the matter, we were told, "There is no need for you to see the plant floor. I can answer whatever questions you have in my office."

I pushed my way into the rotting Iraqi infrastructure, past scowling doctors and idle managers, stepping over the decay I insisted on recording. Government orders: they had to tolerate us. They had to answer our questions, to endure the same ugly probes that journalists had put to them the day before and the day before that. In any other culture, such intrusions might have put us in danger. Yet we went merrily on, gathering details for what we called a "humanitarian story," feeling righteous because so few journalists even bothered to report on the hardships we described, direct from the field.

The farmer stood his ground at the gate to his farm.

During this twenty-minute visit, I uttered barely a word. When I finally replied, I told Fathel I agreed with much of what he had said. My government was brutal, dishonest, arrogant, and deceptive. I said I disapproved of U.S.

military actions. I admitted my work could do little to help Iraq. But words were useless, and my defense was unacceptable.

I never got further than the front entrance of the man's farm. I did not feel that I was in physical danger. But to press forward called for a fierce arrogance that I simply did not possess. (Perhaps I was not yet a hardened war journalist.) I had to respect this man. He did not want me there. I turned and left.

The officials accompanying me back to the city spoke in hushed sentences in the car. I did not ask them to comment on Fathel's actions, perhaps because I supposed they were in full agreement with him.

Within months, following reports in the press, I observed a major shift in Iraqi policy, one that really emphasized this blunt villager's sentiments. The Iraqi leadership said, "No, we will not accept the UN inspectors back here." They admitted a new reality to their people: "The sanctions may never be lifted." This was a new approach to their problems. It was more realistic. Perhaps this would save them.

Black Cactus, by Burhan al-Mufti, 1998.

Sha-ko Ma-ko? A Story

George W. Bush wanted to understand why Iraqis were so clever, so he decided to go to Iraq himself to find out. He called his CIA director to get a briefing, and he told him, "We have determined that the secret of Iraqi's intelligence capacity is the term *Sha-ko Ma-ko.* They use it as a password for top-secret intelligence."

With this knowledge in hand, the American president got ready to go to Iraq. He had his face streaked with red mud, and he was dressed in a deshdasha with a scarf folded around his head, in the same style as local Iraqi men. His chin and mouth were carefully hidden by the cloth. A U.S. spy plane flew over Iraq and parachuted Bush right into the Sunni Triangle. Landing in a palm grove, he quickly hid his parachute as he had been instructed. There wasn't a soul to be seen.

Striding along in his usual gait, the president made his way through palm groves to a nearby village. There he found men sitting in a market square, so he went and sat among them drinking sweet tea and playing dominos. At some point he decided, "Now is the time to begin my research. What a great opportunity. These folks haven't shown any suspicion about my joining them. They look as if they would trust me." Leaning toward the old man beside him, he whispered, "Sha-ko Ma-ko."

"Ah, didn't you hear?" replied the Iraqi, turning to the stranger. "George Bush has just arrived in Iraq!"

Part 3

15

"Him!"

The more the enemy battered away at their country, the more powerful the Iraqi leader became. This is how it seemed to Iraqis and how it was portrayed by journalists such as T. D. Allman writing in the influential *New Yorker* ("Letter from Baghdad: Saddam Wins Again," June 17, 1996). Even so, by the end of 1998, some Iraqis even believed Saddam Hussein's early defiant stance was preferable to the humiliations forced on them. Compliance and acquiescence had produced nothing. Iraq had more hardship and less sovereignty.

The president and his family were infinitely richer due to the roaring out-of-sanctions trade. His sons were more powerful, and Uday, the elder, was totally out of control.[1] The siege drove millions into poverty; it also created a new wealthy class indebted to the leadership. It was more advantageous than ever to be a party member.

From the start of the crisis, some Iraqis were convinced that their leader was working with the Americans. As the embargo wore on, more and more asked, "How could the CIA, who helped bring him to power, not capture him?"

Iraqis read what the western press charged: that all their problems stemmed from their mad dictator. They didn't buy it. He was a tyrant, yes. But just as the United States had a role in his ascent, it must be safeguarding his survival.[2] In 1984, Donald Rumsfeld had met with the dictator. Washington had used him to battle and to contain Iran. The United States and United Kingdom had supplied him with arms, including biological agents.[3] He had worked with them against his people. He would do it again.

But as the years passed, Iraqis shifted responsibility for the country's woes from their leadership to the United States. As the embargo wore on, if greater numbers of Iraqis subscribed to this view, it did not mean they liked their tyrant more. Yet they succumbed as before to his crude manipulations.

Thirty-five couples, each pair surrounded by clapping women, lurched forward, like children waiting for their cue to proceed onstage. Led by a band of noisy musicians, they moved from the hotel courtyard into the lobby. It was Thursday evening—wedding night—at the Palestine Hotel in Baghdad. I paused on my way to my room to watch the parade. Something unusual was under way. This was not a regular weekend marriage celebration. It was a presidential decree!

"The president is giving them this party," whispered Khalid. The bellboy, standing nearby, had noticed my interest. I gazed at the passing couples more closely.

Each young woman, elegantly coiffured, wore a glittering white gown. Her arms embraced a grand bouquet of flowers. A young man, the groom, walked a pace behind his bride. Attentive mothers and sisters hovered near each bride, and excited children rushed in and out among the dresses and around the musicians.

Pair by pair, each set of newlyweds was ushered onto an elevated platform to be photographed. This was when I noticed that many of the bedecked girls were limping. One had a damaged eye; another suffered from a cleft pallet. A wheelchair bearing another bride was pushed into place. Several of the grooms stumbled forward to stand beside their new wives with the aid of crutches.

The bellhop leaned toward me again. "In our Arab society, no one wants a handicapped girl. See. The couples are all handicapped. Pity."

The excitement continued until each pair was escorted to the elevator and deposited in their room.

"These unions are our president's idea. He says such unfortunates are not to be discriminated against. Everyone deserves a marriage partner and a wedding. All this is financed by Him!" Khalid's eyes widened as he informed me of the best part of the deal: "Every couple receives a gift from Him! Hundreds of thousands of dinars to start their lives."

The legacies of Saddam Hussein are many and disparate. That mass wedding was one episode from the bizarre experiences of the Iraqi people with their president of twenty-five years. His largesse continued in good times and in bad times. His seemingly compassionate quirks were as impulsive as his executions.

Who conceived Saddam's bizarre social projects? What did their beneficiaries feel? What long-term benefits accrued? It is hard to say. Were these gestures a peace offering? A media ploy? The decision of a council of bedouin chiefs? Were these marriages his "democratic" solution to a sociologist's report? Were these simply gimmicks or a heartfelt response to the plea of an anguished mother? Whatever their logic, dispensations like this group wedding were part of the character of Saddam Hussein.

This was the populist dictator whose name few dared to utter. For most

Iraqis, Saddam Hussein was simply "Him." Tens of thousands of military widows sang his praises. He knew how to comfort the humble and exploit the geniuses: a scientist whose work he studied and funded, a writer whose poems he endorsed, a handicapped girl for whom he commissioned an entire new school for the deaf, a wounded shopkeeper whose attacker he condemned to death. This was Him!

Rigid as a Board

I can't understand this kind of populist tyrant. My confusion may seem absurd. After all, Saddam Hussein is no enigma for millions who have never been near Iraq, never read more than a sentence about him. Watching television in the safety of their living rooms thousands of miles away, most people in the West agree, "He was a very, very bad guy." They can cite at least one example of his atrocities to his own people. There's no argument. There was no argument after the invasion of Kuwait in 1990, and there was no argument fourteen years later when he was captured by American forces.

Throughout his rule, the Iraqi ruler was presented to us, posed rigid as a board, trussed in his Baathi military suit. His hairy, puffy Arab face was highlighted by a gnarled grimace. Every portrait suggested he was issuing yet another execution order—a common occupation of his. Even from afar, he looked villainous. This was not a man you could reason with, says the picture. A dangerously simplistic view, but it's difficult to counter. Even if he did shake hands with Donald Rumsfeld two decades ago, if he refused to accept some development schemes that would have been more beneficial to U.S. contractors than to Iraq, if he proposed to Gulf financiers in 1990 that they withdraw their assets from British and American banks, if he announced that his oil would be sold only for euros—no one could refute or justify his murderous history.[4]

His misdeeds eclipsed Saddam's intelligence or any personal merit. He offered plenty of opportunities to demonize. He made it easy for political analysts, the media, and his enemies to convince Americans that this single individual, Saddam Hussein, threatened nothing less than "the American way of life." (Did you ever suppose that U.S. capitalism and democracy were so fragile?) The claim must have further swelled the Iraqi presidential ego.

Saddam was such a threat, we were told, that the United States sent half a million troops to Iraq's borders, backed by thirty-two other nations, to oust his army from Kuwait. Yet forty-two days later, on February 28, 1991, U.S. military commanders signed a cease-fire with his generals. The agreement was codified in UN Resolution 687, leaving Saddam Hussein head of his government. He stayed there for another twelve years until American troops actually entered Baghdad and occupied the country.

Since 1990, compared to a decade earlier, Western media portrayal of the Iraqi leader has been singularly negative.

In the West, we are overwhelmed by Saddam's enemy-ness, even while he was a captive. But the Iraqi leader was not the first to receive this treatment. A recent *Guardian Weekly* article noting the fiftieth anniversary of the Suez War, by Jonathan Steele and Ian Black, draws parallels between British demonization of the nationalist Egyptian leader Gamal Abdul Nasser and his Iraqi counterpart half a century later.[5]

I never met Saddam Hussein, and although my life was never thwarted or threatened by any action of his, the mere mention of him somehow unsettled me, too. His face conjured up no inspiration, no willingness to converse, no capacity to comfort, no source of information, and not much curiosity. His rule was displayed in extravaganzas like the mass wedding at the Palestine Hotel, volleys of bullets at public reviews, and construction of the largest mosque in the world. Yet he seemed to be an impoverished man.

A few others and I, writers and filmmakers, tried to portray Iraq's human face in order to arouse a more reasonable and realistic view of the country so that we could have a fair debate about Washington policy toward Baghdad. Twenty million people lived here. We stood to benefit from their experiments in civilization, from their companionship, from their energy and wit. They would make good partners in peace and development, art and science. Today they are lost to us. They are not named people we can share humor and passions with but simply casualties, sect members, and "insurgents."

Throughout the blockade, Iraq was Him!—just as the crude Shia-Sunni divide is meant to represent Iraq under U.S. occupation. Saddam Hussein took responsibility for Iraq's modern history and achievements in health and education as well as its military expansion. But he was also behind the fiasco in Kuwait, the failings of Iraq's minorities, and the UN siege. He aroused U.S. interests in the Middle East, and aggravated Israel's insecurity. His image was easy to embellish and exploit.

Saddam was omnipresent inside Iraq. And from his lofty status there, reinforced by a strong military, he took up Pan-Arab causes. (Again the parallel with the Egyptian leader, although the two men were not allies.) The manner in which the Iraqi chose to project Arab national values could be seen by others as threatening: demand for Palestinian statehood; protection of oil resources. Those could be dangerous. Indeed, those positions surely contributed to Israel's and Washington's determination to do away with Him![6]

The Man Who Needs No Name

Him! I found myself adopting the appellation all Iraqis used when speaking about their president. As they whispered a comment about him, the citizens of Iraq reflexively lowered their voices and raised their eyebrows. Their president was a haunting presence. He hovered above everything and everyone in Iraq.

That so many people avoided mentioning the man's name and simply uttered "Him!" was an indisputable sign of the fear he had hammered into them. Frankly, the expression was ominous, and it frightened me. Iraqis tried to avoid any reference to him altogether. It was not always so, just as Iraq was not always America's nemesis.

On my first visit to Iraq in 1989, following the cease-fire with Iran, I found people refreshingly optimistic about their country's future. The war was over, and it was time for some democratic reforms and open parliamentary elections. Saddam Hussein himself had announced these would soon take place. Grateful that the war had finally ended, Iraqis may have been ready to forgive his executions and intolerance and his blunders as a military leader.

In those quiet months when hope was rekindled, people recounted their leader's escapades with some pleasure. They recalled his habit of appearing unannounced in a humble neighborhood and entering the home of an ordinary family to meet with them and eat from their table. It was well known how he welcomed delegations of common people petitioning him on local matters as they would a family elder. He sought out the lowly worker and dedicated mother, they said; he dropped into a school unannounced and gave a lesson to a class. He often drove his own car through the streets of the capital. He reportedly asked penetrating questions when he visited engineers and scientists at their work sites. On television, the president demonstrated the merits of brushing one's teeth. He visited the widows of martyred soldiers. He invited common people to come and sit with him and tell him what they needed and what their worries were. He let old women put their arms around him and pinch his cheeks. He asked them to sing their traditional songs to him. He asked women if their husbands were kind to them. He joined a line of dancing young men. He spoke the thick Iraqi dialect that his common people used. He rested his forearm on the shoulder of civil servants as he spoke with them, conversing about their work. If a worker offered a proposal for a project, he turned to his secretary to note the details. The expert was invited to the palace for further discussion; a grant would be awarded. To his public, Saddam could appear to be an affable and simple man, not very different from them. (Just as whimsically, he might do something unspeakably brutish.)

This kind of populist character can be appealing. It certainly pleased many Iraqis. Most important, he assured his people that Iraqi oil was a national resource and that no foreign power would never, *ever* be permitted to own and control it.[7] Saddam Hussein convinced Iraqis of this. They loved him for it.

The Iraqi dictator never instituted his promised political reforms after 1988. Instead, he plunged the nation into another war, and after that, more hardships, more enmity, more dissent, and therefore more executions.

"How is it that we find ourselves with such brutish leaders time and time again?" ask Iraq's bewildered, hapless citizens. "In all our history, we have been ruled by iron-handed, stubborn men—fighters more than thinkers," remarked one woman. "Why have we always had harsh and unkind leaders? We are a civilized people, highly educated. What is wrong with us? Such a progressive people, yet we have bad leaders." She and her friends had no solution, although they knew the widely accepted explanation, namely, "Iraqis are so fierce and independent as individuals that it takes a particularly overbearing leader to control us and channel our energy."

"Each of us can be heavy-handed and obdurate," many Iraqis agree. "This is our character. The one among us who is the most domineering becomes our leader." Their fellow citizens concur; compared with Egyptians, Syrians, Gulf Arabs, Indians, or other Asians, they are a fierce people. If so, they say, only a fierce leader can rule them. And if this is really the case, they are surely doomed as a nation.

Saddam Hussein was a major political figure in Iraq beginning in 1968; ten years later, he became president. Most Iraqis knew no other leader. "What does it matter what I think about him?" asked a youth. "I am just tired."

His people's opinions were more diverse than we might expect: "He is a great Iraqi." "He is my president." "He is a monster." "He is a folly." "He is a king." "He *thinks* he is a king." "He thinks he is Hammurabi" [Babylonian king, 1792–50 B.C.]. "He never listens." "He's just an uneducated farmer." "He was never a military man." "He has no knowledge of law and no respect for law." "He is bold." "He made Iraq great." "He is unafraid." "He is a reasonable man." "He is a man of the people." "He thinks everyone is his enemy." "He loves Iraq." "He loves war." "He is our leader." "He is the only Arab nationalist left." "He is the only Arab leader willing to challenge Israel." "He stood and fought against thirty-three countries. That's something, isn't it?"[8]

The former dictator was so omnipotent and his personality so intrusive that barely a day passed without a presidential decree or a radio announcement or a nationalist quotation from him. Publicly and privately, Iraqis could never forget

Him! From birth to death, the life of every citizen was somehow circumscribed by Saddam Hussein. He was there with his directives, declarations, awards, receptions, parades. He was found on television screens, on the cover of a newspaper, in school texts, and in office memos. Even when they reflect on their woes, his people cannot forget Him! It was his decision that precipitated their misfortunes in 1990, leading to the embargo that continued to plague them for more than a decade following the humiliating war.

Whatever his sons did, whatever the generals decided, whatever budget the university got, however wheat production was increased, wherever a new bridge was installed—all Iraq's policy decisions ultimately went back to Him! Good and bad, the source of everything in Iraq was Saddam Hussein. This is the nature of totalitarian rule.

At another level, the majority of Iraqis held the United States and Britain accountable for their misfortunes. They were convinced that Iraq was misled, or entrapped, or betrayed by their "friends," mainly Britain and the United States. Yet they recognized that they, too, made mistakes.

Since this ruler was the final arbiter over everything in their lives, his mistakes were behind the country's failures. Saddam erred in attacking Iran. He erred in assuming he would permanently enjoy Washington's favor. He erred in his judgment of America's response to his claims over Kuwait. He erred in allowing his troops to occupy Kuwait as they did. He erred in subsequent negotiations, in interviews with mass media, in holding foreign workers as hostages. Iraqis had more than two decades to think about these mistakes.

Not a Matter of Disinterest

As a trained anthropologist, I knew I never needed to directly inquire about this country's leader. I merely listened. Ample comments were volunteered. Remarks were casually voiced when his image appeared on television, when we passed one of many portraits on billboards and walls across the country, when we heard about another tragedy or passed the site where his eldest son Uday was riddled with bullets.

No one shrugged with disinterest when it came to Him! Invariably some reaction was aroused: defense, loathing, stillness, anticipation, or embarrassment. I sometimes detected a feeling of uncertainty, a feeling of being put on the spot.

In public, everyone was obliged to assert his or her loyalty. Silence was not an option when it came to Him! The unfortunate citizen felt: "What can I say to assure others that I am a patriot, a loyal follower, and an unquestioning admirer of our noble leader?" The result? A tiresome flood of praises for their ruler's wise guidance: "We have accomplished more in the last twenty-five years than in the past century." "Thanks to our leader, Iraq is a steadfast Arab nation, uncorrupted by blah, blah, blah." "Our leader saw how western powers were consolidating control of global resources when he . . ." "Our great and generous leader has decided to grant amnesty to all those Iraqi sons who return to the motherland." It was incumbent on a citizen to join in the approbation. In word or deed, each man and woman outdid the next. This frightful competition drove the demonstrations, the poems, the sculptures and paintings, the songs and essays in his honor. Every public space was consumed by yet another face of Saddam. To a visitor these portraits appear silly. They insult the intelligence of the Iraqi people. "How many more paintings of *him* do we need?"

Exasperated by the ubiquity of these offending portraits, I put this question to some associates. I doubted if a response was possible. But I was fortunate. My colleagues explained it this way: "The process of aggrandizement starts with someone seeking to ingratiate himself or herself or to affirm their national pride. Who can reply, 'No, we don't need it,' when a union, class, or club director declares he will offer a portrait in honor of the president? No one. The club accepts; the school assents; the department ratifies. To reject such a proposal is to reject the leader.

"Likewise, when a sponsor seeks out an artist to paint a portrait, who can reply, 'No, I cannot,' 'No, I do not like this guy, and I will not put my name to his glorification'? No one dares. The same with the poet, the musician, the sculptor."

His appeal to a foreign delegation worked the same way. A protocol officer would ask, "Do you wish to meet our president?" (Certainly every journalist dreamed of bagging an interview with the dictator.) And predictably an audience was arranged, videotaped, and shown on national television. Thus Iraqi citizens witnessed the world paying homage to their leader.

"Those groveling fellows surrounding him are responsible for this," my companion spat. A pitiful, unstoppable process, it destroyed personal dignity and doubtless did little for the ruler's genuine popularity.

Why Is He Still Here?

As his years of rule went on and on and on, theories spread as to how he survived. The western press was certain he did it by crushing any opposition and with the help of a pervasive security organization. No one could deny the system's effectiveness.[9]

Iraqis and many of their fellow Arabs also subscribed to a conspiracy of complicity between the unconquerable Iraqi leader and the American intelligence agency. They theorized that Saddam's survival was ensured by foreign agents. "The Americans are keeping him in power," they charged. "The CIA supported his coup in 1968. Americans gave him arms and intelligence support against Iran; Washington supported his militaristic ambitions; it encouraged him to become a regional power; U.S. administrations excused his murderous solutions; they said nothing when he crushed the communists; the West supplied him with chemical weapons to use against Kurds and Iran." Many Iraqis argued that their leader could not possibly have foiled the many internal plots to overthrow him without outside intelligence support. So, the reasoning goes, a foreign power must have been protecting him, informing him of coup attempts, and pointing the finger at ambitious generals or other culprits. Remember, they warn, "Your foreign companies installed Iraq's electronic intelligence system and his personal security system. There wasn't an inch of his palaces that western intelligence agencies had not mapped. They know his security codes, hideaways, and escape routes. How can U.S. satellites fly across our land able to read car plate numbers yet cannot find Him!"

Why would Washington want to keep the dictator where he was? Indirect control of Iraq and the region, they retort. The Americans needed to buy oil and sell arms. They had to control Iraq. First they kept Iraq at war with Iran. Then they precipitated the Kuwait thing. Then the embargo. To keep sanctions in place, they needed Saddam. "Sanctions will remain until Saddam is removed," said Madeline Albright. Bill Clinton too.

Apart from any conspiracy beliefs, after a decade of the punishing, grueling embargo, Iraqis had ample evidence that the United States and United Kingdom really didn't care how Saddam Hussein treated his people.

A Local Theory

If you spend much time in Iraq, you begin to feel there may be some validity in that theory. After 1993, the Iraqi ruler was unable to appear in public except at well guarded official functions. But his top brass, civilian and military, were known mortals with families, friends, and personal habits. The movements of the inner circle were no secret. The public knew the identity of the president's mistress. Family members appeared in public. He received foreign delegates inside his palaces. He continued to invite ordinary citizens for private council and fellowship.

The conspiracy theorists believe that their president's whereabouts could be readily accessed by an outside intelligence agency intent on locating him. And, the reasoning goes, they had not caught him because they really didn't want to.

According to the same argument, U.S. policy toward Iraq also served a wider goal of maintaining global control. The bully Saddam was an asset to the Americans because, as long as he appeared to be a threat, Kuwait and its wealthy neighbors purchased billions of dollars in U.S. military equipment. At the same time, Iraq was presented as a warning to others who might assert their national interests over the U.S. agenda. The message: Raise your head as he did, and you will get the same punishment. Everything works to Washington's favor. Thank you, Saddam Hussein.

Differing Opinions, of Sorts

Within limits, Iraqis could argue publicly about their leader's policies.

A: Today the Americans bombed Basra. They say they are defending their aircraft. Humph. The president is right to refuse the return of the UN-SCOM spies. Just as we said, they were indeed spies. Long after we exposed them, the U.S. press reported that Butler's UN weapons inspection team was loaded with American agents. They have their satellites, their bombers. Alas, we have nothing.

B: We have the right to build defenses. What do they expect? Israel is waiting for another chance to attack. Shall we let it, or Iran, or Turkish troops walk all over us?

C: When I was in the army, we were the best-equipped Arab force in the region. Saddam is right. You get respect only when you have a strong military.

A: We are strong because we have good engineers, and our universities have high standards because we have good brains and we work hard.

B: But would we have any of this without the money that our leader put aside to build our schools and our roads? Saudis have oil, but they don't have universities and scientists like Iraq does. Saddam Hussein built us.

A: We have oil. We built what we needed because of oil income.

B: Yes, and we shall keep it. We have not allowed the British to come in and operate our fields. We control our oil. That is only because of Saddam

Hussein. He said, "Iraqi oil belongs to Iraqis." We will never give it up to the foreign companies.

C: But why should we be watched like we are children? You can't have both. You can't give us good schools and then forbid us to question party decisions. We are expected to cower like animals.

B: We are not like children. We are fierce. We are fighters.

A: Face it. Today nobody gets promoted, even in a hospital, without joining the Baath Party. All the ministries are now oozing with incompetent people who sold themselves to the Party. My brother retired rather than join.

C: It's the sanctions. We had good people running things before the embargo.

The Leader of a Formidable People

Iraq is not a big country. Yet within three generations it became highly modernized with a skilled, educated, and forward thinking middle class. I met so many fine people in Iraq who cared about their country, who worked tirelessly to raise their children and hold on to their dignity. Iraqis proved to be perceptive, ready, and capable. They had much to contribute to the development of a strong civil society.

Seeing this professionalism and noting the basic goodness of the majority, one could not help asking: "Did no one listen?" The reply was swift and unequivocal. "No. He didn't listen. He just did not listen to anyone."

How could that be? He held council; he invited delegations; he made himself accessible to a wide representation of citizens; he took pride in reaching out to the common man and woman.

"He only *seemed* to listen," declared Iman despondently. Iman is one of those ordinary Iraqis who met the president face-to-face and spoke with the leader privately. Not once but several times, Iman was invited to offer her opinions directly to Him! Iman made suggestions to the president about reforms to television programming, about reaching out to expatriate Iraqis, about cutting back on favors to party members. She spoke frankly about the corruption, the complaints of women, and rampant emigration. The president did not interrupt her.

Iman was a dedicated Iraqi nationalist, although not a Baath Party member. She was convinced that Iraq could achieve much, much more. She used her opportunities with her president to speak candidly about some of Iraq's domestic problems. As she recalled those meetings, she shook her head dolefully. "He paid close attention to what I said. But he didn't listen. He really didn't listen to anyone.

This may explain many political blunders—the holding of thousands of westerners working in Iraq during the autumn of 1990, the military blunders of the war itself, the detonating of some of Kuwait's oil wells, the excessively long press conference with ABC's Diane Sawyer, and other missed media opportunities.

Iraqi policies became erratic at the height of the crisis in 1990 and following the bombing. Their representative at the UN was on record as saying: "My president says, 'No, we will not allow, not accept, not agree.'" A few days later, we would hear that the Iraqis had capitulated. The Foreign Ministry had to direct its attention to damage control. Two years after the war ended, according to inside sources, the Foreign Ministry felt it had made some progress. "We have finally convinced him that it is best that he not appear on foreign television and that conferences with delegations be kept brief." In other words, "We convinced him to let us handle things." These ministers and aides never gained complete control over policy strategies, but on the diplomatic side, things were improving for Iraq as the 1990s came to a close.

After the 1998 bombing ordered by Clinton until 2001, when the Bush administration began talking about an attack against Iraq, Iraq seemed to move with new determination to reshape its foreign policy, especially vis-à-vis the United States. Although deeply angered by UN Resolutions 661 and 986, which took control of Iraqi revenues and exploited the isolation of the nation, Iraq exhibited a more studied approach—not conciliatory, but rather more realistic. Instead of saying, as Iraq's UN representatives did when Washington was threatening harsher measures, "We want to trade with the Americans. We can be friends as we were before," Iraqis stepped away from the United States and Great Britain.

Earlier, Iraqis had sought to assure their enemies that they bore no enmity toward the U.S. administration. After 1998, Iraqi officials abruptly abandoned their conciliatory posture and openly called the United States and Great Britain aggressors, and they announced that they would be awarding their UN contracts to other countries, to people who had stood by them.

Iraq began to defy the U.S. blockade, sending oil tankers out through the Persian Gulf. Many of these ships were boarded, and their cargo was seized by U.S. frigates, but the Iraqis continued, and some shipments reached their destinations. Iraq also began to court neighboring countries, notably Turkey, Syria, and the United Arab Emirates, but also Vietnam and South Korea. Iraq facilitated the travel of its pilgrims to Saudi Arabia for the Hajj and established a dialogue with Iran. Iraq entered into trade outside the UN scheme, finding partners willing to engage in private commerce that bypassed the embargo. Gradually Iraq had reestablished diplomatic relations with dozens of countries, and many foreign embassies had reopened in Baghdad.

By 2000, despite U.S. intransigence and continued hardships and uncontrolled corruption, there was general acknowledgment that the embargo was crumbling and the American plan to "contain" Iraq had failed. All this was possible, in large part because Iraqi ministers and others in the inner circle had managed to persuade Saddam Hussein to confine himself to military matters and his private business, leaving trade, finance, diplomacy, and the media to them. In return, they would attribute all their successes to him.

No one can confirm this is what happened. But anyone with firsthand experience with Iraqi ministers would have to agree that some of these men could competently guide any ship through the hurricane that battered Iraq over those years. Apart from a few high-ranking party officials who were reputed to be incompetent and self-serving, the cabinet of ministers was composed of highly competent, sophisticated people—acknowledged experts in key fields. Iraq's ministers of oil, trade, health, foreign affairs, the directors of the Central Bank and the national airlines, and several ambassadors were all articulate, able, urbane people.[10] They were highly trained and hard working; all proudly participated in shaping modern Iraq and were credited with its extraordinary social and economic achievements.

Had Saddam Hussein and his sons somehow been cleanly removed, could these men have saved the nation? How did they manage to build modern Iraq, and take it through the calamitous embargo still intact? We need the memoirs of men like Tariq Aziz, former foreign minister, and deputy prime minister, trade minister Mohammed Mehdi Saleh to reveal the inner workings of Iraq's governance during the thirty-five years of Baath rule. Many of those who could write that history are either dead, ailing, imprisoned, in exile, or in hiding.

Two Camels at the Border: A Story

Two camels met at the Iraqi border, one on his way into Turkey, the other entering Iraq.

"Why are you coming to Iraq?" asked the Iraqi camel.

"Don't you know?," replied the other camel. "We have so much terror in Turkey. If they suspect I am a Kurd, it is worse. I am sure Iraq will be safer. But what about you? We heard things are getting better in Iraq; you have more food, you are even using cell phones, and you have a few computers nowadays. Why are you heading for Turkey?"

"Well, you know life is hard," replied the other camel. "No one trusts anyone here. Saddam has declared that all camels with three testicles are under suspicion."

The Turkish camel looked under the belly of the Iraqi camel and said, "But you have two balls. That is the normal number! You have nothing to worry about."

"Ah," said the Iraqi camel. "In Iraq, we kill first, and then we count."

Sabaar and the Boys at the Office

Journalists call them "minders." Foreign reporters assume any Iraqi office they deal with is crawling with spies. Anyone at the Ministry of Information (MOI) who accompanies journalists must be a police informer. Don't trust them.

My experience was different. I had been coming here since 1989. I worked with these men year after year. This was a vital ministry, true. I did not doubt its directors had considerable political clout and worked with security. Doubtless, information from here was sent to the Ministry of the Interior and the police. Probably the sharpest employees were assigned as intelligence agents. One assumed that secret police were everywhere, noting everything. Dangerous, suspecting eyes followed everyone, Iraqi or alien. Everything we did was likely documented somewhere. But MOI's Press Center itself was primarily staffed by low-level civil servants. They surely worked harder during these years of crisis than other ministry clerks.

I was not naïve. Saddam Hussein's intelligence had a fearsome reputation. At the best of times Iraq's secret police were plentiful and active. With the nation at war, it was reasonable that any foreign visitor was suspect. Washington openly declared its goal of toppling the Baath leadership. Iraq could expect infiltration through any route. Journalists and scholars, relief workers and poets would not be exempt.

Like every journalist in Iraq, I was obliged to register at the MOI Press Center on my arrival.[1] As a reporter, I relied on these men—minders, facilitators, or guides—to arrange any interviews I needed with officials and to accompany me to that office. Beyond the city limits, when my minder produced his pass at a checkpoint, the soldier waved us through. I did not consider these employees hostile or devious. I expected they were debriefed about any unusual inquiries we visitors might engage in.

I became aware over time that Sabaar and his colleagues had young families, sick parents, broken cars, and bills they could not pay. They often had to work on Fridays. And they could not resign. Occasionally one managed to persuade a foreign journalist to help him obtain a visa, and he slipped out of Iraq. Esho phoned me when he reached Chicago; Muayad got to Madrid. Sometimes a woman resigned to take care of her family, but Iraqi men had few options.

The five men I worked with at the Press Center in 2003 were the same clerks I met in 1991. Some I liked; some I didn't. On an assignment, we spent long hours together, crossing the city to seek out an official, a manager, a doctor. We sometimes spent an entire day together, traveling to a distant farm or school, interviewing locals, then returning to Baghdad.

Their names were Sabaar, Hassien, Ali, Mohammed, and Karim. None said much about his personal life, and none asked me about mine. But over our twelve-year association, we learned some details about each other. Before the embargo, each possessed a car and a bungalow. Some lived with their parents. Only Karim was unmarried in 1991. As the blockade progressed, three of these men took a second job helping a relative manage small shops. They kept their press office job because it gave them extra food rations. At the office they were obliged to wear a suit and tie; Hassien's clothes were always newly pressed, his shirt fresh, his ties dazzling. Sabaar seemed to have just one suit (it sagged on his shoulders; the cuffs were frayed); Ali liked yellow shirts or dark blue shirts with a sharply contrasting tie.

Over the years, I actually looked forward to seeing these men. Our reunion at their office was always warm, although their welcoming smiles did not mean their lives had improved.

No one was assigned to this department on the basis of party membership or because they were Sunni Muslim. They qualified because of their foreign language skills. Hassien had studied Spanish; Ali, English; Mohammed, Russian. They were interested in world history, or they were inspired by an unforgettable book read at school. Had there been no war they would surely have traveled abroad. Some might have joined the foreign service or a university faculty. I once asked each man what his first career choice had been: Mohammed had intended to become a teacher, Ali a journalist, Hassien a foreign service translator, Karim a travel agent. Sabaar had wanted to work for a publisher.

Wars intervened. Instead of moving to Barcelona or London, each man found himself at a desk, assigned to the busy Press Center.

When Iraqi forces invaded Kuwait, the international media became a priority for the MOI. Although they failed to make the impact they wanted, Iraq's leaders (rightly) judged that their struggle against the embargo was going to be a media war. Hundreds of journalists from around the world were pouring into Iraq to cover the crisis; camera crews and writers needed translators and guides. The MOI became almost as important as the Foreign Ministry.

Sabaar, Hassien, Ali, Mohammed, and Karim were among 15 to 20 men assigned to the foreign press. They were smart, energetic, coolheaded, and broad-minded. They seemed to have only a basic knowledge of their guests' countries. Except perhaps in military service, most had not traveled widely within Iraq. This would change. As far as I knew, none had been beyond Iraq's borders.

I found these men cheerful companions, adaptable to my moods, ready to pursue my often-inexplicable lines of inquiry. Their wards were sometimes impetuous; they had to silently tolerate very bad manners from some foreigners they accompanied.

From a Love of Literature to Guiding Journalists: MOI's Press Center Transformed

I met Ali and Karim in the autumn of 1989 when this was a small public relations office for intellectual, cultural, and sporting events. In the course of a single month, the al-Marbid Poetry Festival, the Babylon Music Festival, and the Pan-Arab Medical Association conference were hosted in Baghdad.[2] The men's jobs were to receive guests and arrange the program.

Two years later, they found themselves assigned to the foreign press center; this office expanded to fill the entire ground floor of the MOI building; satellite dishes were planted on balconies and in courtyards. CNN's Peter Arnet and ABC's Ted Koppel came through here.[3] Activity at the center waxed and waned according to political vagaries. A lull did not last long during those years. A new diplomatic confrontation, an ultimatum from Washington, another Security Council vote, or a bombing brought a new rush of journalists. They needed to dateline their report "Baghdad." Some filed their stories from press center phones; others took a taxi out of the country to prepare their dispatch on the assumption that inside Iraq they would be censored.[4] Whenever Tariq Aziz, Iraq's foreign minister, then deputy prime minister from 1990 until 2003, gave a press briefing, reporters dashed to the conference hall in search of a front seat. Aziz was good "copy." During political lulls, correspondents pumped their minders for an inside scoop. When there was no political action, they might try a human-interest story—a begging child, a hospital ward. Without exception, every reporter in Iraq dreamed of an exclusive with "Him!" Nothing would win a journalist more recognition than an interview with the hated dictator. Sometimes a journalist admitted he was in Iraq solely for this. And if no reply came from the palace within a fortnight, he left. CNN and Reuters set up permanent offices at the center in 1991. By 1998, they were joined by a dozen others—Korean, Turkish, other Arab agencies, Brazilian, European, and American—radio, print, and television.[5] Bombings always attracted journalists.

Sometimes weeks passed when no foreign reporter was seen. While the blockade silently did its killing in Iraq, blood spilled more graphically elsewhere and took the headlines.

The translators lounged in their quiet office in Baghdad those days, amusing themselves with stories of their departed quests. There was the *Guardian* reporter who was frequently heard parroting, "Saddam, yah, Saddam, good man!" (He vigorously, although in vain, pursued the minister in search of an interview with Him!) There was the lady from Brazil with two colors of hair; she was here, she said, to collect Iraqi art for an exhibition in Prague. Why Prague, they did not know. There were priests and nuns who inquired only about Christian Iraqis. One correspondent asked every Iraqi he met what they thought of Saddam. To the MOI clerks, it was not a dangerous question; it was silly. One ABC network producer arrived in Baghdad boasting about the "exclusive" he had; a week later, he had slipped away without his promised special audience, too chagrined to say good-bye. Budget-conscious freelancers sidled up to the network journalists seeking a free phone call. All the Press Center staff pitied the Canadian reporter whose dream it was to be in Iraq but who fell ill on his second day and had to be bundled into a taxi and sent home.

From the outset of the Iraq crisis, CNN was the media star. In the early 1990s it had a staff of three hardworking women and men. All eyes followed the tall, sturdy CNN camerawoman, dressed in her white jeans and jacket with her shirtsleeves rolled above the elbow. Iraqi staff amused themselves with speculations about whether she was lesbian. They rarely saw the British TV team; everyone supposed they were in Iraq solely to cover a coup d'état, whenever it might materialize. Those foreigners rarely left the bar at the al-Rasheed Hotel. In 1998, the crew departed without their coup.

Sabaar and the rest of the press staff had seen them all—the bossy ones, the know-it-alls, men in search of fame, those lured by the $1,000/day danger pay, the flirts and hustlers, the cowards, and the timid, poetic types.

Karim admitted he had grown to prefer moments of crisis to periods of quiet. Iraq was in perpetual crisis. Quiet times were no more than interludes in the months and years of raging storms that battered Iraq remorselessly. They felt more nervous on those calm days. They knew it was no more than an interlude.

The inevitable renewed crisis brought journalists back for a week or longer, en route home from the Congo, Colombia, or Sri Lanka. "Get over to Baghdad. Go via Amman; it's the only way in. Saddam is up to his old tricks. See if you can get a story on that scurrilous son of his. Remember, everything is censored, so carry the story by hand to Amman."

Sabaar's office sprang to life once more; his men worked around the clock, crisscrossing the capital, on the road south to Basra or north to Mosul. They found themselves unwittingly caught up in the rush to meet deadlines, in the excitement of the search for more evidence, testimonies, and expert opinions. Tired stories were revived—an epidemic of breast cancer in young women, a bombing in the "no-fly" zones, a seized shipment of computers, the escape abroad of a high-level official, rumors of more executions by Him!

The press aides adroitly managed to put their own questions to the visitors. "How does the world see Iraq now? Is public opinion abroad shifting? Did the memorial anniversary coverage of the victims of the Amariya bombing reach the United States? Which countries are still with the Americans? Do your people say anything about Israel's role in Washington's Iraq game? What position does your main opposition party take on Iraq?" They tried to sound impersonal. (Don't we all make this effort?)

In the early years of the blockade, these men trusted visiting journalists to tell the truth—a concrete graspable truth. They were certain that foreign visitors had an "inside track," that we really knew what Washington, London, and Tel Aviv were up to.

From the Iraqi side, they expected that some reporters would write straightforward realities: how Iraqis were suffering, how educated and reasonable they were, how they felt no ill will toward the American people. They could not ascertain which journalists were really anti-Iraq and which were not. They could not believe that editorial offices abroad replaced a correspondent in Baghdad if they found him or her sympathetic to the locals or that an editor could (and did) alter what a reporter wrote. They were uncertain how influential the freelancers could be, although they saw how independent reporters seemed to grasp the issues best, traveled frequently to areas beyond the capital, and worked the longest hours.

Underlying every exchange with these Iraqis was the question "When do you think the embargo will end?" Sabaar and his colleagues asked all of us, "When will it end?" I was convinced that his question was more personal than political. The men may have been directed to poll us. Yet they could not veil the personal anxiety on their faces as they waited for the answer. Once or twice I replied: "Look at the embargos against Vietnam, against Cuba." I did not have the heart to admit to Sabaar that I could not see the end of the Iraq siege. I myself could not imagine how it could go on for another three or four years, yet I also could not see real efforts against the embargo by the American public and not a hint of a crack in the U.S. position.

Patriots in the Media War, Then Observers

For the first three years of the siege, Sabaar and his colleagues appeared to sustain their energy and their belief that they could make a difference, politically, through their work with us.

As the embargo wore on, Iraqis privately became less forthcoming. They did not refuse to meet us, but they were distinctly cool. The press officers argued that this was wrong. They urged citizens to speak frankly about their hardships. They pressed men and women to allow us to photograph their tattered clothes, wasting bodies, useless water pumps, and cracked car windshields. If a journalist needed him on a Friday, Sabaar lost his only day with his family in order to help. These men were as dedicated as the journalists they assisted. They believed media was the essential weapon in their redemption.[6]

Inside the Baghdad Press Center, one often felt it was the hub of the universe. Reports from here were being transmitted to every part of the globe. We believed the entire world's attention was focused here. Correspondents seemed confident of their importance. So Iraqis working closely with us must have believed we could reverse the tide. Their observations told me this: "American people are different from the government. If they know the truth, things will change." "The Europeans intend to override the Americans and force the UN to lift sanctions. Is it true?" "If Carter is appointed special envoy to Iraq, will the Americans drop the sanctions policy?"

Sabaar and the others at the Press Center continued with their duties. It was clear by 1997, however, that their energy and their trust in the international press were fading. Physically they were weaker. Family and health problems became their priority, although they tried not to show us. They knew how bad things were across their country. Iraq was on the verge of famine, and warnings to the outside world were not being heard. The medical situation was catastrophic, and there was hardly a whisper outside over the rising deaths.

Only months earlier, the UN Security Council had passed Resolution 986 and instituted the food-for-oil program. The plan did not gratify Iraqis (see chapter 10). Ali said it might help. Karim and Mohammed were cynical. Others were just too weary. The men debated endlessly among themselves.

One by one, their cars failed. They began to arrive at work in a bus. Hassien could not confirm an early morning pickup because his phone at home was broken. Everyone had lost weight. Both Sabaar and Karim now had white hair. Like every Iraqi, these men searched for medicine. Each had an ailing relative. Each had been to a funeral that week. They could no longer avoid mention of personal difficulties. Once when I came to the office to pick up my exit letter, Ali and Mohammed slipped pieces of paper into my hand; on each was the name of a specific medicine. "If you can find this, please try."

By 1999, no one asked when the sanctions might end.

Who Wants the Hospital Shift Today?

I could not have gone to the hospitals year after year like these men did. Since 1994, after news finally reached the outside world about the rising death toll, Sabaar, Hassien, Ali, Mohammed, and Karim were assigned to accompany journalists and delegations wishing to visit hospitals. They had no choice. They returned time and time again to those dreary halls and smelly wards.

Peace and solidarity groups had succeeded in drawing international attention to Iraq's health crisis. Foreigners had to witness the ruined lives firsthand; journalists added health reports to their agenda.

Once I accompanied Hassien as he guided three newly arrived reporters through a cancer ward. I had seen the "objects of interest" before, so I stood aside, observing the group with the MOI clerk. Since the doctor spoke English well, Hassien stood beyond the circle of curious, hushed visitors crowded beside the physician. "This child could die?" More cases of miasma . . ." "Medicine is unavailable." "We lost two this week." "Infections, contaminated water, cooking accidents, car accidents . . ." "No ambulances." "Local health centers closed." "No polio in Baghdad since . . . " "No food." "Medicine is not available . . . not available . . . not available . . ." The doctor spoke with professional calm. It was her eighth interview in a week. Finally, she concluded with a sigh, reluctantly, wearily, half-heartedly, "It's the sanctions." (It's not *really* dirty water or lack of medicine or malnutrition. It's the sanctions, stupid.)

Hassien followed the group to the next bed. A grandmother was stroking a child's forehead. She sat up as the tour approached her. She tried to smile as cameras focused on her.

The facilitator from the Press Center stepped forward to translate. His voice was steady, his expression numb: "She says her grandson is four. He has been here since last month. She says, 'We ask God for mercy.' Her village is in Yussefiyya. She says, 'The doctor says there is no medicine.' She says, 'The baby's mother died two months ago.' She says, 'I stay with him in the hospital.'"

A year later, Hassien was translating the same cursed questions. Answers were unchanged, too. More cases were doomed; the ungodly death toll was higher. Sabaar and the rest of the press staff hated the hospital shift.

Doctors and other hospital staff protested to the Health Ministry. These tours must cease. They are useless and humiliating. In response to their demands, some hospitals set up a small "exhibition" ward for the convenience of journalists. This helped relieve the doctors, but not Sabaar and Hassien and Mohammed. Their duty was to assist the foreigners.

The Agenda Is Adjusted

Journalists would continue to arrive in Baghdad because there was sure to be another confrontation with the United States. Iraq refused to allow the weapons inspection team into the country unconditionally.

Meanwhile, Iraq was permitting a number of foreign carriers to fly in, flaunting U.S. threats. In the Persian Gulf, U.S. policing ships found they could not combat black market trafficking by sea, so extensive had it become. In the north, thanks to the Kurdish warlords, oil traffic into Turkey was unhampered. In Baghdad, traders were arriving in larger and larger numbers, ignoring the ban on trade.

With this, Sabaar's attention shifted to visiting delegations of sanctions-busters, athletes, artists, overseas Baath Party delegates, and Arab Youth clubs. Three tourist groups had arrived: one was from India, one from Belgium, and another from Germany. Jordanian and Syrian solidarity groups were arriving more frequently. The office hosted a team of Austrian-Arab doctors who would assist in a series of operations. A conference of travel agents from nearby Arab countries was under way and needed help. The al-Marbid and the Babylon festivals were on the Press Center agenda every autumn; the twice-annual Baghdad Conference in Solidarity with Iraq, convened by Tariq Aziz, was coming up.

Ali's oldest daughter married. Karim divorced. Sabaar and his wife had a seventh child. Hassien still had one boy but was troubled by a falling out with his brother. Mohammed became a very devout man, and his English greatly improved. He was appointed to the Iraq News Agency office at the UN in New York.

On my last visit, all of them remarked on how my hair had become white, too. They knew that I had divorced, that I had had surgery for breast cancer, and that I had moved out of Manhattan. They seemed to care more about these things than the copy I had brought to Baghdad of my interview with the UN ambassador or my report on the downing of the U.S. spy plane over Iraq.

Spring 2001—no one asked when the sanctions might end.

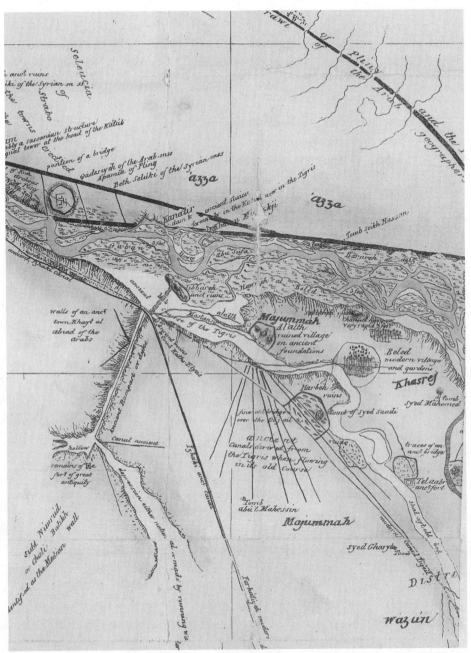

Nineteenth-century Brithish map of the River Tigris. *Source:* Map of the River Tigris (1850), *Memoirs of Baghdad, Kurdistan and Turkish Arabia 1857,* by Cdr. J. F. Jones, Bombay, 1857. Reprinted by Archive Editions Limited, UK.

The Heaviest of Battles

The heaviest of battles broke out last night
with the echo of explosion.
A halo widened around the moon.
A rose, not feeling the safety of fragrance,
raises its head.

You are getting ready, preparing tea for the half-supper,
singing a song about corn ears,
feeling happy with what's left of the salary
like wet hay in your pocket.

When the heaviest of battles began,
you said good-bye to me and
turned to another and kissed a third.

Unknown soldier 1, 1991, Iraq

17

The Pharmacy

I don't really know how I was able to face these women and men year after year. Perhaps being Arab myself, I felt enough like family that their admonitions could not alienate me. We were family. Indeed, being from the same tribe enhanced my commitment even as it increased my pain.

I was also an independent writer. Thus I was able to affirm my own moral agenda as well as my professional program. And I was clear in my resolve to do what I could to see the sanctions lifted. I would not leave before that happened. Being freelance had its limitations. Independence had some advantages as well. No editor in New York or Los Angeles could reassign me to East Timor or Bolivia. In any case, by 1998 and that confrontation with Fathel, the poultry farmer, I had already endured and survived a lot of emotional upheavals.

Going into Iraq back in May 1991 in search of the few people I knew from a better time had not been easy for example. One reunion was with Mahmoud al-Sagar. He was a witty fellow; he liked to deliberate with me, to challenge my devotion to Iraq, to expose my naiveté. We had a lot of joyful evenings together, his family and me.

I felt compelled to see them. Even if we are on contrasting sides of misfortune, we mustn't retreat. Seeking out one's friend is a way to say, "I have not forgotten you." It counts.

I arrived in the crippled, dust-filled, and numbed city to find the entire telephone exchange down. (Bombs took out the system the first nights of the attack.) Al-Sagar's pharmacy, I remembered, was near the statue of a noted mid-twentieth-century poet, Marouf al-Rasafi. "Of course! Find the bard, and I will locate Mahmoud."

I drove up al-Rasheed Street and slowly circled the bronze statue in the middle of the square. I spotted the pharmacy and stepped out, walking apprehensively toward shops lining a colonnade. A sallow-faced man reached the pharmacy just ahead of me. He paused at the door, a box clasped in his fingers. I waited.

The bombardment of Iraq ended after forty-two days (January 17–February 28, 1991). After that came the rebellion that swept through southern Iraq. Then the Baathi military's counterattacks. Then silence.

Across the country, people moved in a daze. The war had not been a war but a shameful routing. How could Iraq have marched into Kuwait as it had? Silently or openly, the country admitted they had erred. They had been badly beaten. What lay ahead? What would the UN do about the embargo? No one knew.

In the shade of the colonnade near the pharmacy door, two thin Moroccan men leaned against a wall. I spoke to them. They had come to Iraq during better times, they said dispassionately. They had worked on farms while Iraqi men their age fought Iran. Now these foreign workers were unemployed. Their Iraqi currency was worthless outside; they did not know where to go. (Possible claimants to the UNCC? See chapter 10.) They didn't expect their own government would repatriate them. Nearby, on the pavement, a woman sat in front of a tray of cigarette packs she hoped to sell. She looked hungry.

Meanwhile, the man holding the small colored box seemed reluctant to proceed into the pharmacy. When the white-coated proprietor behind the counter noticed him, the visitor shuffled forward. He pointed the box toward the pharmacist. The man needed a refill of medication for someone in his family. This was probably not the first drugstore he had visited that day. He looked embarrassed, tentative. He paused, one foot on the pavement, one foot inside the shop. Proceeding deeper into the drugstore would mean he had farther to retreat, and he could not bear walking out empty-handed.

The druggist seemed to know which medication the man was seeking. He did not pretend to check his supplies. He shook his head. "Sorry, I have none left." The response was all too familiar. The would-be customer managed a feeble smile, then withdrew.

Mahmoud al-Sagar managed to greet anyone arriving at his pharmacy with the same quiet sympathy. He spoke to his sad customers as if things were normal, as if he hadn't turned away other supplicants—thirty, forty, sometimes more, a day. Each wanted medicine for his child, for his wife, for his father-in-law, for himself.

"I've nothing to sell them," the pharmacist said, turning to me finally. I had stepped in after the old man left, and I stood in the middle of the shop. I glanced at its shelves. Not only were they empty of medicines but they were also dusty. No one had cleaned them since the bombing. The attacks were especially heavy here because of the nearby telecommunications tower and two bridges at either side. They were frequent targets of the American bombers.

Barely a week had passed since al-Sagar had reopened his shop. He had replaced the plate glass windows and cleared the floor of debris. But he couldn't restock his shelves. Whatever medicine boxes you saw there were decorative. They had nothing in them.

Every day since the bombing ended, the pharmacist had come here. Gazing at Marouf al-Rasafi's statue, he and other proprietors met in the portico to take tea together, then shuffled into their shops.

"I must come to work. I must try to help my people," he had told his wife in reply to her urgings that he stay home.

That had been in April, the eighth month of the embargo. In every house, people were falling ill. Government pharmaceutical stocks were depleted. Some drugs arrived from Turkey through black market channels, but al-Sagar said they were unreliable. "I won't deal with smuggled drugs. Most of it is expired or adulterated. I sell what's left of my stock. That's all." He shrugged.

Before Sanctions, There *Was* a Life

From our first encounter, I was attracted to al-Sagar for his wit and sagacity. Two years ago you could find me at his house at least once a week. How he enjoyed repartee and playing with language. He had been a violinist, skilled enough to play in a chamber group in Baghdad. He was a great enthusiast of European classical music as well as English literature. He nurtured his children's interest in western civilization. He wanted the whole family to speak English well. But he was emphatic that none of them—three girls and a boy—should leave their homeland to settle in the West. "Our country has far more to offer you," the man insisted.

All the family was university educated, including Umm Sagar. She was proprietor of a lingerie shop and worked there every day. Haidar, their son, and Mona, the youngest daughter, were still in school when I first met them in 1989. Haidar was studying agriculture, and he intended to become a forester. Everyone had high expectations for Mona. She was an outstanding student.

Leila, the oldest daughter, helped her mother in her shop and her father at the pharmacy. She had failed to persuade her father to let her emigrate to Australia. Neither had she given up the idea.

The family had a modest collection of paintings, all of them by contemporary Iraqi artists. Al-Sagar was proud of those twenty or so canvases. He could tell me a story about each of the artists.

Everybody in the house drove, using one of the three family vehicles. They kept two dogs as household pets. Fresh flowers from the garden were always set in the vases around the house.

Al-Sagar's middle daughter, Shedah, was engaged to Nazir, a love partner. A refugee from Lebanon in 1982, Nazir had become a successful restaurant manager in Baghdad. After Shedah accepted his proposal, he endured two years while the rest of the family persuaded Mahmoud to agree to their union. Nizar hadn't been to Lebanon for nine years, nor to Brooklyn, where a brother and sister lived. When these New York relatives learned I would be traveling to Baghdad, they urged me to see Nazir. That's how I met the whole family. We spent many delightful evenings together during my visits in 1989 and 1990.

Then the war came.

The Agony of a Pharmacist

With almost no medicine manufactured in Iraq, pharmacists and hospitals relied heavily on imports. Medicines were to be excluded from the UN embargo. But with foreign assets frozen, Iraq had no funds to buy anything from outside, not even drugs.

No one would sell to Iraq on credit after Washington warned that commercial exchange with the country was illegal. U.S. patrols of the Persian Gulf prevented ships from docking in Iraq, and flights had been banned since the beginning of the embargo, effectively blocking off Iraq from the rest of the globe. Doctors and pharmacists were shocked by the blockade: "Orders of drugs, books, and medical equipment paid for before the embargo and ready to be shipped were held back! We wrote the companies whom we had paid in advance, but they still refused to ship the order! Medicines! Medicines!" they repeated in disbelief.

Iraq's Ministry of Health showed me documents for $50 million worth of medicines whose delivery they were awaiting. Iraq had paid in advance for the drugs, and the shipments should have been en route when the embargo was imposed. "The shipments were intercepted by the Americans. We do not know what happened to them. Maybe they were stolen, maybe resold, maybe dumped in the sea. We were never compensated either," said the health official.

"This is the policy of your democracies?" Iraqis asked. It was unfathomable. "We could not believe Europeans would do this. Even when we found a friend outside who would put up the cash for critical drugs, medicines for chronically ill patients, for people who would surely die or suffer terribly if their treatment was interrupted for long, we were refused. The drug companies wrote us saying, 'We are not permitted to send you anything.' Period."[1]

It took many, many months before Iraqis realized the embargo was part of an overall military strategy.[2] It was a campaign specifically designed to reverse all their accomplishments. Iraqi doctors, officials, and ordinary citizens were astonished at the temerity of their former business associates, teachers, and friends abroad. "Not a single country would challenge the Americans who fiendishly policed this blockade. For seven horrendous years, until 1997, everyone turned his back on us. No one would send even basic medical and educational supplies!" Through the entire decade to follow, I would hear these bewildered cries again and again.

During the 1991 assault, it was dangerous to move around the city. Mahmoud al-Sagar's children urged him to close the pharmacy. While bombs rained on their city, al-Sagar and his family slept huddled together in a hallway of their house. They ventured into their garden in the mornings to whisper to their flowers and trees. They went there when nature called. The enemy had bombed the water system, cutting off water supplies to 5 million people in the capital. Like everyone else with a small garden, al-Sagar and his son dug a toilet among the bushes.

Meanwhile the pharmacy sat in darkness facing the poet's statue. Al-Sagar imagined his shop flattened by bombs and the statue in shreds. As soon as the cease-fire was signed on February 28, 1991, the pharmacist and his daughter went to the shop. They cleaned away the rubble and brought in whatever stock they had stored at the house. Al-Rasafi was unharmed but covered by fallen debris. Within two days the pharmacy was opened, and whatever medicines al-Sagar had were sold. "Snapped up as if this place were some cheap bargain basement," grumbled the old man. The same panic had occurred at every pharmacy across the city.

Although he now had hardly anything to sell, the pharmacist continued to arrive at the shop every morning. He simply needed to get out of the house, to determine something in his own life, even if it were only to cross the city and sympathize with his people.

A Reunion, So to Speak

Al-Sagar is tall and thin. His eyes are constantly flitting, following sounds and movements around him. In contrast to his eyes, his body moves lazily.

Thanks to al-Rasafi's statue, I had found my way to the pharmacy. I was delighted to find him alive. I beamed with pleasure as I moved toward my friend. My smile soon dissolved. Al-Sagar stared back at me without saying a word. His eyes were filled with an awful pain.

I stood there in the gloomy space. Another customer came in and departed. Al-Sagar still said nothing to me. His glare was searing. I wished I could retreat and slip away.

Silence. When would he ask when I had arrived, what I was doing here, or how was the family in Brooklyn? So I began. "Nahida was worried," I quietly offered. "They were unable to phone."

"Phones?" he cut in. This was his first word to me. Al-Sagar had lost his playfulness, but his wit was undiminished. "You have phones in America?" he said stingingly.

I had remained standing in the middle of the pharmacy. Perhaps realizing I was determined not to leave, al-Sagar gestured to me to take a seat. He moved a battered, limp floor fan closer to me. The instinct for hospitality moved his hands, but he was still reluctant to speak.

It was up to me. After all, I had invited myself here. I suppose I really wanted to know how they fared through the bombing. The answer was apparent. So I inquired about his youngest daughter. She had been studying for her college entrance exams when I last saw them. "Did Mona graduate?" I ventured.

Now al-Sagar turned slowly to face me. After an awful stillness, he spoke. His voice was almost inaudible, but it had a thunderous tone. "We are starving," he hissed. "All of us," he added, to emphasize that he was speaking for his beloved country. I felt as if I had been slapped. I fell silent. What could I offer in the way of help or solace?

Looking around him, the old man continued. "Everything was smashed. Everything." He stepped back as if checking an urge to hit me. But his anger was like a smack. "You've heard bombs like that, haven't you?" He knew I had not.

Interrupted by a Soldier

I was saved further humiliation by the arrival of two customers. The first was an unshaven, middle-aged man wearing a suit that sagged badly around his body. Al-Sagar stepped forward to meet him as if to shield the man from me. He took a piece of paper the customer handed him and read it. He then handed it back, shaking his head. Shortly, another customer appeared at the door. He, too, held out a small bit of paper to al-Sagar.

My eyes stayed on this young man. He was a soldier's age. His thick brown hair was clipped with the all too familiar military precision of a soldier. He was no more than twenty-five. His face was soft, and he had warm gray eyes. He wore a tropical suit, soft blue in color. It was freshly pressed. On his feet were black sandals. His right arm rested against his chest. With his free left hand, he reached around to his trouser pocket and pulled out an empty vial. "Do you have this as well?" he asked quietly. He acted a little embarrassed. The druggist took the bottle and read the label as he walked past me and behind the counter.

The handsome youth now looked at me. But he did not speak. His right arm seemed to be troubling him, and he winced and pulled it toward him as if it were a child and he were urging it to be still.

My eyes were focused on the fresh white bandage wrapped several times around the young man's right wrist. Below, there was nothing. He had no hand.

When al-Sagar returned to the soldier, he held a second vial and offered it to him. About the prescription on the paper, he said nothing.

The soldier took the vial. He was not ready to leave. Slowly and with tenderness he lifted that arm away from his shirt. He held it toward the druggist, as if to introduce the subject of his missing hand. Perhaps he wondered if the older man had noticed the freshly bound stump. Al-Sagar said nothing, but the youth wanted to talk. They spoke in Arabic.

"I was in Kerbala for some days," he volunteered. "This is what I got there."

Al-Sagar shuffled nervously but said nothing.

Kerbala is the city south of Baghdad. Together with Najaf, it was a center of the popular rebellion—news reports call it the "Shia uprising"—that erupted across the south at the end of the 1991 bombing and ground attacks. The rebels were armed, probably supplied (although not backed up) by the Americans during their advances overland. They were no match for Saddam's troops. If they had been promised some kind of additional support from the Americans, they were betrayed.[3] They must have fought hard, since it took twenty days for the Iraqi army to crush them. The deadly counterattack was another example of the mercilessness of Iraq's leaders.

Standing before me was a member of that ruthless military force—a wounded young soldier. He, too, had come to al-Sagar's drugstore in search of medicine.

With his bandaged stump, the young man lifted the corner of his shirt, and with his remaining hand, he pushed down the waistband of his trousers. "Here, here is one bullet hole." I could see the small dark mark on his flesh below his waistline. Raising his shirt now, he pointed to a spot on his chest. "Here is another. They did three operations on me altogether."

The soldier seemed ready to talk on, but al-Sagar stopped him. "Shame. Lower your shirt. I'll try to get you that medicine. Please."

The soldier smiled shyly. Turning to leave, he nodded a greeting to me. The older man seemed relieved that he was gone. When he took his seat near the counter, he said nothing about what I had just witnessed. (He knew that I had followed the exchange in Arabic.)

"There is nothing to eat," al-Sagar said finally. His voice was cold, disembodied.

We sat in silence until a neighbor, the owner of a nearby cloth shop, appeared. He was carrying a circular plastic tray bearing three small glasses of Iraqi tea. He sat with us as we sipped the hot drink.

If anyone along the street had a few coins to buy a couple of cigarettes from the woman seated on the pavement, or two glasses of sugar tea from the street vendor, they found someone nearby to share this with. There was nothing else to do.

A month after the wars and rebellions and counterinsurgencies ended, some of the city's people had returned to the routine of arriving at their shops by ten in the morning and staying there until dusk. No one knew how long the embargo would go on.

Iraq, fifty-one days before September 11, 2001

Dear Nimri:

I wish you are in good health doing your job in the press and radio.

We opened our CCU, and it is beautiful, supplied with essential requirements to serve our patients. We are striving to update our medical knowledge.

I read your notes about America (unchanging in its policy against Iraq) its work against our people. Yet I want to tell you and if possible, through you, to those Americans who can listen, that Iraq is now recovered from the insult that America did to us and we Iraqis as citizens feel that we are strong enough to rebuild our country and to grasp the best knowledge, in spite of the meanness of the now sunken blockade.

Our summer this year is more merciful, less hot and intolerable; we wish to see you in the autumn. Babies and all my family are greeting you.

Sincerely, KN

July 16, 2001

Facing the Children

If you don't visit the pediatric wards, where do you face the children?

They said we had to travel to Basrah to witness how southern Iraq had taken the full force of the 1991 assault that drove Iraqi troops from Kuwait. "The battlefields are still raw, and the odor of death hangs in the air." This was what they meant.[1]

I teamed up with a Japanese correspondent, Takashita, and we stopped at Kerbala on our way south. The city center lay in rubble. The hospital, too, was damaged. Battles had raged between Shia rebels who had taken over the city and Iraqi troops who would "do their job"—as American soldiers describe their own killing work. The silence of women and men walking past the wreckage testified to their intimacy with martyrdom in this place.[2]

The area around Basrah also lay in waste. Passing through Basra city, I gazed at a ravaged landscape. Many of the city's factories had been bombed. These were not arms depots but food warehouses. Water plants and electric supply centers lay in ruins. City pipelines were laid open by blasts, and water, even in May, flowed freely through the streets. This was the handiwork of the American-led bombers.

Nasiriyya lies on the main route northward to Baghdad. The handsome suspension bridge at Nasiriyya is famous across Iraq. This city is a major center in the south; a few weeks earlier, it had been "liberated" by southern rebels, then crushed; its inhabitants were still in a state of confusion. People we approached did not want to talk with us. They seemed unable to direct us to any official to interview.

Somehow my fellow traveler and I found ourselves in a high school. We were ushered into a classroom of fifteen-year-old girls. The teenagers fell silent when they saw us enter. Yet the room bristled with their excitement. It is not easy for me to forget their bright and welcoming faces. Yes, welcoming. School had reopened only three days before this—three weeks after the rebellion ended and government troops regained control of the streets. Ransacked Baath Party offices were burned, and defaced mural paintings of the president looked onto the eerie streets. Perhaps those charred façades caused people to feel insecure. His portraits were gone—but not Him!

I looked at the young faces in the classroom. Each was flushed with anticipation. Twenty-eight teenagers, the pounding crash of war not yet faded, waited for my companion and me to speak. I was introduced as a journalist from New York.

Wait, I thought. Addressing children is not part of my journalistic agenda. I do not consider myself a war reporter either. I had begun my tours in Iraq to record its people's achievements, to feel the glow of a war's end and to help create bridges between Iraqis and Americans. Instead, I am surveying battlefields, smelling death, feeling some responsibility for the devastation, as if my own body were tainted. Instead, I am standing in a bare classroom confronted by twenty-eight young Iraqis. How can I soften the grief? What can I say to answer their hopes? I hesitated.

"I'm sorry," I finally blurted out.

No one had suggested an apology was necessary. Yet I was overcome, and I uttered these words spontaneously. I willed back a rush of tears and forced myself to speak on. "I was against this war. I believe Iraq was entrapped, then punished and humiliated." I stumbled on. "This terrible war against you is really a demonstration of America's new leadership in the world. It is not about Iraq's ambitions or mistakes. Your country was entrapped, and Iraq is being used as an excuse for the United States to assert a new world order."

The girls remained silent. Had they not understood? Why did they not applaud me for what I perceived as a statement in solidarity with them?

Takashita also took a moral position. But he did not apologize. Instead, he admonished the young Iraqis for the nation's lack of civil awareness. "Your leadership was ill-prepared. You were not given evacuation procedures. Your food supplies were not secured. There were insufficient bomb shelters." The gulf between Takashita and me on one side and the Iraqi youngsters on the other was vast.

My companion and I had no understanding of what the nation had just experienced. Whatever our sentiments, we were free to come and go, free to speak our minds, and free of sanctions. We were not here to lecture Iraqis, especially young people. I was sorry I had accepted the invitation. We were journalists in search of stories. I should be gathering evidence that they were suffering, asking which men in the family were soldiers, which were dead or wounded, if their mothers covered their heads, and how much less they had to eat this month. Two years ago, it would have been different. We might have piled into a bus and headed for a picnic on the edge of the city and gone swimming together in the great Euphrates. What kind of dialogue was possible under these conditions?

Fresh from the Battlefield

After Takashita and I had witnessed the damage in Basrah, we drove north along the notorious, truly ghostly "highway of death" where Iraqi ground forces retreating from Kuwait were pounded by U.S.–led air assaults on February 26 and 27, 1991. Viewing the shells of burned tanks, passing mile after mile of trucks and jeeps, buses and pickup trucks, heaped in disarray along the roadside, we were stunned. The carnage unnerved me, but the silence disturbed me more. The entire landscape was a vast graveyard. It was surely contaminated by the depleted uranium fires and ordinance. I could not see a living soul. I did not want to peer closely to glimpse the corpses hanging out of charred windows or half buried in oily sand.

Because those sights had demoralized me, I had no energy to conduct interviews by the time we reached Nasiriyya. Eventually, a local security officer was assigned to us. He was sullen and suspicious, understandably so. I remember thinking how odd that the Iraqi authorities permitted us to come here at all.

Driving into the city, we encountered the once magnificent Nasiriyya Bridge. It had spanned the Euphrates in a great arc. Now it hung in shreds. Many women and men had died during the barrage of air attacks on this structure, we were told. Bombers would have seen civilians on it when they aimed their guns.

Ten weeks later, city dwellers stepped hesitantly along a wooden pontoon bridge floating on the emerald green water. Enormous clean swathes of metal hung behind them. The twisted steel looked freshly painted. It was the same color as the river. On a mound of mud on the riverbank where pedestrians stepped off the makeshift bridge, a boy was selling cigarettes. Should I ask him why he is not in school? Before bombs, before the sanctions, before the invasion, before the occupation, no children could be found in Iraqi streets during school hours.

There were few cars in these war-soaked streets. A layer of brown dust lay over the city; a burning odor hung in the air. Exploding rocket fumes imbued every street and room that we entered.

In Nasiriyya, as in Basrah, we learned how the bombers had targeted fertilizer plants and acres of warehouses filled with emergency food supplies.[3] The stores were blasted repeatedly from the air until their contents lay in ruins. Water supplies were destroyed as well, more targets for U.S. gunners. The catastrophe that was to decimate Iraq's health system was not apparent yet. But malnutrition had already struck many households, and the water was contaminated. This was just the beginning.

We went to the municipal office to introduce ourselves. I chatted with anyone I encountered during our wait, despite my reticence to record this war. There was no other subject. Electricity had not been restored, so little office work could be accomplished. One clerk told me food was so scarce that everyone had lost weight in these weeks. His wife had died shortly before the bombing began, he said; he decided to ask his two oldest girls, twins, to leave school. He had younger children who needed to be cared for at the house. Another worker volunteered that her husband was a prisoner in Iran. Here she was, in the midst of a new war, while her life was dislocated from the Iraq-Iran war!

In 1989, not long after that war had ended, Iraqis talked about those losses. There were few bombs then; for eight years men had confronted each other in the marshes and on the desert frontier in face-to-face combat. This woman's husband was among thousands of Iraqi men still imprisoned in Iran. Iraq also had many thousands of Iranian POWs. Now more Iraqis, captured in Kuwait, filled prison camps under U.S. control in Saudi Arabia. The south had been through so much more upheaval than the rest of the country. The Iraq-Iran conflict was focused near Nasiriyya; the recent assault was heaviest in the south, and the American-supported "Shia uprising" that was eventually crushed by the Iraqi army happened in these cities and towns.

Getting Closer to the Truth

The southern governorate I was touring included the recent battlefront. It offered journalists graphic illustrations of the damage. We could supply our editors back home with testimonials. "Yes, it had really hurt them. Yes, your troops did a thorough job. Here are some human interest stories to illustrate death."

After Takashita and I had finished our remarks to the secondary school students, the girls were invited to put questions to us. They did not admonish us; neither did they offer testimonials of their war experience. They talked about their country's beauty and its achievements. One girl asked that her nation be recognized for its contributions in science; she noted how interested Iraqis are in language. "We are proud of our schools and museums and hospitals and monuments of civilization," she added. A classmate asked me what my impressions of Iraq were, since I had visited the country three times. I replied that I was deeply impressed by the universities and research centers, by the international art exhibits, by the highly educated middle class who lived as comfortably as Americans did. I had been moved by the design of the ancient Mustansiriyya Madrassa, an exquisite architectural wonder, a prized museum

and cultural center in Baghdad. I told her about the many Iraqis I met who
had traveled to my country, how many women I met who were professionals
—teachers, doctors, archaeologists, and office managers. I was impressed, I
added, by the government's care and commitment in preserving the art and
monuments of Iraq's early civilizations. I recall saying, "I feel that Iraqis share
more with America in its standard of living and its joy for living than any other
Arab country I have visited."

"Then why have you destroyed this?" retorted the fifteen-year-old. Her reply
was gentle, but her voice was very clear and her tone was firm.

I did not try to answer. I could not. I later realized that the child was refer-
ring not only to the immediate past but to her future, too. A society's dignity
and progress include a clear sense of the future, and to build a future, one needs
hope. I did not grasp all this at that moment.

I could not imagine that what we saw in these weeks marked the first infiltration of Iraq. It lay the groundwork for a later, deeper assault on the nation.
The American-led campaign against Iraq that had been initiated with these
bombings would be augmented by years of punishing, decimating, humiliating
economic, intellectual, and social embargo. The blockade was to prove itself
an ugly, poisonous disease—its murderous capacity unseen—descending on
Iraq. It would soon penetrate every house in the nation, ripping its social and
economic life apart, causing infinitely more damage than had been done to the
four families represented by those raised hands whose men had perished in the
battles.

Children Grow Older

I doubt if I could face those young people today. They would be nearly thirty
years old now. They would have a great deal to tell me. Most would have begun studying the Qur'an and wearing headscarves as a sign of their increased
piety—piety embraced by a search for hope, piety grasped to sustain them
through year after year of suffering, piety that emerges from questions on the
meaning of our existence. Some of these children would have finished college.
Some may be ill with cancer; their children may have died in infancy or succumbed to one disease or another. Some may have fled Iraq. Perhaps a few have
become beggars. I refused to return to Nasiriyya to gather those statistics.

In subsequent visits to Iraq, I stopped at another girls' school, al-Aqeeda, in
Baghdad. There, too, the students wanted me to know of Iraq's achievements in
technology, arts, and science. "The Americans think we are barbarians, that we

live like desert nomads, that we have nothing," Raada charged. Several students at al-Aqeeda, one of the top-ranked schools in the country, made a point of telling me about their holiday excursions to Paris, London, and Los Angeles. When I visited the homes of two girls whose parents invited me to dinner, I could have been in any cosmopolitan city. Those modest Baghdad residences had private libraries; contemporary art hung on their walls; the scent of jasmine rose from their gardens. What distinguished these homes as Iraqi were the paintings, all by Iraqi artists, and the fragrances in the evening air.

Other young Iraqis I faced no longer lived in their homeland. Tens of thousands of them reached Amman, Beirut, Ankara, London, Toronto, and Los Angeles. They were mainly from the cities—Basrah, Mosul, and Baghdad—from the urban middle class. And everyone I met had left home unwillingly.

Their first stop was Amman, Jordan, or Ankara in Turkey. There they joined lines of applicants at visa offices, filling out forms. "I'll go anywhere," said a despondent young man. He was making immigration applications at eight embassies in Amman. "I don't even care if it is America." Imagine! He didn't *even* care if America accepted him. His name was Yasser. "I do not want to leave Iraq," he added sadly, his voice low and angry. "After the war I stayed in my country while my school friends left one by one. But there are no jobs. There's no future for me there. Many of my classmates are already in Australia. Maybe I will go there."

I found two sisters in Amman whose father, an archaeology professor, had died from cancer shortly after the war. They had already been accepted as emigrants to Canada and were awaiting the final papers. Neither showed interest in her new homeland. I asked if they were reading books about Canada during these idle months. "No," they shrugged. "We have to leave Iraq. That's all."

As the years passed, I sought out Iraqi children less eagerly. I did not need to. They were increasingly vocal, much more critical than their parents and their teachers. They felt cheated. They discounted the errors of their government and focused instead on the American campaign to destroy their country. "Our president was your friend. You bought our oil. Our scientists studied in your universities. You sold us guns to kill Iranians. Why are you destroying our future?"

Being less reticent than their parents, these Iraqi youths would be excellent ambassadors abroad. Since they were not in any way associated with the Baath Party, they could not be held accountable for its wrongs. They could not be dismissed as Baathi lackeys. They had not yet served in the Iraqi military. They were not employed in government service. They were untainted and clear thinking.

Touring the world, speaking to the public, meeting other young people, they might make a convincing case against the blockade. If they could speak to the world with the same moral conviction and knowledge that I heard them utter, they might counter the demonization of Iraq by western media. Schools, religious centers, and clubs would surely be receptive to these youngsters. Yet they were not recruited. Perhaps U.S. policy makers and partisan journalists feared the redeeming power of these young people.

Washington never issued visas to this class of Iraqis for lecture tours and seminars, as far as I am aware. Foreign doors were open only for immigrants ready to work hard and keep their mouths shut while they toiled toward their citizenship exam in the "free world." Bright, proud Iraqis who might campaign on behalf of their country need not apply.

No More Healthy Children

The healthiest ones left first. The rest entered the West's consciousness only around 1995, four years into the sanctions. By then large numbers of children were perishing. These were not the bright-eyed and inquisitive girls I met in Nasiriyya Secondary School and al-Aqeeda in Baghdad.

The Iraqi children who came into our field of vision, still limited though it was, sat on the broken pavement offering to shine our shoes; they stood at traffic lights with their hands out. They were not in school but more likely in a hospital. They stared at us—groaning, gazing with empty, tired eyes—from soiled hospital beds, in rooms filled with repellent odors.

By 1995, a trickle of foreign humanitarian delegations arrived to examine Iraqi children, victims of the embargo. It took years to break through the propaganda screen erected by the pro-war lobbyists. Most journalists, especially Americans, focused on political stories, misdemeanors of the Baath, odious debates at the UN. News stories about Iraq's "crumbling infrastructure" were so superficial and so impersonal that the term actually contributed to a complete misconception—perhaps intended—of the crisis.[4] Infrastructure was roads and bridges. This was a society of 20 million educated and capable souls, a civilization, and a nation with a major role to play in the world. Its collapse was a policy success.

Those independent-minded investigators who began to recognize the scale of the disaster focused on children to demonstrate the calamity under way. Reports about the spread of diseases, the malnutrition, and the cancers found their way out of Iraq. A surprising number of sympathizers actually feared visiting Iraq.[5] "How did you get your visa? How will Saddam let you in? Aren't you afraid of the secret police?" Some, few though they were, fortunately insisted on witnessing conditions for themselves.

By 1996, embargo-related deaths of Iraqis had reached well beyond a million.[6] Increased malnutrition and disease infecting the entire population was alarming; health needs were soaring while care was less and less available. Hospitals found themselves with no medicine, inadequate diagnostic tools, broken machines, and no blankets or bed sheets.

Faulty light fixtures and broken heart monitors did not interest those visitors. Nor did the rising number of auto accident injuries, diabetics, or dog bite victims.

Newly arrived humanitarian investigators were drawn to the children. Lines of foreign delegates insisted on seeing the pediatric wards. Some carried pouches of useless sample drugs gathered from unenthusiastic friends and religious people; others clutched teddy bears they had collected. Many of the visitors sobbed over the small, wasted bodies of little Iraqis. Men and women alike became inarticulate and stammered as they searched for a recipient of their petty gifts (see chapter 8).

I occasionally followed a group of those solicitous pilgrims to a cancer wing or a contagious diseases ward; invariably, the guests were horrified, then embarrassed. Some wept openly. Others reached out smiling, trying to comfort the wasting little bodies. They asked the doctor what the patient's name was, how old each was—anything to suppress their own discomfort. Some took photos, while others slipped into the hallway to sob in private. Soon the group shuffled out, relieved to end the ordeal.

For most visitors, a tour into Iraq under embargo was their only experience with the country. It was their first encounter with the Middle East as well. The delegations were never large. But being in Iraq, they met up with sympathizers from other countries and worked together to take on the media giants who colluded with the pro-blockade policy makers. Italian, British, Greek, Belgian, and American teams such as Un Ponte per Baghdad and the International Action Center under Ramsey Clark, Sara Flounders, and Brian Becker worked with Kathy Kelly's Voices in the Wilderness, the Organization for Peace and Solidarity with Iraq in Belgium, and Jean-Marie Benjamin's project for Iraq in Italy and France. They gained the confidence of enough Iraqi officials to proceed, few as they were. The last time they were together was in late 2002 for the Baghdad Conference in Solidarity with Iraq.[7] These supporters knew the power of a young healthy Iraqi representative. They grasped the political potential of Iraq; they saw behind exaggerated western claims of a new Hitler in Saddam and Iraq's military might. They were engaged in a campaign to bring balance to the political debate about Iraq. For the most part, their work was overlooked in favor of gratuitous humanitarian reports where children seemed to be the only victims.[8]

Only Dying Ambassadors Succeed

The Ministry of Health capitulated to public demands and directed hospitals to publicize children's suffering. Some of Iraq's medical staff disapproved. They objected to exhibiting their sick and dying patients to visitors; they might be seen as incompetent or uncaring. But they found themselves overruled. Officials had by now understood how these pitiful boys and girls lying in broken hospital beds were less threatening than healthy, defiant children. In their dying weeks and months, unable to utter anything but cries of pain, these little martyrs might become more powerful ambassadors. So the tours went on, despite protests by physicians.

Successive delegations of witnesses arrived to "observe the deadly sanctions" at work. Tour leaders—doctors and government escorts accompanying delegates—tried to interest them in a regular hospital ward where they might encounter a man with kidney failure, or a heart attack victim (coronary cases rose by 400 percent between 1990 and 2003), or a woman with bone cancer.[9] An intestinal blockage (many are fatal), or the sight of burn victims (these, too, had soared, due to faulty electricity and makeshift kerosene stoves used after the war), or casualties from auto accidents (caused by faulty car brakes and stoplight outages or blowouts), or crippling eye diseases could not stir foreign visitors. They needed to see children to feel war's terror. One could not deny that the sight of those little souls had a powerful impact on visitors.

Perhaps at the government's insistence, hospital press tours were augmented by meetings with health and industry ministers, hospital engineers, and medical researchers. These women and men furnished not ideological arguments but empirical evidence of massive suffering. Their testimony statistically proved the breakdown of a health care system. Along with their memory of a dying child, each witness carried away sheets of facts (even when paper was scare), assembled at great expense, about the extent of the bombings, the reappearance of once eradicated diseases, and summaries of studies linking environmental toxicity caused by the war to rising cancer rates. Eventually UN agency reports validated the findings of these missions; even then, few politicians would be swayed by the alarming statistics.

Successive delegations visited Iraqi hospitals. One year their focus was on childhood cancer. The next year they sought out examples of birth deformities. Iraqi doctors grew more impatient and objected more strongly to the parades of peeping foreigners, first because their work was interrupted and second because they saw no concomitant relief, no fresh supplies of essential medicines. United Nations Security Council Resolution 661 held fast.

I gave up my occasional tours of hospitals after an encounter at Mosul Maternity Hospital in the northern city. At the entrance to a pediatric ward, an attending physician barred my passage. With her arms folded defiantly across her chest, she dared me to proceed. She did not care if I were a medical expert, a journalist, or an anti-sanctions activist. "What have you brought with you to help us?" she asked, her eyes fixed on me in rage. When someone who had accompanied me intervened to explain my mission as a journalist, she shot back: "What good will it do to tell you anything? When will the sanctions be lifted?" For her, this question was the only one worth discussing. Her voice was almost a whisper, seeping out through her rage. "When will the sanctions be lifted?" she repeated, stepping toward me.

I backed away and found myself confronted by another hospital official but one with a more kindly face. This was the hospital's chief engineer. He was less truculent than the pediatrician. On his urging, I followed him to the hospital's basement and into the boiler room. He pointed out the broken lift, the leaking pipes, bits of electrical fixtures, and a room full of useless air conditioners. In this inert pile of machinery lay a demon waiting to take its toll. Not only was medicine insufficient. The entire health system of Iraq was falling into ruins. It would soon be completely unable to cope with hundreds of thousands of people yet to be stricken.

On my return to the United States in the spring of 1995, I began to speak out more determinedly against the siege, augmenting that physician's rage with my own. I voiced the plea of that hospital engineer. I decided to approach possible donors for funds to mend the decrepit facilities in two regional medical centers. With just $10,000 we could make some really life-saving repairs.

Even five years into the embargo, not many American audiences would sponsor a talk about Iraq that did not highlight the misdemeanors of the government. Hardly any invitations would permit an appeal for humanitarian support, since sending help was thought to be dangerous. The few groups I managed to speak to needed real drama to overcome their fears. My reports and photos of soiled mattresses, broken elevators, and mangled air conditioners did not touch any hearts. At one such lecture my host candidly counseled, "No one will donate money to repair beds or replace mattresses and light fixtures. Just tell us about the children and ask us for money to buy medicines."

If they did not perish or emigrate, these children grew up. And soon these sanctions-hardened youths scorned our searches for yet another infrastructure story.

Basic Black

"Oh, yes, college girls are dressing in black. It's the new fashion," replied Hanna icily. The young woman lifted her head to signal her termination of the interview, then turned away. ("So there, Miss Nosey Journalist.") I was dismissed. There was nothing else to say.

I was not satisfied. By 1997 black had become a fashion across Iraq. Absolutely everything in the country had been transformed by the creeping pestilence called economic embargo. Besides being thinner, with more white hair, people dressed differently.

Seven years into the blockade, I noticed a change in how girls dressed. Students continued to wear standard blue-and-white striped uniforms. But increasingly more college girls and women working in ministry offices, schools, and shops were dressing in black: black slacks, skirts, and blouses, sometimes set off with a colored scarf or vest.

Hanna was right about the "popularity" of black, if we can call it that. But the choice of black outfits in Iraq did not originate with fashion-setters in women's wear. No magazines had broadcast this trend among young Iraqis. Neither had Muslim clerics declared a *fatwa* on color. Perhaps someone had unloaded a shipment of markdowns from Iran?

On a casual stroll through Bab Sharge market in old Baghdad, I understood. In shop windows and on the street I found racks and racks of black garments. Most were skirts, some ankle length, some with buttons, some with pleats, some ribbed, some narrow and sleek, others in an A-line. There were also stands of vests, blouses, shirts, jackets, and coats—all in black. Women's shoe stores stocked mainly black shoes. Handbags were black, too.

Of course! These garments were mourning clothes! The trend sweeping the country was "death."

Women who passed near me examining the racks were not on any recreational visit. They were not shopping for something fancy for a concert, festival, or wedding. Each must have lost someone in the family—another victim of sanctions. According to custom, Arab women display the family's grief with black attire. They eschew colored clothes for a week, for forty days, or for a year, depending on their relationship with the deceased. Sometimes a brokenhearted wife or mother vows to dress only in black for the rest of her life.

One needed no better evidence than this of how many young Iraqis were in mourning. With 1.5 million (or more) deaths caused by sanctions between 1991 and 1999 (in a population of 20 million), along with deaths from normal aging or disease, every Iraqi would have twenty or more deaths in his or her immediate circle of friends and kin. Take my own social network of 130 or so Iraqis. (This is an estimate of how many people I had sustained contact during those same nine years.) They were not subjects of my research but friends—women and men to whom I felt close. Among them, eight had perished—"sanctions-related deaths." None were babies, and none had died of old age. Eight out of 130! (In the same period, two among my network of friends and family in the United States and elsewhere had died.)

I knew those Iraqi women and men well enough that I was personally moved by their deaths. I saw the women of each family in her normal clothes, then noted the change into black mourning garb. Bahija was one. I was with her one day when she answered her home phone. "Another death, in my husband's family, in Basrah," she confided. Her shoulders dropped. "I am never out of mourning, given the combined size of my family and my husband's. Hardly one forty-day period is over and another begins."

People saw little point in shopping for bright outfits. In any case, many families had become so poor that new clothes were a luxury. It was entirely sensible and enterprising for girls to use their colored accessories with basic black. Created from pain, young Iraqis found themselves in step with the black fashion craze overseas.

After six or seven years of the blockade, many jokes were circulating about Iraqis' massive misfortunes. What appealed to them was the privacy these jokes afforded them. Much of the humor was based on idiosyncratic Iraqi words that were definitely not suitable for prying cameras.

They had talked to journalists half their lives. They had smiled, pleaded, quantified, testified. Then they had stopped. "Let the journalists and television crews run after the billowing *abaya* of our village women," say these wizened youths. Iraq's rural ladies are by tradition less patient with intruders.

These Iraqi women must have felt vindicated when, before long, the world's hungry television networks would rush to capture the more spectacular blue shroud of Afghan women.

Arguments

consider the infinite fragility of an infant's skull,
how the bones lie soft and open
only time knitting them shut

consider a delicate porcelain bowl
how it crushes under a single blow—
in one moment whole years disappear

consider: beneath the din of explosions
no voice can be heard
no cry

consider your own sky on fire
your name erased
your children's lives "a price worth paying"

consider the faces you do not see
the eyes you refuse to meet
"collateral damage"

how in these words
the world
cracks open

by Lisa Suhair Majaj, first published in *Al-Jadid* 4 (Winter 1998).

19

Empty Playgrounds

Between 1991 and 2003, in the course of my visits to pediatric hospitals, ill-equipped schools, and rundown neighborhoods, and even when walking through the streets of Baghdad or Basrah, I saw a lot of sick, unhappy, and idle children.

I saw little corpses, newly cold, held limply by their weeping mothers, or carried in a grandfather's arms toward a car, taken for washing before burial. I saw newborn infants with badly deformed bodies who would soon die. I saw underweight babies lying in small cots, a row of them, waiting for a free incubator. I saw a boy who had been bitten all over his head by a hungry dog, one of many such cases. I saw a handless girl who had picked up a cluster bomb left by the bombardiers in 1991. I saw the remains of a boy who had stepped on a landmine. I saw a skinny girl burned when a makeshift stove overturned, her sores turning from first to third degree because she was too wasted to restore her body tissue. Then there were the hairless children sitting on their cots in the cancer wards, hollow-faced and waiting.

Somehow, none of those sights troubled me as much as a place without children at all—a playground. Those meeting places had become vacant over the years. Their children's pre-occupations lay elsewhere. Playgrounds sat empty all across Iraq. Playgrounds and parks are meant especially for children to run and screech, slide and scamper. So their abandonment is poignant.

As soon as the war began, playgrounds emptied. As far as I knew, none had been bombed. They were not smashed by missiles or riddled with bullets. They were simply vacant.

I Know I Saw Them Here Once

Wooden and plastic frames, once brightly painted, faded in the hot desert glare of the sanctions. In the countryside, outside schools, in the middle of parks, along roadsides, the washed-out childrenless slides, swings, and frames stood tenantless. They were ghostly places because one remembered the sounds and images that once filled them.

I may not have seen this park or that playground before. Yet, witnessing that emptiness, I see the dusty surface where feet had skipped. I detect the faint sounds each held not long ago and hear the squeals caught in the lift of swings. In 1989, when I was moving through the besieged occupied Palestinian territories, I noted this same emptiness. War emptied playgrounds there, too. They were the first victims. The yards that the parents of Ramallah, Hebron, and Jalazone had set aside for the young to run free were overgrown with weeds, their gates barricaded. I did not know if the Israeli occupiers locked them, or if local Palestinians closed them down, knowing that those exposed places had become part of the battlefield. They were unsafe for anyone, especially old folks and children dilly-dallying, vulnerable, absorbed in their joy.

Only after the Oslo Accord, following withdrawal of the occupying troops, did they reopen, brightly painted and well guarded. Flowering shrubs were planted. Those restorations I saw turned out to be just an interlude; the gates there closed again until the search for justice was really won.

Some Iraqi schoolyards, of course, continued to be used during school hours when children gathered there for their sports period or at lunch break. But the fields looked cheerless and unwelcoming to a passerby. Like the schools themselves, the yards were neglected. It was an achievement if a school managed to have a single soccer ball for the children. For years, if I saw children along a roadside, they were hauling carts of battered propane tanks or sitting at a rickety stand selling sweet colored water, cigarettes, or tea.

Idle in the Hot Sun

Playgrounds are not high on a journalist's agenda when reporting on Iraq. But I had passed them, noisy, crowded, and brightly painted in those two years before the embargo war. I had not forgotten the sounds of life there. After the war, my eye caught a particular playground on a hillock in clear view from the route I was traveling. On the main road out of Baghdad, heading toward Kerbala and Najaf cities, I passed a small hill on my excursions southward. I remembered it well because the crest of the hill was leveled, fenced, and made into a playground with tall trees all around it.

I'd remarked, "What a delightful place for a park, on the ridge, full with trees, and away from the road." Now it was abandoned, like the others. I peered at the remnants of a history with its little people: slides and tunnels, swings and sandboxes, benches and tables, all assembled during those years when government funds poured into recreation, art, and education. Iraqi boys and girls from the neighborhood dashed through there every day. Older brothers and sisters gathered in a corner to gossip or examine someone's find, possibly a magazine or a piece of jewelry, while grandparents sat together watching their little ones. They preferred soft grass to the cement benches that were provided for them. Lemon trees and shrubs lined the paths, and tall palm trees stood like sentinels over the gleeful innocents. Clumps of willow trees offered shade. A guard was always present, not far away, watching, bemused by the children or absorbed in his weeding around a flowerbed. He was on the lookout for lads with soccer balls who, if they had their way, would commandeer any flat field.

Similar to playgrounds worldwide, these parks were built of plastic and fiberglass tubing—winding, sliding, laddering, in and out, up and down—set among shade trees and benches. Some had colorful sculptures situated among the trees, while others were populated by statues of animal characters resembling Disney cartoon dogs, ducks, and mice. They stood firm, anchored confidently while children clambered on and off their comforting, smooth shoulders.

Under embargo the slides and tunnels were still visible, but the skeletonlike toys lay cracked and bleached. The municipal guard never came back after the war. No one knew where he went. Every one of the trees had become stumps. Long ago, they were attacked with saws and axes and carted off for firework by families too poor to repair their electric stoves or unable to buy propane from the market.

Every time I passed that hillock I swallowed hard, seeing it so forsaken. I had not seen a child in it for six years. Or a family. Not a sound uttered from that place. It was as much a graveyard as a cemetery.

Where had the children gone? Surely not all were dead or stricken?

No, but things were different now. The playground represented something that no longer existed, something pushed under by the war. Noel and his family left for Sweden, and Farah was sent to live with her aunt in another country. Alia was gone, dead from lack of medicine. Samira, although barely eight, was working with her mother in the market. Alaa sold newspapers on the road with her brother, and Hanan was too sick to go out at all.

Some of the children who once stretched their muscles and bruised their elbows in these parks must have been rushed into adulthood as soon as the war came, pressed into jobs vacated by the dead and wounded.

They were at work now. You could see them in the streets from early morning with their fathers, pushing a cart, or you found them alone on a curb hawking small things. Some were shoeshine boys who set up their platforms along the pavements where there were people who could afford a restaurant meal passed. If you met these lads in the street, would you say, "Boys, why don't you go to the park to play?" If you dared to question them, they would likely look at you, puzzled or openly hostile. "If you really cared, lady, you might lift the sanctions." Many children were too busy to play or too weary when the day was over, and they wandered homeward counting their takings as they went. Some youngsters handed over their earnings to their mother to help her buy food. Other girls and boys had no home to return to. Either they had been put out and had to make their way as best they could, or they ran away. A few were orphans, so they told us. Girls were sometimes lured into crime, and some lads became thieves, working for others or managing themselves.

"Street children" were unknown in Iraq until the sanctions arrived. The government was embarrassed and dumbfounded by these waifs and didn't know what to do at first. They became so numerous they could not be ignored. By 1998, they were a menace with their thievery and gang fights. So municipalities finally began to build shelters where they could sleep in safety and have a few hours of schooling a day. In 2001, working with Un Ponte per Baghdad (A Bridge to Baghdad), an Italian NGO, Baghdad municipality opened a limited number of small centers for these boys and girls.

So you will understand how thrilled I was when traveling through neighborhoods in Baghdad to see boys who had found a ball and split into teams to hit it back and forth in the dusty street. I didn't care if they had proper shoes or if the streets were dangerous. (I was disturbed, however, that their sisters could not join them.) Traveling outside Baghdad, I was similarly enchanted to watch lads splashing in an irrigation canal that ran alongside the road. They yelled happily as they leapt from the riverbank onto one another in the water. Again I chafed, finding no sisters thrashing in the water with them.

The boys' glee was irrepressible, and I envied them splashing about in the canal. This was the everlasting Tigris nourishing its young.

Postscript, 2004. "They stole our playground," said an eight-year-old resident of Sadr City, Baghdad. He pointed at six American tanks parked in a soccer field near his home. Those were the U.S. occupation forces preparing to confront the growing Iraqi resistance to their presence. The same spring of 2004, another soccer field was commandeered in Fallujah. It was annexed to serve as a graveyard for the city's martyrs gunned down by the occupying army.

Daddy Is Going to the Front

When my leave is over and
I get ready to return to the front,
my little girl embraces my luggage, saying,
"Daddy is going to the front."
I watch her and try to hold back
a tear between my eyelashes.
My mother, meanwhile,
Pours her blessings on me.

"Daddy is going to the front."
Yes, dear one. I am going to the front,
To protect your childhood,
To protect the joy in your lovely eyes.
"When will you be back, Daddy?"
Very soon, dear.
Very soon.

Abdul Karim Salam, 1991, Iraq

20

"Ah, the Border"

The tour bus carrying twenty American college students was parked outside the passport control. This was the Allenby Bridge, the border between Jordan and Israel as well as the main entry point to the "Occupied West Bank."

Jordanian officials were taking a few moments to process the busload of travelers. Nevertheless, the Americans were impatient. Four young men stepped from the bus carrying an American football. Theirs was the only vehicle in the parking area, so there was ample space for them to play. Laughing, they proceeded to toss the ball among themselves. Their friends inside the bus watched approvingly.

I don't know what the Israeli guards visible one hundred meters beyond at the end of the bridge thought. They kept their rifles firmly in their hands.

The Americans continued with their sport.

A lone Jordanian policeman emerged from the passport bureau. Smiling, he nervously circled the frolicking Americans. He hesitated for a moment. Either he was trying to summon the courage to (politely, of course) tell the boys this was forbidden, or he sought to show his appreciation for the American version of football. He slipped back into his office, unwilling to interrupt the Americans' pleasure.

A poignant expression of empire—American empire! Here we were at an international border, a sacred line where many had lost their lives in its defense.

Somewhere, along any nation's frontier, martyrs' blood has soaked into the earth. How many were killed trying to flee? How many perished fighting to enter? How many sacrificed their lives to defend it? For some people, this line marks the perimeter of a prison; for others, it is a glorious threshold, promising fantastic opportunities. It welcomes home the citizen. For those inside, it represents pride, security, hope, or confinement—depending on your politics and class. Above all, a border symbolizes the attainment of sovereignty. It is an especially charged place for those whose sovereignty is frustrated or denied altogether. These Americans playing with their toy football at an international boundary as if it were their neighborhood in Seattle or Miami had no concept of this. Here, out of all the frontiers in the world!

This border is especially poignant for Palestinians. Five of them, including our driver, sat in the service taxi with me a few yards from that cluster of frolicking foreigners. Our eyes fixed on them. I suspect my fellow passengers glared at the Americans with conflicting feelings of contempt and envy. The tension in our taxi grew with each flip of the ball.

No one spoke. We were already nervous over how we might be treated at the enemy gates beyond, the same gates those gleeful tourists would bound through ahead of us. Palestinians face abuse and insults whenever they pass this way. They are crossing into their own homeland. Yet they may be denied entry. Some will certainly be humiliated, delayed, possibly sent back to Jordan. Even after the 1993 Oslo Agreement, Israel controlled all access to Palestinian lands; any visitor, entering through any gate, had first to pass though Israeli immigration and customs. A separate VIP gate existed for foreigners, although a foreign citizen of Arab origin might be directed to the "other" line.

Today Muslims everywhere, especially after laws instituted following the September 11, 2001, attacks on the United States, face the same fear when they leave their home for an overseas trip. The arrogance of the young Americans is as much the face of empire as an Abrams fighting tank, an oil rig, the glimmering façade of an international bank, or a military satellite far beyond your reach, mapping your home from above. Imagine living in your country, hearing an airplane engine or seeing a light in your night sky, knowing it can only be a hostile fighter jet or a spy satellite.

The arrival of flights into Baghdad's International Airport holds immense symbolic power for Iraqis. On many sides, Iraq's borders have been violated. The southern frontier was "adjusted" (authorized in SCR 687 adopted April 3, 1991) to the advantage of Kuwait. The provincial border of Iraq's Kurdish provinces of Dohuk, Irbil, and Sulaimaniyya marks the limit of Baghdad control in the north. Iraq is almost landlocked. Its few kilometers of sea access are at Umm Qasr. There U.S. ships stop and search Iraqi boats at will.

The gateway at Treibeel, on the western frontier between Iraq and Jordan, was the sole friendly crossing throughout the embargo years.[1] In 1990, Treibeel became the primary access point for goods and travelers entering and leaving Iraq. At first, the passport and customs office was hardly more than a shed serving meager overland traffic. Iraq's diplomats on urgent missions had to cross here just like ordinary citizens traveling to Amman for respite or medical treatment. Journalists passed through Treibeel, too, along with a trickle of foreign humanitarian delegates.

"Saddam!" shouted one of the passengers.

It was almost midnight. Nevertheless, her fellow travelers rushed to peer out the bus windows. They, too, saw the huge portrait of the Iraqi president. It seemed suspended in the night air. Seeing "Saddam" meant they had arrived in Iraq! It was their first sight of the country.

Anyone arriving at this post during the blockade had already spent five hours on the pitiable, two-lane road from Amman. Another six hundred miles—ten hours or more—across a windy, almost vacant desert route lay between here and Baghdad.[2]

Tonight's arrivals were American and European sanctions-busting activists. (I had met up with them in the Jordanian capital and accepted their invitation to accompany the group.) We occupied two buses; a small truck packed with gifts of medicine followed. These women and men had joined the meager efforts in the activist community to inform Americans about the duplicitous nature of the UN siege and its deadly effects. Despite their political commitment, for most, this was their first visit to Iraq. The party had left Ramtha, the last point in Jordan, a half-hour earlier.

Treibeel was not a town but a collection of single-story sheds—the passport checkpoint, a customs house, some staff barracks, a health post, tax office, toilets, a currency exchange, and a modest duty-free shop. I saw no café and no sign of shops or houses.

Approaching the border at night, one could barely see a light marking the outpost. The cement arch over the gateway highlighted by the spotlighted painting of Saddam Hussein at its apex signaled one's arrival in Iraq. I was so accustomed to this place that I had ceased to notice just how commanding the portrait was. It was an unmistakable statement to first-time visitors.

This delegation was headed by former U.S. attorney general Ramsey Clark. The well known American civil rights attorney is founder of the New York–based International Action Center (IAC), which had organized the trip, the third of what would become many delegations. Since the outset of the U.S.–Iraq confrontation, IAC had campaigned vigorously (and with few allies) first against the 1991 war and then in opposition to the embargo.

IAC's publications and films offered the first English-language documentation available about the devastation and casualties created by the 1991 war, especially the long-term health effects of depleted uranium weaponry used by the U.S. military.[3] Much later, critics of the Bush administration and the Iraq war would refer to the imperialist goals behind the 2003 American invasion and occupation of Iraq. IAC identified the wider American agenda from the inception of the embargo, spelled out in SCR 661 and SCR 687. Few journalists had studied it carefully, or if they had, they could not grasp its long-term implications and its unprecedented punitive intent. At the time, Ramsey Clark's group was the lone American voice campaigning against the sanctions policy and exposing war crimes of the 1991 assault.

First-Time Visitors

Clark and sixty campaigners had left New York the previous day. They were joined by another ten activists from Italy and Belgium. In Amman, Clark gave a press conference. It was largely ignored by the international media, a common policy toward anyone sympathetic to Iraq. The group proceeded undeterred. Without resting after their international flight, the delegates set out for Iraq by road.

As the vehicles passed under the Treibeel archway, the travelers peered through the darkness into Iraqi territory. A few moments later, they found themselves at the door of Iraq's immigration office. This was the VIP lounge, erected not long before (1996) to receive Iraqi and other officials and foreigners like this group, as well as journalists.

The travelers handed over their passports and were ushered into a spacious air-conditioned lounge. In a moment tea would arrive.

On one wall, no one could avoid looking at yet another portrait of Him! It was twelve feet wide and extended from floor to ceiling. Smaller canvasses, mainly landscapes and all carefully framed, hung on other walls. A splendid collection of modern Iraqi ceramic art, carefully mounted, dominated the spaces between the sofas. Like the small paintings, these were clearly works of art.

In the far corner of the lounge stood the ubiquitous TV; customs agents usually gathered there, especially if a football tournament was being broadcast. Tonight the television was running on mute while the staff attended to our group.

Clearing seventy visitors would take almost four hours. A quiet, smiling man served glasses of sugar tea, and we could use the office phone to contact Baghdad—if we knew someone there who would welcome a call after midnight.

Usually I traveled through here alone. Sometimes I shared an SUV taxi— these replaced the 1980s Dodge sedans that until recently ferried travelers— with one or two Jordanian businessmen or an Iraqi returning from overseas. Then the process took under an hour and I was usually directed to the VIP reception.

Most travelers with Arab passports were checked at a second office nearby.

Shia pilgrims from Lebanon, for example, entered by that route. So did regular Iraqi citizens. There was neither tea nor air-conditioning for them at first, and their possessions were subject to scrutiny. I know, because once when I found myself in that line, I was scrupulously searched. I used that opportunity to note how others were questioned and how their belongings were searched for gold and foreign currency.

A third gate processed transport vehicles ferrying food and other civilian goods into Iraq. Empty oil tankers passed through there as well. They often waited at the border for many hours. The exit line for trucks at the far side of the control center was similarly long. Heading for Jordan, those oil tankers were fully loaded.[4] Apart from shipments of phosphate, nothing but oil could be exported from Iraq.[5] After Resolution 986 food-for-oil was signed, traffic through Treibeel into Iraq soared. Passing long lines of trucks along that route, I began to grasp just how much 20 million besieged people need. The sight of those convoys was the closest I have seen to the eighteen-wheelers roaring along a U.S. interstate.

Passenger cars were sparse at this crossing point; sometimes only one or two arrived in a day. By global standards, Treibeel was probably one of the quietest international crossing points anywhere.

The VIP lounge was pleasantly outfitted, doubtless in part because of the clientele it served. Yet the place was also designed to manifest, in unambiguous terms, Iraq's sovereignty. Treibeel was more than the entrance to the land. It was the threshold into their nation and into their civilization. Whatever hardships the population experienced, this gateway was well maintained. The officers were more than courteous. They were gracious. If a car arrived at 3 a.m., perhaps carrying the only visitor they saw all night, an immigration officer stood at the door or stepped into the small parking area in front to greet the traveler. He was always dressed formally in a suit, a clean shirt, and a tie. More than once, the agent in charge recognized me, although six months or more had passed. "Ah, you are here again. Welcome," he said, smiling, as he took my papers. It was Mr. Hameed.

Exiting Iraq at Treibeel was conducted with similar dignity. Baggage inspections were more rigorous here. Agents searched through the car for artwork, modern as well as ancient, gold, and perhaps other contraband. Once an unusually curious official read a set of my news articles on Iraq in my computer and copied one diskette. Another time I was harassed by three young men who insisted on taking over from the immigration staff. I quickly surmised that they were not local hoodlums but city boys. They were more like criminals of the sort I imagined Iraq's chief gangster, Uday Hussein, commanded. I became alarmed when I saw how the regular officials stood by, apparently intimidated by the intruders. There was no sign of other travelers. No police could be summoned. I was alone, and my driver and I passed some anxious moments before the three let us proceed. Looking back, I am amazed I came out of the encounter alive, since the men had clearly commandeered the outpost. They could have done anything they wished to us there on the edge of the desert, for there was no one to control them.

For a number of years in the mid-1990s, bandits hijacked night travelers—generally they were ordinary Iraqis traveling for personal reasons—and stole jewelry and cash. Sometimes a lone driver returning to Jordan was killed. The route was especially dangerous at night, but sometimes the six hundred miles could not be crossed during daylight hours either.

This was another reason to feel welcomed by the Treibeel authorities. How or if they managed to escape the temptations of bribes and payoffs, I do not know. By 2002, it seemed that every civil servant, policeman, and soldier in Iraq had succumbed to corruption. In earlier times intimidation was political, involving the threat of jail or torture. After twelve years of embargo, coercion was applied mainly to make money. It was not always carried out cruelly or clumsily, as one might suppose, since Iraqis were new to bribery.

Road Tolls

"*Habibi, shlonak?*" the soldier asked as he flipped quickly through the car's registration papers. He smiled warmly as he leaned into the open window: "*Aini,* I see you have a lady passenger today. Congratulations."[6] Without looking at me directly, the soldier continued his chat with the driver. An Iraqi bill slid from the driver into the soldier's hand.

This was our fifth checkpoint since leaving Baghdad's city limits. We had been driving for barely an hour; Fallujah was ten kilometers beyond, and darkness had fallen. His rifle hanging at his side, the soldier had signaled our car to halt. We were heading toward Jordan and Syria, directly west out of the capital.

With Jordanian plates on the car indicating we were destined for Amman, I did not expect delays. The soldiers' interests were not official. I did not need to reach for my passport. Leaving the two men to their exchange, I sat back.

"How's your health, Abu-Chebab?" responded the driver. "Good? How is the wife? Send her my regards." He appeared delighted to see the soldier. He was a regular on the Amman-Baghdad route, making the trip two or three times a week. It's part of his job to know the guards, and the modest payment is part of the fare. The driver waved into the night to a barely visible figure on the verge. The soldiers worked in pairs.

"Come again. Peace to you and your family. Have some tea?" called the soldier, as if inviting us to stay a little longer, even as he stepped back and waved us on. (It is common for an Arab host to invite a passerby to a meal or drink as they separate.) Guard and driver dispatch the routine with thorough good humor. It is a well rehearsed pirouette by now. No threats. No protest. A reassuring exchange on a lonely night.

There was no secrecy in the negotiation, and it took only a moment. A 250-dinar Iraqi note was the standard tip at each checkpoint, and every driver carried a stack of these bills in the pocket of his car door.

The tender from my driver's fingers to the soldier's was barely perceptible. It was dark outside. There was no one watching except the soldier's partner in the pillbox. Why so circumspect? I thought. Could it be simple courtesy?

What's Twelve Cents?

Two hundred and fifty dinars were barely twelve cents at the exchange rate that year. Split between the two guards, each man's share was 125 dinars from each passing car. Every soldier would allocate 25 dinars out of this for his superior officer. That left him 100—hardly enough to buy even a liter of milk, an orange, four single cigarettes, or a glass of tea. How many tips would he need to afford a new pair of shoes for his sister?

To me, twelve cents seemed not worth risking your job or your dignity. But that was me. I had several $100 bills in my wallet when I left Iraq.[7] These soldiers knew how much a visitor paid for the taxi to Amman ($60) and what the cheapest hotel room rate was ($50). At the highway restaurants along this route, where fat men sat at the reception desk counting their day's take, I would hand over 3,000 dinars for a plate of food, bread, and tea. It wasn't unreasonable for a humble sentry along a lonely road to demand 250 dinars for himself and his partner.

Before the blockade, no one felt a need for these kinds of supplements. Unlike his Syrian or Egyptian counterpart, the enlisted Iraqi soldier owned a late model car and his house. He took his family away on holiday. He could help pay for his sisters' marriages, and he could buy gifts for his mother and his favorite aunt.

A New World View

More than poverty had overwhelmed Iraq. Sanctions made everyone a cynic. "Who cares? It's only twelve cents," they would say. "I have to get it one way or another." Each man and woman had to find a way to manage. Refuge in another country was not an option for 20 million people. And if a top Baath Party official needed more, so did the foot soldier.

All faced a bizarre turn of fate. Iraq was still producing and selling its oil. However, this was controlled from outside. Moreover, Iraq's oil income was enjoyed by others (see chapter 10). The dinar was also cheap. Anyone passing this way—journalists, taxi operators, oil truckers, visiting delegates, sports teams, humanitarian workers, even the busloads of simple Iranian pilgrims—had a lot more than 95 percent of Iraqis.

How cheap their country had become for any visitor with dollars in their pockets! A taxi ride across town was only 75 cents, a five-minute phone call to the United States was $2.50. Two dollars would cover a meal of meat, appetizers, soup, and vegetables at a middle-class restaurant. A leather jacket was $15, a 4" x 8" woolen carpet, $80. Golly, with dollars you could buy a fine bungalow in the city for $15,000 that year! With $40,000, you could rebuild and equip an entire school![8]

Yes, Iraq had become cheap—for others. Small wonder that any Iraqi in a position to extract these puny tolls did so. All he wanted was a new shirt or an occasional restaurant meal. He had to help his abandoned sister or another brother.

I understood these men. Bribery was new to them. They did not know how to intimidate a rich traveler. They looked shy; their quiet eyes seemed to apologize for the inconvenience. Through much of that embargo decade, Iraqis were amateurs at corruption, and many could not wear it well. When a taxi driver said that he had no cash, one customs officer sadly asked, "What have you that you might give me then?" (That humility would eventually disappear.)

Spinning Tables of Fortune

Jordanians, many of whom are originally Palestinian, had a lot in common with Iraq. Palestinians knew what injustice was. They, too, had been pounded by an overwhelming military power, humiliated, and their resources plundered. But their sympathy gave way to new political and economic realities after 1991. Because of Yasser Arafat's support for the occupation of Kuwait, tens of thousands of Palestinians working in Kuwait were evicted. They arrived in Jordan in a state of desperation, scrambling for housing and jobs. They did not like the Kuwaitis, but now they held Iraq responsible for their latest misfortune. For some of them the embargo would be a boon.

Following the food-for-oil agreement, Jordan would become an even busier trade route into Iraq. More shipments of food had to be transported by road, and more oil would be carried away through Treibeel. The largest beneficiaries were Jordanian suppliers. But the transport from Aqaba port (at the tip of the Red Sea) to Baghdad called for thousands of drivers. Palestinians were first in line for the jobs.

I found it hard to listen to their pitying and critical remarks about Iraqis. "They are all smugglers now," they charged, even though Palestinians were often in partnership with them. These well-paid truck drivers told stories about Iraqi girls leaving school and working in Jordan, about the pitiful lines of Iraqis outside embassy gates in Amman, and street beggars in Baghdad.

Iraqis visiting Jordan, the only place they could find respite, faced derision. "Too much for an Iraqi," said the Palestinian shopkeeper. The Iraqi visitor shot back: "You regard us as penniless! You dare speak like this to us, a country that gave so much to Palestinians. Iraqi soldiers died preparing to defend Jerusalem. We gave a home to 50,000 refugees in 1948 and still more in 1967. We donated millions to families in Gaza and the West Bank. Most of all, among all the Arab states, we spoke loudest against Israeli injustices."

Even into the blockade, Iraqi support for Palestinians did not stop. While in Amman, shopkeepers were exchanging stories about Iraqi corruption and crime, and Palestinian drivers were giving handouts to former patrons and teachers. Palestinians on Iraqi scholarships were studying in Mosul, Baghdad, and other Iraqi universities.[9]

Features of the Journey

Our payoffs to the young men at the checkpoints were mere road tolls. Nights on the desert are cold. The man's sole shelter was an unlighted wooden shed. The rifle he shouldered might be used in self-defense.

Looking into the eyes of those lads as they flipped through our papers and offered us a few friendly words, I sensed that they themselves were frightened. Throughout the cold night, with neither radio nor phone that we could see, nor much food, they waited. Perhaps three cars passed during their shift. Surely the approach of our lights, spotted many miles off, was a comfort to them. Brigands were common on some of these lonely stretches where the nearest village or encampment was thirty to forty miles away.

They could have delayed us, demanded to inspect the car, or hauled us out into the cold night to interrogate us. None ever did. They were welcome to any small toll they extracted.

On one visit in 2001, by the time the morning sun was appearing over the eastern horizon behind us, my driver had paused for a few cordial words at a dozen more checkpoints on our way out of Iraq. Finally, we arrived at the Treibeel VIP post. Unlike the busy transport crossings, this center served both arriving and departing visitors.

"Ah, I see Mr. Hameed," I sighed. I recognized the lone figure in the doorway. His brown suit hung loosely on him. He waited at the curb while I disembarked, then pointed the way into the lounge where, with his customary grace, he ordered tea for me. He then disappeared to inspect my documents.

Thirty minutes later Hameed returned with my passport in hand. He hesitated before he passed it to me. "Do you mind?" he said, reaching for my left arm. I always wore my favorite silver bangles when I traveled; some of them are rather old, and all are traditional in design. "Where did you get these bracelets?" he asked, looking from the jewelry to me, meeting my eyes directly.

"Oh, dear," I thought. "Does he suspect me of smuggling an antiquity?" I tried to stay calm. "This is from India, and these are from Nepal. This is from Oman, this is Egyptian, and this was a gift from Jerusalem."

Hameed sighed, relaxed but not satisfied. "And where is your Iraqi bracelet?" He appeared disappointed at the omission.

"Ah, that one is here," I explained as I pulled up the other sleeve.

"Please," Hammed appealed as he gazed at me. "Don't carry it alone. Link it with the others." He smiled warmly, took the lone Iraqi bangle, and placed it on my wrist among its partners. Only then did he hand me my passport. "*Allah maeek*. Allah be with you."

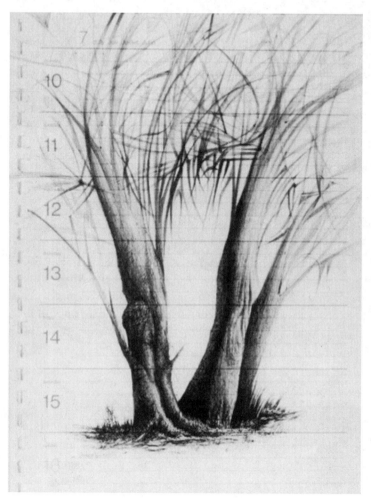

Winter Trees, pencil, by Hazem al-Mawally, 1991.

21

Gravesites: Environmental Ruin in Iraq

It was a sunny spring afternoon in 1996 in northern Iraq. The blockade had been on Iraqi backs for five and a half years. I stood on a gently sloping verge overlooking meadows of what was supposed to be young wheat. A cover of green tinged with waves of soft yellow extended as far as one could see in all directions, and from a distance it appeared to be an undisturbed pastoral setting.

Had I traveled 250 miles just to escape the ugliness of Baghdad and the sight of beggars there? Did I come to this fresh green landscape to shut out those endless complaints about food prices and the tedious questions put to me as a journalist about when the embargo might end? As much as I could, I had addressed those issues. Now I was pursuing my own agenda—to investigate agricultural production.

I wondered how the economic embargo, imposed in 1990 and strictly enforced, could hamper local food production. So I traveled to Iraq's northern wheat-growing region beyond Mosul and to small family farms both north and south of Baghdad.

With me were agronomists from the agricultural office in Mosul, the administrative center for the northern governorate. The region was Iraq's breadbasket. It is a glorious expanse of rolling hills extending as far as one can see. All of it is green in spring, yellow in summer. Normally.

The Iraqis agreed to show me the farms so I could see for myself. We drove fifteen miles outside the city. When we pulled off the road and walked up the slope, I waited for my guides to proceed further, to those fields where wheat grows. The men did not move beyond where we stood. Impatiently, I asked to see the wheat fields.

"This is it," murmured the officer, looking from me to the earth around us. "This is the crop."

I looked down at the growth at my feet, then across the hill, and finally at my Iraqi hosts. I was confused. "I don't believe this is a wheat field," I remarked impatiently. But why did I say that? I felt embarrassed. It was as if I had accused the men of deception.

Mohammed Sheet is chief plant protection officer, a trained agronomist.

Neither he nor his assistants responded to my observation or to my rudeness. What were they to reply?

I broke the awful silence and asked if we could move deeper into the field, as if our proximity to the thoroughfare somehow was responsible for the sickly growth around us. They obliged and led me up the slope and away from the road. It was the same. This time I said nothing. "Yes, this is also wheat," explained the official. This growth was no different than what we had observed earlier. Now all of us were silent, gazing at the ground, as if standing on a grave.

Recovering from the shock, I apologized. I knew what healthy, ripe grain fields looked like, and I could recognize young stands of wheat. In other countries, I had witnessed diseased crops and drought-stricken grasslands. I had observed thin fields planted with bad seeds or crops eaten back by pests. But I had never seen anything as bad as this.

I asked Mr. Sheet to point out which was the wheat plant. He bent down and touched some green shoots visible among the growth. The grass was hardly more than four inches high, whereas a normal crop should reach eighteen inches by now. Low yield is one thing. But this wheat was so badly infested, it was virtually destroyed. Most troubling of all, this tragedy was neither mismanagement nor natural calamity.

The growth at our feet was largely mustard weed and another ugly, thick-leafed plant. Together, the weeds almost obliterated the wheat. There was no possibility of separating these from the food crop, explained the agronomist, not even when the fields were harvested. Weeds had also consumed whatever fertilizer the farmers had spread there.

Weeds, of course, are a threat everywhere. If not controlled, they destroy. They cannot be cut out by hand. Machines are useless. Only chemicals can control them.

Normally, herbicides and pesticides would be applied here. Any amount would have been helpful. But they were unavailable in Iraq. Why? They were embargoed by the United Nations along with other agricultural supplements and machinery.

Those essential chemicals can only be obtained with permission from the UN's 661 Committee in New York. For several years none was available; the weeds flourished, uncontrolled. After the passage of SCR 986 and pressure from the UN's own Food and Agricultural Organization (FAO), limited supplies of herbicides were authorized. Yet somehow shipments were tardy. This year (as in the next and the next) the critical time for spraying had passed before the FAO office in Baghdad received approval to import some of the chemicals that might have saved the wheat.

The crop was lost. Again. The experts knew this. Farmers feared it. Starving Iraqis would soon find out.

Upon returning to Sheet's office from our inspection of the fields, I was astonished to see a line of irate farmers outside the agricultural center. Those were not starving mothers and children. They were portly men who would profit from a good crop. Having prepared the soil and planted the seed, they feared the coming disaster. "Daily they descend on us to plead for pesticides before all is lost," said Sheet, shaking his head and scurrying past them. This was no Baathi conspiracy. FAO officers assured me of that when we discussed my experience in Mosul on my return to the capital.[1]

Should I have asked those farmers if they were Shia, Sunni, Kurd, or Christian? Don't forget Turkman.

The Really Scary Part

The chain of death created by the 1991 Gulf War was a scary thing.[2] I'm not talking about black skies above the blazing oil wells of Kuwait, or the charred remains of soldiers on the sand, or incinerated families who had sought protection in a bomb shelter. Those are familiar images of death, and however painful, they are finite. With the end of hostilities, they disappear.

The really scary part comes later, when we find that things which looked alive are really dead or doomed. I refer to a chain of deadly pollution, the kind that creeps up on us, first with vague complaints, then with the persistence of strange illnesses, then with testimonials from increasing numbers of sick people describing similar odd symptoms. We slowly recognize that disparate reports which first appeared unrelated are in fact connected.

We have the sickening sense of something spreading, without limits, of something embedded so deep within the system that it is unreachable. Our inquiries are met with denials. To begin, we simply seek to confront it. We just want to stand on the gravesite as if it were a known, finite place.

This is our feeling, I think, as we read irrefutable evidence of Gulf War Syndrome and its link to the use by the Pentagon of depleted uranium weaponry in the 1991 bombardment of Iraq. Evidence is mounting of harmful side effects.[3] More and more soldiers are stricken by inexplicable illnesses after their term in Iraq. The veterans are conducting research and gathering facts that the U.S. Veterans Administration would not. They refused to accept government disclaimers that the U.S. Army had employed dangerous materials in the Iraqi battlefield.

In the United States, prompted by war veterans, a public movement to ban the use of depleted uranium in weaponry slowly began to attract some media attention.[4] Inside Iraq, for a long time, nothing was said publicly about what the physical effects on humans of exposure to depleted uranium might be. When asked by a few informed journalists about possible radiation-related diseases, initially health officials were mute. Many Iraqi soldiers were killed outright by uranium-encased weapons when vehicles and bunkers were blasted. Those who survived the onslaught must have ingested and carried with them the fumes and dust created by the bombardments. There is also the uranium waste, three hundred tons of it, according to reports, left on the battlefield inside Iraq. What about the radiation that remained in the air and drifted across the nation?

Today the entire population of Iraq is besieged by diseases. Waterborne parasites and bacteria and malnutrition in Iraq are responsible for many recognizable ailments and deaths. But what about reports of a sharp rise in spontaneous abortions, cancers, and other "new diseases"? The Iraqi Ministry of Health had begun systematically documenting some of these health problems.

Before 2001, only Dr. Siegwart Günther, president of the Austrian Yellow Cross, had published evidence scientifically linking possible Gulf War Syndrome inside Iraq and the high incidence of abnormal births and aborted fetuses.[5] Some Ministry of Health staff and university faculty were engaged in related research, although they said little about their work at first. Their silence may have been an effort not to further traumatize the public. Or, like the Pentagon, Iraqi officials may have sought to downplay the troubling illnesses that soldiers were experiencing. Iraqi research was in any case limited because of inadequate diagnostic instruments.

Iraqi Scientists Most Concerned about Radiation

Nonetheless, probably no one is more concerned about radiation and other kinds of pollution than Iraqis. The pollution is concentrated in their land. It will affect the future of every soul born here for generations.

Essential comparative data should be gathered by Iraqi researchers. Only they have firsthand access to data. Before the blockade, Iraq had a highly capable community of biologists, environmentalists, energy specialists, cancer researchers, etc. Most had advanced degrees in their fields from the United States and Great Britain. They were capable of conducting the necessary research.

Until the embargo and war, these scholars were active in the international scientific community; they published widely, and they took part in international conferences. But their ability to keep abreast of developments and share their work was also blighted by the embargo.

First, their government could no longer afford to finance the expense of overseas travel for its experts. Even if the money could be found, there was another obstacle: Iraqi scientists were unwelcome abroad. They had more reason than ever to consult with their peers about their research findings. It took some years before they understood that the embargo essentially barred scientific exchange with Iraq. First, they were not invited to consult with others abroad; second, even when they learned about a conference and applied to join, they could not obtain visas to attend. When Iraqis finally realized that a ban lay behind their exclusion, they were incredulous. Once again, their own teachers were abandoning them. Science was being politicized.[6]

Inside Iraq, disease control was desperately needed. Conditions were deteriorating rapidly; hazardous conditions generated by the war were spreading. A catastrophe of accelerating proportions and unknown ramifications was under way. Iraqi experts tried to alert their colleagues worldwide about the contamination. They had firsthand data and important comparative material to report. No one seemed to care.

The Pentagon, which has been trying so hard to suppress information about the extent, occurrence, and possible source of Gulf War Syndrome among its own personnel, would doubtless want to keep any Iraqi source silent on the matter as well. A prohibition on scientific exchange in general was in effect throughout the blockade; the Pentagon had additional reasons to see that the ban was in place.

Dr. Huda Ammash was an Iraqi scientist eager to share her research on war-related contamination with international colleagues. Ammash, an environmental biologist, completed her PhD in microbiology at the University of Missouri. After graduate studies in the United States in the 1980s, she returned home and joined the University of Baghdad faculty. She taught and was engaged in cellular research.

Working with governmental departments of agriculture, health, and environment, Ammash studied the health effects of pollution caused by the 1991 bombings. When I met her in 1996, she kindly shared her report with me. Her research focused on the enormous energy emissions and light energy from the massive bombing in the forty-two days of war in 1991 and the resulting radiation.

"We know that ionization causes radiation," she explained. "It is now diffused throughout the entire airspace of Iraq and likely has spread to our neighbors as well, possibly as far north as the southern border of Russia. The prolonged effect of this ionization, over a period of more than ten years, is equal to one hundred Chernobyls."[7]

Dr. Ammash and others identified an outbreak of meningitis in children, concentrated in one Baghdad locality. "This is highly unusual and may be a manifestation of high ionization levels. It has never been seen in Iraq before, and under the circumstances of the embargo, we are unable to provide immunization against it." Ammash noted the alarm among doctors she interviewed who report that 99 percent of the victims of this disease are children. The microbiologist's research on the incidence of cancer indicated that "the disease is increasing at rapid and abnormal rates. Childhood leukemia is especially rampant, with some areas of southern Iraq exhibiting a fourfold rise in these few years. Breast cancer in young women (ages thirty and under) is also many times higher than before 1990 in certain parts of Iraq."

The professor explained how "the Iraqi environment is subject to a mass of other chemical and microbial pollutants released into the atmosphere, indirect results of the war. This further aggravates conditions." Ammash pointed out, for example, how "damage to bombed and crippled industrial plants resulted in the leakage of millions of liters of chemical pollutants—black oil, fuel oil, liquid sulfur, concentrated sulfuric acid, ammonia, and insecticides—into the atmosphere. Fumes created by the bombardment of more than 380 oil wells produced toxic gases and acid rain.

"Bombardment of chemical factories damaged their gas purification units and thus created tremendous air pollution as well. If these filters can't function, dangerous gases are allowed to escape from cement factories, for example. Up to the present, the imposition of sanctions prevents repair of these industrial filters. Untreated heavy water from industrial centers is the medium for growth of microbes, mainly typhoid, malta fever, and other pathogenic bacteria."

Ammash also identified fourteen new crop diseases never before recorded in Iraq's history. "They include covered smut, sazamia moth, yellow crust, spiculated drought disease, gladosporium disease, and epical bent. These are now infecting date trees and citrus trees. Nothing is immune to these toxins," she warned.

The Iraqi biologist was becoming increasingly disturbed about what she realized was a determined goal by the United States to keep Iraq's scientists isolated and to prevent their research findings from reaching others. When I first met Ammash in 1996, she had completed the first phase of research and expected her work would soon be distributed internationally and that scientists worldwide would be alarmed by the incipient health hazards of a continued blockade. As the years progressed and her efforts were sabotaged, she became increasingly and openly critical of American policy. This may have been a factor in her appointment to the Revolutionary Central Command, headed by Saddam Hussein, in 2001. At the time of the American invasion, she was targeted by U.S. authorities, arrested, and held in a U.S. military jail in Iraq for thirty-one months. The professor was never charged for any crime, and when asked about her imprisonment in 2005, a U.S. spokesperson told Lenora Foerstel, "We have nothing on her." In a 1997 radio interview (www.RadioTahrir.org/iraq.php), Ammash explained her research on war pollution.

Now let's return to those wheat fields. In Baghdad I followed up my research in Mosul by contacting agriculture officials and visiting small farms engaged in mixed agriculture. Farming had declined during the Iran-Iraq war, which is why the FAO office in Baghdad was engaged with Iraqi agricultural experts since before the embargo to increase food production.

With imported food unobtainable, Iraq was obliged to attend to its neglected agricultural sector. Somehow it had to bring more land into grain production and improve irrigation; the FAO was there to help.

Iraq Could Be Self-Sufficient

FAO officials were unequivocal about prospects. "Iraq could be self-sufficient in grain," said director Amir Khalil. "It has the water; it has the land; it has the expertise." Yet, despite enhanced efforts and the growing food crisis, production was not increasing at the rate it could. Why?

Agriculture experts and farmers agreed on the answer: "No herbicides, no pesticides, no fertilizer, no improved seed." It was that simple. And everyone knew why they were unavailable—the UN embargo.

Iraq's animal husbandry and poultry industries were as crippled as grain farming. The reasons were the same. "Without vaccines and other medicines, all of which Iraq cannot produce at home and can no longer import, animals—like people and plants—cannot survive."

According to an FAO report, dairy herds in Iraq declined by 40 percent after 1990.[8] Before the war, dairy cows numbered 1.512 million. By 1995, the figure had fallen to 1 million. Water buffaloes suffered an even worse fate, and goat herds declined from 1.3 million to less than a quarter of a million. Iraq's poultry system with 106 million hatching hens in 1990 was virtually wiped out overnight by the bombing when electrically run poultry sheds across the country—8,400 units—shut down. Without temperature-controlled sheds, vaccines, and specialized food, moreover, hens could not survive long.

Why such massive devastation? Bombing was not that widespread. No; it was the embargo. The UN banned almost everything. Lack of essential supports in food production in any modern economy sets another landslide in motion.

Like plant infections, animal diseases were spreading uncontrolled. The 1995 FAO Survey on Iraq, itself commissioned by the UN, provides documentation of the catastrophe. This is the same UN whose 661 Sanctions Committee either refused to allow those imports (including items requested by its own FAO) or somehow could not manage to facilitate approval and shipping when the agricultural cycle demanded.

If we are to believe the FAO's own reports, it seemed that another weapon in this secret war was the denial of agricultural essentials—a kind of sabotage—to ensure that Iraq could not become self-sufficient.

Many wind-borne diseases, unimpeded in Iraq, were expected to infect every part of the region. They could reach beyond Iraq. Officials in Baghdad hoped that Turkey, Jordan, Iran, and others would become sufficiently alarmed to call for international action. Thus far, say Huda Ammash and other concerned Iraqi specialists, Iraq's neighbors were doing nothing to control these developments. Iraqi biologists were unaware of related research being carried out in Jordan, for example. "We are totally disconnected," Dr. Ammash said with distress. "We have no means of communication with our counterparts."

Before They Are Even Born!

Farms, like hospitals, provided us with the first ominous signs of a problem. Rashdiyya is a farming community two hours north of Baghdad. Before 1990, it was a wealthy agricultural district. There I found shocking evidence of a plague in the human population that, up to this point, had received no outside attention. It turned up during my visits to family farms outside the capital. I found myself dismayed as I passed the thin fields of Rashdiyya. The gardens were overrun with weeds. Even orchards were untended. Broken tractors lay idle outside the farm sheds. Shortage of fertilizer had reduced yields of apples and grain as well as vegetables by half. The hand spraying machines were in disrepair, too. Even if they worked, where were farmers to get chemicals to spray? After my experience in Mosul, I saw no point in asking why things were so rundown.

I accepted the invitation from one farmer to sit inside his home rather than tour the fields. I wanted to gather information about the workers themselves. Before long we were joined by my host's brothers, cousins, nephews, and other villagers. (Most were relatives, and all were men.) Soon twenty men sat with us; they represented a valuable store of knowledge about their community.

We began talking about social life in Rashdiyya. When one of the men remarked that fewer couples were marrying now, I was curious to hear his explanation. Without hesitating, he said, "Young people fear having stillbirths and babies with strange abnormalities."

How had they come to this conclusion? "Look around our village. We all know couples here who had such babies in the last four years." The other men nodded in agreement.

With the help of several farmers and the local schoolteacher, I took an ad hoc survey of the 160 houses in this village. The men reviewed each household, one by one, discussing the family history. They counted twenty families where babies with malformations had recently been born. Most stillborn and abnormal babies were fathered by men who had been soldiers during the Gulf War, they said. They also pointed out that spontaneous abortions were more common. These were in addition to stillbirths and birth deformities.

Later, doctors in Baghdad confirmed that spontaneous abortions were far more frequent since 1990. These specialists were cautious in their assessment, but more and more evidence was forcing them to admit that these were not localized phenomena but a countrywide epidemic.[9]

My subsequent inquiries at five hospitals (in Mosul, Baghdad, and Kerbala) revealed the same alarming trend; the number of abnormal births recorded in hospitals had dramatically increased. Where statistical records were unavailable, anecdotal evidence told the same story. Doctors whom I interviewed estimated that they were seeing ten times more abnormal births than five years earlier. Dr. Nawal in Mosul confessed, "Before 1991 I saw no more than two cases a year. Now I see four or five examples a month!"

Babies were born without ears, without eyes. Their limbs are missing or are stunted; their genitalia were undeveloped. There were more instances of cleft palate, club foot, and enlarged heads. There was one case of congenital leukemia reported by an alarmed doctor.

"How Can I Have Any Plans?"

A professor of poultry science had accompanied our party to the wheat fields in Mosul. I noticed at the time how slowly he walked and how ashen he looked. I suspected he was unwell. As we drove back to the city, I inquired about his plans for further research. His expression turned from passivity to bewilderment. Like the agronomist, he had every right to lash out at this upstart journalist's naiveté or arrogance. They could have directly accused the United States of sabotaging the wheat crop. They did not.

The professor paused as if to contemplate my question. Or was he just weary? His voice was low and pained. "Plans?" he said softly, gazing at me as if confused. "Madam, I am trying to feed my family. I am looking for a medicine for my ill father. How can I have plans?"

I would ask Dr. Ammash the same question in her office at the university. We had been speaking about her research program, so the question seemed pertinent. Perhaps because she knew me better and was a researcher herself, she took time to explain. "It is difficult for anyone to have a plan." Her voice, although not resigned, was calm. She was aware she was speaking to someone who had little inkling of the conditions under which Iraqis lived. "You have a plan when you have a settled situation, when you have known circumstances. We don't have that anywhere in Iraq. My immediate plan is to provide tomorrow's means for life for my children, to help my students into another successful day. After that, I don't know."

As for her ongoing research, this soft-speaking, committed professor said, "One major study is complete. I want to enlarge the project, concentrating on electromagnetic fields. But that research requires instruments and expertise from outside. Because of this blockade, I cannot plan the next necessary step." She ended our interview with a call to scientists from outside Iraq. "We ask them to join us in demanding that those powers imposing sanctions allow this research to be undertaken; we urgently need to begin collaborative work with experts in countries bordering ours."

Author's note: A previous version of this essay appeared in *Metal of Dishonor: How the Pentagon Radiates Soldiers and Civilians with DU Weapons*, ed. Sara Founders (New York: International Action Center, 1997), 155–63. Another version was published in *Anthropologists in the Public Sphere: Speaking Out on War, Peace, and American Power*, ed. Roberto Gonzalez (Austin: University of Texas Press, 2004). Used with permission.

Asking Iraq to Comply

A decade ago the words: comply comply comply,
hundreds of thousands of Iraqi men dead, generations
of Iraqi children sanctioned to graves.
Iraq is Assyrian, is Mede, is Persian, is Babylonian,
is the origins of human narrative flowing into the Tigris,
flowing out of the Euphrates, flowing into Eden, into Genesis,
into Adam and into Eve, into Ur and its Kings;
Iraq is the first science, the first math, "al-jabr,"
"algebra" meaning "restoration"; Iraq is the first
universities—"madrassa" of once glorious Baghdad,
Iraq is the first Christians of the East,
who lived among Muslims, together as Arabs,
now forced to comply, to line up for rations,
to beg in the streets of Iraq,
the once-learned center of the Abbassids, of al-Rashid;
the first written history of the middle ages is Iraq,
the bearers of medicines and astronomies,
of logarithms and philosophies;
Iraq is Chaldaean and Kurds, Nestorians
and Turkman, is the place of the first laws
of Hammurabi's code giving order to the first societies—
now forced to comply, the place of the first Kings saying
to their sons over 3,000 years ago, "how long will it be necessary for us
    to continually guide you?" is like my father
saying to me, is like all parents forever worried
and hopeful about the future of their children—
is Iraq saying now, so how? how do you go about demanding
compliance, without first having made amends.

Zaid Shlah, *Taqsim* (Calgary, Alberta: Frontenac House, 2006)

22

Targets, Not Victims

If any American were asked to consider ceding New York State to Canada, the reply would be a resounding "Never." In a 1996 conversation with Mustafa al-Mukhtar, we pondered aloud the real motive behind Washington's retribution against his nation. We arrived at the subject of oil. Playing the naïve journalist, I asked him if he thought Iraq might privatize its oil industry.

"Never." The man did not hesitate for an instant. It was unthinkable. The proposition was tantamount to relinquishing sovereignty. His conviction was deeply rooted in his knowledge of world history and in Iraqi nationalist logic. It was as sacred as a constitutional right.

This man was dangerous! If American strategists targeted benign fields of ripening Iraqi wheat, why should they not also want to eliminate devoted and industrious Iraqi men and women? Mustafa al-Mukhtar would unquestionably be identified as a major menace to U.S. interests. He was a brilliant man, a proud Iraqi who believed in Baath economic principles. Those included his nation's determination to control its resources.

An Iraqi Target

Nasra al-Saadoon recalled that her husband was completing an article on the inconsistencies in United Nations sanctions regulations against Iraq. "It was an illuminating piece. He had been examining the documents for months to identify the skewed logic. Finally he understood; he was preparing his critique for publication. We had talked about it that morning."

That afternoon, Mustafa died of a heart attack. Sudden, uncomplicated, painless. "Mustafa had a medical checkup only weeks earlier. Our doctor said he was in good shape. He felt excellent. He was at work." By the time Nasra reached the hospital, he was gone. "He collapsed at his desk, they said. I went to his office that very day to collect his papers. I found the essay. He had essentially completed it, and I felt so good for him. It will be published. I will see to it."

Nasra talked about her husband's mission and his unfinished work rather than her personal grief. As an intellectual, perhaps it was her way to deal with her terrible grief, at least publicly.

As far as we knew, Mustafa was not suffering from any illness. He was fifty-three. Like everyone in the country, he felt stressed by difficulties stemming from the blockade. As the hardships weakened people around him, he assumed greater responsibilities. He and Nasra had two teenage children. Her sisters' children depended on them as well. If he could not help them materially, he might offer them hope.

Many people across Iraq had become confused and angry about the sanctions. Mustafa, too, was perplexed. Amazingly, he showed no bitterness. I never heard him scorn Washington, London, or the United Nations during our many political discussions. He was a critical man—intellectually, not personally. He pointed out specific falsehoods and inconsistencies, and he researched historical precedents for current American and British military and economic policies. He viewed Iraq's position critically.

Mustafa al-Mukhtar seemed to possess limitless energy. He saw potential in everything around him, from the fragrances in his garden to the books in his library, from the foreigners at his door to a false news report that must be corrected.

As outside pressure on Iraq persisted and with no progress toward easing the blockade, Mustafa continued to argue against the American policy and its manipulation of the UN. He likely sought a domestic solution as well. Al-Mukhtar was not afraid to question a decision by Saddam Hussein or suggest how Iraq's approach might be adjusted and improved. Support for his Baath Party was never in doubt. I mention this because I know it is hard for the general public who hear only about Baathi repression in Iraq to imagine intelligent, independent-minded people devoting themselves to the party. Amazingly, thousands of critical Iraqis like Mustafa wouldn't give up. Despite their government's blunders and mounting personal hardships, Mustafa and others believed that the country was on the right track and could overcome present obstacles, even dictatorship. This must have become apparent to American and British strategists after their failed coup attempts and when inventive and resourceful Iraqi moves succeeded, step by step, in eroding support for the embargo.[1]

Mustafa and Nasra generally worked from offices at home. Their private library, a fine collection of historical, literary, and political books in several languages, was surely unique in the country. Mustafa was adding to it all the time. The walls of several rooms were lined with bookshelves; any free wall space was dense with paintings and sketches by Iraq's major contemporary artists. There were lots of framed photographs of Nasra and Mustafa, their two children, and other family members.

Working against the World Embargo from Home

The couple were available to receive almost any visitor. They welcomed them at the house. Mustafa prepared the snacks and beverages. Conversations moved from politics to food, to stories of friends, to student reminiscences and pre-blockade fantasies, to Sumerian mythology and archaeological discoveries, Arab semantics and American history.

. Both Mustafa and his wife read profusely, reviewing literature in Arabic, English, and French. Both relished intellectual combat, testing their assessment of issues against anyone, Iraqi or foreign. This in itself did not distinguish them, since Baghdad has always been home to a robust community of writers, performers, and artists. But this family was unusual in its decision to remain in the margins of Baghdad's intellectual circles. They found those cliques sometimes a little pretentious, "more social than scholarly," according to Mustafa. Sanctions gradually decimated those groups; many painters, archaeologists, musicians, and professors either died, moved away, or became too depressed or impoverished to continue. This couple persevered. Their vigor seemed unabated.

They each had their own projects. Hers was economic theory, and his was Iraqi political economy and nationalization policy. As a team, they collaborated and shared ideas. Nasra told me how, whenever they met a journalist or author, whenever they screened a film or read a book or article, they later compared notes. They did not always agree, and probably this made them more effective partners.

Being an easygoing, engaging family, they attracted a considerable following of foreign visitors. Their house remained open during the embargo years, and through their open door came vigorous debate. Political questions nourished this couple. Not only did they try to set falsehoods straight. They also studied the logic of the foreigners. Gradually they became more selective whom they spent their time with.

One found Japanese, Italian, Spanish, or French television crews at the house in the early years of the crisis. Mustafa was happy to have Nasra take the spotlight. She was a powerful critic of U.S. policy. Nasra could challenge and set straight any journalist or scholar. She could handle the most arrogant foreign journalist. Mustafa's style was different. He would quietly engage one or more producers on the other side of a room while the cameras were on Nasra.

As the embargo war continued, many Iraqis gave up arguing with foreigners. This couple became more determined to resist. Like international anti-sanctions advocates, Nasra and Mustafa were driven by the conviction that the

American and British campaign against Iraq was deceitful and illegal. If their schemes were exposed, Iraq would come out on top. They believed they were right, despite knowing about their president's awful intolerances. The foreign press could be educated. It was up to Iraq to set the record straight.

I was never convinced that oil was the primary concern of American and British aggression in the region. Other economic motives were behind their attack on Iraq. For example, Iraq's resistance to the U.S.–led global privatization program troubled Washington. Iraq held steadfastly to its Baath philosophy and showed no readiness to abandon its particular variety of Arab nationalism. Iraq sought greater regional influence and was ready to take up the Palestinian cause. Coming out of the war against Iran, a war fought on behalf of other Arab states, Iraq saw itself as a leader of Arab nationalism.

In 1988, following its cease-fire with Iran, Iraq turned its attention to defining a new economic shape for the Arab nations. At home, it had begun to open possibilities for increased private enterprise; the Baath administration encouraged what Mustafa described as cooperative government/private industry. Iraq had already agreed to the sale of limited shares of some secondary industries. Sectors of transport and tourism, agriculture, fisheries, and even the oil industry appendages such as gas service stations and oil transport could be partially held by private companies. Oil production was a special category. It remained under government control. This was a Baath principle universally shared by Iraqis.

The administration also focused on international affairs after 1988. Iraq sought to improve its position as a member of the Non-Aligned Movement, a major counterbalance to the western bloc. It became a major financial supporter of the *intifada*, the Palestinian resistance movement. Baghdad felt it had defended Arab interests through its costly war with Iran. After the cease-fire, it moved to reinforce Arab solidarity by establishing regional cooperative economic councils. Baghdad led the Arab states in rehabilitating Egypt, ostracized after its 1979 treaty with Israel. It proposed that the Arab League office be moved from Tunis to Cairo, and in 1989 it was. A summit of twenty-one Arab countries convened in June 1990 in Baghdad was consistent with its goal of asserting its new regional status.

I visited Iraq three times between 1989 and 1990 and found the level of energy phenomenal. Inside the country, postwar reconstruction moved at a fierce pace. New festivals and conferences were being planned. Visitors were welcomed, although few took the opportunity to visit. Travel restrictions were eased. But the effort assigned to these projects and to international diplomacy was not matched by domestic political reform. There was no plan for promised elections, and the Iraqi parliament was powerless.

Could Iraq Have a Destiny outside Saddam Hussein?

Mysteriously, Saddam Hussein focused on Kuwait. Iraq had lost many young men in battle, and it was deeply in debt, mainly to Kuwait, by 1988. Outstanding liabilities and suspicions that Kuwait had been siphoning off Iraqi oil near its frontier were behind Iraq's confrontation with Kuwait. Kuwait refused to negotiate. Iraq moved militarily. When Iraq invaded its southern neighbor, this became a watershed moment in world history with ramifications continuing into the present day.

Western ideological strategists went to work. Few Americans had heard of Kuwait until this time. No earlier inter-Arab dispute had warranted such profound, immediate international interest. Suddenly Iraq was a formidable world force. It was a looming threat to peace everywhere. To convince the world public of this danger, American mass media and Washington's political machine set out on a remarkable campaign. Within weeks they served up an image of Iraq that was truly demonic. Fed by exaggerated reports and outright fabrication about Iraq's biological and chemical weaponry potential, world opinion continues to this day to harbor excessive fear about Iraq. Like Islamic fundamentalism, Iraq was "out of control" and had to be thwarted.[2]

We may dispute the degree to which Iraq was unjustifiably demonized. Most will agree nevertheless that it was singled out for extraordinary punishment. Political critic Noam Chomsky, who has long understood the process of imperial conquest that underlies military action, has written about this for years. In his preface to his updated edition of *Fateful Triangle,* Chomsky tries to pinpoint the source of American frenzy: "In reality, the 'threats to our [U.S.] interests' in the Middle East, as elsewhere, had always been indigenous nationalism, a fact stressed in internal documents and sometimes publicly." Chomsky is concerned with Palestinian-Israeli relations, and this particular discussion focuses on the "indigenous nationalism" of Islamic fundamentalism manifested in the resistance movements of Hamas and Hizbullah. He reminds us of "American campaigns aimed at ostracizing and destabilizing nationalism—except, of course, where it can be used to garner opposition to another nationalism, as in the case of Afghanistan." Chomsky invites us to note how an "indigenous nationalism" becomes labeled "ultranationalism" or "radical nationalism"—an enemy—when it is out of sync with U.S. policy. In 1991, the nation that Washington armed and supported in its war with Iran had moved into the category of ultranationalist. This justified war.[3]

Iraq was easily driven from Kuwait and overpowered militarily in 1991. Its air power was neutralized. Yet the assault would not halt with military victory. Despite Iraq's handy defeat and the destruction of the country's infrastructure, the U.S. and British governments insisted that Saddam Hussein was a danger and that Iraq had to be contained by additional means. The sanctions must remain. It did not matter that the blockade created civil chaos, killed hundreds of thousands of young people, decimated the education system, crushed people's dignity, and drove out its creative and professional class.

As the years wore on, Iraq became increasingly isolated. Culturally, Iraqis relied both on interaction with the West, whose accomplishments and arts they greatly admired, and on Arab sister states. That exchange ground to a halt with the blockade. Intellectually, Iraq was cut off; it could not import books or obtain paper to manufacture its own. Iraqis received no invitations to professional conferences abroad. This was particularly debilitating for a society whose progress depended on active dialogue with the United States, Europe, and the Middle East. I recall a senior professor asking me to bring him a textbook in political science. When I asked which title, he replied, "Anything, anything." He was desperate from lack of contact. At moments like this, I began to grasp the terrible loneliness from civilization that was engulfing the nation.

Somehow, Mustafa was able to surmount this isolation. He somehow managed to locate news of new publications even when Iraq lacked Internet access. (The late introduction of the Internet in Iraq was due not to censorship but to weak phones lines, crippled in the 1991 war, and to embargoed technology.) He learned about current specialist publications as well as new general books on political science and economics. He had a librarian's passion for compiling sources. He took on a project to expand the bibliography of the Academy of Science newsletter, listing titles of whatever new books he could identify. It did not matter that he probably could secure very few titles among those he listed. He argued that even if Iraq's scientists, diplomats, and researchers could not obtain these books, they could at least have some sense of the directions in which others were moving intellectually.

As economists and social critics, Mustafa and Nasra were admirers of Chomsky. Mustafa heard about *Year 501: The Conquest Continues* within months of its appearance in 1993.

Mustafa knew the U.S.–led global economic campaign could weaken countries like Iraq. It would work against nationally controlled energy sectors. Yet

Iraq's oil must never return to private or foreign control. Mustafa maintained that "Iraq's economy is flexible; we have become more pluralistic to accommodate private business and investment. Privatization is acceptable—outside the oil industry."

Mustafa and Nasra were born into landowning families, in a class whose privileges and resources ended with the monarchy and colonial rule over Iraq. That was a past era, and they held no nostalgia for it. They fully embraced the policies of land reform and the benefits of nationalization when Iraq became independent. Although many economic schemes had failed and improvements were needed, they believed postcolonial Iraq had managed to redistribute wealth fairly and to provide outstanding facilities in education, research, and health.

This prosperity nourished Iraqi national pride, but it could not be sustained under the sanctions. To hell with national pride when you can't find even a used tire for your wretched Toyota. To hell with my son becoming a civil engineer like his father; let him try to get a visa for New Zealand. To hell with guarding a museum when I can't find some simple antibiotic to save my mother. Desperation swept aside work and civic ethics. People killed to steal a car tire; civil servants abandoned any notion of efficiency and service. Emerging from their mosque, worshippers would find their shoes stolen. Women stopped going to the office because they could not dress properly and still provide the few school items their children needed.

January 1999 marked a year since Mustafa al-Mukhtar's passing. Nasra, his wife, was his partner of twenty-nine years. Their daughter, Duaa, was born in France when they were studying there. She graduated in French and English literature from Baghdad University. Their son, Dhirar, was studying for his high school finals even during the forlorn days following his father's death.

I often thought when I met these youngsters over the years: "What a wonderful environment for a boy and girl to grow up in." In the extended family alone, they had a host of experts, a rainbow of opinions, and abundant love. Duaa was close to her father's sister, who lived next door; half the time she was living with her. In recent years, Duaa and her brother had joined their aunt in fasting during Ramadan. Was this a sign of their maturity, or was it an outcome of the calamities created by the sanctions? I did not know.

No one escaped the sanctions. The entire family's fortunes changed dramatically when the sanctions took effect. Even when they were not driven into poverty, everyone's dreams were somehow thwarted. Duaa, who had the alert watchful eyes of her mother and relaxed composure of Mustafa, decided not to attend graduate school abroad.

Nasra closed the bookstore she had opened two years earlier and took up government service after the 1991 war. Mustafa abandoned his plans to start his own publishing company and concentrated on research and writing. The family ceased traveling, and the car was a wreck, although somehow they kept it running. When they stopped eating meat, Mustafa took it as a challenge and began showing off his new vegetarian dishes.

All around them, this family witnessed the rising death toll. "Every week I get a call from someone in the family who has passed," Nasra said. "Mustafa, too. I decided I am not going to wear black anymore. Otherwise I will never take off my mourning clothes." Yet here she sat, a few days after Mustafa's death, in her black *abaya*. For forty days she would greet the many Iraqis who came to praise Mustafa, to accept Allah's power, and to give her and the children some comfort.

Was Mustafa a Victim of Sanctions?

Each of us likely knows someone our father's age who has been struck down by a heart attack. Heart disease is a common outcome of stressful living anywhere. So it was not calculated among the diseases resulting from Iraq's embargo. But speak to any cardiologist in Iraq, and he or she will tell you there has been a doubling of the rate of heart attacks. That is linked to a tripling of the mortality rate among heart patients since 1991 because of the collapse of the health system.[4] Doctors no longer have the machines and medicines needed to treat these attacks.

Was Mustafa a victim of sanctions? Ask his forlorn wife and children. Ask Mustafa's sister, Ferdous. (Mustafa was very proud of her cookbook, the only modern cookbook documenting Iraq's unique cuisine up until then.)[5] Ask the women at the Academy of Science, where Mustafa worked. Ask journalists at *al-Jumhuriyya,* where he occasionally published his work. Was Mustafa killed by sanctions?

Across the nation, all Iraqis knew that every one of them—dead or alive—was a victim of the sanctions. It was simple and unequivocal for them because the sanctions deprived the whole society of its intellectual strength and vigor, its self-sufficiency, its dignity. It was more than the grinding poverty. It was deprivation at every level. As the eminent economist Amartya Sen explains in his groundbreaking 1999 book *Development as Freedom,* poverty created by deprivation of food and health means deprivation of a freedom. Whatever political rights the Iraqi system has denied them, Iraqis once possessed quality health care, education, and food. Now that has been taken away by the very powers that claim they set the world standard of democracy and freedom.

Moreover, Iraqis had begun to understand that they were indeed the targets of an ongoing war designed to destroy them. As Pam Africa, a prominent Philadelphia activist who has led the campaign to free Mumia Abu-Jamal, says of the police harassment of African Americans, "We are targets, not victims."

Not unexpectedly, with the accumulated effects of the deprivations and the feeling of being targeted, a malaise was overtaking Iraqis. This fact was behind rising petty crime; it was the source of rampant and hitherto almost unknown corruption; it was responsible for the smuggling of museum antiquities and the pillaging of archaeological sites. It lay behind the readiness to betray friends or to sell one's daughter. It was the source of a new greed, of unprecedented jealousy among brothers. It was the motive for the prevailing question "How can I get out of here, and how can I get my child out?"

Denis Halliday, former head of the UN humanitarian program in Iraq, toured the world speaking about the breakdown of Iraqi civil society, a breakdown that goes far beyond the lack of food and medicines. This breakdown, he warned, was leading to a greater reliance on religious duty and faith and could lead to a radical religious social system in the future. Halliday was the only international commentator on Iraq at that time who spoke out about the colossal scope of the sanctions.

The sanctions penetrated into a sphere beyond the personal. The sanctions rendered professional excellence obsolete; they made knowledge redundant; they made Iraq's great history irrelevant; they mocked the value of its abundant oil resources. Those endowments, as much as Baath Party machinery, had accounted for "indigenous Iraqi nationalism." By 1999 the Baath Party and its military could still hold together a semblance of a society; they could offer farmers and merchants fortunes to produce wheat and to smuggle in essential light fixtures for the poor and luxuries for the elite; and they could spout a bizarre kind of nationalism that rings hollow to many Iraqis and most foreigners. But the real elements that made Iraq modern, dynamic, and capable were threadbare. The administration could organize, coerce, and order, but few Iraqis had hope. Few were able to plan. Fewer could follow the example of Mustafa Al-Mukhtar and others like him.

The United States and Britain devised the embargo plan and maneuvered the UN into implementing it with alarming speed after the military invasion of Kuwait. Washington established a regime of worldwide compliance and ongoing policing that was truly formidable. Nine years later, this embargo remained rigidly enforced under U.S. leadership, despite other nations' attempts to circumvent or ease it. Meanwhile, the terms of compliance kept shifting so that no progress seemed underway toward any resolution.[6] While smuggling and corruption continued to grow, a new small class of farmers and smugglers had emerged who worked with the regime and were completely beholden to the Baath Party for their fortunes.

Periodically, the sanctions policy was discussed in the United Nations, but there was no serious debate about its removal. Compensation was paid out of Iraq's escrowed revenues in New York to Vietnamese, Sri Lankan, Egyptian, Australian, British, and other nationals who lost their jobs because of the Kuwait war. Iraq also paid for all UN operations related to the country—from the salaries of the sanctions committee at the UN headquarters to the UNSCOM inspectors who engaged in illegal spying while on duty in Iraq, to the $100,000 salaries of hundreds of UN-appointed monitors who supervised distribution of the food that was permitted into Iraq. Iraqis were so outraged by the opulence they saw exhibited by UN employees inside Iraq that their property had to be protected from public attacks and UN staff had to carry special devices to protect themselves.

It was increasingly clear that the U.S. and British sanctions policy was a war not to remove a leader but to decimate a society. Kathy Kelly, head of Voices in the Wilderness, who for years was engaged in a campaign to lift the sanctions, has rightly called the embargo "a weapon of mass destruction." Its effect was to destroy Iraq's culture, modernity, and history. In other words, the sanctions were a mechanism to decimate the human resources that would carry out that indigenous nationalism which Iraq represented.[7]

Washington worked with Saddam Hussein before the invasion of Kuwait. The Iraqi leader was as despotic and as ambitious militarily during those years as he was in 1990. Iraq, moreover, never challenged or suggested anything but continued cooperation with Washington. Even though it was an unfailing critic of Zionist policies, when Israeli planes attacked Iraq's Osiraq nuclear plant on June 7, 1981, Baghdad did not retaliate. But Washington was not satisfied with a military defeat at the end of the Gulf War. It had to get at the roots of society; it had to eliminate people like Mustafa who made Iraq modern and forward looking, people who possessed the skills and desire to define another political path. Iraq had the technological and educational tools that could have established it as a pivotal regional leader.

This is not to say that one wanted to see Iraq's type of government flourish. Baathi intolerance of individual liberties should be soundly rejected. But Iraq's leadership could have been a force of some significance, for example, in the Non-Aligned Movement, in which Baghdad had been a major force, and it could have threatened U.S. global economic interests or its domination of the United Nations. In that respect, Iraq represented an "indigenous nationalist" potential, and Washington decided Iraq had to be neutralized, not just militarily but also technologically and economically. Thus Iraqis with education, skills, and ambition became policy targets. Institutions that supported them—museums, schools, medical colleges, fish hatcheries, the solar energy research center, clubs and seminars, and professional journals—had to be decimated, too.

A high-ranking U.S. military officer asked his planners and experts on Iraq what was unique about Iraqi culture that our military could target?[8] The embargo is phase two of this targeting strategy. Through it, Washington told men like Mustafa that his library would be sold and might disappear from the country, his car would become useless, his phone would not work, and his life span would be halved. His educated children would not find work, or they would go to farms to pick potatoes with other hungry young men and women. Meanwhile, the mosque would replace their electronics seminar.

The UN instituted a relief program (SCR 986) paid for by Iraq that ensures most of Iraq's population would not die of starvation. Yet Iraqis had become so weak that few could think beyond how to find enough food for their family. The food-for-oil scheme that the U.S. government allowed the UN to put in place merely kept famine at bay so that Washington and its friends could not be accused of genocide.

Was Mustafa just a victim? Or, like the millions who have died or fled Iraq, was he a target?

Author's note: An earlier version of the essay appeared in *Iraq under Siege: The Deadly Impact of Sanctions and War,* ed. Anthony Arnove (Cambridge, Mass.: South End Press, 2002), 127–36. Used with permission.

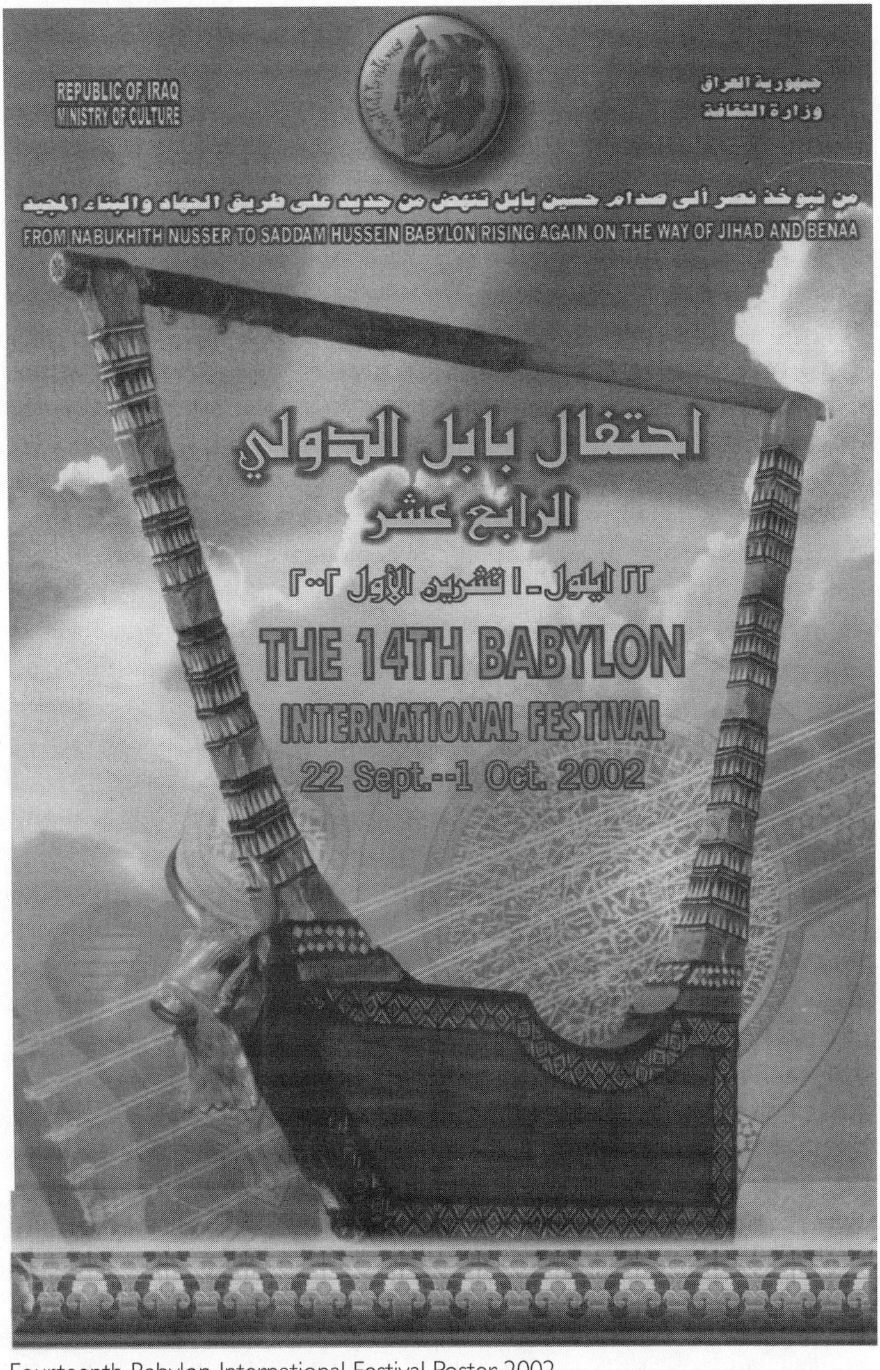

Fourteenth Babylon International Festival Poster, 2002.

23

Where Is Amaar?

By early April 2003, Iraq had been conquered. Military defeat followed by occupation was established across the land.[1] Assertion of U.S. military force was
only one aspect of Washington's conquest of Iraq. It had followed two preparatory steps, launched in the final months of 2002, psychological warfare against
a defenseless nation, accompanied by intrusive weapons inspections. Preparing
the military assault against Iraq, Washington had finally managed to force the
imposition of the inspectors through the UN agency, UNMOVIC (successor to
UNSCOM) headed by Dr. Hans Blix. Their mission was to verify that Iraq possessed no weapons of mass destruction. (Even during the final UNMOVIC tour,
American and British aircraft, which had been bombing Iraq almost daily since
1991, also intensified their terror campaign over northern and southern Iraq.)

Those exercises rendered Iraq—the theater of war—ready for the final land
and air assault, beginning March 19 and culminating in the arrival of foreign
troops in the Iraqi capital April 9, 2003. On the ground the assault had encountered some opposition, but within a few weeks invading forces declared
Iraq "liberated."

Widespread plundering ensued. This was explained as a spontaneous outburst of public anger or relief among the Iraqis. But that is questionable. The
looting and plunder actually marked a new phase in the process of conquest
—de-Arabization, an invidious course of action rendered by the occupiers as
de-Baathification. Following the April 9 "liberation," Iraqi state authority dis-
integrated. The invading forces "secured" Iraq's oil installations, presidential
palaces, and strategic ministries. Meanwhile, chaos ruled in the streets, where
men hunted down known Baath Party leaders and military officers. Public
buildings were attacked by gangs. Some of the looting that ensued may have
been a spontaneous release of hatred from a tormented people. (At last, their
dictator was gone.) Crowds smashed open public buildings and carried away
furniture and other equipment. The rampage went beyond the 1991 torching
of Baath Party offices and murals of Saddam Hussein in the south. In 2003,
universities, hospitals, and schools did not escape plunder. Ministries were also
attacked, although the invasion forces secured at least four key agencies: oil,
defense, internal affairs (security), and the Central Bank of Iraq.

With the real booty, Iraq's oil fields, controlled by occupying troops, the American forces apparently made little effort to prevent civil mayhem and pillaging. Foreign media focused on the plundering of Iraq's museums and libraries, repositories of Arab and earlier civilizations.

It appeared as if Iraqis themselves carried out this shocking abduction of their nation's treasures. But information from within the country soon indicated that those raiders were not all Iraqis. The mayhem seemed to be a sinister foreign plan, part of the overall strategy to destroy Iraq's vital role in Arab national history.[2] Al-Jazeera Television is among many reliable sources that reported the raids on Iraq's museums were undertaken by foreign gangs, probably hired by outside plotters. According to well-informed observers, this scheme was in part executed with the cooperation of Kuwaiti authorities who made a deal with criminals imprisoned in Kuwait: "Carry out this mission in Iraq, and you will be released." (Recall how in 1990, Iraqi troops had looted Kuwait's museums and libraries.) According to my sources inside Iraq, those attacks on museums and libraries also took place with the complicity of U.S. troops; in one case, occupation soldiers reportedly opened the barred doors of the museums for the thieves. Elsewhere, U.S. forces stood by, unconcerned with the plundering. Trucks were in place to tow away the booty; the same haul is reported to have been seen at the Baghdad airport, crated and ready for (unknown) foreign destinations. After the thieves completed their assignment, they seem to have evaporated. Burned books and historical documents were lost forever; Jewish documents and treasures that the Iraqis had proudly held as a sign of their respect for the Jewish heritage of Iraq are rumored to have been collected, then dispatched forthwith across Iraq and Jordan to Israel. Lists of the lost antiquities were assembled by international experts, but it is unclear how many were retrieved.[3] Meanwhile, angry Iraqi crowds were reported moving through neighborhoods and into any public buildings in their path. Officials simply disappeared; even the notorious Republican Guard, the reputed elite battalion, was nowhere to be found.[4] At the same time, the thousands of civilians expected to flee did not materialize, although temporary camps were readied to house refugees at the frontiers with Jordan, Syria, and Kuwait. From the dusty roadsides near their homes, traumatized Iraqi families watched the invading army proceed into the land. They had neither flowers nor songs of welcome for the self-professed "liberators."

Everyone could watch television relays of waves of devastation by the mobs. Behind these scenes the occupation forces began to dismember Iraq. Billions of dollars in cash and gold were removed by occupation forces. The American Coalition Provisional Authority enacted one hundred laws that laid the groundwork for the privatization of the country, awards of multibillion-dollar reconstruction contracts to Washington friends, while Iraqis helplessly watched their nation being plundered by the invaders, now well documented in investigative studies, among them *Iraq Inc.* by Pratap Chatterjee and *Imperial Life in the Emerald City: Inside Iraq's Green Zone* by Rajiv Chandrasekaran (New York: Random House, 2006). "Liberation" brought bitterness, deepened resentment, and soon sparked resistance. Attack, counterattack, retaliation, and sabotage accumulated and spun rudderless, sucking in more energy with the momentum of the rising death toll and the abuses in homes, offices, and prisons—in their Iraq. There is no use in asking who the victims are today, compared with yesterday, compared with under the blockade.

With so much violence, fear, and fragmentation, who could concern themselves about Ahmed Sousa's library, or the lost work of contemporary Iraqi masters, or the incidence of birth defects, or the shortage of professors? For a week in 2006, media attention focused on reports about assassinations of 250 professors and more kidnappings. Long lists of names were circulated. American and British academies composed petitions. "Why should we be so concerned about professors and not the tens of thousands of others? Every one is an Iraqi mind, every one an Iraqi hope," asked an American interviewed about the reports. In any case, these recent reports and petitions demonstrated a belated awakening inside the Western academic community. During the sanctions war, its voice was barely heard. Today, Iraqis face hard, hard decisions. Should they cooperate with the occupying power in order to obtain work and feed themselves? Should they look for employment with any foreign company without asking questions? Should they search for a way to get out of Iraq and forget about their homeland? Join the resistance movement against occupation? Become a posse to avenge the bombing of their holy place, their uncle's house, their farm? Follow a gang of thugs to take whatever they can by any means? Or inform on a neighbor whose brother may be a resistance fighter? Should they believe in some form of democratic process? If so, which political party should they join? How could they make a difference if the walls of their homes might be blown away any hour?

Many choices lie before Iraqis. None contain the stuff of dreams. From all sides, dangers crush in, hour by hour. Every woman and man faces some awful choices.

Where is Sabaar from the Press Center? He had been with the Ministry of Information through the first Gulf War and during the entire embargo war.[5] I never knew whether the man was a Baath Party member, although it was said that any new face in the office midway through the embargo must be Baathi. As the blockade progressed, government posts were increasingly filled by Party loyalists. Fidelity to the government took precedence over any other qualifications. Where daily life was increasingly hard, families needed the little bit of economic security that Baath Party membership promised. Thus, after twelve years of siege, in contrast to before 1990, partisans and not technocrats ran Iraq; this reduced efficiency and probably contributed to more corruption.

Where is Souad, still vigorous and vocal at eighty-five? Daily, she would follow French, British, U.S., and Arab radio and television news reports, then seek out journalists to pass along and test out her own political analyses. "You can quote me," she would say at the end of her commentary—what she considered a brilliant assessment. Ignoring pleas from her children abroad, Souad insisted on remaining in the country. Perhaps she needed to guard her house and family memorabilia. Perhaps she was simply fearless. She had already seen so much in her Iraqi lifetime.

And where is Amaar, who drove me from Baghdad to Kerbala in the family car? (The excursion with me was a treat from his father.) Amaar had completed his military service only a few months earlier and was sure he would be called to fight. The family discussed whether half of them should flee to Jordan; ultimately none left. Everyone knew the American assault would begin any day. No one could comprehend what military occupation might involve. Driving together southward toward Kerbala, Amaar asked, quietly, apologetically, perhaps fearing the question might reveal his faltering patriotism, "Will America bring us freedom?"

Waiting for the invaders, many Iraqis armed themselves. Saadoon was one of them. He insisted he would use his pistol. Did Saadoon know whether he would point it at the foreign invaders or at marauders at his door in search of booty?

Where is Dr. Saad? As newly appointed director at Kerbala General Hospital, he proudly took me on a tour to show me recent improvements. He was especially pleased about the renal center, where he was department head. "We are working toward making this a medical college connected with the new university in the city," the surgeon explained. "Next time you visit, perhaps it will be well under way. Yes, in the past two years, we have been able to make some progress." Saad thanked me warmly when we parted. My visit to Kerbala General, a hospital whose fate I closely followed, was testimony to remarkable achievements since 2001.

Iraq's hospitals were looted, too. I found this unfathomable, and I wanted to believe the stories were untrue. Even if pillaging of health centers was less than reported, I felt deeply troubled by the news. No government sector suffered along with civilians more than Iraq's medical profession. Handicapped as they were by unavailable equipment, hospital staffs had painstakingly assembled medical records during the embargo years. Their hard work recorded patient histories as well as the murderous history of the blockade. Why would raiders want to destroy medical records? They were just sad, sad records of the afflicted and lists of death certificates of those who could not be saved.

Where is Rouah, whose epilepsy could only be controlled with regular medical treatment? There was no hospital or special school left in Iraq where she could receive the treatment she needed. She had had to leave school. At home, her care rotated among her brothers, her mother and father, day after day, year after year. The family had been trying to find help for her in Germany. The year before, they sold their house to raise money to take Rouah to the United Arab Emirates for diagnosis. They returned with a diagnosis but no medicine and began the search for help all over again.

What about Omaya and her husband? They were waiting for her cancer diagnosis from a hospital in Amman. Her tissue samples were dispatched to Jordan by road courier. (Flights, which had recommenced only a year earlier, were halted in anticipation of the invasion.) If the result of Omaya's tissue diagnosis were positive, she would need a specific drug. She was a doctor herself and knew it was unavailable in Iraq. The laboratory promised they would send their report by e-mail. When the bombing began, it hadn't yet arrived.

Invading American and British troops set up checkpoints on all major roads across Iraq. Phone lines within the capital were cut and would not be restored for months. Communication between cities became difficult. Journalists, anticipating the cuts, had brought satellite phones and video transmitters with them. The outside world could closely follow the progress of the invasion. Inside Iraq, local television service stopped when the communications towers were bombed. If a family had a transistor radio, they picked up fragments of the war from the BBC, Tehran Radio, and French Arabic services abroad.

Where is Maher Feisel? On that sunny spring morning he had successfully defended his MA thesis in French literature at Mosul University. What has happened to him and to his classmates, who celebrated his success with ice cream and cake in the university garden?

Nisreen and her sister Nawal both said good-bye to their students when they closed down their school a week before the invasion. The two women hunkered down in their house with cartons of water and jars of preserves. They made one call to their brother in Germany, saying they were determined to remain, whatever happened.

What about Manal? She's seventeen now. Her 1995 spinal operation in Los Angeles prolonged her physical life. But no one talks about her returning for the recommended follow-up procedure that would make it possible for her to walk. Her cousin Mohammed so envied Manal's stay in California; he desperately wanted a pen pal in America.

And where is Farida, who studied Spanish in college? She was trying, even as the American president gave his last warning to Iraq, to somehow get to Madrid. She had been awarded a scholarship from the Spanish government to continue her studies there.

Where is Salem, the archaeology department guard? He was posted at the university field station at the Abu Hatta archaeological site for twenty-eight years. Excavation at the site never resumed after 1991, but Salem stayed on to thwart vandals.

Where is Ahmed? A veteran of two wars already, he was a gatekeeper at the ancient garrisoned city at al-Ukhaider when I met him. Although almost no visitors arrived to see the remarkable architecture he was eager to share with them, he went to work every day.

Where is Nada, the translator, journalist, and painter? The Ministry of Information Press Center would not hire Nada—they employed no women working as guides—so she moved here and there hustling journalists for translation assignments, and she tried to sell us her paintings. Nada had to support six brothers and sisters.

And Omar? He was a zealous and accomplished zither player and a graduate of the Institute for Classical Music. To earn extra money for his upcoming marriage, he opened a snack shop on the second floor of the Ministry of Information. Omar had the widest, most joyous smile in all Iraq. Could he have lost it in the invasion?

And where is Nasra, who was furious about the embargo after her husband died of a stress-related heart attack in 1998? Without him, she no longer gave interviews and never again welcomed visiting journalists into her home. Instead, she embraced the Baath Party more wholeheartedly. She became editor of the sole government daily newspaper. Its quality greatly improved under Nasra's editorship, but tiresome quotes by Saddam Hussein still appeared on the front page. Most of her employees were young women whom she trained in computer technology and journalism. Nasra had many dreams to fulfill.

The invaders arrived with the names of all Iraqi scientists in hand, especially nuclear physicists and other specialists of "strategic" interest. The list was a gift from the UNMOVIC inspectors, who had wrenched the names from the government during their searches before the invasion. (In 2002, Iraq permitted UN inspectors to enter on the dim chance that it might avert a war against them.) U.S. military commanders argued that Iraqi women and men on the list were needed "to help locate the whereabouts of Iraq's weapons of mass destruction." These Iraqi scientists were identified by American authorities as "resources to produce weapons." Their existence in their homeland might enable Iraq to retain its "capacity to build nuclear weapons."[6] In other words, they wanted Iraq's brains, one way or another.

So where is Ali's uncle Mustafa, one of Iraq's youngest atomic scientists? He had refused the UNMOVIC order to appear for an interview. When members of UNMOVIC inspected Mustafa's office in December 2002, they ransacked his research files and seized his ID card, making it impossible for him to travel.

Where is Dr. Huda Ammash, microbiologist and professor at Baghdad University? She had spent twelve years desperately—but without success—trying to inform fellow scientists abroad about atmospheric and other contamination resulting from the 1991 bombings. Spurned by her peers, yet determined to help her country, the professor was obliged to accept nomination to the Republican Central Command in 2000. When the Baath government fell, she found herself on America's list of the "fifty-five most wanted." Was her crime being "a f--cking intelligent Iraqi"? She was detained for thirty-one months by the occupation authorities. No charges were ever filed, yet when she was released, the authorities immediately imprisoned her husband, Dr. Ahmed Makki (at the time of writing, Makki had not been released). Ammash's name was probably on another "most wanted list" of Iraqi scientists.[7]

Where is Dr. Basil? He finished his PhD in agronomics at Colorado and became deputy minister of agriculture in his homeland. He was a distinguished and capable scientist who admitted what he most wanted was to continue his research in irrigation. Administering the country's agricultural policy under siege was almost impossible for him to bear.

Where is Dr. Zouba, another American graduate and an Iraqi war hero who had lost an arm in combat with Iranian soldiers? He was sent into that battle barely three years after returning in 1979 with his American PhD in business management. Zouba was determined to do whatever he could to thwart the imminent invasion. In 2002, he helped launch a program to mobilize world youth organizations to support Iraq. He directed the conference of youth in Baghdad in February 2003 while, overseas, millions protested the impending war. Both were in vain.

What about Nazim, barely eleven when I first visited his house in 1989? He had become very tall and lanky when I last saw him at the family's farm near Yussefiyya. With the same bright, saucy eyes and a wide smile, he was twenty-four and newly married. I cannot imagine him a soldier, or a prisoner, or a resistance fighter.

I recall young Zena's declaration. "I will not leave auntie's side if Mosul is bombed," she announced to the family. The teenager lived with her mother's sister Bushra, a professor at Mosul University. Child or adult, they were resolved.

Louay ran a small furniture factory outside Mosul. Arming himself and his workers in the weeks before the war, he said, "Of course, I will take up arms to defend Iraq. Men who are my father's age are ready to join the army. I, too, must defend my country, and my son will do the same."

Author's note: An earlier version of this essay appeared under the title "After the Conquest," in *Toward Freedom* (Vermont), Spring 2003. Used with permission.

I'll Tie My Mother's Shawl

I'll tie my mother's shawl
to the muzzle of my rifle
and carry the laughter
and happy looks of children
in my pack.

Unknown soldier 2, 1991, Iraq

24

"You Are My Guest"

I settle into the taxi, heading north on Kindi Street. It is early 1989 and I am wrapping up my first visit as a journalist to Iraq. "Mustashfa al-Yarmouk," I announce to the man at the wheel.

The driver's heavy shoulders fill much of the space in front of me. I note the trim black line of his hair above the collar of his red shirt. He is young, under thirty, I guess. He doesn't peer at me through his rearview mirror as most drivers do when I enter a taxi in Baghdad.

He pulls his car into the road quietly. After a moment I hear him sigh, as if gathering his strength to speak.

Gentle English words roll back from where he sits. "Yarmouk Hospital? Are you going there for a blood test?" He seems to know that these procedures are required for visitors to his country.

"You are exactly right. Thank you." I relax, confident he will deposit me precisely at my destination. He drives on. The wide road is lined with tall sheltering date palms on either side of us.

I have been in Baghdad three weeks. The hostilities with Iran ended five months ago, in August 1988, and Iraq is welcoming visitors like me—writers who are more curious about social and cultural life than about death tolls and weaponry. The war with Iran went on for almost eight years, and the human losses were tremendous. Yet, passing through the streets, visiting museums and galleries, hotels, shops, and universities, I note that the city has miraculously been spared. Baghdad has grown while the war raged on the eastern frontiers of the country. I am impressed how, during those hard years, Iraqis have built up their civilian sectors. Elegant new underpasses channel streams of cars from city to suburbs. Traffic is dense during the mornings and evenings. People seem to be in a great hurry, leaving their offices, shopping, and driving, especially going in the direction of Mansour suburb to the west and Kadhimiyya in northern Baghdad. New hotels, constructed in the last decade, rise twenty stories to overlook the great, silent river Tigris. *Allah ala ayyamak ya Dejli.* Haifa Street and Abu Nawwas Drive, where old Ottoman-style family houses were shaded beneath heavy palms, are now almost treeless. Only two houses remain, both converted into museums. Lining Haifa Street is an uninterrupted row of modern apartments and townhouses. Although they are modestly priced, these apartments are unpopular with the garden-loving Iraqis. (Most of these units get assigned to Baath Party members anyway, they say. And *they* don't like them either.)

The war is over, *al-Hamdulillah*, and Iraqis seem to need to talk. They remember the unsettling silence of rockets that flashed high over the palms. They saw the streak arch through the skies over Baghdad, then heard its deathly crash. Not many missiles hit the city. But those months and months of battles in the southern front found their way, weeping, into Baghdad homes. Cars carried coffins on their roofs almost every day, bringing young soldiers back to their families. When Iraqis speak of those lost men, it was not as casualties. They were martyrs.

The American press labeled that killing "a war of attrition." At first I was confused by the phrase. Later, when I learned how their weapons were supplied by outside powers, I understood the politics of the term. "Let them kill each other until they have nothing left; meanwhile our pockets are full from weapon sales."

Because of that war, Iraq became heavily indebted to its suppliers and supporters. It grew dependent on imported food; it bought killing tools from Europe and the United States, then sent its maimed young men to French hospitals while Iran's broken boys were patched together by British medics.

I eventually realized that the western powers, along with their ally, Israel, were happy to keep the killing machines going, profiting from arms sales to both sides, keeping the two neighbors fighting each other and weakening their economies. It was one way to contain the newly established Islamic state of Iran and to drain Iraq of its oil revenues.

Eight years is a long time to be at war. The entire population, far from being exhausted, seems, within a few months of the ceasefire, to be overflowing with energy. Travel restrictions have been lifted. People can visit their families in Manchester and California. They can motor to Turkey, then to Italy, for a holiday. They can join conferences in heart surgery, nuclear physics, solar energy, and endocrinology or exhibit their sculptures and paintings in Havana and Vienna.

Whenever I drive with friends along Mansour and Sadoun streets, they recall the scene that hot night in August when they heard that a cease-fire with Iran had been negotiated. Disbelieving, children and their parents rushed from their homes to sing and cry the news to their neighbors. They danced and paraded every night for a week. Even six months later, their references to the war focused on changes to come rather than on past sufferings. Baghdadis are delighted to see visitors in their city. The American Information Office has reopened, and a lecture series is scheduled to begin.

Today, the spring morning is balmy. Hardly anyone is on the roads because by 10 a.m. most people have reached their workplaces. I am to leave Iraq the next day. I am certain I will return, seeing that there is much to write about. Iraq is on the cusp of a new era.

My driver interrupts my thoughts with another short question. "Bulgarian? Are you from Bulgaria? Or Yugoslavia?" Foreigners whom Iraqis had met in the city during the war were likely to be Yugoslavs, Bulgarians, or Hungarians. Many East European companies were contracted to build roads, hotels, and hospitals. Quite a few Iraqi students went to Yugoslavia, Poland, and Bulgaria for graduate studies.

"Do I look Bulgarian?" I laugh, intrigued. What does a Bulgarian look like? "No, I'm from New York."

When Iraqis learn I am American, interest often perks. They name their relatives in the States—in Texas, Indiana, California, New Jersey.

"Ah, USA," replies my driver. I can feel his interest grow. He glances back at me through his mirror. "I'd like to visit New York. What do you do there?" When I reply that I am a journalist, his big shoulders fall and he is silent again. His attention refocuses on the road ahead. We speed past the exhibition ground. When he stops at a red light, he decides to try again. "Do you write about politics?"

"Not at all. I'm an anthropologist. My interests are in social and historical things, not archaeology, but rather contemporary Iraqi society. I know nothing about Iraq's people, and I want to write about your cities and farms, your exhibitions and universities, your industries and irrigation systems. I want to meet your writers and artists too."

He seems to approve. "Overseas, not many people know about our great civilization and what we have built in these years since I was a boy. Journalists usually write about oil and our battles. Well, the battles are over now. Sports is a good subject. Soon there will be international competitions here. Or you can write about people like me. We have a lot of stories to tell."

He has something else to tell me. But we are not in a café sitting face-to-face. We shall soon part. As if knowing my thoughts, he notes that the hospital is not far ahead of us. He reduces the speed long before we reach the intersection. We proceed at barely more than a crawl for the next five hundred yards.

This man is too young to have studied in the British or American schools operating here in the past. I ask him, "How is it that you, such a fluent English speaker, drive a taxi?"

He is so still I can almost hear him breathing. His eyes dart upward to glance at me through his mirror, then refocus on the road. "Look," he says, and I can detect the movement of his left hand as it slides off the steering wheel. I lean forward to peer over the seat that separates us. His hand is resting, trembling, on his thigh. "I have no leg here." He wants to explain. "Before the war, I was a lecturer in English at Baghdad University. But now it's difficult for me to move around." He continues speaking softly, enunciating every syllable with care, as if he has practiced the report. "How can I continue at the university in this condition? I have not decided what is best for me. In the meantime, I drive this taxi."

I know the Iraqi government compensates its fighters well, and no expense is spared to rehabilitate wounded men. He would have possibilities to retrain and find suitable work.

Ahead, in the street, white-coated men and women are crossing at the intersection. We have reached Yarmouk Hospital, but I am not eager to disembark. I do not want my conversation with this man to end. Even as he slows and pulls over to the curb, this war veteran is similarly not ready to leave me. He continues the story about his leg. "Of course, I have an artificial leg; it was made for me in France. I was sent there by my government for therapy as well." He pauses, then sighs, "But these legs, you know, are never as good as those which Allah gives us."

We have come to a full stop. I have to leave. Another passenger is waiting on the curb. I fumble in my pocket, then hold out the fare—two one dinar coins. As I extend my hand toward him, the driver turns and we look at each other directly for the first time. His face is chubby, and his eyes are warm and trusting. He pulls back, a little upset by my gesture. "No, I would be ashamed to take money from you," he says. Then he volunteers his noble farewell: "My name is Kamal Abbas Hussein. Hussein is my grandfather. Abbas is my father. I am Kamal. And you, you are my guest." His smile broadens.

Kamal gently pushes my hand away. Traffic passes us, unconcerned. People flow out of the gate of the hospital. I open the door and step onto the curb as the white taxi with its orange fenders pulls away into the current of Baghdad history.

Postscript: A brief encounter between a visitor and an Iraqi soldier took place in Baghdad early in 1989. For the American, the exchange was an introduction to war, personal dignity, generosity, and new possibilities for a dialogue. Did Kamal Abbas Hussein ever remember the New York journalist? And what did he take from that conversation into the coming years of his life inside Iraq? On my side, I wasn't sure if I needed to actually see him again.

Author's note: An earlier version of this chapter appeared under the title "Baghdad Interlude" in *Jusoor, The Arab-American Journal of Cultural Exchange* (2/3 Summer 1993), ed. Munir Akash (Bethesda, Maryland). Used with permission.

I'm from Palestine

I'm from Palestine.
Some people go for Bush.
Some people go for Iraq.
I just don't want anybody killed.

Sanaa, age 10, 1991, Brooklyn, New York

25

Birds of a Feather

"You Iraqis are fucking intelligent bastards!" growled the American to three Iraqi professors he was charged to investigate. He was a member of an UNSCOM Weapons Inspection squad in 1998, and his agents had just overrun Baghdad University's biology department. They had disrupted classes, hurled books from the windows, and pawed through office files.[1]

Why was that UN employee so angry? Was it because his Iraqi charges appeared more intelligent than he? Or undeservedly intelligent? Or because he had not found whatever evidence he had been sent to discover? Or because he had been unable to intimidate them? Or because they had managed to hide their evil "weapons" from him? Perhaps he saw what fine work they had managed to do, even under siege. In any case, "intelligent bastards" is how one U.S. intelligence agent characterized the people of Iraq.

And what did I think of Iraqis? This question was put to me in New York in 1995 by two expatriate Iraqis I barely knew. As far as I was aware, they were not U.S. agents. They were professors long settled in the United States. The woman and her companion had read my dispatches and heard my broadcasts (www.RadioTahrir.org) from Iraq over the Pacifica Network (www.Pacifica.org) during the earliest years of the siege.[2] Between 1991 and 1995, few journalists were reporting from the ground, and when they did, they seemed to applaud punishments being dealt to Iraq. Whereas Pacifica listeners found my unbiased reports refreshing. "They stimulate thought rather than anger," said one reader. She was typical of our many regular listeners who keep themselves well informed. Their perspective of American policies is realistic. They remember American history.

As a responsible journalist, I had concentrated my efforts on informing Americans about startling changes wrought by the embargo. I had first-hand experience with Iraq and I knew it had accomplished much beyond the golden era of the Abbassids. I concluded that Iraq was an American target, not a victim. This was evident to anyone who had witnessed recent developments inside the country firsthand.

Reluctantly I had become a war correspondent, and war and siege did not offer me the luxury to reflect on the Iraqi personality. So I had no riposte to these interrogators. I could have readily responded to other questions: "What do you think of Saddam, Baath ideology, or the cease-fire with Iran? What do you think of Iraqi health centers, schools you saw, or today's standard of living? The Babylon festival? The FAO program in Iraq?" I had opinions on each of those, but none about Iraqi people in general.

I had never pondered the concept of "Iraqis." Few others had, either. In the West, all debate on Iraq was fixated on Saddam Hussein, oil production, and what Washington should do about both. Some strategists have even gone so far as to argue that Iraq is really a twentieth-century creation, that Iraqi nationality is a post-Ottoman construction. Even its name is modern, they claim. Those arguments are spurious. But this approach supports divide-and-rule strategies by powers with imperial interests in an area. If they can convince others that inhabitants of a region they covet are not "a people" or "a nation," it is easier to dispense with them. ("Iraq is not a real nation" is increasingly voiced in the U.S. press, perhaps in preparation for the dismantlement of the state as we know it.) Anthropologists on this side of the debate always stress the minorities—e.g., Marsh Arabs, Turkman, and Kurds in Iraq—and this serves certain political agendas. Maybe that's why we read few formulations about "Iraqis" by the political pundits.

The two visitors in front of me had not come to discuss political science or anthropology, however. They wanted to know why I was so committed to their nation. "You were not born in Iraq. We know you are not Baathi. You are not a disgruntled civil servant or an American agent. You have no party affiliation or history of political activism elsewhere." (They were unfamiliar with my work on Nepali political history, a biography of two twentieth-century dissidents.) "We know your experience with Iraq is new. So what do you think of Iraqis in general?"

I had to mull over this question. In my professional life as an anthropologist, I have opposed character summaries of whole nations. It is limiting as well as dangerous to speak about "the Arab mind" or "nomadic family values," "the gentle Balinese" or "the conformist Dutch," "the spiritual Tibetan" or the "traditional Indian." At the same time, we can recognize national variations or leanings, peculiarities that distinguish a country.

Iraq *is* different; Iraq *is* unique. This was obvious to me from my first encounters inside its borders. Without preparatory studies in Iraqi history or earlier experience with the country, from the start I felt myself confronting a people of extraordinary energy, curiosity, joie de vivre, love of experiment and risk. Here was a nation striving for excellence, it seemed.

Iraqis are unarguably Arabs. Besides language and religion, they share many customs and ideals with their neighbors. Nevertheless, I find them different from the Palestinians, Syrians, Egyptians, or Lebanese among whom I have also lived. From my first encounter with Iraq, I have been smitten with the energy of these people. They have fewer inhibitions than I have found in neighboring lands. What I most appreciate is their indifference to class and pedigree.

These visitors to my home were still not satisfied. "But what do you think of *Iraqis*?" Zeineb repeated. Was she looking for some political statement? She and Gassan, her companion, glared at me, impatient for an answer. I felt pressed to respond and, without deeply considering my reply, I said, "Actually I find Iraqis very much like Americans."

Hmm; a startling analogy. Why did I say this? I began to explore the inspiration, thinking about all the women and men I have met, from shops along Sadoun Street in Baghdad to Kirkuk, from Treibeel's immigration office to farmhouses in Rashdiyya and Hillah to the townsfolk of sleepy Ein al-Tamr.

"Try It" People

We know Iraq is an ancient land compared with the United States. Iraq is almost landlocked, while the United States has abundant seacoast. The United States is a land of immigrants, whereas Iraq is not. Wait. Dissimilarities and contrasts are endless. Let's put aside how we are different and look at what we might have in common. Let's consider our temperaments and spirits rather than our traditions and geography:

Everyone knows how Americans say, "Let's go for it," when faced with a new idea. There's always a solution. Well, Iraqis often have the same approach to a problem. In Iraq, one doesn't find the hesitation and conservatism we encounter with Syrians or Egyptians, the British or Danes, who can quickly offer up reasons why something couldn't work. "Try it," reply Iraqis, and like Americans they will jump in to help make it happen. These people are not afraid to take a risk. Because of this, visitors have always liked working with these Arabs.

Iraqis are tough like the classic early American pioneer, the cowboy, the streetwise New Yorker, or the tycoon. They share American doggedness. Iraqis are not timid if presented with a challenge. Few will retreat if the going gets tough. On the contrary, Iraqis plod on with determination, eager to beat the odds. Aren't Americans similar?

My First Encounter: A Late-Night Escapade in Baghdad

Just as Iraqis work hard, they also play hard. I've tried, usually with limited success, to match them at festivals, picnics, and banquets. I often spent hours with friends in their homes, eating, drinking, and chatting pleasurably. Around midnight, satiated, drowsy, I would suggest returning to my hotel. "What? Dinner is almost ready. You must eat with us." A huge meal followed. By 2 a.m. I might manage to depart.

My very first week in Iraq in 1989, I found myself piled into a car of revelers setting out for somebody's country house outside Baghdad. It was past midnight.

I had met these merrymakers at an art exhibition in a smart downtown gallery. It had been an exuberant evening; most guests had departed by 11 p.m. Having stayed on, I found myself with friends waiting for Sousa, the director, to lock up. Being a gracious host, she would not allow me to cross the city alone. She must deliver me to my hotel herself, she insisted. No matter that her Toyota Corolla was already occupied by five friends waiting for her to take them to her farm.

With Sousa driving, we would be seven in the Toyota. "My hotel is not far away. I'll find a taxi. No problem," I said. Baghdad could not be as hazardous at midnight as Manhattan is. (I did not want to delay them.)

"Unthinkable. Hop in. Your hotel in on our way." The farm was an hour's drive beyond the city, and it was 11:45 already. My companions were not teenagers or even young adults (I somehow doubted that they were married couples). All appeared to me to be in their forties, not much younger than Sousa. Lamea I knew to be a widely loved writer. The tall, thin man was a well-known surgeon. A second man, already seated in the front passenger seat, was a ranking diplomat (Baathi, of course) and a celebrated translator. A couple I did not know was already firmly secured in the back seat beside the surgeon and the writer. I was gently maneuvered onto the lap of the smiling diplomat. He was gracious, fortunately, and not in his Baathi uniform.

Sousa announced that she needed gas. We drove around the city for half an hour, with me clutching the dashboard to balance myself, and my fellow passengers rollicking and musing about who else they might call on to join them at the farm. All offered Sousa a locality where gas might be obtained and no one advocated that the party be canceled. (Nor did anyone suggest the Party officer with us should commandeer a passing car.) Sousa drove on, passing one darkened station after another, until at last we found a pump open. After filling up, we went straight to the Baghdad Hotel. It was almost 1 a.m. I waved thanks and wished them well as they drove off into the Baghdad night.

None of this will surprise a western reader. Americans enjoy spontaneous escapades anytime and anywhere. You do not think much about a carload of middle-aged singles heading to a late night party at someone's cabin in the countryside. But this was in an ancient Arab city. It is a city where parties frequently begin after midnight.

Who Are *You*? Not Who Is Your Family?

Like Americans, Iraqis do not invoke class priorities as a rule, at least not city people. I found women and men expressing more pride in their personal achievements than in their provenance. Admittedly, the individuals I spent time with were the products of the 1960s and 1970s, when educated young people had limitless opportunities in Iraq.[3] This may not apply in rural society, where tribal rank and patriarchy predominate (although women, as elsewhere in the world, often manage the farm as well as the family, despite public invisibility).

In cosmopolitan Iraq, when a woman is introduced to me, I am advised not of her pedigree but of her educational degree. I am told about *her* achievements, not her husband's rank. I hear about *her* awards, not her son's scholarship. This also applies to men. Compared with protocols observed by other Arabs, in many Asian cultures, and in parts of Europe, there is little formality here and little regard for one's family background. You will recognize this as characteristic of the American culture, too.

I often enjoyed an evening with Osama Gailani at the home of another Baghdad family. Together he and his host conversed about the quirks and whereabouts of their old friends, commenting on books and television programs, telling stories about their students or nieces and nephews. Only after I had met Osama several times did someone mention he was from the once wealthy and powerful Gailanis. His father or uncle was Rashid Ali al-Gailani, former prime minister of Iraq. In 1941, he led the decisive coup against the Iraqi monarchy (and therefore British rule, a great victory). Except in the United States, such provenance is the first item of an introduction, is it not?

Doubtless class-consciousness persisted in some social circles. Hardly two generations of republicanism had replaced the established structure. Expanding cities attracted the classless generation.

Artists and academics with whom I associated were of diverse origins and cared little for pedigree. Key officials in ministries and directors of institutes were self-made women and men. Personal merit, not family background, had become an established political ideal. Many highly capable, well-educated ministers, directors, etc., like Americans, came from humble origins, men and women who earned recognition and appointments on the basis of individual merit. Scions of families who lost their fortunes in the revolution moved freely with the new elite where they were accepted for their own accomplishments. (Under the embargo, this merit-based culture crumbled; for example, people were appointed increasingly on the basis of party loyalty and little else, with fealty to the president being paramount.)

This openness didn't apply to Saddam's innermost circle. From the outset of his leadership, probably obsessed by the issue of security and loyalty, Saddam Hussein mainly confined himself to his blood kin and other men from his hometown, Tikrit, to fill important military and security posts. It seems that his rule was based on a complex structure of links to his person. We are told that he manipulated tribal leaders, bringing them into his web.[4] Appointments of the many "minorities" to high posts were said to be token gestures, to demonstrate that his was an open society.

Yet there was abundant room in Iraq for smart, skilled, and ambitious people to move into positions of social and administrative, if not political, influence. Before 1990 women and men from all corners of Iraq, from cities and villages, from Shia, Christian, Kurd, Turkman, and other populations occupied important posts. As the embargo wore on, this changed. Many capable people were pushed to the margins of Iraqi society, and they emigrated if they could find a way out. I often heard them say that, compared with the past, "Iraq is now run by men and women with no training; they are but lackeys of the president, his sons, and other thugs in their gang." The threat of a coup was ubiquitous; it generated purge after purge. (Could this have been an aim of the highly publicized American calls for toppling Saddam throughout the embargo?)

Iraqis, like Americans, eschew formalities. Immediately they get down to business or pleasure. They shun the awkward, elaborate preliminaries that many modern Asians as well as Arabs seem unable to completely abandon. First names apply throughout the Iraqi social system: department directors and professors are Dr. Ali, Dr. Bahija, Dr. Muna, Dr. Muhammad, and so on. Last names are discarded, and often Doctor and other titles are dropped altogether.

"Hey, Look, It's Huda!"

In Iraq, informality is the norm. We are spared long-winded introductions about the status and achievements of a guest or host.

One witnesses few awkward silences and hardly any shyness at social gatherings. Iraqis, like Americans, are in-your-face people: "Have a drink! What can I get you? Come over here. I want to talk with you. Give me a quick kiss."

In the spring of 2000, I was dining with Huda, a friend, and her husband, Ahmed, at Baghdad's Alwan Family Club, a union popular with the city's professional class. Its doors reopened not long after the 1991 bombing, even though liquor was no longer served and the pool was unusable. Alwan's dining tables were arranged in a large open space—no hidden private corners. That night the room was crowded. Partway through dinner Huda noticed friends arriving. They waved across the room and shouted greetings. On our way out an hour later, Huda stopped at their table to say hello. But that was not enough. Chairs were brought in for us to join them. I was introduced to someone I recognized: a cabinet minister. (Same open shirt and rolled up sleeves, nothing to distinguish rank.) During our meal, departing diners had stopped at our table. Other guests waved from across the room.

"Any time is a good time to enjoy yourself," says an Iraqi. In this country, people seem ready to join anything that looks like fun. If you are in search of a good time or simply something new, you can count on an Iraqi to accompany you. Mosul picnics are planned "at the drop of a hat," as Americans say.

Iraqis give high priority to performance. One hardly found a sloppy worker across the whole country before the 1991 war and embargo. If a bridge had to be finished, or a patient treated, or a report sent out, you could count on an Iraqi to do it without delay, whatever the obstacles or conflicting duties. I never heard a civil servant or other worker say: "It's five o'clock, and I'm going home" or "It's Friday, my only day off in the week, and I promised to visit my mother, or be with my children." Completing an assignment took precedence, it seemed.

As a result of that dedication and industry, Iraqis excel at what they do. Around the world, their excellence is highly regarded and in demand. In the 1920s, Iraq set up a first-rate educational system that was maintained and improved upon by each subsequent government. In 1985, Iraq won the UNESCO prize for wiping out illiteracy. In 1986, the now pariah nation received the UNICEF award for the lowest infant morality. In 1990, Iraq doubled the number of medical schools from seven to fourteen.

Iraqis strive to be first. They want to win, and they expect to take top prize, just like Americans. They want to be the best, just like Americans. That drive, I think, is associated with a keen sense of excellence. Where else do we find such resolve?

In 1999, when preliminary rounds were under way in the world soccer tournament, Iraqis, still under siege, were smitten with the possibility that they might get into the quarterfinals, where they had a chance to be pitted against the American team. Iraq had beaten Saudi Arabia. They next had to face Iran and several South American clubs. All had teams far superior to embargoed Iraq. But Iraqis were fixed on a face-off with the Americans. Everyone followed the competition closely. All fiercely hoped that Iraq would have that fortune. Their goal was not necessarily to beat the Americans but simply to be matched with them. When Iraq was eliminated in a game with Morocco, the public was less disappointed by that defeat than by the lost chance to engage the Americans.

Iraqis watch others, learn, and then move ahead on their own. They believe they can do it better. But this is not expressed through arrogance. Perhaps it is somehow associated with their ten thousand years of civilization.

Finally, I have to say something about these two people's shared sense of patriotism—fierce patriotism, a sometimes irrational patriotism. Only if you travel beyond its shores do you become aware of how extreme American nationalism really is and how it swells with war. Its people love it, despite its abuse.

How easily we forget how American authorities also have killed "their own people" by the millions. America's mistreatment of its black population is well known, not to forget the Native Americans or citizens of Japanese origin during World War II. Even when slavery ended, after the "Jim Crow laws" were overturned, after racism continued and opportunities were unrealized following the civil rights movement in the United States, most African Americans did not hate their country. In fact, many felt deeply attached to it. One of the most severe critics of America, James Baldwin, an author who lived many years abroad, declared, "I love America." And the Delany sisters, who lived with American racism every day of their century-long lives, loved their country best of all: "Lord, ain't it good to be an American."[5]

As American military aggression and foreign policy follies enrage and dismay so many people inside the United States and abroad, its citizens somehow remain fiercely patriotic. There is hardly a people as nationalistic as Americans are today. Few may be as violently dedicated to their sovereignty. Alternative Radio's David Barsamian quotes a comment from a U.S. army colonel: "It was a big mistake to discount the Iraqi resistance. If someone invaded Texas, we'd do the same thing."[6]

To many of us, Iraqis have many reasons to abandon their nation or to betray their leaders. They endured unspeakable brutality under their dictator. They do not like war; they do not like foreigners taking their resources, or their educated class; they do not like cruel men; injustice, chains. Yet they continue to love their country.

Scientist and engineer Ahmed Sousa left a loving family in the United States in 1930 to return to his homeland, then a British-managed monarchy, to a city badly flooded every year, to study and to write important books about its waterways, its history, and its treasured Arab values. Literary critic and author Jabra Jabra, originally Palestinian, remained in Iraq and never considered another homeland. Hala, twenty-four, waiting in line along embassy walls in Amman for a visa to "anywhere, even the United States," preferred to live in her own land, Iraq. Adnan, even after bringing his son to be with him in California, could not forget Iraq. Amal, who insists that every item in her art gallery be genuine Iraqi and who wants people to own Iraqi-made things, sometimes cannot bear to part with the treasures she has gathered. Buthaina settled in Cairo and returned year after year for the al-Marbid poetry festival. The millions who remained during the blockade desperately welcomed news that someone who had gone away "did not forget Iraq." If Americans ponder on their delight when they return home from a voyage, when they compare their land with others, when they sail along its endless motorways, maybe they will understand how much Iraqis love their country.

The Boxer Dog

There was a boxing match between an American dog and Iraqi dog in Jadiriyya, Baghdad. The Iraqi dog was scrawny, hungry, and utterly pathetic looking. The American dog on the other hand had a glossy coat of fur, was beautifully groomed with firm muscles and a fierce growl.

The match began. After the first round, it seemed the Iraqi dog was winning, knocking the American dog to the mat several times. The same thing happened for two more rounds, with the American dog gasping and shying away from his adversary. By the end of the fifth round, the Iraqi dog had knocked out the American animal. He was declared victor.

The American trainers were astonished and wanted to know what was the secret of the haggard Iraqi dog. So they brought a lie detector machine to question the Iraqi. The American machine asked it, "What's the secret of your victory. You look so emaciated, hungry and without any energy at all.

The Iraqi animal replied: "It's because of the embargo that I became a dog. Do you know what I was before?"

Now, the American machine was very excited and it asked, "Tell us the truth. What were you?"

The Iraq dog answered: "Ah Sir; before the embargo, I was a lion!"

Words and calligraphy by Ghani Alani. Translation: "We do not live in a country so much as its language lives in us."

Notes

Introduction

1. In numerous articles and now in in *Iraq Confidential: The Untold Story of the Intelligence Conspiracy to Undermine the UN and Overthrow Saddam Hussein* (New York: Nation Books, 2005), Scott Ritter insists that Iraq had been disarmed by UNSCOM. As late as 1997, International Atomic Energy Agency head Hans Blix reported that Iraq had complied with demands for disarmament and that the IAEA had no evidence that Iraq was concealing nuclear weapons or materials. In early 1999, three UN Security Council panels were studying ways to end the blockade, suggesting that the weapons verification program was an obstacle rather than an aid and admitting it was heavily biased by U.S. members. Ian Williams, "Panels Report Back," *Middle East International*, April 1999, 12.

2. Richard Drayton, "Shock, Awe, and Hobbes," *Guardian Weekly*, December 28, 2005. This interpretation was articulated from the outset of the embargo by many Arab commentators, among them Abbas Al-Nasrawi, professor of economics at the University of Vermont.

3. Ottavio Piccolomini, "A Long History of Abuse: The U.S., Iraq, and the United Nations," *Middle East International*, February 12, 1999, 23.

4. Pratap Chatterjee, *Iraq, Inc., a Profitable Occupation* (New York: Seven Stories Press, 2004); Naomi Klein, "Baghdad Year Zero: Pillaging Iraq in Pursuit of a Neocon Utopia," *Harper's Magazine*, September 2004, 43–53. Bob Woodward's *State of Denial: Bush at War, Part III* (2006) records Paul Bremer's administrative blunders according to Washington sources.

5. Klein (ibid., 48) and Sara Flounders, "The Corporate Looting of Iraq," *Workers World News Service*, July 24, 2003.

6. Chalmers Johnson, "The Smash of Civilizations," <www.tomdispatch.com> (accessed July 15, 2005). A less scrutinizing but more comprehensive study of this scheme is Milbry Polk and Angela M. H. Schuster, eds., *The Looting of the Iraq Museum, Baghdad: The Lost Legacy of Ancient Mesopotamia* (New York: Harry N. Abrams, 2005).

7. Drayton, "Shock, Awe, and Hobbes," 5.

8. Jose Bustani, director general of the Organization for the Prohibition of Chemical Weapons, was removed after intense U.S. lobbying for his replacement. The reason, according to BBC News, was that Bustani was negotiating with Iraq to join the OPCW and allow inspections, thus offering an alternative verification system to UNSCOM.

9. Ramsey Clark, January 5, 2005, press statement, International Action Center, New York. From the time of the 1991 Gulf War, Clark was an outspoken critic of Washington's Iraq policy. He exposes disingenuous American aims in *The Fire This Time: U.S. War Crimes in the Gulf* (New York: International Action Center, 1992, 2002).

10. Jeremy Smith, "U.S. Seeking to Totally Re-Engineer Iraqi Traditional Farming System into a U.S.–Style Corporate Agribusiness," *Ecologist*, January 21, 2005. For more on these lost seed banks

and warnings of threats to the world's genetic heritage, see Fred Pearce, "Returning War-Torn Farmland to Productivity," *New Scientist*, January 22, 2005. An October 20, 2003, online article by Firas Al-Atraqchi (www.IslamonLine.com) reports destruction of Iraqi flora and crops by American troops as a systematic campaign (using methods that recall Israeli attacks on Palestinian farms).

11. See <www.sciencemag.org>, September 30, 2005. Reversing its earlier (September 2003) optimism for what the U.S. occupation would mean for Iraqi education, the *Chronicle of Higher Education* would later make an appeal for the protection of Iraqi academics. Belatedly, in April 2006, U.S. academics joined European academics' calls for action to save Iraqi scholars. <www.brusselstribunal.org/Academics.htm>

12. Interview on WBAI Radio, May 10, 2005, with Mohammed Alomari, Detroit-based investigator who made frequent visits to Iraq to gather human rights data. He is the author of *The Blockade and Destruction of Iraq: Crimes against Humanity* (Southfield, Mich.: FAAIR, 2002).

13. The best-known report and analysis of the Iraq prison abuses is Seymour Hersh, *Chain of Command: The Road from 9/11 to Abu Ghraib* (New York: HarperCollins, 2004).

14. Ghali Hassen, a frequent commentator on developments in Iraq, calls the trial "a farce." Ghali Hassen, "The Show Trial of the Century," <www.globalresearch.ca>, October 20, 2005.

15. Barbara Nimri Aziz, "Iraqi Scientists outside History," *Natural History* 105, no. 7 (1996): 14–17. Also see audio excerpts from my 1998 interview with Ammash on <www.radiotahrir.org/features.php>.

16. Huda Ammash, "Toxic Pollution, the Gulf War, and Sanctions," in *Iraq under Siege: The Deadly Impact of Sanctions and War,* ed. Anthony Arnove (Cambridge, Mass.: South End Press, 2002), 169–78.

17. Patrick Cockburn. "Iraq Election Spells Total Defeat for U.S.," December 25, 2005, Counterpunch.org.

18. Hassen, "The Show Trial of the Century."

19. Noam Chomsky, "Beyond the Ballot," *Khaleej Times*, January 6, 2006.

20. Scott Taylor, *Among the Others: Encounters with Forgotten Turkmen of Iraq* (Ottawa: Esprit de Corps Books, 2004).

21. Harold Pinter, "Art, Truth & Politics." Nobel Prize acceptance speech, 2005, published on nobelprize.org.

22. Phyllis Bennis, *Calling the Shots: How Washington Dominates the UN* (New York: Olive Branch Press, 1996).

Chapter 3. Adnan in America

1. Even if government support was politically motivated, the quality of work exhibited in public places, including ministry halls and lobbies, was excellent. Iraqi art was, for the most part, not the often garish propaganda selected by bureaucrats. As late as 2000, the Ministry of Culture commissioned an extraordinary set of charcoal sketches of Iraq's outstanding musicians. At the time of the 2003 invasion, eighty-four tastefully framed pictures recently sketched by three artists, hung in the corridors of the ministry's third floor. The exhibition was initiated by Ali Abdullah, director of the Ministry's Music and Art Department during most of the embargo period.

Chapter 4. Mehdi

1. Iraq was widely recognized for its accomplishments in education and health care. In 1985, Iraq won the UNESCO prize for wiping out illiteracy; in 1986, UNICEF honored Iraq for

achieving the lowest infant mortality in the world. A WHO report noted that before 1991, health service reached 97 percent of Iraq's urban population and 78 percent of rural inhabitants. Its overseas delegations focused on development aid. Iraq was also advancing its political ambitions through economic strategies and military strategies. Step by step, Iraq was also consolidating its leadership in newly formed Gulf/Arab state regional alliances.

2. The Baath Socialist Party was founded in Damascus in 1954. Sandra Mackey traces its development in Iraq in *The Reckoning: Iraq and the Legacy of Saddam Hussein* (New York: Norton, 2002); Christine Moss Helms, *Iraq: Eastern Flank of the Arab World* (Washington, D.C.: Brookings Institute, 1984) describes the party's ideology and rise in greater depth. A useful summary is included in Dilip Hiro, *The Essential Middle East: A Comprehensive Guide* (New York: Carroll and Graff, 2003), 66–69.

3. Iraqi class structure at the time of the revolution is described by Marion Farouk-Sluglett and Peter Sluglett, "The Social Classes and the Origins of the Revolution," in *The Iraq Revolution of 1958: The Old Social Classes Revisited,* ed. Robert Fernea and William Roger Lewis (London: Taurus, 1991), and by Phebe Marr in *The Modern History of Iraq* (Boulder: Westview, 1985).

4. For a useful account of how Saddam Hussein manipulated tribal structures and values to support his government, see Mackey, *The Reckoning,* 204–12, 317–26. Although Mackey glosses over the depth of Britain's perfidy in Iraq, her analysis suggests that Baath Party membership or Sunni religious identity alone could not account for the hardiness of the dictatorship.

5. Twenty million is the 1990 figure provided by Iraq's Ministry of Trade based on their food rationing system. Twenty-three million is most often quoted by outside sources as Iraq's population during the 1990s. While the net population probably increased despite massive deaths and out-migration during the decade, I retain the figure twenty million throughout this book.

6. Largely ignored in the press, and forgotten in the world courts, in late August 1990, U.S. agents stormed, pillaged, and destroyed Iraq's embassy in Washington, D.C. The embassy building (Iraqi property) was then "taken over by the U.S. government" until 2003. In an interesting contrast, throughout the long and bloody Iran-Iraq war, the Iranian embassy in Baghdad was untouched and remained opened and functioning.

7. Iraq held more than five thousand foreign nationals who had been working and living in Iraq for several months while they were negotiating the Kuwait crisis. Eventually, at the end of 1990, all were released unharmed. The Iraqis called them "guests" and tried to demonstrate how well they were treated, but the action was a public relations disaster for Iraq.

8. Worldwide, only five nations did not endorse UN Security Council Resolution 678, November 29, 1990, supporting military action to oust Iraq from Kuwait. On August 2, 1990, the Security Council voted 14–0 in support of Resolution 660 and 13–0 four days later for the far-reaching (sanctions) Resolution 661. On August 3, 1990, the majority of Arab League foreign ministers voted to condemn Iraq.

9. On August 12, 1990, Saddam Hussein agreed to withdraw from Kuwait if Israel withdrew from territories it occupied in Palestine, Lebanon, and Syria. Years later, Iraq tried to link its cooperation regarding weapons with the removal of Israel's nuclear weapons. These moves only heightened U.S. resolve against Iraq.

10. Although generally overlooked by the press or referred to tangentially, bombing Iraq's essential civilian targets was a well-established fact, as reviewed in Carl Conetta, "Reconstructing Iraq," *Project on Defense Alternatives, Memo #28,* April 25, 2003 <www.watchingpolitics. com>.

Chapter 5. "I Love My Country"

1. On those two visits, I met artists Laila Attar, Mohammed Ghani, and Samira Abdul Wahab, Dr. Souad Khalil Ismael, minister of higher education, archaeologists Bahija Ismael, Doni George, and Gaya Rahal Ghani, economists Nasra al-Saadoon and Mustafa al-Mukhtar, publicist and journalist Asia Turaiki, her father, Mohammed Turaiki, poet Lamea Abbas Amara, critic and translator Jabra Ibrahim Jabra, and veterans of the war with Iran such as Kamal Abbas Hussein.

2. Perkins claims American economic "advisors" were unable to convince Saddam Hussein of the merits of their scheme, one subtly designed to take control of Iraq's economy. John Perkins. *Confessions of an Economic Hit Man* (San Francisco: Berrett-Koehler, 2004), 182–89.

3. In September 1988, although the House of Representatives approved this bill to boycott Iraq, President Ronald Reagan did not ratify it. In April 1990, months before the Kuwait crisis, another bill, HR 4585, was introduced, calling for economic sanctions on Iraq and the destruction of its weapons.

4. The Iranian embassy in Baghdad remained opened during the Iran-Iraq war, whereas U.S. authorities sacked the Iraqi embassy in Washington not long after Iraqi troops had marched into Kuwait. Soon after the 1988 Iraq-Iran cease-fire, although thousands of POWs remained to be repatriated, Iranian pilgrims resumed traveling to Iraq in large numbers.

5. A major agricultural policy innovation under embargo was the obligatory planting of wheat on all arable land. See chapter 21.

6. Abdul Kadhum al-Aboudi, professor of biotechnology at Senia University in Algeria (in personal conversation, March 2006), joins other Iraqi scientists who dispute charges of political motives behind Iraq's draining the southern Iraqi marshes. Al-Aboudi (himself from the marsh region) maintains marsh drainage schemes were driven by agricultural needs. For more on the "marshes controversy," see "The Iraq Marshes: Drying or Development?" (July 10, 2005) by A Concerned Iraqi Engineer, <http://zennobia.blogspot.com/2005/04/iraqs-marshes-beyond-politics.html>. Al-Aboudi concurs with many Iraqi experts (e.g., Ahmed Sousa, "Books Break Sanctions," chapter 8) that irrigation technology, the foundation of all civilizations, was especially important in Iraq's historical development.

7. Halliday resigned in 1998 and von Sponeck, in 2000, in protest of their agency's Iraq policy. Following the bombing of the UN headquarters in Baghdad in August 2003, Halliday posited the unthinkable: that Iraqi anger toward the UN was understandable. "When you think it through, why not?" he said. "We, the UN, have been tainted and corrupted by our presence in Iraq and the work we have done in Iraq at the beck and call of the Americans and the British." Jeff Guntzel, "Sanctions Gone from Discussion of Dark Era," *National Catholic Reporter Online,* December 26, 2003.

8. A worldwide outpouring of grief over lost antiquities arose because of looting following the toppling of the Baathists. Yet little was said before that about the archaeological sites ravaged by thieves and subject to neglect due to the embargo. The blockade eroded civic pride and impoverished the universities.

Chapter 6. There Goes the Medical System

1. For a summary of United Nations Resolution 687 and others relating to Iraq, see Dilip Hiro, *The Essential Middle East,* 544–45.

2. This policy is laid out in Phyllis Bennis, *Calling the Shots,* and addressed by Geoff Simons in *Targeting Iraq: Sanctions and Bombing in U.S. Policy* (London: Saqi Books, 2002).

3. This is the civilian death estimate published in 1998. It continued to be quoted by the media even though the deadly sanctions went on for five additional years. Even this appalling figure cannot explain or suggest the suffering of the rest, some 20 million, who somehow stayed alive. And it does not include the unknown military deaths of Iraqis in the 1991 Gulf War.

4. In the mid-1990s Iraq began sponsoring an annual trade fair in Baghdad. By 2000, 1,500 companies representing forty-five countries were participating, as reported in *Crescent International* (Toronto, November 16, 2000). In 2002, attendance was even higher.

5. UN Resolution 661 prohibited import of computers, scientific journals, and other educational supplies on the "dual use" argument that Iraq could apply these to military use. The western press accused Saddam Hussein of running these import schemes for his personal profit. No doubt Saddam and his family used this trade to personal advantage, but not to the exclusion of basic essentials for the general population and to keep the ministries working.

6. Examples are al-Ferdous and al-Hamra hospitals, both in Baghdad. Each began with fewer than fifty beds, but they were refurbished and expanded in 1994 by senior physicians with access to capital. Al-Ferdous's twelve shareholders were all surgical specialists (orthopedics, ophthalmology, gynecology, etc.). Each of the clinic's patients had a private room, the halls were quiet and uncluttered, and its staff of eighteen nurses represented a high ratio compared to decrepit government hospitals where seventy to eighty patients shared one nurse.

Staffed by well-known consulting physicians, al-Ferdous attracted some patients from neighboring Arab states. As government hospitals deteriorated, more ordinary Iraqis somehow found the fees for treatment at these private clinics. By 2000, these clinics numbered fifty in Baghdad. In spite of their air-conditioned rooms and superior operating facilities, these upscale centers were deficient in drugs. As of 2001, private clinics, like general hospitals, were not permitted to import their own drugs. They also lacked ambulances and up-to-date diagnostic equipment. Patients were required to pay cash in advance of admission, and because drugs were scarce, they were given a list of medications to bring with them at the time they were admitted for surgery. They also had to find suturing materials, syringes, and blood bags for themselves. (Some were obtainable in the open black market.)

7. I prefer to call this plan "food-for-oil," rather than adopt the commonly known term "oil-for-food." The plan may have helped Iraqis better survive the embargo, but the West's interest in oil supplies from Iraq was doubtless a major factor in the plan. See chapter 10 and Lee Siu Hin's report, "U.S. Using the UN Program to Steal Iraq's Oil," *CovertAction Quarterly,* Spring/Summer 2000, 32–33.

8. FAO and UNICEF, both UN agencies, a small Red Cross operation (through the Red Crescent), a one-man Christian church relief agency, and two Islamic relief organizations had limited projects in Iraq. Ad hoc groups of concerned citizens from Algeria and Jordan arranged medical shipments but maintained no offices in Iraq. Beginning in 1999, more Iraqi individuals living abroad undertook small-scale projects on an ad hoc basis.

9. When I suggested to physicians and senior officials of Iraq's health ministry that they explore possibilities of technical assistance from China and Cuba to import and develop alternative medical treatments, they felt insulted. Those sources of treatment were never seriously considered. At the same time doctors were disturbed that desperate families increasingly resorted to what they regarded as dangerous "local" treatments for their ailments.

10. See UNICEF, *Situation Analysis on Iraq,* 1993, 1995, and 1998; M. S. Fawzi and S. Zaidi, "Public Health in Iraq after the Gulf War," mimeo (Cambridge: Harvard University, May 1991). The Iraqi Ministry of Health published numerous reports after 1995, all of which affirmed find-

ings of outside investigators. See also UNICEF, *Joint Government of Iraq–UNICEF Program Review, 1990–2000.*

11. Rumors circulated through the American medical community that any physician communicating with Iraq might lose his or her license; the same threat was made to physicians who wanted to join a humanitarian delegation to Iraq. Medical journals were halted at their point of origin when editors received (and obeyed) instructions to abide by the embargo.

12. In 2000, Iraqi doctors confided to me that they had heard about a "hospital surcharge" being levied on oil contracts. According to those rumors, a foreign company would be obliged to rebuild a hospital for every major oil purchase it made. The scheme, which would not have been costly for a foreign company, perhaps $2–3 million, could have helped Iraq immensely. However, there was no evidence of any hospital construction. Meanwhile, the international press repeatedly accused Saddam Hussein of levying a surcharge on oil sales for his personal profit. Barbara Crossette, "Iraq Running Payoff Racket," *New York Times,* March 7, 2001; David Teather, "Volker Lays Abuse Claims against 2,400 Firms," *Guardian Weekly,* September 16, 2005, 11.

Chapter 7. One Iraqi Child and Her Father, 1996

1. Immigration to the United States, Britain, and Australia during the embargo was relatively easy. Tens of thousands of Iraq professionals were welcomed during that period. See chapter 18.

2. See chapter 23 for more information on Manal.

Chapter 8. Books Break Sanctions

1. Sympathizers with Iraq may have felt, erroneously, that the Baath government banned outside literature. My Iraqi associates assured me they were never questioned about books I shared with them. Remember that anti-Baath propaganda produced in the West was widely distributed directly from Washington through television and broadcast over CIA-funded radio stations set up in neighboring countries to support foes of Saddam Hussein. (As for an Iraqi resident criticizing the leadership, that was another matter. Iraqis were executed for far less.) Why did western donors overlook school supplies? Perhaps medicine has more symbolic, emotional value for westerners whereas literature is not central to western culture as it is for Iraqis. See B. N. Aziz, "What to Take to Iraq," in *Challenge to Genocide: Let Iraq Live,* ed. Sara Flounders (New York: International Action Center, 1998, 113–18).

2. The link between Palestinian aspirations and Iraq was made at critical points by western and Israeli politicians. More than once, Israeli commentators asserted, "The road to Palestine is through Baghdad." In the months leading to March 2003, Israeli leaders and the press demanded that Iraq must be attacked and its leadership removed. Arab commentators argue that the fates of the two peoples are intertwined in Israeli–U.S. policies. After 2003, western analysts dropped the Israeli factor from their commentaries on Iraq. In his recent book, *A War Too Far* (London: Pluto, 2005), Paul Rogers includes a chapter concerning the "Israeli factor." Rogers's attention to Israel here is a gloss and distracts from the realities of Israeli interest in Iraq; Rogers provides no documentation or rationale for the policy significance of Iraq to Israel. James Petras and Robin Eastman-Abaya provide a detailed article documenting U.S.–Israeli collaboration in the buildup to the 2003 invasion of Iraq ("Excess of Evil: Israel–U.S. Connections against Iraq," *CovertAction Quarterly* 77 [Fall 2004]: 2–5, 37–46). See also "The Israeli Factor" in Geoff Simons's *Targeting Iraq.*

3. In 2001 a delegation of Arab literary figures led by luminaries such as Egyptian author

Nawal el-Saadawi joined politicians, actors, and others on a solidarity mission to Iraq. In February 2001, the Iraq Museum organized a six-day international conference, The Emergence of the Written Language, which was attended by 100 experts from abroad (Reuters, March 1, 2001).

4. Reliance on imported paper created problems for Iraq when the embargo struck. Paper remained on the sanctions list. The paper shortage circumscribed avenues of cultural expression in Iraq. Even the import of textbooks for schools was banned by the blockade.

5. Ishtar's list of publications includes Mehdi Essa Al-Sakar, *East Wind, West Wind*, 1998; Hameed Taha al-Shabeeb *The Sixth Tale*, 2001; and *Before Breaking the News: Three Generations of Iraqi Poets*, 1998. All are Arabic-language texts.

Rachida Mohammedi, an Algerian intellectual and poet working with Iraqi writers during the blockade, collected and translated important new Iraqi works into French for Editions Latour. Among them are *L'orgueil des années trés Irakiennes*, 2001; Kudaer Meere, *Les jours de miel et de la folie*, 2001; and Kistru al-Djaf, *Le chien*, 2001. *Banipal, Magazine of Modern Arabic Literature* featured six Iraqi novelists in its summer 2006 issue. Europeans and Americans, including sympathizers who consistently supported Iraq under embargo, showed little interest in Iraqi literary life. In the late 1990s, France opened a cultural center in Baghdad with a fine galley, language lab, and computer center; it focused on films and visual art, especially the work of contemporary Iraqi painters.

6. This literary energy is manifest today in the vigorous journalistic work of Iraqis living under military occupation while simultaneously subject to enormous daily obstacles. Best known among them is the blogger "Riverbend." *Baghdad Burning* (New York: Feminist Press, 2005) is a collection of her dispatches.

7. Israel had not yet been founded. Sousa's studies in Zionism led him to oppose Zionist ideology in its early stage. He was convinced it would lead to the destruction of Arab culture and Arab nations. Sousa's religious orientation was affected at a young age by his Islamic environment and Muslim friendships. A favorite uncle had also embraced Islam. Sousa's critical writing on Zionism strained his relations with his family. His father, a wealthy landlord, nevertheless supported Ahmed financially throughout his studies in Lebanon and the United States where, in 1928, he became the first Iraqi engineering graduate of an American university. (Sousa's overseas study was not government funded.)

8. Baghdad, up to the mid 20th C, was plagued by annual floods, as it had been throughout history; thus the city's planning in modern and ancient times grew around the need for flood control and water management.

9. Sousa encouraged his daughter to go to France for advanced training, and they kept up a steady correspondence throughout their separation. Those letters were also saved in his library.

Chapter 9. Just Business

1. Turkey's border with Iraq offered prospects for trade. Iraqis who most benefited from commerce moving into and out of Turkey were Kurds. They were well placed to control the north-south land route. Out-of-sanctions oil leaving Iraq by land transport into Turkey was especially lucrative. Kurds did not suffer the despair and poverty that plagued the rest of Iraq. But conditions were still bad and made worse by widespread corruption, documented in detail by Rizgar Khoshnaw in *Nothing Left but Their Voices* (private publication, 2001). Syrian trade with Iraq was initially slow, restricted by their long political standoff. When that ended in 1995, Syria also benefited from sales to Iraq. By 2001, Syria had instituted regular air service to Baghdad to facilitate commerce in Iraq.

2. As soon as the Iraqi food-for-oil deal was signed in May 1996, world oil markets were affected. When Iraq threatened cutoffs in response to U.S. and British bombings in its north and south, oil prices were again destabilized. Resulting fluctuations were noted in the press.

3. Author interviews in 1996 with Mohammed Mehdi Saleh, Iraqi minister of trade, and economist Mustafa al-Mukhtar.

4. Campaign Against Sanctions on Iraq offers a useful guide with commentaries (www.casi. org.uk/guide) to all United Nations sanctions resolutions concerning Iraq.

5. By the mid-1990s, the plummeting Iraqi currency had stabilized at around 1,500 ID to the dollar, 1/6,000th of its value before the invasion of Kuwait and the embargo.

6. In *Iraq, Inc., a Profitable Occupation,* 98–101, Pratap Chatterjee identifies Iraqi families, the "Barons of Baghdad," who profited from Iraq's economic crisis under U.S. occupation. Neither his account nor Naomi Klein's excellent investigation of profiteering by U.S. firms in Iraq and the sale of Iraqi state companies mentions Jordanian counterparts. Klein, "Baghdad Year Zero."

Chapter 10. Who Gets What

1. The U.S. administration called for investigations of UN collusion with the Iraqi government, mismanagement of funds, and the abuse of their mandate. It was known as the Volker Report, named after its chairman. The United States raised suspicions about the UN secretary general himself. Earlier, Kofi Annan had suggested that the 2003 U.S.–led invasion of Iraq was not legal.

2. To answer reports of massive deaths as a result of the embargo on Iraq, apologists for American policy charged that responsibility lay with the Iraqi president. Press accounts of Saddam's extravagances suggested that the nation's oil revenues were usurped by him and that he was holding back medicines and food intended for the public.

3. Food production became a priority at the outset of the embargo. Engineers, chemists, industrialists, doctors—anyone with access to capital—leased land and began growing wheat. New fortunes were made, but a famine was also averted. Also see Pratap Chatterjee, *Iraq, Inc., a Profitable Occupation.*

4. Handouts of oil contracts seem to have been based on the ruler's whim: a poet he fancied who praised his rule, a foreigner whose service to Iraq impressed him. The windfall could have lured some sanctions opponents, and rumors circulated about an occasional beneficiary. When it came time to name recipients, American enemies were listed. One was a British MP, George Galloway. A strong critic of the embargo policy and a supporter of Iraqi people, Galloway suffered repeatedly from nefarious attacks. He fought back and cleared his name. After he had publicly stated that the 2003 invasion was "illegal," Kofi Annan found himself indirectly implicated in the scam. Annan also cleared himself of any involvement. For differing press summaries of the Volker Report, see David Teather, "Volker Lays Abuse Claims against 2,400 Firms" *Guardian Weekly,* September 16, 2005, 11; and Ian Williams, "The Volker Report," *Middle East International,* September 16, 2005, 10–12. As Williams points out, the report did not address U.S. profiteering and manipulations of oil prices during the embargo or Iraq surpluses taken over by American occupation authorities. See Lee Siu Hin, "U.S. Using UN Program to Steal Iraq's Oil," *Covert Action Quarterly* 69 (Spring–Summer 2002): 32–33; Sana Kamal, "Feeling the Pinch," *Middle East International,* July 2001.

5. According to a 2000 Iraqi Ministry of Trade report, the value of goods received between 1997 and 1999 in various sectors was as follows: medicine 53 percent of its needs, communications 0 percent, oil 19 percent, education 12 percent, water and sanitation 9 percent, electricity 13 percent, and food 75 percent.

6. Gazwan Mukthar, Baghdad, confirmed by the Ministry of Trade. This calculation was made on the basis of a Ministry of Trade 1990 Iraq population of 18 million. Other sources put the population at 20 million in 1990 and at 23 million in 1999. If 18 million was an underestimate, the allocation per person would be even lower than calculated.

7. Before 2000, per diem was $300. Author interview with UN-Iraq project employee Hans von Sponeck, who resigned in 2000 to protest UN sanctions. See also Alain Gresh, "Oil for Food: The Real Story," *Le Monde Diplomatique,* October 2000, 1–4; Geoff Simons, "Compensation or Theft?" in *Targeting Iraq*; and Suzi T. Kane, "Where Does Iraq's Money Go?" *NonViolent Activist, the Magazine of the War Resisters League* 19, no. 2 (2002): 6–7, 11. Kane notes that as of 2002, the UNCC had received 2.6 million claims.

8. The UN employed several hundred local staff, mainly Iraqis, to assist more than 220 foreign nationals at their jobs on-site. Local staff monthly salaries ranged from $50 to $200.

9. Minister of Trade M. M. Saleh, a brilliant, affable, and exacting man when it came to his job, was credited by the UN and others with the development of a fair, manageable, and efficient rationing system for the entire population.

10. The three Kurdish governorates (Dohuk, Irbil, and Sulaimaniyya) were free of Baghdad control, and they received a generous allocation (nearly 17 percent) assigned to them in SCR 986. The rest of Iraq, including the southern "no-fly" inhabitants, was administered by Baghdad. I never heard that their rations were less than anyone else or were undelivered. "No-fly" meant that Iraqis could not fly in those areas. If and when Iraqi radar tracked the intruders, they were subject to attack and were in fact regularly bombed with considerable loss of life.

11. In "Iraq and the Corruption of Human Rights Discourse," *Middle East International,* February 11, 2000, 22–24, Abdullah Mutawi contrasts human rights condemnations of Iraqi officials while ignoring the genocidal effect of UN sanctions.

12. Jeff Guntzel. "Sanctions Gone from Discussion of Dark Era," *National Catholic Reporter Online,* December 26, 2003.

Chapter 11. Trade or Aid?

1. See chapter 13 for details of confrontations between mainly European airborne sanctions-busters and U.S. authorities. By the end of 2002, flights from sixty nations had arrived in Iraq, and half a dozen airlines were operating scheduled flights to Baghdad.

2. The American and British argument was that if Iraq could trade, it would rearm itself and pose a danger to the world. UNSCOM had to certify that Iraq was totally free of weapons before the sanctions could be lifted, they said. (UN resolutions also specified this.) Later, "regime change" was announced as a condition for ending the sanctions.

3. Author interview with the director of a small international New York–based NGO who took a one-ton shipment of milk to Iraq in 1992 and decided not to return to the country. In August 1999, the Indian government was prevailed upon by British and U.S. authorities to abandon its plan to loan Iraq money in order to purchase buses. This is one of numerous cases of attempted aid to Iraq being halted by Washington's threats to foreign governments.

4. Amariya is the neighborhood in which a bomb shelter where up to 1,000 civilians, mostly children and women, sought safety during the 1991 U.S.–led bombing. Hundreds perished when it was struck by two 500-pound bombs. The shelter was later made into a shrine to which visitors were brought—a reminder of the indiscriminate targeting of civilians. Overlooked were equally appalling attacks outside Baghdad such as the devastation of a mental hospital. Its occupants' fates are documented by Kudaer Meere in *Les jours de miel et de la folie* (Paris: Latour, 2001).

5. This is the theory of the "white man's burden," which lies behind much north-to-south or developed-to-underdeveloped aid. The Baath government resisted NGO assistance, arguing against foreign interference. It was also suspicious of possible anti-Iraq political motives. Only a handful of non-Arab organizations were permitted regular access to Iraq and then only on a symbolic scale. These included Voices in the Wilderness, Un Ponte per Baghdad, the International Action Center, a French association, and an Africa-based Islamic relief agency. What actual supplies they delivered to Iraq was insignificant in practical terms, but for both sides their presence had a political and educational purpose.

Chapter 12. A Little Loot

1. *Gaamar* is an Iraqi delicacy, a rich blend of clotted cream made from the milk of water buffalo. It is eaten chilled and topped with honey or the syrup of dates. Although not expensive, *gaamar* is not always available in cities. It must be brought from farms. During the months after the war, Baghdadis yearned for it. Rhyming with Bremer, it was used in verses to mock the despised American viceroy Paul Bremer III, who was appointed by President George Bush to head the Coalition Provisional Authority after the removal of Gen. Jay Garner in May 2003.

2. Following the cease-fire on February 28, 1991, the Iraqi army moved against the Shia rebellion across the south, putting it down ruthlessly. The American forces had withdrawn, abandoning their promise to aid the southern rebels. For three weeks, while this massacre was underway, Iraq closed its borders. I was among the first small group of journalists to re-enter the country, witness the damage, and hear the anger and bewilderment of citizens.

3. When Kuwait eventually returned property to Palestinians resettled in Jordan, those assets reportedly amounted to over $5 billion.

4. See Suzy T. Kane, "Where Does Iraq's Money Go?" *NonViolent Activist, the Magazine of the War Resisters League* 19, no. 2 (2002): 6–7, 11.

5. Alain Gresh, "Oil for Food: The Real Story," *Le Monde Diplomatique,* October 2000, 1–4.

6. These suppliers had to accept payment in Iraqi dinars or goods rather than in dollars. Payment could be a shipment of oil. Iraq managed to slip extra UN-sanctioned oil through the northern route (heavily taxed by Kurdish agents) to Turkey. In 2000, Syria reopened its oil pipeline with Iraq. Iraq paid for repairs to the line, which had been out of use for years; it had also financed a new Jordanian highway up to the Iraqi border at Treibeel to facilitate trade along that route. Oil was shipped by tanker out of Umm Qasr, a southern Iraqi terminal near other Persian Gulf ports. U.S. patrols frequently boarded those ships and confiscated their loads. It became a game of cat-and-mouse. Merchants continued to operate in this channel, accepting the losses as part of doing business under siege. Trade via this route was economically viable and not really hazardous for embargoed, suffering Iraqis.

Chapter 13. Skies Over Baghdad, 2000

1. John Pilger, *The New Rulers of the World* (London: Verso, 2002), 76.

2. In 1999, three planeloads of Iraqi pilgrims landed safely at Jeddah. Each succeeding Hajj, these religions missions continued, although the number of planes was not more than two. After 2001, when a new regulation prohibited Iraqi planes from staying over to take their passengers home, pilgrims were forced to return to Iraq by land.

3. The AmeriCares team, upon its return to the United States, reported to the press that there was no real humanitarian crisis in Iraq. Ramsey Clark issued a statement pointing out that the U.S.–based organization included Barbara Bush on its board of directors. Just what the specific flight accomplished in relieving Iraq's problems is uncertain. It carried only 100 tons of foods for distribution, but the flight was apparently "blessed" by President Clinton.

4. In August 2000, Venezuelan president Hugo Chavez, then chairman of OPEC, flew into Baghdad. He was the first foreign leader to meet with his Iraqi counterpart after the 1990 crisis. (This action, some say, officially marked the start of the erosion of the sanctions.) Certainly the American press (Jon Lee Anderson, "The Unvanquished," *New Yorker*, December 11, 2000) gave considerable coverage to foreign aircraft arriving in Baghdad. John Burns (*New York Times* Sunday World Section, March 4, 2001) wrote of these flights as signaling a seismic shift in Iraq's international status.

5. Author's interview with Benjamin, November 2002, Baghdad.

Chapter 14. One Farmer's Message

1. Establishment of a euro currency for Iraq oil purchases was a profound measure, even though the American press essentially ignored it. The move doubtless had a tremendous impact on U.S. policy toward Iraq. One radio report from Europe notes the seismic shift at the time (Charles Recknagel. Radio Free Europe/Liberty Radio <rferl.org/feature/2000/11/01112000160846.asp>, November 1, 2000). Otherwise press references appear only in 2003, and then on alternative news websites—Gavin Putland. "The war to save the U.S. dollar," http://www.trinicenter.com/oops/iraqeuro.html, (2003, accessed July 15, 2006). Cóilín Nunan. "Oil, currency and the war on Iraq," http://www.feasta.org/documents/papers/oil1.htm.(January, 2003) (accessed July 15, 2006).

2. William Clark discusses the role of the petroeuro in U.S. hostilities toward Iran and Iraq in "Revisited—The Real Reasons for the Upcoming War with Iraq," <www.ratical.org/ratville/CAH/RRiraqWar.html>.

3. When Richard Butler succeeded Rolf Ekeus in July 1997, he introduced vigorous and confrontational tactics after which relations between Iraq and UNSCOM deteriorated. UNSCOM member Scott Ritter details this relationship in *Endgame: Solving the Iraq Problem—Once and for All* (New York: Simon and Schuster, 1999), and *Iraq Confidential*. In these and other writings, Ritter claims that early UNSCOM inspections had disarmed Iraq of chemical and biological weapons and that UNSCOM passed information to U.S. and Israeli intelligence. For a useful summary of the UNSCOM and Iraqis confrontations, see Dilip Hiro, *The Essential Middle East,* 557–59.

4. Mail service halted on August 6, 1990, with the first UN Security Council Resolution 661. Land phones were unworkable for three months after the first Gulf War ended; cell phone networks were installed only after the 2003 invasion, which probably allows easier scrutiny by U.S. occupation authorities. Internet service became available around 1998, and satellite television was possible for citizens after 2003. Before that, satellite TV reception was restricted by the Baath government, while other broken communications services were a result of the blockade.

5. My source, an Iraqi diplomat speaking on condition of anonymity, reports that a few trusted associates eventually persuaded the president to give fewer interviews and press conferences. To a lesser degree they were able to moderate his claims of victory in the 1991 Gulf War.

6. General public understanding, helped by a biased U.S. media, was that the inspectors had been ejected from Iraq. This is erroneous. Once they left voluntarily, Iraq refused UNSCOM reentry without agreed preconditions. One condition was a timetable for compliance and lifting the sanctions. This, I believe, was a reasonable position. Their justification was reinforced by documents that came to light only after the 2003 invasion (see Ritter). People who read the events carefully knew the claims made against Iraq were false, but their voices were weak.

Chapter 15. "Him!"

1. Uday, the eldest, had a fearsome reputation. It is widely believed inside Iraq that his father had him bullet-riddled from the waste down to curb his sexual appetite. I never heard anyone dispute the awful stories of Uday's murderous behavior. In my opinion, he was more reviled than even his father.

2. The 1963 coup that ousted the leftist leader Qassim and the 1968 coup that paved the way for the rise of the new Baathists, in which Saddam Hussein was a key player, are widely reported to have been aided by the CIA. Dilip Hiro, *The Essential Middle East,* 216; Tariq Ali and David Barsamian, *Speaking of Empire and Resistance* (New York: New Press, 2004), 139–40.

3. Senator Robert C. Byrd refers to earlier U.S. shipments to Iraq of chemical and biological weapons in an interview in *Minaret,* November/December 2002, 39–41.

4. Details of Saddam Hussein's crimes are discussed in Andrew Cockburn and Patrick Cockburn, *Out of the Ashes: The Resurrection of Saddam Hussein* (New York: HarperCollins, 2000); Said Aburish, *Saddam Hussein: The Politics of Revenge* (London: Bloomsbury, 2000); and Sandra Mackey, *The Reckoning.* All concur regarding the ruthless character of the former Iraqi president. So much of the man's intelligence was devoted to eliminating perceived or real enemies.

5. Throughout the 1990s, Israeli leaders urged a regime change for Iraq; in an unequivocal statement to British parliamentarians as late as November 2002, State Department official and Israel advocate Richard Perle among other pro-Israeli policy makers declared that the United States must attack Iraq, no matter what the weapons inspectors found.

6. One cannot overemphasize the public appeal of a strong nationalist policy regarding oil resources. More than oil revenues, nationalization of oil represented sovereignty and real freedom from European colonization. It is a sentiment that Baath philosophy incorporated. One only has to note Hugo Chavez's rising status worldwide to understand its appeal in Iraq in the 1960s. Much of Chavez's popularity stems from his nationalist policy regarding Venezuelan oil. In *Confessions of an Economic Hit Man*, John Perkins refers to failed attempts by the United States to recruit Iraq into its perfidious development schemes (182–89). Regrettably, Perkins provides no details of that policy. We learn nothing of what American agents proposed, how Saddam Hussein rebuffed them, and how this tied into later U.S. policy decisions over Iraq. In 1990, in a speech he gave in Jordan, the Iraqi leader urged assembled Arab delegates to withdraw their assets from U.S. and British banks; in 2000, he announced that the euro, not the dollar, would be accepted for Iraqi oil. Although these policy announcements were buried by the western press, they must have been critical to Washington's aim of "regime change" in Iraq. As Perkins notes, where the economic hit man fails, the jackals are called in.

7. I never asked for an opinion about Saddam Hussein. If I waited, opinions were volunteered. Iraqis could not be entirely frank with outsiders about their leader. Any remark about him in my presence was qualified. Yet people found ingenious ways to convey their feelings.

Together, these collected remarks said a great deal and helped me better evaluate any reports about Saddam Hussein. As a field anthropologist, I understood the value of passive dialogue: participation-observation.

8. In *Iraq Confidential,* former intelligence agent Scott Ritter records in considerable detail how the CIA tried to use UNSCOM to penetrate Iraq's high-level communications system. He confirms what Iraqis had suspected—that the CIA was seeking access to the Iraqi president's communication system and that UNSCOM worked closely with Israel. Both were violations of UN and UNSCOM protocol.

9. Mohammed Mehdi Saleh, trade minister, Omed Medhat Mubarak, health minister, and Abdul Munim, director of the Central Bank of Iraq, are three high-ranking authorities whom I met and interviewed at length. Their reputations were already well established, and many who knew the work of Saleh and Mubarak praised their skill in handling the daily damage of the embargo. The determination and loyalty of these highly qualified administrators always confused me. It is hard to believe that they were kept in service by fear alone.

Chapter 16. Sabaar and the Boys at the Office

1. From August 2, 1990, when Iraqi forces entered Kuwait, until the bombing began on January 17, 1991, hundreds of journalists flooded into the country. Only a handful, including CNN, stayed throughout the assault.

2. This is an annual Pan-Arab convention, hosted in rotation by different Arab capitals. After the war with Iran ended, Iraq was chosen to host the 1989 meeting in Baghdad.

3. The Press Center and the protocol office of the MOI were staffed by Iraqis with foreign language skills. Both offices dealt with foreign visitors, mainly journalists. As the crisis mounted, the center installed facilities for direct TV transmissions, satellite phone connections, and the Internet. Journalists registered their equipment upon arrival and could use them only at the Press Center. Media companies also paid a daily installation fee that could amount to hundreds of dollars. After 1998, foreign media were taxed more heavily; some paid daily stipends for their "minder." In 1997, a private "business center" opened in the otherwise idle Iraqi Airways office in downtown Baghdad. It facilitated the work of Iraqi and foreign businessmen, and some journalists used it. After 1997, it was possible to make international calls from some hotels. One assumed that all outgoing calls, from any locations, were monitored.

4. U.S. media outlets often qualified reports originating in Baghdad as "checked by Iraqi censors." They did not acknowledge U.S. military censorship as judiciously. In any case, Iraqi oversight was not as rigorous as one might expect. In 1991–92 I was asked to submit a copy of a written dispatch but not the text of my radio transmissions. Over the years these regulations were relaxed perhaps because the authorities realized they had little control over what was ultimately broadcast or printed. Perhaps they understood that nothing a reporter dispatched from Iraq was as damaging as reports originating in the United States by commentators who had never set foot inside Iraq.

5. In late 2002, as the U.S. and Britain prepared for another war on Iraq, the Press Center expanded to accommodate a new flood of foreign television crews. Regulars now included Fox, NBC, Al-Jazeera, and several other Arab networks.

6. Iraqis' confidence in journalism seems undiminished even under current (2006) hazardous conditions. Because of dangers posed to foreigners under occupation, most on-site journalists are

Iraqis employed by foreign news services. Their risks are high, and casualties are high. Canadian reporter Dahr Jamail (www.dahrjamailiraq.com) is an outstanding independent print journalist covering occupied Iraq. Enterprising Iraqi writers today employ Internet blogging to offer the world otherwise unavailable accounts of the occupation. Arab television channels also offer excellent alternatives to the limited and biased western news services. Several Web sites, e.g., <www.albasrah.net>, <www.uruknet.info>, as well as individual blogs, provide up-to-date and alternative new coverage one cannot find in mainstream media.

Chapter 17. The Pharmacy

1. Western doctors and publishers were initially skeptical of this report. Such behavior was contrary to western medical ethics. Iraqi authorities showed me authentic letters from European suppliers that explicitly said they were prevented from delivering anything to Iraq. My early research discovered how editors of medical journals also suspended deliveries of private subscriptions to Iraq ("Iraqi Scientists outside History"). Nothing angered and demoralized Iraqi doctors, many of whom were trained in the United Kingdom, more than their realization that their own teachers had turned their backs on Iraq.

2. Before President George W. H. Bush ordered the 1991 assault, his secretary of state, James Baker, meeting with the Iraqi foreign minister, Tariq Aziz, warned, "We will bomb you back to the stone age." One could say the plan was ultimately not carried out by tanks or missiles but by the UN economic blockade, a veritable "weapon of mass destruction."

3. As U.S. forces weakened the Iraqi army, it also encouraged the southern opponents of Baghdad, the disgruntled, restive Shia population, to revolt. When U.S. military support did not materialize, the rebellion failed. In *The Great War for Civilization: The Conquest of the Middle East* (New York: Knopf, 2005), 662–65, journalist Robert Fisk reviews the doomed uprising. This soldier would have been among the Iraqi troops engaged against the rebels. That he was seeking medicine in a private shop may have signaled military supplies were also unavailable.

Chapter 18. Facing the Children

1. In *The Fire This Time,* Ramsey Clark provides one of the earliest firsthand accounts of the assault. Unlike normal (pro-American) press accounts, Clark's detailed report suggests that the behavior of the U.S. military amounted to war crimes.

2. After the American-led bombing campaign ended February 28, 1991, a rebellion rose across southern Iraq. If not instigated by them, it was certainly encouraged by American forces. Western allies did not move into Iraq to support the rebels as had been expected. The insurgency, finding itself overwhelmed by government forces, was swiftly defeated. It is possible that tens of thousands were killed. This defeat was considered a betrayal by the U.S. government of Iraqi Shia people. They expected the United States to help them overpower an already weakened Iraqi military following their rout in Kuwait.

3. This took place during the February 1991 air campaign to destroy Iraq's strategic targets, but much more was laid waste (see Ramsey Clark, *The Fire This Time,* 59–84). Altogether 86,000 air sorties were mounted on Iraq during the five-week campaign. Dilip Hiro, *The Essential Middle East,* 160.

4. "Crumbling infrastructure" became a politically correct catch phrase, a conveniently disembodied image, widely employed by journalists to refer to what was really a social, health and

civilizational catastrophe. Editors and others realized that this term effectively kept the murderous nature of the blockade out of the news. Infrastructure, unless it is reported in its human dimension, seems to refer only to bridges and roads.

5. The U.S. and European public were misled into believing that travel to Iraq was illegal or that Iraq was reluctant to issues visas. Rumors circulated in the medical community that any physician who traveled to Iraq, even on a humanitarian visit, might lose his or her U.S. license to practice medicine.

6. The actual number who perished is impossible to say; a generally accepted UNICEF estimate (after 1997) for children under the age of five was more than 5,000 a month. Two million, commonly cited as the estimated deaths directly resulting from the twelve-year embargo, has not been disputed. See UNICEF, *Child and Maternal Mortality Survey,* 1999.

7. This conference, convened every six months since 1999 to bring world leaders together, was initiated by Deputy Prime Minister Tariq Aziz.

8. In a much quoted 1996 interview with ABC TV's *60 Minutes* host Leslie Stahl, responding to reports of half a million Iraqi children dying as a result of the sanctions, Secretary of State Madeleine Albright replied, "We think the price is worth it."

9. My sources were Iraq Central Ministry of Health figures and statistics that I assembled randomly from individual Iraqi hospitals. These were corroborated by UNICEF and other health agency studies. See chapter 6 regarding health surveys conducted in Iraq between 1991 and 2000. By all accounts, health conditions across Iraq have worsened since the 2003 occupation. See Ghali Hassen, <www.globalresearch.ca> and Ghassan Attiyah, <www.Bitterlemons-international.org>, along with UNICEF reports on Iraq.

Chapter 20. "Ah, the Border"

1. Iraq's border with Syria opened for general commerce after 1999. The frontier with Turkey was controlled by Kurdish agents. (A few journalists used that route.) The eastern frontier with Iran was open to incoming Iranian pilgrims to Najaf and Kerbala holy sites, and considerable unofficial trade passed from Iran. The Treibeel gateway was really the main access to and from the West, and a "U.S.–friendly" special arrangement was made between Amman and Washington.

2. This particular International Action Center trip lasted twenty hours because of mechanical breakdowns. By 2000, after a new fleet of SUVs was put into service, the 600-mile trip from Treibeel to Baghdad was reduced to eight hours on average.

3. Ramsey Clark, *The Fire This Time;* IAC, *The Children Are Dying,* ed. Sara Flounders (New York: IAC, 1996); IAC, *Metal of Dishonor, Depleted Uranium: How the Pentagon Radiates Soldiers and Civilians with DU Weapons,* ed. Sara Flounders (New York: IAC, 1997), and IAC, *Challenge to Genocide: Let Iraq Live,* ed. Sara Flounders (New York: IAC, 1998). For films produced on Iraq by the International Action Center, see <www.iacenter.org>.

4. By a special 1990 protocol between Jordan and Iraq, $350 million of Iraqi oil at a below market price was shipped to Jordan every year. How much of this oil was consumed within Jordan, and how much is resold to a third party, is not known.

5. The only other export had negligible commercial value: dates and truffle, harvested in considerable quantity from the Iraqi deserts. Iraq's once huge date fruit industry could not be tapped, and many of the orchards fell into disuse.

6. *Habibi, shlonak* (Dearie, how are things?) and *aini* (glory to behold) are popular Iraqi greetings.

7. With no international commerce, credit cards or bank checks were useless in Iraq. All exchange was in cash, so visitors had to carry a lot of cash; TV crews brought tens of thousands of dollars with them.

8. Houses lost value because there were few buyers. Also, emigrating families left secretly and therefore could not advertise their houses for sale.

9. In December 2001, riding a bus from Jerusalem to Ramallah in the West Bank, I learned the young woman sitting beside me was a Palestinian pharmacist recently returned from Iraq. She had received a free education there from 1996 until 2000—during the sanctions era. I met Yemeni and other Arab students in Iraq whose studies there were entirely supported by the government.

Chapter 21. Gravesites

1. FAO officers in Baghdad told me that these delays occurred year after year. The FAO Baghdad director did not hide his suspicions that these holdups were not bureaucratic error but intentional sabotage by the UN itself. These same FAO officials did not deny reports by Iraqis that U.S. and British planes flying over the area had deliberately aimed incendiary bombs into these wheat fields, causing the destruction of hundreds, possibly thousands, of acres. They carried out these raids during the weeks before harvest time.

2. War-related contamination could be equally dangerous following the 2003 military invasion of Iraq. Loss of life from daily violence and general mayhem created by the occupation and resistance eclipses pollution-related problems.

3. First documented in a seminar sponsored by the International Action Center and subsequently published in a collection, *Metal of Dishonor*. The subject of health effects of depleted uranium in weapons has led to numerous follow-up conferences and articles by concerned veterans and scientists. See post-2003 invasion reports by the Association of Humanitarian Lawyers, *San Francisco Bay View*, May 14, 2003.

4. This movement continues up to the present with new testimonies and evidence of depleted uranium use in the U.S. occupation of Iraq and Afghanistan. See <www.gulfwarvets.com>.

5. Siegwart-Horst Günther, "Depleted Uranium and the Gulf War Syndrome," *CovertAction Quarterly*, no. 69 (Spring/Summer 2000): 34–35.

6. See Aziz, "Iraqi Scientists outside History."

7. Author's personal interviews with Huda Ammash in Baghdad, 1996, 1997, 1998, supplemented by a discussion with her fellow Iraqi investigator, environmental engineer Dr. Souad al-Azzawi. Also see Ammash, "Toxic pollution, the Gulf War and Sanctions," in *Iraq under Siege*. Also see further documentation by Ammash delivered at a 2002 European conference at <www.monabaker.com/pMachine/more.php?id=P797_0_1_0_c>.

8. In 1995, as in prior years of the embargo, the FAO commissioned a health report by the Harvard Study Team.

9. The Iraqi Ministry of Health could not provide me with statistics about this development at the time of my research, although they seemed to be aware of the trend. Without data, health officials were unwilling to make any statement. Eventually, it published data that supported my anecdotal findings.

Chapter 22. Targets, Not Victims

1. World opinion against the American policy on Iraq shifted as a result of a growing awareness of an immoral "double standard" applied by the United States and the United Nations, Washington's excessive punitive stand against Iraq, and individual nations' economic self-interest in trade with Iraq. In *Targeting Iraq,* Geoff Simons characterizes the sanctions as a criminal policy designed to target Iraq.

2. As recently as July 2006, Pew Research polls regarding western views of Islam indicated that U.S. public opinion is biased against Muslims. A surprising number of Americans polled continue to believe Iraq possessed weapons of mass destruction and was somehow linked to the September 11, 2001, attacks on the United States.

3. Noam Chomsky, *Fateful Triangle: Israel, the United States, and the Palestinians* (Cambridge, Mass.: South End Press, 1999), x, xii. In Afghanistan, "ultranationalism" was represented by the Taliban. They evolved from the Mujahidin, fighters nurtured and supported by the American CIA to oppose Russian occupation during the 1980s. After September 11, 2001, ultranationalism in this part of the world became identified as "Islamic terror."

4. Based on author interviews with doctors at Kerbala General Hospital, Iraq, in 1995 and 1998.

5. Ferdous Al-Mukhtar and Naziha Adib, *Arabic Cuisine* (Surry: Surbiton/Laam, 1993).

6. Through to 2002, after the exit of UNSCOM in late 1998, Iraq offered to readmit weapons inspectors if they drew up a timetable when the inspections and sanctions might be concluded. The United States refused to consider the proposal and prepared for war.

7. Ramsey Clark, in *The Fire This Time,* and Geoff Simons, in *Targeting Iraq,* argue that the sanctions supported a long-term policy goal by the United States and Britain to completely destroy Iraq. They provide abundant evidence for their conclusions.

8. Rick Atkinson, "U.S. to Rely on Air Strikes If War Erupts," *Washington Post,* September 16, 1990.

Chapter 23. Where Is Amaar?

1. What the U.S. administration and media refer to as a "coalition" was essentially an American force with strong backup from Britain. In *The Essential Middle East,* Dilip Hiro lists the initial number of U.S. troops as 255,000, British 45,000, Australia 2000, Polish 200, and Czech 200, with other countries offering various degrees of technical support (165).

2. This period was not an impulsive burst of wild looting but consistent with a calculated American design to accelerate the process of de-Arabization. The attacks were designed to undermine Arab cultural roots. The United States understands how Arab nationalism and Baath philosophy are intimately linked. To destroy the Baath Party and Iraq, they had to target *all* sources of Arab nationalism, including its cultural roots.

3. Among many foreign experts who made pleas for the return of the treasures were Eleanor Robson (Oxford University) and Neil Brodie (Cambridge University). No western press accounts of an outside conspiracy are recorded.

4. After offering some initial resistance to invading land forces, Iraq's army was swiftly overwhelmed. Some former ministers fled to neighboring countries; others were arrested or killed; Saddam Hussein's wife, daughters, and grandchildren received asylum in Jordan. As for the

Republican Guards, rumors circulated that their leaders fled before April 9, the official end of the Baath regime. Some reports say they shed their uniforms and merged into the general population, later to become a nascent resistance movement. Some have been recruited to help run the new Iraqi army. Many midlevel officials, mainly technocrats, found employment with the American occupation authority within months of the end of Baath rule.

5. Sabaar's ten-year-old daughter scolded her father about his smoking. "What will happen to me if you die?" she implored.

6. Under pressure, Iraq capitulated and submitted a partial list of scientists' names. Some of these were interviewed by UNMOVIC agents, but the Americans were still not satisfied. The UN offered to remove scientists (with their families) to safe places abroad to be questioned, suggesting that if they openly "cooperated" with the UN inside Iraq, their lives were imperiled. From an Iraqi point of view, the UN was trying to kidnap these people, a critical national resource. (A former UN director suggested the UNMOVIC scheme "amounted to kidnapping.") Since the 2003 invasion, scores of scientists have been murdered or kidnapped. Hundreds of professors and doctors have been assassinated. These killings, some observers suggest, are one more tactic in the de-Arabization plan; the aim, they say, is to "cleanse" Iraq of its best-trained people. This would have removed a critical element of Iraq's nuclear "capacity." Since the occupation, many of the nation's most gifted people have left voluntarily because of the rampant strife. A few are known to have accepted American invitations to scientific conferences.

7. More about Huda Ammash can be found in the introduction and chapter 21, also Aziz, "Iraqi Scientists outside History" and <www.radiotahrir.org/features.php>.

Chapter 25. Birds of a Feather

1. This account came from two Iraqi professors, in interviews with the author, 1996. They asked me not to print their accounts to me of shameful, abusive, and destructive behavior by members of the UN weapons inspection teams in Iraq. In an April 2002 conference in Europe, Professor Huda Ammash detailed some of the tactics she observed that Iraqi professors were subjected to by UN weapons inspectors. See <www.irk.be/ned/missiles/ConferenceHuda.htm>.

2. "Iraq voices" and other features from the Pacifica archived news are posted on <www.RadioTahrir.org/iraq.php>.

3. See chapters 3, 4, and 5.

4. It seems others may be applying some of Saddam Hussein's tactics, if a 2004 *Le Monde* report is correct. Patrice Claude, "Washington Puts Trust in Iraq's Tribal System," *Guardian Weekly,* September 7, 2004, 20.

5. Sarah Delany and A. Elizabeth Delany with Amy Hill Hearth, *Having Our Say* (Thorndike, Me.: G. K. Hall, 1993), 298.

6. The quote may have originated in an October 31, 2003, *Wall Street Journal* interview with Lt. Col. Kim Keslung.

Select Bibliography

Aburish, Said. *Saddam Hussein: The Politics of Revenge.* London: Bloomsbury, 2000.

Afzal-Kan, Fawzia, ed. *Shattering the Stereotypes: Muslim Women Speak Out.* Northampton, Mass.: Interlink Publishing, 2005.

Al-Djaf, Kistru. *Le chien.* Trans. Rachida Mohammedi. Brussels: Latour, 2001.

Ali, Tariq, and David Barsamian. *Speaking of Empire and Resistance.* New York: New Press, 2004.

Allman, T. D. "Letters from Baghdad: Saddam Wins Again." *New Yorker* (June 17, 1996): 60–65.

Al-Mukhtar, Ferdous, and Naziha Adib. *Arabic Cuisine.* Surry: Surbiton/Laam, 1993.

Alomari, Mohammed. *The Blockade and Destruction of Iraq: Crimes against Humanity.* Southfield, Mich.: FAAIR, 2002.

Al-Sakar, Mehdi Essa. *East Wind, West Wind.* Cairo: Ishtar Press, 1998. (Arabic text)

Al-Shabeeb, Hameed Taha. *The Sixth Tale.* Cairo: Ishtar Press, 2001. (Arabic text)

Ammash, Huda. "Toxic Pollution, the Gulf War, and Sanctions." In *Iraq under Siege: The Deadly Impact of Sanctions and War,* ed. Anthony Arnove, 169–78. Cambridge, Mass.: South End Press, 2002.

Attiyah, Ghassan. <www.Bitterlemons-international.org>

Aziz, Barbara Nimri. "Gravesites: Environmental Ruin in Iraq." In *Metal of Dishonor, How the Pentagon Radiates Soldiers and Civilians with DU Weapons.* Edited by Sara Flounders. 155–63. New York: IAC, 1997.

———. "International Women's Day, March 2003." *Shattering Stereotypes: Muslim Women Speak Out.* Edited by Fawzia Afzal-Khan. Northampton, Mass.: Interlink Publishing, 2005.

———. "Iraqi Scientists outside History." *Natural History* 105, no. 7 (1996): 14–17.

———. "Targets, Not Victims." In *Iraq Under Siege: The Deadly Impact of Sanctions and War.* Edited by Anthony Arnove. 127–36. Cambridge, Mass.: South End Press, 2000.

———. "What to Take to Iraq." *Challenge to Genocide: Let Iraq Live,* ed. Sara Flounders, 113–18. New York: International Action Center, 1998.

Banipal, Magazine of Modern Arabic Literature 26 (Summer 2006).

Bennis, Phyllis. *Calling the Shots: How Washington Dominates the UN.* New York: Olive Branch Press, 1996.

Chatterjee, Pratap. "Barons of Baghdad." In *Iraq, Inc., a Profitable Occupation.*

———. *Iraq, Inc., a Profitable Occupation.* New York: Seven Stories Press, 2004.

Chomsky, Noam. *Fateful Triangle: Israel, the United States, and the Palestinians.* Cambridge, Mass.: South End Press, 1999.

———. "Beyond the Ballot" *Khaleej Times,* January 6, 2006.

Clark, Ramsey. "Fire and Ice." In *Challenge to Genocide: Let Iraq Live.* Edited by Sara Flounders. 3–32. New York: IAC, 1998.

————. *The Fire This Time: U.S. War Crimes in the Gulf.* New York: International Action Center, 1992, 2002.

Clark, William. "Revisited—The Real Reason for the Upcoming War with Iraq." January 2003, revised March 2003. www.ratical.org/ratville/CAH/RRiraqWar.html.

Cockburn, Andrew, and Patrick Cockburn. *Out of the Ashes: The Resurrection of Saddam Hussein.* New York: HarperCollins, 2000.

Cockburn, Patrick. "Iraq Election Spells Total Defeat for U.S." December 25, 2005, Counterpunch.org.

Conetta, Carl. "Reconstructing Iraq." *Project on Defense Alternatives, Memo #28.* April 25, 2003, http://www.watchingpolitics.com.

Concerned Iraqi Engineer. "The Iraqi Marshes: Drying or Development?" July 10, 2005. <http://zennobia.blogspot.com/2005/04/iraqs-marshes-beyond-politics.html>.

Crossette, Barbara. "Iraq Running Payoff Racket." *New York Times,* March 7, 2001.

Delany, Sarah, and A. Elizabeth Delany with Amy Hill Hearth. *Having Our Say.* Thorndike, Me.: G. K. Hall, 1993.

Drayton, Richard. "Shock, Awe, and Hobbes." *Guardian Weekly,* December 28, 2005.

Farouk-Sluglett, Marion, and Peter Sluglett. "The Social Classes and the Origins of the Revolution." In *The Iraq Revolution of 1958: The Old Social Classes Revisited,* ed. Robert Fernea and William Roger Lewis. London: Taurus, 1991.

Fawzi, M. S., and S. Zaidi. "Public Health in Iraq after the Gulf War." Mimeo. Cambridge: Harvard University, May 1991.

Flounders, Sara. "The Corporate Looting of Iraq." *Workers World News Service,* July 24, 2003.

Fisk, Robert. *The Great War for Civilization: The Conquest of the Middle East.* New York: Knopf, 2005.

Gresh, Alain. "Oil for Food: The Real Story." *Le Monde Diplomatique,* October 2000: 1–4.

Gönther, Siegwart-Horst. "Depleted Uranium and the Gulf War Syndrome." *CovertAction Quarterly,* no. 69 (Spring/Summer 2000): 34–35.

Guntzel, Jeff. "Sanctions Gone from Discussion of Dark Era." *National Catholic Reporter Online,* December 26, 2003. <http://www.ncronline.org/NCR_Online/archives2/2003d/122603/122603c.php>.

Hassen, Ghali. "The Show Trial of the Century." October 20, 2005. www.globalresearch.org.

Helms, Christine Moss. *Iraq: Eastern Flank of the Arab World.* Washington, D.C.: Brookings Institute, 1984.

Hersh, Seymour. *Chain of Command: The Road from 9/11 to Abu Ghraib.* New York: HarperCollins, 2004.

Hin, Lee Siu. "U.S. Using the UN Program to Steal Iraq's Oil." *CovertAction Quarterly,* Spring/Summer 2000: 32–33

Hiro, Dilip. *The Essential Middle East: A Comprehensive Guide.* New York: Carroll and Graf, 2003.

————. *Iraq: in the Eye of the Storm.* New York: Thundermouth/Nation Books, 2002.

International Action Center. *Metal of Dishonor, Depleted Uranium: How the Pentagon Radiates Soldiers and Civilians with DU Weapons.* Edited by Sara Founders. New York: International Action Center, 1997.

————. *The Children Are Dying: Reports by Ramsey Clark and the UNFAO*. Edited by Sara Founders. New York: International Action Center, 1996.

————. *Challenge to Genocide: Let Iraq Live*. Edited by Sara Flounders. New York: International Action Center, 1998.

"Interview with Senator Robert E. Byrd." *The Minaret* (Nov.–Dec. 2002): 39–41.

Jamail, Dahr. <www. *dahrjamailiraq.com*>.

Johnson, Chalmers. "The Smash of Civilizations." <www.tomdispatch.com/indexprint. mhtml?pid=4710> (accessed July 15, 2005).

Kamal, Sana. "Feeling the Pinch." *Middle East International,* July 2001.

Kane, Suzy T. "Where Does Iraq's Money Go?" *NonViolent Activist, the Magazine of the War Resisters League* 19, no. 2 (2002): 6–7, 11.

Khoshnaw, Rizgar. *Nothing Left but Their Voices: The Plight of the Iraqi People*. Annandale, Va.: Privately published, 2001.

Klein, Naomi. "Baghdad Year Zero: Pillaging Iraq in Pursuit of a Neocon Utopia." *Harper's Magazine,* September 2004, 43–53.

Mackey, Sandra. *The Reckoning: Iraq and the Legacy of Saddam Hussein*. New York: Norton, 2002.

Meere, Kudaer. *Les jours de miel et de la folie*. Trans. Rachida Mohammedi. Paris: Latour, 2001.

Marr, Phebe. *The Modern History of Iraq*. Boulder, Colo.: Westview, 1985.

Mohamad, Qassim, Awatif Naeem, and Abdul Khaliq al-Rikabi. *Four Iraqi Plays*. Cairo: Ishtar Press, 1999. (Arabic text)

Mohammedi, Rachida, ed. and trans. *L'orgueil des années trés Irakiennes*. Brussels: Latour, 2002.

Mutawi, Abdullah. "Iraq and the Corruption of Human Rights Discourse." *Middle East International,* February 11, 2000, 22–24.

Nunan, Cóilín. "Oil, Currency, and the War on Iraq." January 2003. http://www.feasta.org/ documents/papers/oil1.htm (accessed July 15, 2006).

Pearce, Fred. "Returning War-Torn Farmland to Productivity." *New Scientist,* January 22, 2003. http://www.newscientist.com/channel/earth/mg18524831.000.

Perkins, John. *Confessions of an Economic Hit Man*. San Francisco: Berrett-Koehler, 2004.

Petras, James, and Robin Eastman-Abaya. "Excess of Evil: Israel–U.S. Connections against Iraq." *CovertAction Quarterly* 77 (Fall 2004): 2–5, 37–46.

Piccolomini, Ottavio. "A Long History of Abuse: The U.S., Iraq, and the United Nations." *Middle East International,* February 12, 1999, 22–23.

Pilger, John. *The New Rulers of the World*. London: Verso, 2002.

Pinter, Harold. "Art, Truth & Politics." Nobel Prize acceptance speech, 2005, published on <nobelprize.org>.

Polk, Milbry, and Angela M. H. Schuster, eds. *The Looting of the Iraq Museum, Baghdad: The Lost Legacy of Ancient Mesopotamia*. New York: Harry N. Abrams, 2005.

Putland, Gavin. "The War to Save the U.S. Dollar." Revised April 18, 2003. http://altnews.com. au/nuke/article.php?sid=4645 (accessed July 16, 2006).

Recknagel, Charles. Radio Free Europe/Liberty Radio, Prague <rferl.org/feature/2000/11/ 01112000160846.asp> November 2000 (accessed July 15, 2006).

Ritter, Scott. *Endgame: Solving the Iraq Problem—Once and for All*. New York: Simon and Schuster, 1999.

————. *Iraq Confidential: The Untold Story of the Intelligence Conspiracy to Undermine the UN and Overthrow Saddam Hussein*. New York: Nation Books, 2005.

Riverbend. *Baghdad Burning*. New York: Feminist Press, 2005.

Rogers, Paul. *A War Too Far*. London: Pluto, 2006.

Sen, Amartya. *Development as Freedom*. New York: Knopf, 1999.

Shlah, Zaid. *Taqsim*. Calgary, Alberta: Frontenac House, 2006.

Simons, Geoff. *Iraq-primus inter pariahs: a crisis chronology, 1997–98*. New York: Macmillan, 1999.

————. *Targeting Iraq: Sanctions and Bombing in U.S. Policy*. London: Saki Books, 2002.

Smith, Jeremy. "U.S. Seeking to Totally Re-Engineer Iraqi Traditional Farming System into a U.S.-Style Corporate Agribusiness." *Ecologist*. January 21, 2005. <http://www.theecologist.org/archive_article.html?article=487&category=52> (accessed July 20, 2005).

Taylor, Scott. *Among the Others: Encounters with Forgotten Turkmen of Iraq*. Ottawa: Esprit de Corps Books, 2004.

UNICEF, *Child and Maternal Mortality Survey, 1999*

————. *Joint Government of Iraq–UNICEF Program Review, 1990–2000*.

————. *Situation Analysis on Iraq*. 1993, 1995, and 1998.

Williams, Ian. "Panels Report Back." *Middle East International*, April 1999, 12.

————. "The Volker Report." *Middle East International*, September 16, 2005, 10–12.

Woodward, Bob. *State of Denial: Bush at War, Part III*. New York: Simon and Shuster, 2006.

Index

Barbara Nimri Aziz is a freelance journalist and research anthropologist based in New York. She hosts a weekly radio program at Pacifica-WBAI, New York (*www.RadioTahrir.org*) and has broadcast and written widely from across the Arab lands since 1989. Aziz completed her Ph.D. in social anthropology from the School of Oriental and African Studies, University of London. After a successful research career in anthropology focused on the peoples of Tibet and Nepal, in 1989 she turned her attention to the Middle East, beginning with Iraq. She has recently been awarded a Fulbright professorship.

Related-interest titles from University Press of Florida

Against Islamic Extremism: The Writings of Muhammad Sa`id al-'Ashmawy
Edited by Carolyn Fluehr-Lobban

American Oil Diplomacy in the Persian Gulf and the Caspian Sea
Gawdat Bahgat

Biblical Interpretation and Middle East Policy: The Promised Land, America, and Israel, 1917–2002
Irvine H. Anderson

A Fevered Crescent: Security and Insecurity in the Greater Near East
James F. Miskel and P.H. Liotta

Islamic Societies in Practice, Second Edition
Carolyn Fluehr-Lobban

The Many Faces of Islam: Perspectives on a Resurgent Civilization
Nissim Rejwan

Nadir Shah's Quest for Legitimacy in Post-Safavid Iran
Ernest S. Tucker

The Veil Unveiled: The Hijab in Modern Culture
Faegheh Shirazi

Woman's Identity and the Qur'an: A New Reading
Nimat Hafez Barazangi

For more information on these and other books, visit our Web site at www.upf.com.